To Christine,  KW-442-682

UNIVERSITY OF PLYMOUTH
LIBRARY SERVICES

Item No.	900 1813043
Class No.	332 . 094 HEN
Contl No.	0077077 296

90 0181304 3

EUROPEAN FINANCE

Roger Henderson

*Reader in International Finance
at Leeds Business School*

McGRAW-HILL BOOK COMPANY

London · New York · St Louis · San Francisco · Auckland · Bogotá · Caracas
Lisbon · Madrid · Mexico · Milan · Montreal · New Delhi · Panama · Paris
San Juan · São Paulo · Singapore · Sydney · Tokyo · Toronto

Published by
McGRAW-HILL Book Company Europe
Shoppenhangers Road, Maidenhead, Berkshire, SL6 2QL, England
Telephone 0628 23432
Fax 0628 770224

British Library Cataloguing in Publication Data
Henderson, Roger
European Finance
I. Title
337.94

ISBN 0–07–707729–6

Library of Congress Cataloging-in-Publication Data
Henderson, Roger
European finance / Roger Henderson.
p. cm.
Includes bibliographical references and index.
ISBN 0–07–707729–6–
1. Finance—European Economic Community countries. I. Title.
HG186.E9H46 1993
332′.094—dc20

92–39448
CIP

Copyright © 1993 McGraw-Hill Book Company International. All rights reserved. No part of this publication may be reproduced, stored in a retrieval system, or transmitted, in any form or by any means, electronic, mechanical, photocopying, recording, or otherwise, without the prior permission of McGraw-Hill International (UK) Limited.

1234 CUP 9543

Typeset by Wyvern Typesetting Limited, Bristol
Printed and bound in Great Britain at the University Press, Cambridge

CONTENTS

PREFACE

The subject matter of this text is currently of immense public interest, and debate whether in academic, business or parliamentary circles or in the bars, *bierkellers* and pavement cafés throughout the European Community. Financial issues are at the heart of major changes to the market and institutional environment in which Europeans live and work, most notably in the context of the completion of the internal market with effect from January 1993 and the conflicts surrounding economic and monetary union

Certain recurrent themes exist at various levels throughout this book. Resource allocation problems occur with the changing nature of the Community budget and the debate over the future 'widening' or 'deepening' of the European Community in the light of opportunities and pressures from neighbouring countries. Conflict exists between supranational 'federalism' and the potential loss of national sovereignty implicit in the single-market programme, economic and monetary union, and moves towards fiscal federalism. Moreover, after a decade during which market philosophy and liberalization have been promoted in many Western nations, the appropriate role of government involvement in various spheres of the economy remains under scrutiny, as is manifest in areas such as public-sector funding, privatization, central banking operations and financial-sector supervision. Within the private sector, a common theme is that of competition or cooperation as banks, building societies and other financial institutions seek methods of servicing their customers' needs, while the emerging financial capital and derivative markets battle for technological and regional supremacy.

This book aims to address such issues within the common framework of finance. As a discipline, this is often subsumed within economics, through a focus on macroeconomic policy, or under financial management, with its emphasis on the sources and uses of funds within the firm. Although here the focus is mainly upon the former, especially at the Community level, reference is also made to the problems of business funding. Part 1 highlights the two fundamental issues that will form a backcloth to European financial developments in the 1990s. Chapter 1 examines the process of EC integration and the need to complete the internal market, given the continued existence of non-tariff barriers to trade and factor mobility, and the costs of 'non-Europe'. The liberalization of financial services is seen as a key element in this process to raise efficiency and choice and to lower costs for consumers. Chapter 2 considers the contentious issue of monetary union from the foundation and operation of the European Monetary System (EMS) to the September 1992 currency crisis. The problems of defending an overvalued pound, the role of the central banks and dealer power are discussed. The chapter also focuses on the theory of monetary union, the Delors Plan and the Maastricht Treaty, with its tight timetable and possibility of a 'two-speed' Europe. Prospects for a future single currency are examined, including varying proposals for the European Currency Unit (ECU), although its relative lack of operational acceptability is seen as a constraint, irrespective of current difficulties in implementing economic and monetary union.

In Part 2 the focus is on the interaction between finance and the government sector, largely through two distinct areas: public-sector funding, and central banking. The former is seen as playing an important role in formulating economic policy both at the national level (Chapter 3) and in the context of the EC budget (Chapter 4). The coordination of national budgets is a fundamental aspect of economic and monetary union, whereas the EC budget has long been a source of concern, whether in the decision-making process, the allocation of expenditure with its emphasis on agriculture, or the method of funding and its incidence on member nations. The relationship between a government and its central bank gained prominence with the September 1992 currency crisis, which highlighted the differing pressures on the Bank of England and the Deutsche Bundesbank, and in debate over the future European Central Bank (Chapter 5). Equally, the advent of the internal market emphasizes the need for adequate banking supervision and investor protection in Europe, a problem underlined by the ramifications of the BCCI collapse (Chapter 6).

During the existence of the European Community there have been far-reaching changes to the nature of the financial system. Part 3 refers to private-sector developments, notably the adaptation of financial institutions and markets in the major nations to the forces of innovation, deregulation and competition (Chapter 7). Future institutional product-market strategies are considered in the light of the single-market programme, along with technological and structural influences on delivery systems. With regard to financial markets, competition has intensified and liberalization, aided by technological advances, has fostered the development of derivative markets in many centres. Nevertheless, the dominance of London remains for the foreseeable future, although doubts exist as to whether it will capture the 'prize' of the site for the future European Central Bank. In Chapter 9 various types of company finance are examined together with the problems of small-firm funding. Relationships between firms and their suppliers of funds are considered in the context of the availability of finance, governance and short-termism. Debate persists as to whether UK firms are more disadvantaged than their overseas counterparts, although the level of communications may play a role.

In the final part, the growth of the EC is charted in terms of its membership and financial resource implications. The 'southern extension' continues to present problems of 'cohesion', namely the development of the weaker EC members, and the broader issue of trade and aid relations with the Mediterranean basin lands as a whole. The 'eastern focus' represents a severe challenge to EC skills and finance, an insight into which has been gained from German unification. The single-market programme and the changes in the former USSR have provided a new dimension to EC–EFTA relations formalized in the free trade zone EEA (European Economic Area) Treaty, although the poor state of the Nordic financial sector may hinder the integration process. Nevertheless, the potential exists for a major European financial and trading bloc effectively to rival Japan and the United States.

This book is intended mainly for university and college students following second- or third-year courses in finance and accounting, European business or economics, including foreign students from mainland Europe here on exchange programmes. It is hoped that it will also assist those students undertaking postgraduate and professional finance courses, together with general readers who desire an appreciation of financial developments in the EC. The text was essentially completed in the summer of 1992 but was amended to incorporate the ERM currency crises of autumn 1992, events that illustrate both the rapidity and the importance of change in the European financial environment.

Roger Henderson
Leeds Business School

ABBREVIATIONS

ACP	African, Caribbean and Pacific Countries (Lomé)
ACT	Advanced Corporation Tax
ADR	American Depository Receipt
AFB	Association Française des Banques
AFDB	Association of Futures Dealers and Brokers
AGF	Assurances Generales de France
AHC	Acceptance Houses Committee
APACS	Association for Payment Clearing Services
ATM	Automated Teller Machine
BCCI	Bank of Credit and Commerce International
BELFOX	Belgian Financial Futures and Options Exchange
BES	Business Expansion Scheme (UK)
BFI	Bank Financial Intermediary
BIS	Bank for International Settlements
BNP	Banque Nationale de Paris
BRITE	Basic Research in Industrial Technologies in Europe
BSA	Building Societies Association
BSI	British Standards Institute
CAC	Cotation Assisté et Continu (France)
CAP	Common Agricultural Policy
CATS	Computer Aided Trading System
CB	Commission Bancaire (France)

CBI	Confederation of British Industry
CBOE	Chicago Board of Options Exchange
CBOT	Chicago Board of Trade
CBV	Conseil des Bourses de Valeurs (France)
CC	Community Charge
CCAH	Credit and Commerce American Holdings (Netherlands Antilles)
CCAI	Credit and Commerce American Investment (Amsterdam)
CCB	Commission de Contrôle des Banques (France)
CCC	Competition and Credit Control
CCF	Crédit Commercial de France
CCIFP	Chambre de Compensation des Instruments Financiers de Paris
CD	Certificate of Deposit
CDC	Caisses des Dépôts et Consignations (France)
CEN	Comité Européen de Normalization
CENELEC	Comité Européen de Normalization Electro-technique
CET	Common External Tariff
CFP	Common Fisheries Policy
CGA	Credit Guarantee Association
CGFD	Central Government Financial Deficit
CLSCB	Committee of London and Scottish Clearing Banks
CIS	Commonwealth of Independent States
CME	Chicago Mercantile Exchange
CMEA	Council of Mutual Economic Assistance (also COMECON)
CNC	Conseil Nationale du Crédit (France)
CNMV	Commision Nacionale de Mercado de Valores (Spain)
COB	Commission des Operations de Bourse (France)
COREPOR	Committee of Permanent Representatives (Comité des Représentants Permanents de la CEE)
DTB	Deutsche Teminbörse
EAGGF	European Agricultural Guidance and Guarantee Fund
EBA	ECU Banking Association
EBRD	European Bank for Reconstruction and Development
EBTA	Hellenic Industrial Development Bank (Greece)
EC	European Community
EC9	EEC6 plus the UK, Eire and Denmark
EC12	EC9 plus Greece, Spain and Portugal
ECB	European Central Bank
ECP	Euro-Commercial Paper
ECOFIN	European Council of Finance Ministers
ECSC	European Coal and Steel Community

ECU	European Currency Unit
EDC	European Documentation Centre
EDF	European Development Fund
EEA	European Economic Area
EEA	Exchange Equalization Account
EEC	European Economic Community
EEC6	Belgium, France, Federal Republic of Germany, Italy, Luxembourg, Netherlands
EEIG	European Economic Interest Grouping
EES	European Economic Space
EFTA	European Free Trade Association
EFT–POS	Electronic Funds Transfer at Point of Sale
EFCM	European Financial Common Market
EIB	European Investment Bank
EMCF	European Monetary Cooperation Fund
EMF	European Monetary Fund
EMH	Efficient Markets Hypothesis
EMI	European Monetary Institute
EMS	European Monetary System
EMU	European Monetary Union
EOE	European Options Exchange (Amsterdam)
EOTC	European Organization for Testing and Certification
ERASMUS	European Action Scheme for Mobility of University Students (and Staff)
ERDF	European Regional Development Fund
ERM	Exchange Rate Mechanism
ESC	Economic and Social Committee (also known as ECOSOC)
ESCB	European System of Central Banks
ESF	European Social Fund
ESPRIT	European Strategic Programme for Research and Development and Information Technology
ETSI	European Telecommunications Standards Institute
EUA	European Unit of Account
EURATOM	European Atomic Energy Community
EUROFED	see ESCB
EU	European Union
EVCA	European Venture Capital Association
FAB	First American Bankshares
FGB	Financial General Bankshares
FOF	Futures and Options Fund
FRG	Federal Republic of Germany
FSE	Frankfurt Stock Exchange
FSLIC	Federal Savings and Loans Insurance Corporation

FTA	Free Trade Agreement
FTA	Financiale Termijnmarkt Amsterdam
FTSE	Financial Times Stock Exchange Index
GAN	Groupe des Assurances Nationales
GATT	General Agreement on Tariffs and Trade
GDP	Gross Domestic Product
GDR	German Democratic Republic
GEMM	Gilt-edged Market Maker
GEMSU	German Economic, Monetary and Social Union
GFOF	Geared Futures and Options Fund
GMP	Global Mediterranean Policy
GNP	Gross National Product
GSP	Generalized System of Preferences
G10	Group of 10 Industrialized Nations
HOBS	Home Banking Service
HSBC	Hong Kong and Shanghai Banking Corporation
IBIS	Interbank Information System (Germany)
IBRD	International Bank for Reconstruction and Development (World Bank)
ICCH	International Commodities Clearing House
IDB	Inter-dealer Broker
IFS	Institutions Financières Specialisées (France)
IGC	Inter-governmental Conference
IMF	International Monetary Fund
IMP	Integrated Mediterranean Programme
ISD	Investment Services Directive
ISE	International Stock Exchange of the United Kingdom and the Republic of Ireland
ISRO	International Securities Regulatory Organization
LAFD/S	Local Authority Financial Deficit/Surplus
LCB	London Clearing Bank
LDC	Less Developed Country
LGS	Loan Guarantee Scheme (UK)
LIBOR	London Inter-bank Offered Rate
LIFFE	London International Financial Futures Exchange
LIFFOE	London International Financial Futures and Options Exchange
LTOM	London Traded Options Market
MATIF	Marché à Terme International de France
MATIS	Makler-Tele-Information System (Germany)

MCA	Monetary Compensation Amounts
MEFF	Mercado de Futuros Financieros (Spain)
MEFFSA	Mercado de Futuros Financieros SA (Spain)
MEP	Member of European Parliament
MIDAS	Market Maker Information and Trading System (Germany)
MMC	Monopolies and Mergers Commission
MNE	Multinational Enterprise
MONEP	Marché des Operations Negociables de Paris
MPL	Maximum On-line Publication Level
MQS	Minimum Quote Size
MSS	Maximum SAEF size
MTAS	Medium-term Assistance Scheme
MTFS	Medium-term Financial Strategy
NAFTA	North American Free Trade Area
NASDAQ	National Association of Securities Dealers (USA)
NBFI	Non-bank Financial Intermediary
NCB	National Commercial Bank (Saudi Arabia)
NCT	New Control Target
NIF	Note Issuance Facility
NMS	Normal Market Size
NTB	Non-tariff Barrier
OECD	Organization for Economic Cooperation and Development
OPEC	Organization of Petroleum Exporting Countries
OTC	Over-the-Counter
PCFD/S	Public Corporations Financial Deficit/Surplus
P/E	Price-earnings Ratio
PEDIP	Programa Especifico de Desenvolvimento da Industria Portuguesa
PEP	Plan d'Épargne Populaire
PHARE	Poland and Hungary: Assistance for the Restructuring of their Economies
PIBOR	Paris Inter-bank Offered Rate
PLC	Public Limited Company
PSBR	Public Sector Borrowing Requirement
PSDR	Public Sector Debt Repayment
PSFD/S	Public Sector Financial Deficit/Surplus
PW	Price Waterhouse (Accountants)
R&D	Research and Development
RIE	Recognized Investment Exchange
ROCE	Return On Capital Employed

RUF	Revolving Underwriting Facility
S&L	Savings and Loans (USA)
SAD	Single Administrative Document
SAEF	SEAQ Automatic Execution Facility
SBD	Second Banking Directive
SBF	Société des Bourses Françaises
SEA	Single European Act
SEAQ	Stock Exchange Automated Quotation
SEAQI	Stock Exchange Automated Quotation—International
SEM	Single European Market
SEPON	Stock Exchange Pool Nominees
SERPS	State Earnings Related Pension Scheme
SFA	Securities and Futures Association
SIB	Securities and Investments Board (UK)
SMEs	Small and Medium-sized Enterprises
SIM	Societa di Intermediazione Mobiliare (Italy)
SPRINT	Strategic Programme for Innovation and Technology Transfer in Europe
SRO	Self-regulatory Organization
STABEX	Stabilization of Export Earnings Scheme
STMS	Short-term Monetary Support
SVT	Spécialistes en Valeurs du Trésor (France)
SWIFT	Society for Worldwide Interbank Telecommunications
SYSMIN	System for Mineral Products
TALISMAN	Transfer Accounting Lodgement for Investors Stock Exchange Management for Principals
TAURUS	Transfer and Automated Registration of Uncertified Stock
TEMPUS	Trans-European Mobility in Higher Education
THA	Treuhandanstalt (Germany)
THS	Trading Hors Séance (France)
UAP	Union des Assurances de Paris (France)
UBR	Uniform Business Rate
UCITS	Undertakings for Collective Investment in Transferable Securities
USM	Unlisted Securities Market (UK)
VAT(TVA)	Value-added Tax
VER	Voluntary Export Restraint
VSTF	Very Short-term Facility

ACKNOWLEDGEMENTS

I am indebted to the following for kind permission to reproduce copyright material:

The Association of British Insurers (ABI) for Table 7.4 from data in *Insurance Statistics 1986–1990*.

The Bank of England for Table 7.1 from data in *Quarterly Bulletin*, Vol 32,1, 1992.

The Central Statistical Office (UK) for Table 9.2 from material in Table 8.2 *Financial Statistics*, 362, June 1992; Table 9.1 and Table 9.4 from data in Tables 17.11,17.12, and 17.25 *Annual Abstract of Statistics*, 1992 edn; Tables 3.4, 3.5, and 5.1 from figures in Tables 3.5, 11.13, and 11.14 in *UK National Accounts Blue Book*, 1991 edn.

The Commission of the European Communities, Brussels, for Tables 1.2 and 1.3 based on figures from *European Economy*, 35, 1988.

Gower Publishing for permission to reproduce Table 1.2 from P. Cecchini, *1992–The European Challenge*.

The Office for Official European Community Publications, Luxembourg, for Table 4.1 from data in 'The Facts in Figures, from *The Community Budget*, 3rd edn, 1990; for Table 4.2 from figures in the *Official Journal of the European Communities*, L26, 3.2.92

The Deutsche Bundesbank, Frankfurt, for Table 9.3 from p. 17, *Monthly Report of the Deutsche Bundesbank*, November, 1991; for Table 6.1 from data on p. 34, *Monthly Report of the Deutsche Bundesbank*, July, 1992; for Table 7.5 from material contained within pp. 14–31, *Monthly Report of the Deutsche Bundesbank*, August, 1991.

PART
ONE

EUROPEAN FINANCE IN THE 1990s

THE SINGLE MARKET: LIBERALIZATION OF EUROPEAN FINANCE?

The European Community is now at a crucial stage in its evolution, with the fulcrum for economic development provided by the 1986 Single European Act, which set out a programme to complete the Single, or Internal, Market by 31 December 1992. Although the possibility of slippage in this timetable was acknowledged at the outset, the momentum for change has been such that most of the legislative proposals (directives) deemed necessary to remove barriers to the free movement and exchange of goods, services and resources were effected on schedule. The '1992' programme reflects both the greater appetite for integration and the strength of free-market philosophy in dominant political thinking in many member states. Consequently, the main thrust of Community development is currently on the market and on competitive, liberalizing forces, rather than on achieving political, economic and social goals *per se*.

1.1 EUROPEAN COMMUNITY: FROM CUSTOMS UNION TO SINGLE MARKET

In effect, the Single European Act is an attempt to satisfy the original broad objective of the 1957 Treaty of Rome which established the European Economic Community: to create a Single Market without barriers of any kind between the six founder member states. While a customs union was duly created and internal tariff barriers removed, the Community was not a common integrated market since a plethora of non-tariff barriers remained; indeed, even now it is still far from an economic and political union as envisaged by its founders, such as Jean Monnet.

Table 1.1 illustrates various theoretical states of economic linkage along a spectrum encompassing ever closer integration. On this spectrum, a *trade link* refers to a basic cooperation via the adoption of a preferential tariff on a specific good. Participating nations levy a lower rate of taxation on mutual imports than on those from outsiders. Such schemes existed between the Commonwealth and the UK until the latter joined the EC. A *free trade area*, such as the European Free Trade Association (EFTA) covering Austria, Iceland, Norway, Sweden, Finland and Switzerland, extends the preferential tariff to all imports between members. It is a loose, international association in which members eliminate trade barriers between each other, but retain their own trade policies with respect to outsiders. Thus, they may impose their own restrictions subject to other agreements to which they are party.

Greater interdependence may lead to common policies, as in a *customs union*, where a joint external trade policy is adopted, for example, the imposition of a common external tariff on imports from non-members. The revenue from this will be commonly shared according to a prescribed formula. Thus, the creation of a customs union enhances trade among its members but diverts it from those excluded. As Lintner and Mazey (1991) observe, this infringes basic free trade principles enshrined in the General Agreement on Tariffs and Trade (GATT), which forbids discriminatory tariffs and has had to be amended to cope with customs unions. A *common* or *internal market* extends the customs union principle by abolishing all obstacles to trade between members—not just tariffs but also non-tariff barriers. The free movement of labour and capital is promoted, and integration occurs for what were previously separate factor markets. A *monetary union* represents a higher order of integration, in that the monetary system of the member states is based upon a common currency, or irrevocably fixed exchange rates. The former 'strong-form' monetary union implies policy coordination via a common monetary policy.

Ultimately, economic integration may take the form of an *economic and monetary union*, which implies macroeconomic policy coordination across members, including fiscal as well as monetary policy. Essentially, the member states lose their economic independence, and inevitably a large part of their political sovereignty too. In essence, a central, federal government dominates macroeconomic policy-making, although some devolution can persist, as for example in the USA, with a common currency and the federal government controlling most fiscal policies.

Economic integration is thus wide in scope, and is seen as a process by which independent economies combine. While it is depicted in economic terms, it is evident that political will is required for it to be effected since progressive interdependence implies relinquishing ever more sovereignty over domestic decisions. Indeed, as Table 1.1 shows, intervention via policy harmonization becomes more intensive with enhanced integration. Thus, as the process

Table 1.1 Types of economic association

	Trade link	Free trade area	Customs union	Common market	Monetary union	Economic and monetary union
Preferential tariff	Yes	Yes	Yes	Yes	Yes	Yes
Internal free trade	No	Yes	Yes	Yes	Yes	Yes
Common external trade barrier	No	No	Yes	Yes	Yes	Yes
Free factor mobility	No	No	No	Yes	Yes	Yes
Common currency	No	No	No	No	Yes	Yes
Common economic and monetary policy	No	No	No	No	No	Yes

5

develops there is a shift from negative to positive integration. *Negative integration* refers to the removal of restrictions on trade and is characteristic of free trade areas and customs unions, where the focus is on enhancing trade and the mobility of the factors of production. *Positive integration* implies the building of an institutional framework and includes commonly achieved decisions on macroeconomic policies as in an economic and monetary union. The stages of integration shown in Table 1.1 should not be considered deterministic. For example, if in the future EFTA is assimilated into the full EC common market, this will imply the omission of the customs union stage. Moreover, monetary union, broadly defined, may exist between countries sharing merely a common currency irrespective of their underlying trade policies.

The economic development of the European Community is largely in line with the pattern depicted in Table 1.1, culminating in full economic and monetary union early in the twenty-first century if the Delors Plan succeeds. Thus, progression to the higher stages of integration could be a speedier process than the 35 years it took to move from the customs union stage to the completion of the Single Market. Progress has been erratic; an initial flurry in the first decade was followed by relative stagnation in the 1970s and early 1980s, and then renewed momentum from 1985. Severe economic recessions and enlargement of the Community have delayed the process, but, equally, so have periods of political fervour and nationalist reaction to the federalist principles implied in union. While I am concerned primarily with economic considerations in my examination of European finance, political influences are never far removed. Indeed, the creation of the customs union was arguably an economic expression of the desire for political unity.

The concept of political and economic union in Europe has had a long history. There had been attempts to impose political unity by force, for example by Charlemagne, Napoleon and Hitler, and attempts by peaceful means, ranging from scholars such as Erasmus and Aquinas in medieval times to the 1923 call for a 'United States of Europe' by the Pan-European movement, and the Briand–Stresemann scenario of a 'European Union' within the League of Nations proposed in 1929. Not surprisingly, after the devastation of two European 'civil wars' spurred by national rivalries, there emerged a strong tide of federalism in the late 1940s, especially among those nations that had been overrun. However, translating federalist ideals into a workable structure proved more difficult, as some wanted supranational European controlling bodies while others favoured looser intergovernmental cooperation. In particular, Britain and France continued to voice concerns over the potential loss of sovereignty.

The foundation for a solution was laid by two Frenchmen, Jean Monnet and Robert Schuman, pragmatic federalists who saw the road to unity via specific, incremental economic measures. Their plan aimed to alleviate French fears of a resurgence of German military dominance by focusing on the integration of the crucial coal and steel-making industries via the creation of the European Coal and Steel Community (ECSC). Founded in 1952, this comprised agreement between France, Germany, Italy and the Benelux countries to oversee these industries in a common supranational interest. Thus, the German industrial base would be restored but with its use controlled. Moreover, it was hoped that a more politically acceptable and economically efficient solution would arise if a common market was established among a wider group of countries, overseen by institutions independent of existing governments. The ECSC was soon successful, boosting coal and steel output by 37 per cent and 150 per cent respectively in the decade from 1948. This spurred Monnet to seek further sector-based integration, and in 1955 a committee under Paul-Henri Spaak began to review ways of furthering the 'European experiment'. The Spaak Report, published in 1956, recommended sectoral integration in nuclear energy and, significantly, the creation of a general common market.

The Spaak Report formed the negotiating basis for the Treaties establishing the European Atomic Energy Authority (EURATOM) and the European Economic Community (EEC), signed by the Six in Rome on 25 March 1957 with effect from the start of 1958. Nevin (1990) observes that, although France was unenthusiastic about a full customs union, it was anxious to develop nuclear energy and to share the development costs, thus agreement to the EEC was a price paid for EURATOM. In 1967 the three 'Communities' merged, and as integration proceeded they were referred to as the EEC and later the EC (European Community).

The goal of the EEC Treaty was 'to lay the foundations of an ever-closer union among the peoples of Europe . . . to ensure economic and social progress by common action to eliminate the barriers which divide Europe'. This was to be achieved by the creation of a common market for all goods and services, encouraging the progressive convergence of the economic policies of the member states. The EEC Treaty set out to abolish all tariffs and non-tariff barriers to trade. The tariff had been the mainstay of protectionism, but quotas had become increasingly significant; hence, as Pinder (1991) observes, the removal of these would be a radical venture. The target date for the customs union was 1969.

The Treaty also established various common policies, including those for agriculture and competition, and three funds: the European Social Fund (ESF), to improve employment prospects and cater for related social issues; the European Investment Bank (EIB), to aid long-term investment via the provision of loans and guarantees; and the European Development Fund (EDF), to assist the then associated overseas territories.

The administrative institutions set up in the ECSC formed the basis for those in the EEC, namely the Court of Justice and the Parliamentary Assembly. A new executive authority, the Commission, was created to ensure that member states enacted the Treaty, and to submit proposals to and enforce the decisions of the Council of Ministers. The latter has the final say in EC legislation and consists of ministers from the member states responsible for the subject under discussion; thus, '1992' internal market directives have been dealt with by trade ministers, although the finance directives were discussed by finance ministers.

The decision-making process is illustrated in Appendix A. The principle is that institutions should be independent of national governments, a feature most evident with the Court of Justice, where EC legislation takes precedence over national laws.

The central EC institution is the Commission, the independent executive body seen by Monnet as the key to integration. The Commission was originally conceived to draft legislation put before the Council and Parliamentary Assembly, and to implement the resultant directives. However, it also administers the various EC funds, namely the ESF, the European Regional Development Fund (ERDF) and the European Agricultural Guarantee and Guidance Funds (EAGGF). Over time the Commission has become more powerful, and, with a 12 000-strong army of civil servants, also more bureaucratic, raising questions over its role and relationship with Parliament. In the context of the Single European Act, its position has become crucial as it has been able to originate legislation, and to be involved in monitoring and implementing the directives. This has made the 17 Commissioners and their President, Jacques Delors, powerful personalities.

The European Parliament was not really necessary for the ECSC itself but was perceived as a step towards a federal Europe with members directly elected by the peoples of the member states. Since it is not at the apex of power within the Community, Welford and Prescott (1992) argue that it has had to seek ways of exercising power and influence largely through questioning the Commission and Council. Thus, in the early years it had essentially an advisory role, and arguably it is still embryonic in that the first direct elections were not held until 1979. However, its prominence rose when in 1981 it passed a resolution inspired by Altiero Spinelli for revision of the Treaty aims and operation. This started the process that culminated in the Single European Act, which in turn strengthened Parliament's role by ensuring that on '1992' legislation a second reading of any bill must occur in Parliament. If MEPs then reject it or its amendments, a unanimous vote of Council is required to overrule these decisions. Moreover, Parliament has a final say in respect of commercial trade and association agreements between the EC and non-members. Thus, it is beginning to flex its muscles as integration proceeds. However, real power would require political union.

The discontent that prompted the 1981 Spinelli-inspired resolution stemmed from the seemingly slow progress on many policies. This was due partly to the above bureaucratic, institutional framework, but other factors were also influential. In the early years after the Treaty, the ECSC and EEC enjoyed considerable success as trade grew and their development corresponded to the 'neo-functionalist' theory of integration. Developed by Haas (1958) and Lindberg (1963) in the context of the ECSC, this argued that integration derived from the management of political conflict. In the context of the coal and steel industries, once the decision was made to establish supranational bodies covering that sector, interest groups, political parties and governments switched their attention to the high authority, namely the administrative executive and model for the

EC Commission. When convinced of the benefits of the ECSC, they became advocates of further integration, encouraging interest groups in other sectors to lobby. As other sectors sought to be integrated, their own interest groups would be frustrated by the lack of integration and this would help promote the need for central, supranational policy-making, thus fuelling the integration process.

Neo-functionalists thus recognized the importance of central institutions with policy-making capabilities in the formulation of common policy, and the need for appropriate legislation. While influential, this perspective over-estimated the extent to which powers might be transferred from members to supranational bodies, and sparked the long-running debate between national sovereignty and federal reform.

Progress towards the removal of trade barriers benefited from improved franco-German relations, but plans for political union, such as the 1961 Fouchet Plans for a joint foreign policy, foundered with de Gaulle's concern with national sovereignty and his use of the veto. The latter was first used in 1963 to block British entry, ostensibly on the grounds that the UK was too tied to the United States and the Commonwealth, and was the antithesis of the principle of collective decision-making embodied in the Treaty. Further use of the power of veto in the 1970s, coupled with severe recession induced by the oil crises, slowed the pace of development. Moreover, much of the Community's energy was dissipated in disputes over the budget. Thus, neo-liberalists argue, 'euros-clerosis' had set in, whereby market forces were stifled and member states were preoccupied with domestic issues rather than with liberalizing their own or the wider European market.

The major Community achievement in the 1970s and 1980s was the broadening of membership. In 1973 Britain, Denmark and Ireland joined, followed by Greece in 1981 and Spain and Portugal in 1986. Britain had declined invitations to participate in the founding initiatives in the late 1950s, preferring the concept of a European free trade area with no loss of national sovereignty. However, efforts to create a large free trade area covering the EEC and other, notably Scandinavian, countries failed through differences between France and Britain. In response, EFTA was formed in 1959 consisting of Britain, Denmark, Norway, Sweden, Iceland, Portugal, Austria, and Switzerland, some of which felt that the Treaty of Rome had political overtones not acceptable to their traditional neutrality.

However, Britain's world influence was faltering and political isolation was a possibility. Moreover, the early economic success of the Six offered an opportunity for hard-pressed British firms to find new markets. Thus, economic pragmatism encouraged a political shift, and the UK's first formal application was made in 1961, although de Gaulle's use of the veto ensured that membership was not gained until 1973. These Community enlargements produced further pressure for reform as they failed to generate expected benefits in the face of the prolonged recession. Moreover, the budgetary strains continued, exacerbated by the need to cater for some of the weaker, newer, members.

Thus, by the mid-1980s the European economy was rapidly returning to a series of national markets separated by non-tariff barriers, many of which were geared to support declining industries such as shipbuilding, textiles or steel. Here competition was emerging from the newly industrializing countries in the Far East, while in advanced technologies American and Japanese firms were outstripping European ones. To counter such threats, advanced technology products were increasingly subjected to national specifications and subsidies. The Community seemed to be lurching towards collapse, lacking direction and dynamism.

However, the passing of the Spinelli resolution produced new impetus. The European Parliament wanted more influence on major policy-making and approved a draft Treaty on European Union at Fontainebleau in 1984. The following year the Council of Ministers decided that this should be considered at a special intergovernmental conference.

Simultaneously, the Commission began to investigate the obstacles preventing integration. Before taking up office in January 1985, the new Commission President, Jacques Delors, toured European capital cities seeking opinions on ways of enabling the Community to progress. Deregulation was favoured, and at Brussels in March 1985 the Council charged the Commission to draw up a timetable for the completion of the Single Market by 1992. In June 1985 the Commission presented a White Paper (EC Commission 1985) setting out some 300 separate measures designed to remove physical, technical and fiscal barriers to trade. At the Luxembourg summit in December 1985 the meaning of 'European union' was discussed in the context of changes to the Treaty of Rome, with Italy and France wanting to form an Act of European Union, and Britain and Denmark preoccupied with raising the efficiency of existing institutions and policies (Owen and Dynes 1992). Eventually agreement was reached on the content of the Single European Act to amend the Treaty and codify the White Paper measures. The Act, signed in 1986, took effect from July 1987 after Parliamentary approval in each of the member nations.

1.2   THE SINGLE EUROPEAN ACT AND SINGLE-MARKET PROGRAMME

The 1986 Single European Act is very wide-ranging, going beyond formalizing the economic concept of the Single Market to set out amendments to the original Treaties covering the environment, regional inequality, social policy, research and technology, and monetary integration. Moreover, it modifies the decision-making process and re-emphasizes the Community's ultimate aims. Before considering the Single Market proposals, it is worth dwelling on some of these other features, since the whole Act provides the political impetus and legal framework for the unified market goal.

Reference was made earlier to Parliament's enhanced powers in terms of the 'cooperation procedure' for a second reading of legislation related to the internal market; but the Act also allowed for qualified majority voting in the Council of Ministers on policies relating to the Single Market. This replaces the previous unanimity requirement, thus reducing the damaging power of the veto and speeding up the processing of directives. However, this needs to be extended to other areas of major importance, notably finance, to accelerate the integration process.

The Act sought to revive the objective of economic and monetary union by encouraging members to work progressively to this goal without a specific commitment. While any institutional changes here needed to be agreed unanimously and required further Treaty amendments, the Act spawned the establishment of a committee under Jacques Delors to consider ways of achieving this objective. The 'Delors Plan' was submitted to the Madrid summit in 1989 and was agreed at Maastricht in December 1991 (see Chapter 2).

As part of the integration process, the Act aims to improve cohesion by reducing regional disparities. Its general objective embraces both southern rural areas and northern declining industrial ones. Subsequently it was agreed that the structural funds would be doubled by 1993 to meet these needs. This reflects the recognition that the internal market may enhance the attractiveness of some regions at the expense of others, and that, with factor mobility, resource migration may exacerbate differentials. Detailed provisions have also been made to strengthen the scientific and technological base of European industry in the light of the aforementioned competition from the United States and the Far East. Specifically, the Act promotes programmes such as ESPRIT (information technology and telecommunications) and BRITE (industrial technology). The environment policy is based on the premise, 'the polluter must pay', and sets Community standards, although nations may introduce more stringent criteria if they see fit.

While these measures support the integration process, they are essentially secondary to the main purpose, which was to establish the Single Market by 31 December 1992. The Act describes the internal market as 'an area without internal frontiers in which the free movement of goods, people, services and capital is ensured in accordance with the provisions of the Treaty' (EC 1986). Thus, the Council has not only accepted the White Paper proposals but has also embodied attainment of the internal market as a Treaty objective.

Notwithstanding the wealth of technical legislation, the programme contains two underlying principles: the '1992' time-scale, and deregulation, a reflection of the neo-liberalist emphasis on market forces. Here, the approach has shifted from the 1970s focus on harmonization towards mutual recognition. Harmonization aimed at compliance with fixed European standards, but these took a long time to produce and often threatened national sovereignty. Mutual recognition operates on the basis that a nation's goods and services should get free access to another country if they conform to certain basic requirements. This approach stems from the 1979 *Cassis de Dijon* ruling in the European Court of Justice.

German authorities banned the import of French *crème de cassis* blackcurrant liqueur on the grounds that the drink's content did not conform to German regulations. The Court ruled that French regulations, which had been respected, were an adequate safeguard for health and must be recognized. Thus, the German ruling contravened EC free trade laws.

In planning the internal market, the Commission took up the above principle that, for goods to move about the integrated market unhindered, they should conform to mutually recognized standards. However, practical difficulties have ensued, notably with respect to financial services, since the financial institutions involved must be regulated at EC level if their product sales are to be liberalized. Thus, harmonization has been necessary, with directives setting out what companies can undertake. This issue is addressed in Sec. 1.4 below.

The White Paper identified three broad categories of non-tariff barriers to trade; physical, fiscal, and technical. Physical obstacles are those created by customs formalities and controls which affect the movement of goods and people. In particular, frontier barriers have been a poignant reminder that the Community remains divided into distinct states. Within the new Single Market, people are free to seek work without previous constraints such as work permits. The UK has objected to the removal of border controls, which it sees as necessary to combat terrorism, drug trafficking and other such criminal activity, although other member states argue that the onus should be placed on strengthening the common external frontier. The UK's stance is reflected in its decision to incorporate special customs and immigration facilities into the Waterloo terminus of the Channel Tunnel link (Goodman 1990). In contrast, France, Germany and the Benelux countries signed the Schengen Accord which abolished all frontier formalities between them in 1990, although spot checks remain.

A major rationale for the internal market is the cost of delays in moving goods caused by the customs clearance necessary to collect duties and statistics, enforce quotas and licences, and control the spread of diseases and prohibited products. The introduction in 1988 of the Single Administrative Document (SAD) has considerably reduced the paperwork involved in cross-border, intra-Community transport, and efforts have been made to eliminate the duplicate checking of goods. The freer mobility of trade also imposes obligations on the control of hauliers in so far as common standards and consistent enforcement of lorry safety are required.

Many of the above frontier needs stem from fiscal barriers arising from differences in indirect taxes. Clearly, these are an anathema in a common market since they distort competition. However, fiscal frontiers exist to ensure that the appropriate tax revenues accrue to the correct member state, and to prevent fraud and tax evasion (EC 1989). Thus, by removing frontier controls, the Community takes away the point of administration for the revenues; instead, it needs ideally to levy taxes on products as if they were domestic sales. Hence exporters will charge VAT on sales and importers will reclaim it as import tax. However, to work effectively this requires harmonization of taxation, since significant price differentials between nations would distort trade and competition. In one sense progress was made with the use of VAT as the common tax levied, but its application has remained inconsistent, both in the wide range of rates applied and in the goods and services covered.

In 1987 the Commission put forward proposals to approximate VAT rates aimed at reducing disparities to a level where they did not in themselves encourage cross-border trade distortions. For VAT two broad bands were suggested: a standard rate band of 14–20 per cent, and a reduced band of 4–9 per cent on 'items of basic necessity'. However, a fierce debate followed, notably in connection with the abolition of zero-rating, which in the UK covers key items of consumer spending such as children's clothes, food, energy, drugs, water and newspapers. New proposals incorporating concessions were advanced in 1989, but British reaction was that the market should determine VAT rates and it was not until June 1991 that final agreement was reached. This was for a minimum standard rate of 15 per cent from January 1993; harmonization of excise duties on mineral oils, alcohol and tobacco so as to ensure that the price differential is not an incentive to cross-border shopping; a lower band of around 5–6 per cent chosen by member states for basic items; and zero-rating to be temporarily retained for selected products but subject to biannual review. Efforts to end zero-rating and shift the onus of VAT from the country where goods are consumed to the one where they originate was not agreed. Thus, the imposition of the tax on imports will persist until 1996.

Ultimately tax harmonization is necessary, since a Single Market means that prices cannot differ much between regions, transport costs excepted. In theory, demand, money and jobs would flow from higher to lower tax environments, which are often the more prosperous locations, thus furthering the inequality. However, if taxes are harmonized, then cross-subsidization is needed, which implies a central 'pot' from which expenditure is made, possibly via one monetary authority and thus one currency!

Technical obstacles comprise the third, but arguably the most important and wide-ranging, category of modern non-tariff barriers. These are mainly technical regulations and standards imposed for health, safety, consumer protection or environmental reasons. They might apply to basic items such as electrical wiring and plug specifications, toys, medical products or food hygiene; they might also apply where products must meet differing national standards and certification needs, which are in reality often artificially erected forms of protectionism, such as differing emission rules or food content. Examples include German national 'purity laws', which have prohibited the import of beers brewed elsewhere in the Community, and Italian restrictions on the sale of pasta not made from specified wheat. Technical obstacles may also be embodied in procurement policies adopted by state agencies, in exchange controls, and in services as well as industrial goods. The Community has taken exception to the inefficiency and expense implied by duplication of effort, the failure to benefit from scale economies, and the cost involved in adapting products to meet other nations' criteria. Europe-wide technical standards are seen as important integrating forces, since if these commonly exist people will consider a broader source of supply, and, conversely, will market their goods more widely.

The new philosophy in the White Paper involves a move away from harmonization in the old sense of prescribing detailed, technical Community-wide standards to mutual recognition, such as the *Cassis de Dijon* principle; but specifically, three forms of action are involved. Firstly, efforts are made to prevent new technical barriers. Under Directive 83/139 a member state is obliged to notify the Commission in advance of new technical regulations relating to industrial or agricultural products. The Commission and other members may object if they consider that a barrier to trade would ensue, and can enforce a standstill of up to one year.

Secondly, Community harmonizing legislation will still apply through 'essential requirements' for products where safety, health, consumer protection and the environment are involved. However, the directives will only set out general levels or standards, with the details to be worked out by European standards institutes: CEN (Comité Européen de Normalisation) and CENELEC (Comité Européen de Normalisation Electro-technique), both of which include national standards bodies such as our British Standards Institute (BSI) and also ETSI (European Telecommunications Standards Institute). The directives apply irrespective of whether the products are traded between differing EC nations, and compliant goods will carry a 'CE' mark, on which basis no member state may refuse them market access on technical grounds. By February 1992 directives had been agreed for various items including toy safety, pressure vessels and gas appliances. As an example, the toy safety directive's essential requirements relate to: physical and mechanical properties, flammability, hygiene and radioactivity, chemical and electrical properties.

Thirdly, the above 'approximation' principle is complemented by the mutual recognition of standards by national governments, enforceable as the *Cassis de Dijon* ruling. This avoids unnecessary harmonization and the need for duplicate checking. To this end the European Organization for Testing and Certification (EOTC) has been created to encourage agreements on the mutual recognition of test results and certificates.

The existence of technical barriers can restrict labour mobility, notwithstanding the removal of physical border controls. In particular, differences in education and qualifications are potential constraints, hence the '1992' programme has set out to establish mutual recognition of professional qualifications. Previously directives had set out harmonized training in dentistry and the medical profession leading to the 'right of establishment overseas', but this was laborious; for example, pharmacy took 16 years to effect. Once the general directive on the freedom of establishment is in force, all professionals whose qualifications fall within its scope will have a right to have their qualifications recognized elsewhere within the Community. Where their training and education is substantially like that of the member state, their qualification will be recognized as equivalent; if not, they will have the choice of taking an aptitude test or undergoing a period of supervised practice lasting not more than three years.

Technical barriers also exist in service activities and a major thrust of the Single-Market programme is the completion of a common market in services, given their significance to modern economies. The process adopted is mutual recognition underpinned by local rules, with supervision of the task by the government of the country in which the service firm is based. Apart from the deregulation of financial services discussed in Sec. 1.4, the programme pays particular attention to transport, for example the liberalization of European air travel, and to the promotion of common standards in new technologies such as computing and audiovisual services.

Finally, the programme recognizes that various other legal and administrative barriers persist. For example, in terms of company law the Commission provides for the establishment of European Economic Interest Groupings (EEIGs) to encourage cooperation between businesses across member states. More significantly, it provides for a new form of European company structure; this will allow businesses in at least two member states to form a European public limited company (plc) to be set up anywhere in the EC. However, other directives have been implemented to coordinate the safeguards required for shareholder protection, such as those relating to information disclosure. Moreover, the programme is particularly concerned that intra-Community trade is fully subject to market forces, and that the gains from the elimination of national barriers are not lost to private barriers which fragment the Single Market (DTI 1992). This appears to create a paradox in that on the one hand the Commission wishes to engender cross-border collaboration, economies of scale and the free movement of factors of production, yet on the other it decries anti-competitive behaviour associated with market dominance, mergers and restrictive practices. Consequently, Community competition policy is a vital adjunct to effective implementation of the Single Market programme. This is discussed more fully in the context of Chapter 9.

1.3 THE FINANCIAL RATIONALE FOR THE SINGLE-MARKET PROGRAMME

To provide an impetus for the implementation of the Single European Act, the Commission felt obliged to quantify the benefits it perceived as arising from the Single Market programme. Hence a major two-year research study involving 11 000 firms was undertaken under the direction of Paolo Cecchini, special adviser to the Commission, together with 15 consultancy companies, academics and independent experts as well as Commission personnel. The results are fully examined in EC Commission (1988) and Cecchini (1988). The approach adopted is to argue that the economic benefits of the '1992' programme represent the mirror image of the costs of the 'uncommon market', that is of the failure to integrate. The Cecchini Report may be criticized for, firstly, bias and overestimation of the benefits, given that it was undertaken for the Commission; secondly, understandable inaccuracy, given the nature of the data and magnitude of the task; and thirdly, failure to examine the regional spread of benefits within the Community. Nevertheless, while the detail may be disputed, the general consensus is undoubtedly that completion of the internal market will herald significant gains in the region of ECU174-258 billion (at 1988 prices), or around 4.3–6.4 per cent of GDP.

In examining the costs of 'non-Europe', those relating to frontier controls are readily considered as excessive. Companies face unacceptably tedious administrative formalities, hauliers face long physical delays, customers must often pay more for foreign items, while travellers encounter checks, duties and exchange costs, and governments have the cost of administering such border points. The Cecchini Report estimates that firms pay ECU8 billion in administrative costs and delays resulting from intra-EC customs, or some 2 per cent of trans-border sales. Such costs become relatively more significant as company size falls, since larger companies are often able to reorganize to cater for the paperwork involved and to economize on procedures and staff. The research suggests that customs costs per consignment may be 30–45 per cent higher for companies with less than 250 employees.

Frontier delays also arise from differing national and industry technical, testing and safety standards which create lengthy inspections and higher production costs. In 1983 some 100 000 different technical specifications operated across European industry and, as technical progress has intensified along with greater environmental, health, safety and consumer protection concerns the problem has exacerbated. Such constraints prevent the emergence of genuine Euro-products and economies of scale such as are enjoyed by the Japanese and the Americans. In telecommunications and building products, divergent standards are estimated to cost ECU4.8 billion and ECU2.5 billion, respectively.

The diversity of standards in public purchasing is perhaps even more dramatic. Indeed, whereas private firms have gradually enhanced their intra-EC trade, the national bias of many public purchasing agencies remains, whether in the ordering of basic supply items, such as hospital and school equipment; tenders for public works, such as bridges or road construction; or major strategic industry support, such as aerospace or power generation. Cecchini estimated that total purchasing controlled by the public sector in 1986 amounted to 15 per cent of Community GDP or ECU530 billion, some ECU30 billion greater than the value of all intra-Community trade that year. Even allowing for the goods and services that are effectively non-competitive, non-tradable or too small in volume to warrant non-domestic suppliers' interest, the value of member states' annual procurement contracts was EC240–340 billion, of which only just over 1 per cent was awarded to contractors outside the national frontiers. The futility of national protection in a Community procurement context is seen with the European telecommunications market, worth £5 billion per annum. Owen and Dynes (1992) observe that the market consists of 11 national producers currently installing seven different exchange systems, most of which have been developed by state-owned companies. The opening up of procurement would provide an incentive to encourage linkages and cost reductions.

The total potential public expenditure savings from eliminating such inefficiencies are estimated at some ECU21.5 billion. The 1985 White Paper firstly proposed amendments to existing directives to encourage market entry by non-nationals; secondly, it provided opportunities for suppliers and contractors to pursue complaints about discrimination; and, thirdly, it extended new EC purchasing rules to previously 'closed' markets, notably water, energy, transport, supplies and telecommunications. This latter directive took effect on 1 January 1993. Public bodies will now have to open up all supply contracts above ECU200 000 and public works contracts above ECU5 million, and recognition of Community technical standards is required.

Such aforementioned costs of 'non-Europe' are essentially those that disappear once barriers are lifted, and those inefficiencies should be improved upon as competitive pressures intensify. Whereas the abolition of frontier controls produces relatively modest gains of approximately 0.3 per cent of GDP, removal of barriers arising from technical and material standards, public procurement and service-sector constraints amount to approximately 2.0 per cent of GDP. This is about the same magnitude of gains estimated to derive from integration via greater competition, economies of scale, specialization of production and trade via comparative advantage, and better use of technology.

A summary of the *microeconomic*-level gains suggests that consumers benefit from better choice, and from more consistent and lower pricing. Producers lose the benefit of protectionism, but, if competitive, stand to benefit from greater sales, lower input costs and access to technology. However, within individual sectors the spread of the impact varies considerably, as the following cases illustrate.

The EC *motor vehicle industry* is seen as a suitable case for treatment under the White Paper reforms. In 1987 it employed 7 per cent of EC manufacturing employees and generated 6 per cent of its value added in producing 11 million vehicles, approximately half of which were sold in the producer country. However, this is far from a rationally organized, unified market, and the 5 million vehicles exported across EC borders face considerable technical obstacles. The European Confederation of Vehicle Manufacturers estimates that the removal of these could save ECU2 billion merely through the reduction in transport, storage, marketing and research time. Fiscal differences further fragment the market, and sales prospects would benefit from moves to harmonize VAT around 15 per cent and reduce total indirect car taxes. In Denmark and Greece such taxes represent 195 and 131 per cent respectively of the sales price, compared with only 14 per cent in Germany and 25 per cent in the UK. Clearly, the revenue implications of cuts may be difficult for the Danish and Greek authorities to accept. In accordance with the Single Market aim to liberalize trade, the EC envisages the dismantling of trade quotas for 'third' nations. Currently these affect Japanese investment in car plants in the UK. If the quotas are eliminated, then EC manufacturers will face greater direct imports and the UK, potential future job and investment losses.

The challenge to the motor industry is to remove obstacles, and also the circumstances under which they create large price differentials, such as when technical problems are compounded by distribution arrangements. The weakness of the UK motor industry suggests that it may lack the competitiveness necessary to benefit from the removal of barriers. Although approximately 100 000 more cars were produced in the UK in 1987 than in 1983, the number exported fell by 10 000 over the same period, and the largest UK-owned manufacturer, Rover, held only 4 per cent of the EC market.

The *building products industry* is indicative of important regional differences among EC members. In spite of the fact that many of the products (bricks, glass, cement, etc.) are bulky, with transport costs a major influence, and that in house building national tastes diverge, the industry nevertheless is subject to considerable intra-EC trade. The Cecchini Report found that import penetration was significant in Italy, France, Germany and the UK, but that a wide range of standards persist, holding back further trade. Deregulation is estimated to encourage scale economies and long-term gains of ECU1.7 billion. The report showed that 70 per cent of the industry's products faced foreign technical problems, most notably in the 'northern' nations of the EC, especially France and Germany. Differences in electrical voltage, water pressure and pipe specifications have long proved obstacles. In cement the UK is likely to lose from harmonization, since UK prices are among the highest in Europe, although for other products UK companies may benefit, especially as they tend to be among the larger operators who can gain from economies of scale.

The *pharmaceutical industry* represents one of the more dynamic and profitable, but equally one of the most regulated, of EC industries owing to diverse and lengthy licensing requirements. This reflects the need for controls on product quality and safety, and the concerns of public authorities who bear 50 per cent of the expenditure on pharmaceutical products. The producers, however, have to finance considerable research and development, often with uncertain and lengthy payback. This curious interplay between private and public forces means that the government is often cast in the role of customer, regulator and price-fixer. The EC Commission wishes to end state support for national producers and to stimulate research and development by freer competition, with production on a larger and more cost-effective scale. The Cecchini Report argued that the registration of new drugs differed widely between nations in spite of a convergence in technical standards and agreement on a 120-day decision period. Delays in processing took two years in the UK and Germany and at least three in Spain and Italy. This caused revenue losses for the producers concerned and the total cost of 'non-Europe' arising from registration practice differences was put at 0.5–0.8 per cent of EC industry costs. The UK pharmaceutical industry is among the more profitable in the EC, largely because of its low labour cost–value added ratio, but undoubtedly also because the National Health Service is a major customer.

The impact of the internal market is particularly acute in service-sector operations, since any market distortions are passed on through their servicing role to industry. *Telecommunications* is seen as ripe for deregulation. European suppliers lag behind their US and Japanese counterparts largely because of the fragmented EC market with its tradition of public-sector telecommunications monopolies, national preference in government procurement policies and artificially high tariffs. Limitations that often exist over the compatibility and supply of equipment are such that there is little cross-border trade. The EC Commission proposed a graduated deregulation to 1992 estimated to bring cost savings of ECU2 billion, largely resulting from lower capital investment costs creating lower tariffs. Moreover, given the strongly expected expansion of the world market, the polarization of the industry into a handful of large entities exploiting economies of scale is seen as necessary to match Japanese and US competition. The UK has shown the way with the deregulation of British Telecom (BT) in 1984, and UK companies such as BT and Mercury should benefit from competition in the supply of equipment to support the basic telephone service, such as databanks, electronic mail and electronic data exchange services.

The Single-Market programme comprises a range of microeconomic policy measures aimed essentially at enhanced competitiveness and efficiency. Yet the magnitude of the total perceived benefit, around 5 per cent of GDP in the initial five years, suggests considerable *macroeconomic* effects. These can be separated into effects on the real or goods markets, and effects on the financial markets.

Given that the customs union has been in existence since 1968, notwithstanding the 1980s accession of 'southern members', a reasonable degree of *goods market integration* might be expected. Thus, if the customs union has worked, the macroeconomic effects of abolishing the border controls should be relatively low. This is confirmed in Table 1.2, which illustrates that the major GDP benefits come from the supply side and financial services gains. The impact of the removal frontier controls is via improvement in the general terms of trade as import prices drop under competitive pressure and reduced costs. Abolition of customs posts will have a negligible, if favourable, effect on public revenue via savings in expenditure and the enhanced value of business, although some offsetting short-term redeployment and unemployment costs will ensue.

The liberalization of public procurement has a greater measurable impact via price and competition effects. Public expenditure gains should follow from cheaper supplies and should be passed on to the economy at large. The supply-side 'shocks' on business portrayed by Cecchini are seen via economies of scale and competition creating price benefits from production gains, and productivity improvements fostering efficiency and profitability. These will impact via medium-term demand increases into the macroeconomy, although cost savings

Table 1.2 Macroeconomic impact of the Single Market for the Community (medium-term)

	Abolition of frontier controls	Liberalization of public procurement	Liberalization of financial services	Economies of scale (industry) and competition	Total (average values)
Relative changes (%)					
GDP	0.4	0.5	1.5	2.1	4.5
Consumer prices	−1.0	−1.4	−1.4	−2.3	−6.1
Absolute changes employment (millions)	200	350	400	850	1800
Government borrowing requirement (as % GDP)	0.2	0.3	1.1	0.6	2.2
External balance (as % GDP)	0.2	0.1	0.3	0.4	1.0

Source: Cecchini (1988).

in the factors of production will create short-term, often severe, adjustment issues. Wolf (1988) cites the problem in farm equipment manufacture, where 50 EC tractor manufacturers are competing for a market similar in size to that served in the USA by just 4, and notes that in public procurement there is virtually no intra-EC trade in locomotives, turbine generators and telephones, yet in Germany prices of telecommunications equipment are 50-100 per cent above world market levels. Government regulations are particularly noticeable in *financial markets* and, as Table 1.2 indicates, the greatest sector gains of all are estimated to accrue from financial services liberalization.

1.4 THE EUROPEAN FINANCIAL COMMON MARKET (EFCM)

The financial services sector is both a vast and rapidly growing market in its own right, and a catalyst for the whole EC economy through its interaction with agriculture, manufacturing and other services. However, it is inevitably a highly regulated sector, as individual nations have imposed restrictions on financial services operations across their borders. These constraints, whether for investor protection, revenue or other reasons, have influenced the organization and growth of financial systems often along very specific lines, thus further hindering the integration process.

The Cecchini Report examined the potential gains from financial services integration in a survey of three main areas (banking and credit, insurance, broking and securities) across eight EC nations. Prevailing price differentials were calculated for a range of representative products and the findings revealed considerable divergences, notably in the prices charged for mortgages, foreign exchange drafts, consumer credit, commercial insurance and most securities operations. Various future price levels were then estimated, with the average of the four lowest prices observed taken as the one that would exist with liberalization. The difference between this average and the observed price was then calculated, with the discrepancies converted into *potential* price falls. However, given that differing national circumstances as well as regulations contribute to price differences and would not be fully removed on completion of the Single Market, these potential price falls would accelerate the gains. Thus, these price reductions were scaled down to produce the *expected* price falls shown in Table 1.3.

Table 1.3 Gains from the completion of the EFCM

Estimated potential falls in financial product prices from completion of the internal market

	% differences in selected financial product prices compared with average of the four lowest observations						
	Bel.	Ger.	Sp.	Fra.	Ita.	Neth.	UK
Banking							
Consumer credit	−41	136	39	105	n/a	31	121
Credit cards	79	60	26	−30	89	43	16
Mortgages	31	57	118	78	−4	−6	−20
Letters of credit	22	−10	59	−7	9	17	8
Foreign exchange	6	31	196	56	23	−46	16
Travellers' cheques	35	−7	30	39	22	33	−7
Commercial loans	−5	6	19	−7	9	43	46
Insurance							
Life	78	5	37	33	83	−9	−30
Home	−16	3	−4	39	81	−17	90
Motor	30	15	100	9	148	−7	−17
Commercial, fire, theft	−9	43	24	153	245	−1	−27
Securities							
Private equity	36	7	65	−13	−3	114	123
Private gilts	14	90	217	21	−63	161	36
Institutional equity	26	69	153	−5	47	26	−47
Institutional gilts	284	−4	60	57	92	21	n/a
Theoretical, potential price falls							
Banking	15	33	34	25	18	10	18
Insurance	31	10	32	24	51	1	4
Securities	52	11	44	23	33	18	12
Total	23	25	34	24	29	9	13

Source: 'The Economics of 1992', study by Price Waterhouse in *European Economy* (1988), 35.

These expected price reductions were then used to examine the impact on individual nations, and the greatest expected falls were shown to be in Spain and Italy. The overall benefit for the EC was estimated at ECU21.7 billion, with the largest gains likely in the UK (ECU5.1 billion) since, although UK price falls are relatively modest, they are multiplied by the huge size of the UK financial sector. While such findings are estimates based on over-optimistic assumptions (see Dixon 1991), they nevertheless point to considerable benefits from financial services integration. Liberalizing national financial markets should therefore provide more choice of savings products and more efficient, cheaper, sources of financing. These gains would presumably be even greater if linked to a common currency, thus eliminating intra-Community exchange costs.

Legislation necessary to liberalize European finance has existed for some time. Indeed, the Treaty of Rome catered for the right of establishment and the free movement of capital. However, less progress has been made than in the traded goods sector, largely because of the view that money and capital movements are concerns of national sovereignty and have major impacts on the domestic economy. In addition, the wide range of activities encompassed in financial services and the rapid changes in the international financial environment created complicated moves towards greater integration. The 1987 Single European Act is thus seen as providing the impetus for a European Financial Common Market (EFCM). This implies that banks, insurance companies and other financial institutions can freely establish and provide services, and that customers may borrow, invest and obtain insurance or other financial products in any member state. Moreover, capital circulates freely within the Community, and ultimately a common monetary framework exists, a macroeconomic aspect of profound significance for Europe.

According to the 1985 White Paper, the Commission's aim is that trade in financial products should be governed by three main principles: minimum coordination of individual national rules, mutual recognition, and home-country control. The four areas targeted for integration are: capital movements, banking, securities, and insurance.

1.4.1 Liberalization of capital movements

To achieve a genuine Single Market, efficient and competitive financial markets are essential. This implies full freedom for capital movements, a feature encouraged by disenchantment with exchange controls in the context of globally linked markets. Some larger EC nations have modernized their financial systems, recognizing that their competitive ability *vis à vis* the United States or Japan is enhanced by freeing capital movements. However, in the early 1980s controls remained in Denmark, France, Italy and Ireland, and the accession of Spain, Greece and Portugal further added to the scale of protectionism. Thus, as part of the Single European Act, a directive *Capital Movements* (88/361), removing controls from all capital flows within the EC, was adopted in June 1988 applicable to most countries from 1990. Spain, Ireland, Greece and Portugal were given until 1992 to comply fully with the terms of the directive, and, because of adjustment difficulties with their developing markets, Greece and Portugal were given the possibility of a further extension to 1995.

The directive contained a safeguard clause allowing controls to be imposed where exceptional short-term flows would seriously disrupt monetary and exchange rate policy. This reflected the fact that, in the absence of a common currency, monetary policy is the responsibility of national authorities. In addition, to ease the adjustment process, the Community combined two existing facilities for medium-term assistance for member states facing balance of payments crises. Firstly, loans of up to ECU16 billion are available. Secondly, the directive also made reference to freeing capital movements to and from non-EC members. This was taken up in the Maastricht Treaty on European Union. The new regime, which starts in January 1994, extends the liberalization of capital and payments between EC members, with some exceptions, to movements between members and other parts of the world.

Capital movement liberalization will eventually have greater impact on residents of EC nations that have prolonged their exchange controls, such as Greece and Portugal. Their business with the UK will increase; for example, there will be no restrictions on Greek residents opening bank accounts in the UK, or on Portuguese residents borrowing from UK banks without authorization at home. Market forces should in theory encourage nations to harmonize withholding tax rates on interest rate payments to prevent nations with the most favourable rates attracting large capital inflows. France, which levies high rates, was particularly concerned lest large capital outflows started following the relaxation of its exchange controls, and has sought proposals to harmonize withholding taxes. However, taxation remains one area where agreement is not easy between members, and hence complete liberalization of capital movements is still some way away.

1.4.2 Liberalization of banking

Banking has traditionally been one of the most regulated industries in the EC, hence the challenge facing the Commission has been to formulate a regulatory regime that accounts for the varied practices yet is not burdensome. Consequently a set of directives was established. Initially these aimed at harmonization, but later, following the 1985 White Paper, they came to be built around the concept of a single banking licence with home-country control.

The initial move towards the formulation of a common market for banking services was the *First Banking Directive 77/780* in 1977, which required the member states to establish systems for authorizing and supervising banks and other credit institutions that take deposits and lend money. The directive created a basic right of establishment whereby a bank (or credit institution) in one country could open a branch or offer banking services in any other member state, provided it complied with the conditions and supervision applied to local banks.

To obtain authorization, a credit institution must have separate capital from that of its owners; must meet an initial capital requirement; and must have at least two directors plus a reputable and experienced management.

However, for a real single banking market a basic right of establishment is not enough. Banks (or credit institutions) wishing to establish a branch elsewhere in the EC still required authorization from the host country, which could apply legislation and arduous capital requirements. So in 1989 the Commission produced a *Second Banking Directive 89/646*, which set out the principle of the right of banks to establish branches and to trade financial services throughout the EC, on the basis of a single authorization or 'licence' from their home-country supervisor.

Thus, there has been a shift away from detailed harmonization of regulations towards a principle of home-country control based on mutual recognition by EC nations of each others' systems. The aim is *enough* harmonization to allow for mutual recognition. The directive thus accepts the concept that, provided banks are properly authorized and supervised in their home country, they may take deposits and offer loans in other states without the need for host-country authorization.

There are exceptions to home-country control in that host countries can retain the right to control bank liquidity for monetary policy reasons. Also, banks selling a range of products, for example, consumer credit, savings and mortgages, will still need to ensure compliance with local host-nation consumer protection and similar laws in the public interest, such as the 1986 Financial Services Act in the UK. However, individual EC members cannot discriminate against foreign entrants alone. The directive covers a wide range of activities akin to those provided by all-purpose 'universal banks', including the following:[1]

- Acceptance of deposits and other repayable funds from the public
- Lending to include consumer credit, mortgage credit, factoring, financing of commercial transactions (including fortfaiting)
- Financial leasing
- Money transmission services
- Issuing and administering means of payment (e.g. credit cards, travellers' cheques and bankers' drafts)
- Guarantees and commitments
- Trading for own account or for account of customers in:
  (a) money market instruments (cheques, bills, CDs, etc.)
  (b) foreign exchange
  (c) financial futures and options
  (d) exchange and interest rate instruments

[1]Taken from the Second Banking Directive 89/646/EEC (*Official Journal* of the EC, L386, Vol. 12, 30 December 1989, Annex).

(e) transferable securities

- Participation in share issues and the provision of services related to such issues
- Advice to undertakings on capital structure, industrial strategy and related questions, and advice and services relating to mergers and the purchase of undertakings
- Money broking
- Portfolio management and advice
- Safekeeping and administration of securities
- Credit references services
- Safe custody services

By implication, a bank will be able to provide such services even if the host country prevents domestic firms from offering them. This itself is a spur to deregulation, as those firms tightly restricted in the activities they can provide at home will be disadvantaged *vis à vis* banks from the more liberated parts of the Community.

The directive also harmonizes minimum standards of authorization and prudential supervision. Thus, credit institutions must initially have and maintain capital of at least ECU5 million. The authorities have the right to supervise ownership and control to prevent cross-financing and conflicts of interest, and may refuse to sanction certain group structures deemed inadequate. The institution must regularly inform the authorities of its major shareholders and those investors stake-building with a view to acquisition. Moreover, credit institutions may not maintain a participation in any one non-bank business that exceeds 10 per cent of their own funds; nor may the overall value of such holdings exceed 50 per cent of own funds. The directive also sanctioned the abolition by 1992 of the initial capital requirement of branches, previously a costly disincentive to branch expansion.

The concepts of mutual recognition and home-country authorization, together with minimum standards, thus considerably strengthen relationships between member nations' supervisors. Further provisions are made for consultation before branches are established and for general information exchange. For banks and other credit institutions the directive lowers technical barriers to cross-border trading and heightens awareness of the larger, Single Market. Thus, banks are freer to open branches, to extend their range of services, and to link with other institutions overseas. Such strategic options are considered in Chapter 7.

However, to service the EC market banks must also be adequately capitalized, and thus two important complementary directives were issued in 1989: the *Own Funds Directive 89/299* and the *Solvency Ratio Directive*. Indeed, a provision in the *Second Banking Directive (SBD)* prevented it from being implemented prior to these two rulings. They establish the minimum prudential standards and, together with the *SBD*, provide the basic regulatory framework for banks in the Community. All three came into force on 1 January 1993.

The purpose of the Own Funds Directive is to harmonize the definition of the minimum capital base of credit institutions so that banking authorities know that supervisory standards are broadly compatible. 'Own funds' cushion losses but also indicate the solvency of institutions by forming the numerator for solvency ratios. The Commission considers that minimum harmonization is necessary to avoid distortions in competitiveness. A two-tier classification is used similar to the Bank for International Settlements' (BIS) capital-adequacy ratings. Tier 1 capital includes that at the bank's free disposal and can cushion losses: equity, reserves (legal, revenue, capital), general provisions, and securities of indeterminate duration, for example cumulative preference shares. Tier 2 capital represents funds available but not fully owned or controlled by the institution, such as subordinated loans. By 1995 these Tier 2 elements may comprise only 50 per cent of an institution's own funds.

The Solvency Ratio (*Directive*) aims for a minimum prudent ratio harmonized among banks. These must maintain shareholders' funds at not less than 8 per cent of risk-weighted assets. Borrowers are assigned risk-weights according to their status, such as central banks, local authorities, etc., and are divided between EC and non-EC locations. Both of these directives reflect international agreements between the G-10 industrial nations (Cooke Committee). Thus, the standards apply beyond the EC to Japan, the United States and other OECD nations. Further strengthening of capital adequacy has come with the 1987 *Recommendations on Large Exposures 87/062*, which is the basis for a *Large Exposures Directive* to be adopted. Credit institutions must report annually on all large exposures to individual borrowers amounting to more than 15 per cent of their 'own funds', as well as the largest exposures even if less than 15 per cent.

1.4.3 Liberalization of securities markets

An integral part of an unfettered EFCM is that the issuing and trading of financial securities takes place unhindered across EC boundaries. Given the substantive changes to leading world securities markets brought about by technological advances in dealing systems and telecommunications, product innovation and deregulation, there is an urgent need for Community policy in this area. This is even more acute if the pricing discrepancies uncovered by the Cecchini Report are considered. However, progress in this direction has been somewhat erratic, with resistance to cross-border trading emanating from France, Spain and Italy who fear for their stock exchanges in the face of competition.

Since 1979 the Commission has promulgated a series of directives initially geared to the harmonization of regulations and later with a view to creating a single securities market. The March 1979 *Admissions Directive 79/279* established the conditions necessary before securities could be admitted to an EC exchange; for example the provision of accounts, which meant that countries could not refuse a listing on the grounds that a company has not been listed on another exchange first, although they could refuse it for investor protection reasons. This was the first of four directives (one other covering the listing of particulars and two on mutual recognition) intended to make it easier for companies to list their shares or raise capital on other EC exchanges.

In the mid-1980s two directives on the marketing of units by investment funds, *UCITS Directives 85/611* and *88/220* (undertakings for collective investment in transferable securities), adopted the 1985 White Paper principle of mutual recognition. Thus, a unit trust, if approved in one country and meeting the basic requirements of the directive, can be sold anywhere in the EC without further approval, provided it meets investor protection needs. Thereafter directives began to promote greater transparency in European securities dealings, often requesting more information: *Large Shareholdings Directives 85/791, 88/627* (disclosure of large stakes in companies); *Prospectus (Public Offer) Directive 89/268* (provision of full, minimum information in prospectuses); and *Insider Dealing Directive 89/592* (harmonization of the diverse laws on insider dealing throughout the EC).

However, the most significant development is the *Investment Services Directive 88/778*, which was proposed in 1988 and after much debate finally came into effect in June 1992. Together with regulations on insurance and capital requirements (*Capital Adequacy Directive*), it represents the final stage in the Community's attempts to build a Single Market in financial services by the start of 1993. It works on the same 'passport' principle as the Second Banking Directive. Indeed, although the latter includes securities operations in those activities sanctioned by the licence, the Council accepted that stock market access needed to be widened. Moreover, the Second Banking Directive excludes non-bank investment firms which thus become disadvantaged *vis à vis* cross-border trading. This latter aspect is of vital significance in highly segmented, market-based financial systems such as in the UK, which traditionally have not conformed to the 'universal bank' models, and UK securities houses therefore welcome the Investment Services Directive (ISD).

Under the ISD, investment firms authorized in one member state are able to open branches and provide services in others. They will need to notify their intention to establish, but not any additional authorization. Supervision is by home-country regulators for whom the directive sets minimum standards, but information must be provided to other regulators on request. Investment firms are defined by reference to a broad range of financial service activities: brokerage, market-making, dealing as principal, portfolio management, underwriting, security custody and professional investment advice. In turn, these activities relate to instruments: money market, foreign exchange and interest rate products, futures, options and transferable securities. However, commodity futures and options dealing are excluded from the benefit of the 'single licence' and from authorization, although within the UK such dealing is subject to the Financial Services Act. With the growth of 'off-exchange' trading, the provisions for access have had to be amended. Thus, investment firms may join exchanges without establishment in the member state concerned. The provision allows such exchanges to provide facilities in other member states so that investment firms there may join the exchange.

The accompanying *Capital Adequacy Directive* will impose a framework for minimum capital requirements for authorized investment firms and the investment business of credit institutions. Banks have a choice, in that they may apply the Solvency Ratio Directive to all the bank's activities, or they may separate out the investment trading aspects and subject these to capital adequacy requirements. Investment firms are expected to have a minimum capital of ECU500 000, reducible if no trading positions are maintained.

1.4.4   Liberalization of insurance

The European insurance industry has been subject to a large number of directives in recent years, but has only recently exhibited movement towards the establishment of a single insurance market. Freedom of establishment for insurance companies located in one member nation to set up branches or agencies in others on the same basis as domestic insurers was set out in the 1973 *First Non-Life Insurance Directive* and its subsequent amendments, and in the 1979 *First Life Insurance Directive*. These resembled the First Banking Directive with a focus on harmonizing supervision.

Moves towards a 'single-licence' system have progressed more slowly, notably over the freedom to provide services in another member state without establishment there. Several member states, apart from the UK, imposed substantive restrictions on service provision. In Germany, non-German firms were forced to have a local establishment and to pay tax rates considered discriminatory by the Commission. In 1986 the issue was judged by the European Court of Justice which ruled against four member states, arguing that their restrictions on insurance companies from other states were partly illegal. This judgment, and the arrival of qualified majority voting to overcome the single-country veto, encouraged the formulation of the June 1988 *Second Non-Life Insurance Directive* or *Non-Life Services Directive 88/357*. This took effect in July 1990 and gives EC insurers, wherever based, freedom to cover the risks of policy-holders in any member country. It frees cross-border trade in large risks, namely policies for companies with more than 500 employees or more than £15 million turnover. For these, home-country control exists without the need for special authorization in the host nation. Thus, large corporate customers may buy their insurance where they desire, without being bound by local laws to purchase domestically. For mass risks, such as house insurance, host-country control was prescribed to comply with local regulations, although further changes are expected.

The adoption of this Non-Life directive paved the way for other 'freedom of services' proposals. In November 1990 the *Motor Insurance Services Directive 90/278* was adopted, bringing motor insurance within the scope of the above Non-Life directive. In addition, the *Second Life Assurance Directive* or *Life*

Services Directive 90/305 was enacted. The latter similarly provides two regimes for the provision of cross-border services. A more 'liberal' approach allows 'well-established' companies covering large risks merely to notify the relevant authorities of their intention to provide services, whereby under the more 'restrictive' regime the host country may exercise significant control.

Nevertheless, problems remain with life assurance. Germany is reluctant to cede authority over institutions entrusted with individuals' life savings and has strongly protected its market. However, the growth of cross-border banking is likely to undermine this, given the advent of 'Bancassurance' with mergers or reciprocal business links between banks and insurers. Taxation differences also compound the problems, with different tax relief treatment on premiums creating an element of competitive distortion. Nevertheless, progress towards a single insurance market is gathering momentum, spurred by the Commission's recent 'framework' proposals.

Three 'framework' directives—*Third Non-Life Insurance; Third Motor Insurance* and *Third Life Assurance*—were proposed in 1991 for implementation in 1993. They amend current directives and introduce the 'single-licence' system modelled on the Second Banking Directive, enabling EC branches and agencies to be authorized and supervised by the insurer's home country.

The UK is a major supplier of insurance services, and, notwithstanding problems in the Lloyds insurance market, stands to gain from EC insurance liberalization. In the past many British insurers have been relatively under-represented, operating much of their non-life business via agencies. The special-ism in non-life large risks will offer opportunities via links with local companies overseas, especially in the relatively underdeveloped 'southern' EC markets. In life assurance the high returns on UK policies may attract new custom. However, insurance is clearly one area of financial services where more deregulation within individual countries is necessary before cross-border activity really takes off.

CONCLUSIONS

The reality of the single European market has taken a long time to develop from the principles established in the 1957 Treaty of Rome. With the advent of the customs union in 1968 intra-Community tariff barriers were repealed, only to be replaced by non-tariff obstacles in the form of national specifications, regula-tions and subsidies. For many years the Community seemed to have lost its dynamism and been consumed by national self-interest. The Single-Market pro-gramme is a complex, wide-ranging attempt to marshall the diverse economic forces of Europe and provide the stimulus and direction for future economic, and possibly political, unity.

The 1987 Single European Act is essentially a set of microeconomic policy measures, originally some 300 specific proposals geared primarily to improving the supply side of the economy. The operational focus is on dismantling barriers between member states, and considerable progress has been made with the '1992' time-scale, aided by a climate of belief in market forces promulgated by many developed countries in the 1980s. The Cecchini Report, for all its estimates and assumptions, points to the tremendous costs of 'non-Europe' associated with features such as frontier delays, technical constraints and procurement policies. Equally significant are the efficiency gains from greater competition, economies of scale and the spur to technological innovation.

Much of this micro-level benefit derives from the liberalization of financial services where integration is seen to produce consumer gains via better advice, product availability and favourable pricing, and producer gains via greater profit opportunities generated by a wider market. However, liberalization brings forth difficult decisions which form focal points for subsequent chapters. Deregulation can go too far, and so a major issue for national and supranational authorities is the appropriate level and focus of supervision, an issue addressed in Chapter 6. The wider, liberated market produces important strategic decisions for the major European financial institutions, and in Chapter 7 we consider the product-market options available to them in a period of rapid technological change. The European Financial Common Market impinges heavily upon financial market development, and Chapter 8 focuses on the problem of competition and the scope for collaboration among stock exchanges and derivative markets in the light of deregulation and the drive for efficiency.

The Single-Market programme also has a major macroeconomic impact, estimated in the Cecchini Report to add approximately five per cent to Community GDP in the first five years. One-third of this derives from the liberalization of financial services, where pricing gains are seen to feed through into lower capital costs, fuelling investment and growth. Moreover, deregulation should provide a wider availability of credit and better allocation of finance, issues also central to bank–industry relations discussed in Chapter 9. The logic is that lower-cost finance will stimulate purchasing power, boosting demand and growth. However, the liberalization of capital controls, added to competitive trading across financial markets, will accentuate pressures on exchange rates and create the need for firm currency management. Thus, the European Monetary System will come under pressure; indeed, by implication, the Single European Act threatens its demise.

However, if there is one market, then perhaps we need only one currency? In Chapter 2 this fundamental issue facing the EC is considered, a focal point of the Delors Plan for Economic and Monetary Union adopted at Maastricht in December 1991. Fundamental to the development of such a union is the future role of the central banks. In Chapter 5 the independence of central banks is considered with reference to the *Bund*esbank, the Bank of England and the future European central banking proposals.

The Single-Market programme is not welcomed universally throughout the EC. Although many industrialists accept the potential economic benefits from the wider market and ensuing economies of scale, some fear the consequences for small businesses or vulnerable sectors, such as the car industry. However, a more widespread fear is the loss of sovereignty and the transfer of power to the Brussels 'federalists'—one market, one currency and one government? Moreover, after a decade of the dominance of market philosophy and deregulation in many areas of activity, there is less favour for bureaucratic centralization, issues considered in Chapter 3 on public-sector funding and in Chapter 4 on the Community budget.

Many also disagree about the pace and direction of integration, some want the immediate integration of the existing Twelve, while others favour a broadening of EC membership. Chapter 10 considers the financial aspects of such expansion. Indeed, since the Single European Act and the Delors Plan were formulated, the map of Europe has changed radically: Germany has unified, the Soviet Union has disintegrated, fledgling democracies have emerged in eastern Europe, and applications for EC membership have risen, notably from the EFTA block—all of which make 'Europe' a harder term to define. Nevertheless, the Single Market programme has endured these events, and, indeed, furthered plans for economic and mometary union, to which we now turn.

FURTHER READING

Hitiris (1991) provides a concise overview of regional integration theory which is covered in depth in most international economics texts. For the development of the European Community see Nevin (1990). On the Single Market see EC Commission (1985) (the White Paper) and general guides produced by the DTI (1992), or texts such as Owen and Dynes (1992), Roney (1991) and Budd and Jones (1991). The most comprehensive sources are the European Documentation Centres (EDCs) found in most British universities, which contain all important EC publications. The major assessment of the financial impact was the EC's multi-volume study on the 'costs of non-Europe'—see EC Commission (1988), Cecchini (1988), Emerson *et al.* (1988) or Baldwin (1989).

TWO

EMS AND EMU: ONE CURRENCY FOR EUROPE?

If the Single Market is preoccupying businessmen and politicians in the early years of the 1990s, by the end of the century the focus should be very much on European Monetary Union. Will we have relinquished sovereignty over our economic and monetary policies? Will we have dispensed with our pounds, francs and Deutschmarks for the ubiquitous ECU? If so, then some of the major economic, political and psychological barriers to our becoming one Europe will have been overcome. Moreover, if monetary union is achieved by, or shortly after, the turn of the century, it will be a remarkable achievement, given the chequered history to date of developments in this direction.

2.1 EARLY MOVES TOWARDS ECONOMIC AND MONETARY UNION

The Treaty of Rome made no specific reference to monetary union: rather, its aims lay in the 'foundations of an ever-closer union among the European peoples' via the setting up of the Common Market. The progressive convergence of members' economies was intended but was seen as the business of the individual member states. At the time currency policy harmonization was not a priority, as the Six operated within the confines of the Bretton Woods fixed exchange rate system with currencies linked to the dollar. By the end of the 1960s, however, the stability of the international monetary system was severely disrupted: sterling was devalued in 1967; confidence in the dollar was weakening; and, significantly in 1969, the franc was devalued and the Deutschmark revalued. These latter adjustments had a highly disruptive impact on the Community economy, notably on the viability of the pricing system of the Common Agricultural Policy (CAP). The potential gains from the integration of a large Single Market were clearly being hampered by monetary instability, and so in December 1969 the EEC heads of state decided to pursue full monetary union.

The resultant Werner Plan ambitiously proposed: (1) permanently fixed and convertible exchange rates by 1980; (2) coordinated monetary policy supervised by a common monetary institution; and (3) fully liberalized capital movements. The process was to be split into two stages: an initial phase of improved economic convergence and narrower limits (± 0.75 per cent) of exchange rate fluctuation than the ± 1 per cent prescribed by the IMF, to be followed by a monetarist-led phase to fulfil monetary union.

Implicit in the Werner proposals were two issues that have remained central to subsequent arguments about EMU. Firstly, member states would have to relinquish sovereignty to a central body in areas of exchange rate, fiscal and monetary policy. Secondly, certain economic disadvantages, such as regional imbalances and unemployment, might ensue from members forfeiting sovereignty; to counter this recourse might be necessary to EC social and regional funds.

The broad principles of the Werner Plan were duly agreed and it was launched in June 1971. But the timing was unfortunate, as the ongoing dollar crisis caused havoc on the foreign exchange markets—indeed, caused the short-term closure of certain European exchanges. Ultimately an IMF conference in December 1971 set out the Smithsonian Agreement, whereby the official exchange rate of the dollar was reduced and the existing fixed exchange rate system was modified from currency movements of ± 1 per cent to parity ± $2\frac{1}{4}$ per cent.

Eventually in April 1972 the European Common Margins Agreement (the 'Snake') became operational, whereby members' currencies were to be restrained within bands limited to one half of that required by the IMF—hence the 'Snake' within the 'Tunnel' of the wider IMF band. The reciprocal margins required obligatory intervention points, and the participants' central banks agreed to a system of unlimited short-term financing of interventions through a newly established European Monetary Cooperation Fund (EMCF).

The operation of the 'Snake' was disrupted by the collapse in confidence of the dollar and the oil crisis of 1973–74. The dollar was at the centre of the fixed exchange rate system and its stability was essential for success. When exchange rates became increasingly volatile, severe balance of payments difficulties ensued and the differential effects of the oil crisis increased the variability of EC inflation rates. By 1976 three of the four major currencies had left the 'Snake' and 'floated'; indeed, sterling had left within six weeks of its entry in 1972. In essence, all that remained was an effective Deutschmark bloc consisting of West Germany, Denmark and the Benelux nations.

Thus, the first attempt at economic and monetary union was unsuccessful. While the venture was ill-timed with the demise of the Bretton Woods system of fixed exchange rates, it was weakened by the lack of commitment to, and actual convergence of, participants' economies and economic policies. Moreover, the system placed undue burden of adjustment upon countries with weak currencies. Those with stronger currencies could offer support but were not obliged to keep the value of their exchange rate down. Of course, proponents of EMU argued that it had not been given a fair trial at all.

2.2 THE EUROPEAN MONETARY SYSTEM (EMS)

Somewhat ironically, it was a Briton, Roy Jenkins, the EC president from 1977 to 1980, who revived the concept of economic and monetary union as part of his desire to further the economic and political benefits of the Common Market. At the 1978 EC summit in Bremen, agreement was reached on the creation of a European Monetary System (EMS), a zone of exchange rate stability.

Currency conditions were better for monetary union, as many EC members were disenchanted with the effects of floating exchange rates which had impeded trade, and Germany was keen to protect the Deutschmark from upward pressure from a weak dollar. Fixed commitments with other currencies would lower the attractiveness of the Deutschmark. There were also signs of convergence among members' economies, especially in the fight against inflation. However, their previous experiences dampened enthusiasm for monetary union and the EMS. Ireland was reluctant to join and Italy entered on the wider ± 6 per cent band of fluctuation, while the UK only partly joined and did not join the exchange rate mechanism (ERM).

The original implicit EMS aims might be considered as threefold: firstly in the very short term to stabilize exchange rates and in so doing to form an effective currency bloc against the dollar and yen, while at the same time helping European economies by avoiding frequent currency alignments; secondly, in the short term to promote economic convergence and to force policies on members similar to those of the most successful nations, notably Germany; thirdly, in the long term to encourage economic and monetary union, which was seen as a prerequisite for political union. Economic union via convergence of policies on inflation, interest rates and taxation would encourage trade and the integration of capital and foreign exchange markets, and would possibly pave the way for a common currency.

2.2.1 Operation of the EMS

We can distinguish certain principles underlying the operation of the EMS from its actual mechanics. In the first place, it consists of a set of rules to limit currency fluctuations based on each currency having a central rate parity fixed in

ECUs and thus being indirectly fixed in terms of the other currencies involved. Secondly, members are obliged to curtail fluctuations in the value of their currencies against one another within stipulated margins. These obligations imply intervention to stabilize currencies, both 'intra-marginal intervention' prior to the corresponding currency limits, and 'compulsory intervention' when the ECU-prescribed limits are breached. This principle aims to offset a major defect of the 'Snake', and indeed of the Bretton Woods system before; namely, the lack of *mutual* obligation of exchange rate support. Thirdly, from time to time central rates may be changed, hence the system is not a rigidly fixed one.

The mechanics of the EMS involve three elements: a currency unit (ECU); an exchange rate and intervention system (ERM); and a mechanism for administering the necessary credit facilities (EMCF).

The European Currency Unit (ECU)   The European currency unit ECU is a composite unit of currency based on a basket of the participating currencies, plus sterling. It is calculated as a weighted average of all EC currency values, the weightings originally reflecting the trade significance of the nations concerned, with the proviso for revision every five years. Table 2.1 shows the current composition following the revisions in 1984 (addition of drachma) and 1989 (addition of escudo and peseta).

Within the EMS, the ECU has technically four related roles:

- As a *unit* in terms of which parities are declared
- As a *measure* of the overall strength of currencies against the average of the rest and hence the basis for the *divergence indicator*

Table 2.1 Composition of the ECU

Currencies	13/3/79–16/9/84	17/9/84–20/9/89	Since 21/9/89	Weights based on exchange rates at 10/8/92
Deutschmark (DM)	0.8280	0.719	0.6242	30.62
Pound sterling (£)	0.0880	0.0878	0.0878	12.18
French franc (FFr)	1.1500	1.3100	1.3320	19.32
Italian lira (L)	109.0000	140.0000	151.8000	9.84
Dutch guilder (G)	0.2860	0.2560	0.2198	9.56
Belgian/Luxembourg franc (BFr/LuxFr)	3.8000	3.8500	3.4310	8.17
Danish krone (Dkr)	0.2770	0.2190	0.1976	2.52
Irish punt (IR£)	0.0076	0.0087	0.0085	1.10
Greek drachma (Dr)	—	1.1500	1.4400	0.57[a]
Spanish peseta (Pta)	—	—	6.8850	5.29
Portuguese escudo (Esc)	—	—	1.3930	0.83[a]
				100.00

[a] Notional rates/weightings.

- As a *means of settlement* between monetary authorities
- As a *denominator* for operations involving the intervention and credit mechanisms.

The intention was that the ECU would be used predominantly for intervention purposes to limit the potential for losses incurred when central banks borrowed foreign currencies to maintain their own currency. For example, if the Bundesbank lends DM100 million to the Bank of France to prevent a run on the franc and the prevailing exchange rate is DM1 = FF3.4; it has a claim of FF 340 million on the Bank of France. However, if at the time of repayment the exchange rate has moved to DM1 = FF3.672 (an 8 per cent devaluation), the Bundesbank will receive only DM92 592 592 whereas, if the loan was in ECUs the loss would have been much lower (1.54 per cent), given that the French franc comprises only 19.3 per cent of the ECU.

The Exchange Rate Mechanism (ERM) The ERM is the key element of the EMS, yet the UK did not join it until October 1990. The ERM provides a mechanism for confining exchange rate variability, since for each currency a 'central' rate is fixed in ECUs and these rates form the basis of a 'parity grid' of bilateral central exchange rates between currencies. Provision is made for periodic realignments of these ECU-based central rates following discussions at ministerial level. As with the 'Snake', permitted margins of fluctuation around the central parity occur; however, these are wider (± 2.25 per cent apart from the UK and Spain at ± 6 per cent) than under the old 'Snake'(± 1.125 per cent). Each member is obliged to ensure that it keeps its rate within the prescribed bands by either buying or selling currencies or utilizing the system's credit facilities (see the following sub-section).

However, the use of the ECU further distinguishes the system from the 'Snake', since it is a mechanism for measuring the position of a currency relative to the EC average. This should reduce the problem of the Deutschmark forcing action on the other member countries because of its strength *vis à vis* the others. Moreover, the actual amount that a currency can deviate from the ECU is less than 2.25 per cent because the currency itself is part of the ECU. Thus, a lowly weighted currency like the Irish punt can diverge by 2.2 per cent and the Deutschmark by approximately 1.5 per cent while keeping within the 2.25 per cent limit with other currencies.

The ERM also contains an ECU-based divergence indicator known as the 'Rattlesnake' or 'Amber Light', which signals when a currency diverges from the average of the others. Here divergence is measured by the amount by which a participating currency departs from its ECU central rate, and each member has a divergence threshold fixed at 75 per cent of the maximum range of divergence around the ECU central rate, calculated as $0.75 \times 2.25 \times (1-w)$ per cent where w is the weight of currency in the ECU basket. So for the Deutschmark the limits are $0.75 \times 2.25 \times (1-0.3010)$ per cent = ± 1.1796 per cent. The divergence threshold thus acts as a warning that a currency is getting out of line before the bilateral intervention points of the parity grid are breached at which time corrective action is compulsory. In this way the scheme tries to ensure that the burden of adjustment is more equally shared.

Notwithstanding the 2.25 per cent narrow and 6 per cent wide bands, implying that a currency has a total flexibility of 4.5 and 12 per cent respectively, in reality, each currency is likely to reach its effective limit against other currencies before it can make use of these ranges. The effective upper and lower limits are determined by the currency needing to remain within its bands against all other currencies simultaneously. Thus, the basic rule of the ERM is that no currency may rise by more than 2.25 per cent above the weakest in the system (apart from sterling prior to September 1992 and the peseta, which may rise by 6 per cent). So, if a currency hits its limits against the weakest, central banks will intervene, selling the strongest and buying the weakest to keep them within their trading ranges and avoid the need for realignment. This 'intra-marginal intervention' reinforces the discipline of the essentially semi-fixed EMS. It means that the 'divergence indicator', which measures deviation from ECU-related central rates, is in reality less significant than was anticipated when the ERM was devised.

Figure 2.1 shows the pound sterling's position on entry to the ERM in October 1990 and the percentage that each currency was trading against the lira, the weakest in the system and marked at zero. So, to summarize, this use of the basic rule, i.e. the movement allowed against the weakest, is designed to be a practical signal of the need for intra-marginal intervention, but it should not be confused with the equally correct measure of deviation from central rates. Where these are used, the allowed limit is 2.25 per cent or 6 per cent either side of the centre and the divergence indicator comes into force.

Intra-marginal intervention came into effect with the Basle–Nyborg Agreement in 1987 and was perceived as a major step forward in collective responsibility. However, while there is an assumption that central banks with strong currencies, namely the Bundesbank, will buy weak currencies before they reach their ERM divergence limits, the scope for support is limited. The amount it would be expected to purchase is only twice the weak currency nation's quota in the EMCF short-term facility. For the UK this equates to less than £3 billion, an amount barely sufficient to combat a couple of days' heavy selling, as was seen when intervention failed to hold sterling in September 1992.

The European Monetary Compensation Fund (EMCF) The EMCF was created as a mechanism for administering the 'Snake'. It is a depository for the 20 per cent of each member's gold and foreign currency reserves which serve as backing for the 'official' ECUs that it creates and distributes to members in return. It also administers the extensive array of credit facilities used to finance intervention. The most significant of these are the ECU30 billion of very short-term facilities (VSTF) providing credits for up to 10 weeks with automatic renewal for a further three months to finance temporary balance of payments difficulties and maintain the value of a currency. A further ECU14 billion is

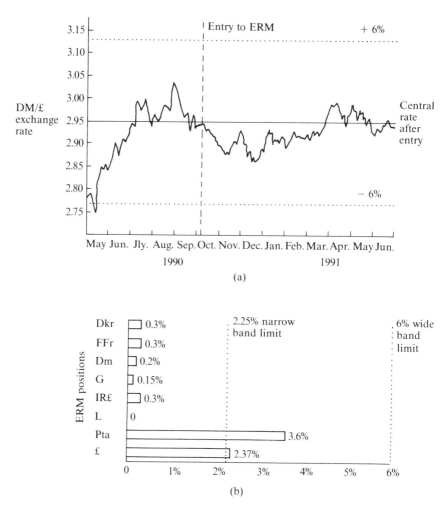

Figure 2.1 Position of the pound sterling on entry to ERM (a) Sterling–Deutschmark position (b) Percentage deviation of each ERM currency from the Italian lira

available for assistance up to nine months under the short-term monetary support scheme (STMS), and ECU11 billion is available on a conditional basis sanctioned by the Council of Ministers for periods of two to five years under the medium-term assistance scheme (MTFA). In reality, these arrangements for intervention are constrained in both time and quantity, and have been used sparingly. Monetary authorities have tended to support each other to a limited extent via intra-marginal intervention, but should compulsory marginal intervention become necessary, these resources are insufficient to prevent a sustained 'run' on a currency without recourse to domestic reserves. Even then, a significant interest rise may be needed or, failing that, devaluation. Such a situation faced the Italian government in September 1992 when one-third of its foreign exchange reserves was used up and eventually a 7 per cent devaluation was needed.

2.2.2 Performance of the EMS

The performance of the EMS can be judged in relation to its original objectives: creation of a zone of exchange rate stability; encouragement of economic convergence among members; and the long-term promotion of economic and monetary union.

Stabilization of exchange rates   At first glance, the high number of realignments of central rates illustrated in Table 2.2 suggests that the EMS has not been successful in its short-term objective of creating a zone of monetary stability. During the period 1979-83 exchange rate movements were marked, mainly because of differences in members' desire or abilities to adjust their currencies and respond to external shocks such as the 1979 oil crisis, which led to a deterioration in most members' terms of trade and encouraged inflation. Within this period there were seven realignments during which the Deutschmark was revalued by 27 per cent on a trade-weighted basis against the other EMS currencies. From 1983 to 1987 the system began to settle down and the four realignments during that time produced a much smaller Deutschmark revaluation of only 8 per cent. From January 1987 to September 1992 the central rates were not changed, save for a technical adjustment in January 1990 when the lira moved to the narrow band. Thus, although the average revaluation of the Deutschmark against the other EMS currencies has been approximately 38 per cent (including a 58 per cent appreciation against the lira and 45 per cent against the French franc), the frequency and magnitude of these adjustments declined significantly until the events of September 1992 detailed below.

   To consider the EMS currencies alone is inappropriate. Comparative tests with non-EMS currencies generally indicate success for the system, in that the instability of the EMS currencies after the establishment of the system was much lower than that of non-members. Admittedly, this partly reflects the key relative stability of the Deutschmark against currencies outside and within the system, the controls over capital flows in France and Italy and the role of political wrangling. At first currency realignments were accepted, but later they became more acrimonious with France threatening to leave the system; indeed, the realignment in January 1987 was preceded by weeks of public argument between France and Germany.

Economic policy convergence   At the start of the EMS various concerns were expressed that fixed rates and the attendant intervention obligations would undermine the ability of the more stability-conscious nations to control domestic

Table 2.2 Currency realignments in the EMS

Realignment date	(% change in central rate)									
	DM	FFr	BFr	DKr	G	IR£	L	£	Pta	Esc
Sept. 1979	+2.0	—	—	−2.9	—	—	—	—	—	—
Nov. 1979	—	—	—	−4.8	—	—	—	—	—	—
Mar. 1981	—	—	—	—	—	—	−6.0	—	—	—
Oct. 1981	+5.5	−3.0	—	—	+5.5	—	−3.0	—	—	—
Feb. 1982	—	—	−8.5	−3.0	—	—	—	—	—	—
June 1982	+4.25	−5.75	—	—	+4.25	—	−2.75	—	—	—
Mar. 1983	+5.5	−2.5	+1.5	+2.5	+3.5	−3.5	−2.5	—	—	—
July 1985	+2.0	+2.0	+2.0	+2.0	+2.0	+2.0	−6.0	—	—	—
April 1986	+3.0	−3.0	+1.0	+1.0	+3.0	—	—	—	—	—
Aug. 1986	—	—	—	—	—	−8.0	—	—	—	—
Jan. 1987	+3.0	—	+2.0	—	+3.0	—	—	—	—	—
Jan. 1990	—	—	—	—	—	—	−3.7	—	—	—
Sept. 1992	—	—	—	—	—	—	−7.0[a]	[a]	−5.0	—

[a] Lira and pound sterling 'temporarily' leave ERM.

monetary policy and inflation, while those nations with higher inflation rates would be forced to use highly restrictive practices to prevent exchange losses. There were also fears that the system was not durable, that it was unreasonable to expect countries with divergent economic policies, growth rates and potential to converge their policies to support the EMS.

In terms of economic convergence the results are mixed, as Fig. 2.2 shows. The overall slowing down of inflation rates is cited as evidence of success, yet the impact of monetary discipline is also evident elsewhere, as in the UK in the mid-1980s. Moreover, during the early years inflation reached record heights, yet members' responses created substantial divergences in prices and costs. Between 1982 and 1987 inflation rates fell markedly in all member states, more significantly, there was a narrowing of the gap between the highest and lowest rates among members. From 1988 inflation rates began to diverge again; implying that the ERM is no guarantee of price stability. Indeed, while nominal exchange rates have stabilized, real rates have not, and hence the competitiveness of individual members differs as those nations with relatively stable prices improve their position while those with inflationary tendencies suffer.

The external accounts of the EMS members have varied, with Germany consistently recording surpluses, both in absolute terms and relative to other EC members. The growing bilateral deficits of partner nations with Germany suggest competitive weaknesses, although admittedly pressures on the exchanges are relieved by the higher interest rate policies of these countries who are thus able to finance deficits by short-term capital flows. However, while for economic union to develop it is desirable that trade should be stimulated, it is questionable whether such continued imbalances are in the long-term interest of the EC. Not surprisingly, growth rates have not tended to converge. While it might be expected that countries with balance of payments surpluses and low inflation might expand more rapidly than those with deficits and high inflation, the converse is apparent, with Italy and Ireland growing rapidly in contrast to the Benelux nations and Germany. In the latter case, the Bundesbank's preoccupation with maintaining the external value of the Deutschmark and avoiding domestic inflation has curtailed the rate of growth of that economy.

2.2.3. The issue of UK membership of the ERM

The UK's attitude towards both the European Community and the EMS has tended to be ambivalent. It joined the Common Market in 1973, 15 years after the founding members, and while technically a member of the EMS since it was set up, did not join its core, the ERM, until October 1990, some 11 years after it began operations. Political reasons are often cited for this delay. The well-worn phrase, 'We will join when the time is right', was used by both major parties when in power. For Labour full EMS membership in late 1978 would have provoked a vociferous anti-EC faction at a time when party unity was needed in the pre-election period. The Tories were lukewarm in opposition and once in power were preoccupied with renegotiation of our terms of entry and budget commitments to the EC. Even as late as 1989 certain conditions were attached to entry: UK inflation to match the European average; capital liberalization in France and Italy; and progress towards the completion of the Single Market. In 1990 Tory attitudes changed and ERM entry was seen as politically necessary for a fourth term in office.

Various economic arguments against ERM membership have been put forward over the years. The surrender of 'sovereignty' was frequently used, as most member countries have had to forgo independence and flexibility in their domestic monetary policy and have had to accept some higher unemployment. The pound's status as a petrocurrency based on the UK's oil revenues was seen to set it aside from other currencies. Indeed, sterling's strength between 1979 and 1981 might have disrupted the ERM bands. However, as world oil prices stabilized in the 1980s and UK oil production fell, this factor diminished. In the early years the inadequacy of the UK's foreign exchange reserves to enable Bank of England intervention was also cited. However, by the mid-1980s these reserves had grown substantially. Throughout the period from 1979, the question of when and at what level to enter was often raised. Fears of a sterling crisis on entry, if inflation was out of control, and of a loss of confidence and competitiveness from defending a falling rate were seen as major constraints.

However, perhaps the overriding disadvantage in the 1980s was the potential politico-economic impact in terms of the fundamental shift required in economic policy. By 1980 the Conservatives were committed to the Medium-Term Financial Strategy (MTFS), geared to creating the conditions for growth by ensuring price stability. They chose to tackle inflation by means of domestic

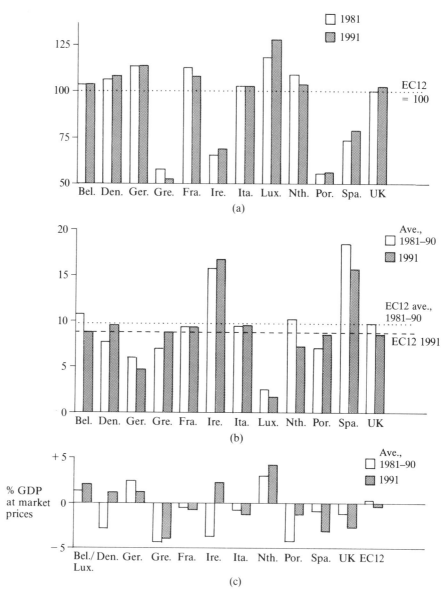

Figure 2.2 Economic convergence among EC members (a) GDP per capita at market prices (b) Unemployment rate (c) External balance (d) Price deflator, private consumption (e) General government net lending (+) or net borrowing (−) (f) Nominal short-term interest rates *(Sources: Eurostat, OECD)*

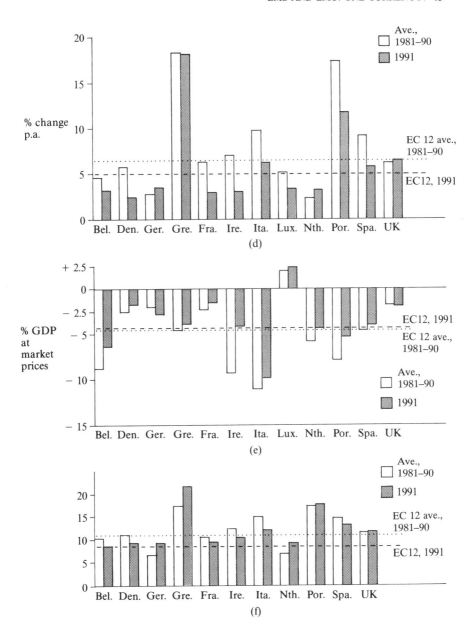

(d)

(e)

(f)

fiscal and monetary restraint with targets for progressive reductions in the rate of growth in the money supply and public expenditure. The exchange rate was allowed to vary in line with interest rates, although towards the end of the strategy it was seen as an additional tool of monetary policy, and ultimately became an objective itself. Thus, although various other economic objectives existed, including the improvement of the 'supply side' of the economy, monetary discipline was pre-eminent. The implication of monetarism is that prices, including interest rates and exchange rates, are market-led and hence must be allowed to move as required for money-supply control. Thus, membership of any fixed or semi-fixed exchange rate system was untenable.

In terms of the UK's economic objectives and performance in the early 1980s, this stance seemed justified. Inflation was brought down more rapidly than in the ERM, albeit at a cost of rising unemployment and lower growth. In the second half of the 1980s the reverse occurred, with reduced unemployment, greater growth but rising inflation. If the UK had entered the ERM in 1979 the pound could not have risen so far, although as a petrocurrency it would have probably been revalued. Inflation might have been lowered more slowly but the impact on output and employment would have been less. If the UK had entered in October 1985, as proposed by the then Chancellor Nigel Lawson, the exchange rate and interest rates would not have fallen so far and inflation would have remained lower. The balance of payments deficits from 1987 onwards and pent-up demand might have been avoided.

The key advantages of UK membership of the ERM were perceived as the confidence factor, external policy discipline and exchange rate stability. It was expected that there would be greater confidence in the global financial markets about the stability of sterling, possibly allowing lower and less volatile interest rates. Membership would mean economic policies geared to lower inflation as the UK would follow those of the most successful and strongest participant, Germany; and, in spite of early currency realignments, the EMS had provided exchange rate stability for members even if it had been less successful in terms of economic convergence. However, in joining the ERM in October 1990, the UK lost considerable monetary independence, with interest rates being managed to control the exchange rate rather than domestic demand. On this basis Sir Alan Walters, former personal economic adviser to Margaret Thatcher, criticized the ERM, along the lines shown in Fig. 2.3. He contended that the system encourages capital flows to countries offering the highest interest rates, usually those with the highest inflation rates. The inflows push up the exchange rate, creating pressure for interest rate cuts, but these make inflation harder to control.

The Treasury argued that, while the Walters critique might apply in the short term, the long-term aim of the ERM was to bring down inflation. Given that an exchange rate between two countries reflects, *ceteris paribus*, relative inflation rates, if the UK's inflation rate did not move into line with that of Germany the pound would have to fall *vis à vis* the Deutschmark. Certainly, in the initial period from October 1990 onwards ERM membership enhanced the

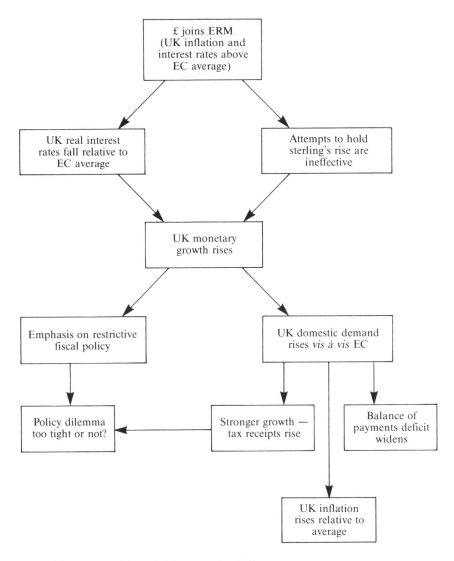

Figure 2.3 Walters's critique of UK entry to the ERM

government's credibility with the financial markets as it assisted the stated anti-inflationary stance. The commitment to the entry parity of DM2.95 required a high interest rate policy which reduced demand and curtailed pay and price rises. However, this also squeezed profits, cut output and raised unemployment. Ultimately, monetary policy became too tight, with the UK being over-zealous in curbing inflation at the expense of growth. The parity of DM2.95 was close to the original prevailing market rate, then a compromise between a high rate necessary to reduce inflation by squeezing export margins and cutting imports, and a low rate needed to reduce the trade deficit. Sterling membership of the ERM on the wider band technically allowed for a ± 6 per cent leeway around the central parity, and there was scope for realignment via devaluation/ revaluation by common consent. However, the Prime Minister consistently ruled out devaluation as a policy option until the currency crisis of September 1992 forced a temporary suspension of UK membership of the ERM and led to downward flotation of the pound.

The sterling crisis began in earnest in the summer of 1992 as the foreign exchange markets foresaw rifts opening up between the EMS currencies. Bundesbank concern with the inflationary effects of unification had pushed up German interest rates in July, and, because it has never been devalued in the ERM, investors moved further into the Deutschmark. By itself this was not enough to create strains, but the weak US economy further stimulated investment in the Deutschmark; thereby enhancing its value. European currencies struggled to maintain their parity, including those outside the ERM that were nevertheless tied economically to Germany such as the Swedish krona. Uncertainty was added by the prospect of a French 'no' vote in their September referendum on the Maastricht Treaty, a move ironically designed to underline wholehearted French support for the EC and the Treaty, but which began to backfire following the Danish rejection of the Treaty in June 1992 and a subsequent rise of nationalist feelings in Europe.

In late August a sharp fall in the dollar was not offset by intervention and the Deutschmark soared. The markets then turned their attention to the weaker currencies in the ERM, notably the lira and pound. The latter was deemed overvalued at its central parity of DM2.95 by virtue of the UK's poor export performance, high domestic costs and political, media and business pressure for interest rate cuts and other measures to stimulate demand. From early July sterling had traded towards the bottom of the ERM grid in a DM2.82–2.86 range before falling steadily to reach DM2.78 by the start of September, when an ECU10 billion support operation was launched (see Sec. 5.2.1). Further pressure arose from the Finnish markka devaluation and a massive Swedish interest rate rise, both of which encouraged Deutschmark buying.

There then followed a remarkable week for European finance, which threatened to undo the work of the previous decade of EMS development and to undermine future steps to EMU. Barely a week after the European Council of Finance (ECOFIN) ministers had refuted suggestions of an ERM realignment, on 13 September 1992 the lira was devalued by 7 per cent, a reminder of the semi-fixed nature of the EMS. Moreover, the Bundesbank seemed to have compromised on its valued independence by yielding to external pressure and cutting domestic interest rates (see Sec. 5.3). However, in reality the magnitude of the cut was smaller than hoped for, and although the pound rallied to DM2.81, within two days heavy selling of sterling ensued. By close of trading on 15 September the full force of market pressure was felt as the pound fell close to its ERM floor of DM2.7780. However, it was overnight rumours that the Bundesbank felt a sterling devaluation was necessary that ultimately precipitated the crisis. The following day, 16 September, the Bank of England spent substantial sums, variously estimated at between £10—£15 billion, in supporting sterling, assisted by £2 billion from the Bundesbank and the Banque de France. The UK government announced the reintroduction of minimum lending rate (MLR) at 12 per cent, signalling a 2 per cent rise in interest rates, then in an unprecedented move announced that a further 3 per cent rise in rates would take effect the following day. Ultimately this was to no avail, and in the face of the then largest assault on the ERM, the pound closed in London at DM2.7500. This prompted the government's decision to suspend sterling's membership of the ERM, thus allowing the pound to float, while cancelling the second interest rate rise.

On 17 September the previous day's interest rate rise was reversed and the pound ended the day at DM2.6279, an effective 10 per cent devaluation from its former central parity. The lira was also withdrawn from the ERM temporarily and the peseta was devalued by 5 per cent. By the end of the week the UK government had vowed to return to the ERM 'as soon as conditions allow', arguing that the exit was a temporary function of exceptional market turbulence, and that the ERM was still seen as the best means of bringing down inflation. However, equally, the Prime Minister expressed concern at seemingly German intransigence which had created many of the tensions inherent in the system, and called for parity changes such that EC monetary policy was operated in the interests of all members and not just Germany.

Further currency turmoil was only partly alleviated by the referendum vote in France on 20 September, which narrowly endorsed the Maastricht Treaty, and the meeting the next day of EC foreign ministers, who reaffirmed that the process of ratification would proceed without Treaty renegotiation; they did however pledge to take cognizance of concerns being expressed by large numbers of Europeans, either directly by referenda or through their elected representatives. Meanwhile sterling continued to edge downwards on the expectations of further interest cuts, and on Tuesday 22 September the base rate was duly trimmed by 1 per cent to 9 per cent and the currency closed at DM2.5382, a 14 per cent devaluation from its old central parity.

This was the situation for sterling at the time of writing, and clearly the fundamental UK policy shift raises uncertainty as to when—indeed, if—re-entry to the ERM will occur. From a medium-term focus upon squeezing inflation using a high interest rate policy to sustain an overvalued pound, the emphasis has switched to a short-term demand stimulus via interest rate cuts and a depreciating currency with seemingly little indication of what level it will settle at. The Chancellor has indicated that while outside the ERM the UK will focus its anti-inflationary policies on the growth in the money supply and asset prices, a move reminiscent of 1980s monetarism. To avoid sustained inflation, the Prime Minister has hinted at public expenditure curbs within a strict fiscal regime, although the inflation threat may be difficult to avoid given the already 14 per cent devaluation against a weak external trade position. The sluggish state of UK exports suggests that considerable effort will be required before the price benefit of devaluation takes effect, and meanwhile higher import costs will ensue.

Moreover, any perceived 'benign neglect' of sterling may be interpreted by the markets as a sign that the UK has given up its anti-inflation strategy, with further adverse consequences for the pound and reserves. The crisis has clearly demonstrated the power of the currency markets to offset monetary authority actions. By selling short pounds they did not hold and buying back at a later lower price, dealers made huge profits, whereas the authorities spent virtually half of the existing UK foreign exchange reserves on 15 September 1992, ultimately to no avail. The exact cost to the economy depends upon when the Bank of England closed out the intervention transactions, converting the sterling bought into foreign currency. However, on the basis of an intervention of £10–£15 billion, it is likely that at least £1 billion was lost.

Some critics might argue that Treasury involvement delayed the raising of interest rates too long and yet also led the authorities to concede the fight too early, especially given the pending French referendum outcome. Moreover, globally, very substantial international support is potentially available from IMF credits in addition to the limited EMCF funds and national reserves. More pressure might also have been brought to bear on other central banks to assist. Such views give weight to the case for an independent Bank of England, an issue returned to in Chapter 5.

Both German and UK authorities have indicated that, if and when sterling re-enters the ERM, it will be on certain pre-conditions. The Germans insist that all ERM members must agree and that the level of UK interest rates must be acceptable, namely not too low. The UK government has implied that re-entry will be considered, firstly, when the UK and German economies show greater signs of convergence, such that the UK is no longer subject to high German interest rates occasioned by the inflationary impact of unification. Secondly, the Chancellor seeks a reform of the ERM so that it is strong enough to withstand such turbulence, with greater formal obligations on central banks to intervene earlier before countries reach their ERM floor. This specifically implies greater onus on strong-currency nations, such as Germany, to share the burden of adjustment; yet it is precisely the problem of the old 'Snake', which the ERM with its 'compulsory' and 'intra-marginal' intervention was in principle supposed to avoid. However, the main method by which a 'run' on sterling could have been avoided was a commitment to existing parities by the Bundesbank enacted through a significant interest rate cut rather than through sterling purchases.

Many UK businesses, especially major exporters, do not advocate a return to the ERM, but a permanent exit is not consistent with expected future European development and Britain's role therein, or for long-term attainment of stable interest and exchange rates. Nevertheless, in the immediate short term the crisis points to either temporary suspension of the ERM or a slimmed-down version of the EMS, possibly consisting of the Deutschmark, the Belgian/Luxembourg franc, the guilder and possibly the French franc, with weaker currencies such as the lira, peseta, escudo, Irish punt and sterling all floating. Indeed, the position of the French franc is crucial to the survival of the ERM in its present form. While a devaluation is quite likely, given that in the immediate aftermath of the French referendum the franc closed barely a centime above its ERM floor, this would be contrary to French policy, which has been based around a strong franc and the ultimate creation of a single currency without changing the existing Deutschmark parity. However, as with the situation facing weaker currencies, this scenario reckoned without the shock of unification and the Bundesbank's desire to resist inflationary pressures by maintaining high interest rates and not printing more Deutschmarks to relieve currency tensions.

Recent events have thus exposed the vulnerability of a rigid ERM. In the early years it was more flexible, since economies were too diverse to prevent regular realignments, but in due course the realignments became fewer, if more acrimonious. By the time that sterling and the peseta were incorporated further realignments were discouraged, since negotiations on monetary union had started. The ERM had begun to be viewed by the markets and politicians as an interim stage to union with the 1987 parities virtually immovable. Moreover, there was more confidence in sterling, in particular, when it entered the system with a firm government commitment not to be devalued from its DM2.95 parity, and in weaker currencies in general when the Maastricht Treaty set out a timetable for union (see Sec. 2.3.4 below). The current ERM situation appears untenable. Thus, movement is likely to be either backwards to a more flexible arrangement, as in the past, especially if Maastricht has to be renegotiated, or forwards towards speedier union and a single currency.

2.3 EUROPEAN MONETARY UNION (EMU)

As we have seen, the first attempts at European Monetary Union foundered. While the political will to establish the ideal was expressed in 1971 with scheduled implementation by 1980, little progress was made until the creation of the EMS. However, the EMS is ultimately limited as an arrangement between members to restrict exchange rate fluctuations. Technically countries can leave the system, as happened in 1992 with the UK and Italy; national currencies exist in spite of the novel creation of the ECU; and there is no collective currency policy *vis à vis* the rest of the world. In theory, however, once all member nations' currencies are operating effectively within the ERM, the technical basis for a single currency and monetary union will have been established.

2.3.1 The theory of monetary union

In theory, a monetary union between various independent countries calls for certain prerequisites. Firstly, complete convertibility of the currencies is required, which in turn implies an absence of exchange controls and the free mobility of capital. Secondly, there can be no possibility of internal exchange rate changes; that is, there must be a regime of complete and irrevocably fixed exchange rates. These characteristics are most easily achieved by the adoption of a single currency, but distinct national currencies may be retained provided they are freely interchangeable at a *fixed* rate. If this is the option chosen, the exchange rates of these currencies must be managed jointly with those of the rest of the world; in other words, their foreign exchange reserves must be operated as a common pool by a single body. However, these requirements bring forward others. Thirdly, in order to control the money supply a common monetary policy is needed, to be either operated by a single central bank or coordinated by a similar body. Fourthly, governments will have to lose some control of fiscal policy as their abilities to finance budget deficits by borrowing are restricted. Finally, a common payments system must exist throughout the union, and the capital market and banking system must both be subject to a common regulatory regime.

Various advantages derive from these characteristics of a monetary union. In the first place, they imply a high degree of integration between the member states in terms of trade, capital and monetary flows. Indeed, adoption of a single currency is seen as a major unifying factor. Goodhart (1991) cites the potential in the private sphere for greater cross-border capital investment as business decisions are made free of currency uncertainties; and with regard to the public sphere he argues that it is difficult to envisage taking on expensive, political decisions (e.g. defence) at, say, a European level and then allocating the fiscal burden without a single currency on which to base calculations. Secondly, trade is enhanced as uncertainty associated with exchange risks is eliminated and there are no transaction costs, such as that for forward exchange cover. Thirdly, if full convertibility at a fixed exchange rate exists, no foreign exchange reserves are needed apart from those held by the central monetary authority of the union regulating exchange rate levels with the rest of the world. Moreover, no balance of payments financing problems or speculative capital flows can arise if the trading partners are using effectively the same currency. Fourthly, interest rates might be expected to be lower throughout the union, with reduced anticipated inflation and the absence of risk premia attached to weaker currencies as an insurance against devaluation. Finally, efficiency gains derive from capital and savings flows being channelled within the union to where rates of return are highest, as there are no impediments to their free flow.

In spite of these seemingly pervasive advantages, the fact that EMU has not yet materialized reflects not only the slow attainment of the prerequisites, but also certain substantive problems associated with the concept of monetary union. The major theoretical issues relate to the loss of sovereignty with regard to both macroeconomic targets (e.g. inflation) and instruments (e.g. exchange rate, fiscal and monetary policy). Given that the policy of any member nation is determined centrally, there is no differentiation to reflect regional economic circumstances; and thus, for example, high levels of unemployment resulting from lack of competitiveness cannot be offset by devaluation. The counter-argument is that, with increased integration and interdependence, the effectiveness of members' individual policy decisions is reduced. The effects of these decisions become dissipated overseas, and, conversely, domestic measures become more influenced by decisions taken abroad. Thus it is feasible that in, say, an EC context greater integration of fiscal policies and budget transfers, allied to freer capital and labour movements, might reduce regional unemployment disparities. However, it is equally arguable that such differentials would not exist if mobility of labour and capital responded perfectly to supply and demand, and, moreover, that the implied enhanced budgetary needs and transfers may be politically unacceptable if they are at the expense of national ones.

Llewellyn (1988) argues that greater interdependence requires more policy coordination as each country has the power to undermine the policies of others. Recognition of this promotes the concept of 'collective sovereignty', and, clearly, the closer the members' objectives are, the less cost there is in surrendering individual positions. Llewellyn argues that EC governments will not give up instruments of policy regulation until they believe they are giving up little effective sovereignty. In a fixed-rate regime, if members' monetary policies are not broadly consistent, then arbitrage and speculative capital flows will put pressure on exchange rates. Consistency can be brought about by acceptance of the policy of a dominant partner, by coordination in advance (collective sovereignty) or by imposition. Within the EMS the former has applied, with the Bundesbank the dominant force.

2.3.2 The Delors Report

The above theoretical perspective implies that the transformation of the EMS into a genuine monetary union requires a permanent transfer of authority, which, while hard to reverse compared with the existing system, could provide a real boost to the fundamental EC goals of political and economic integration. A significant impetus in this direction was given by those who drafted the Single European Act in 1985 and who wrote in the creation of a monetary union as a formal objective. Subsequently the Council of Members in 1988 entrusted the President of the European Commission, Jacques Delors, to 'study and propose concrete steps leading towards EMU'. The subsequent *Report on Economic and Monetary Union* (the Delors Report) (EC Commission 1989), which was presented to the European Council in June 1989 and approved in 1990, envisaged a three-stage approach to EMU:

Stage 1: 'Convergence' (July 1990 start)
- Consolidation of the single-market programme
- Removal of physical, technical and fiscal barriers
- Stronger competition policy; reduced industry subsidies
- Reform of structural funds and doubling of resources
- Deregulation of financial markets—a single financial market
- All community currencies to join the ERM
- Greater coverage of economic and monetary policies
- Greater private use of the ECU encouraged

Stage 2: 'Institutional'
- Transitional phase to reinforce convergence
- Establishment of European System of Central Banks (ESCB)
- ESCB to start transition from independent national monetary policies towards a common monetary policy

Stage 3: 'EMU'
- Irrevocable fixing of exchange rates—ultimately a single currency
- Rigid constraints on national budgets
- Further strengthening of community structural and regional policies
- Assumption of monetary policy responsibility by the ESCB
- Common international policy measures

Stage 1 began on 1 July 1990 and involved strengthening economic and policy coordination and cooperation to secure greater convergence of economies. It included a series of policy measures, some of which were already in force. For example, all four members still outside the ERM were to participate, ultimately on equal terms. Indeed, Spain and the UK joined on the wider bands within 18 months of the Report's publication. Moves towards liberalization of exchange controls were enhanced when those restricting capital movements in France and Italy were eliminated in 1990. Stage 1 also required the completion of the internal market by 1992 so that goods and services can move freely between members, and various directives also needed to be implemented to deregulate financial services (see Chapter 1).

A key aspect of Stage 1 is the introduction of new measures of multilateral surveillance of economic policies and developments following a Council of Ministers decision in March 1990. Surveillance carried out by the Council will cover economic performance, compatibility of economic policies and the impact of global factors using a range of macroeconomic indicators. For example, considerable emphasis is being placed upon fiscal policy, with reviews of the size and financing of budget deficits in advance of national budgetary planning, thus aiming to reduce excessively high deficits and the need for financing. The Council has the right also to carry out *ad hoc* consultations and issue recommendations as it sees fit. In turn, the Council is subject to Parliamentary control of its surveillance activities.

Stage 2 is expected to begin in January 1994 and is seen by Delors as a short transitional stage to enable the establishment of the institutions necessary to take over the functions presently undertaken by national bodies. Decision-making in economic policy gradually shifts to the EC level and policy guidelines are established, for example those relating to the size and financing of budget deficits. The permitted range of exchange rate fluctuations will also be reduced below the existing $\pm 2\frac{1}{4}$ per cent and realignments will be possible only in very exceptional circumstances. The major institutional development will be the laying of the foundations for a European Central Bank. This was envisaged as a single European System of Central Banks (ESCB), similar in concept to the Federal Reserve System of the USA. It would absorb the EMCF, the Committee of EC Central Bank Governors and the permanent secretariat. However, this is a highly contentious issue, to which I shall return in Chapter 4.

Stage 3 is the 'EMU' stage, in which the full implications of monetary union become apparent, notably the irrevocable fixing of exchange rates, and, once integrated, their replacement by a single European rate, possibly based on the ECU. The ESCB would hold and manage all the foreign exchange reserves and be responsible for the conduct of monetary and exchange rate policy. Community bodies would be given directly enforceable powers in areas such as the coordination of members' budgets and the use of EC resources to secure the attainment of structural and regional policy objectives or to intensify members' adjustment efforts.

In addition to these discrete steps, the Delors Report contained very explicit statements as to the nature of EMU. If economic and monetary union implies freedom of movement for goods, services and capital, as well as irrevocably fixed exchange rates and ultimately a single currency, then this in turn implies compatibility of economic policies and a transfer of decision-making power from national to Community bodies. Similarly, monetary union requires a single monetary policy with responsibility vested in a new central institution. In other words, policies are aimed at the Community as a whole rather than its constituent parts, and this implies far-reaching changes to national sovereignty. Thus, while Stage 1 does not require changes to the Treaty of Rome, this is not the case for Stages 2 and 3, which involve new institutions and the transfer of power. Hence one of the key features of Stage 1 was the Intergovernmental Conference (IGC) in December 1990 to discuss these changes to the Treaty.

2.3.3 Responses and alternatives to the Delors Report

Agreement was reached at the 1989 Madrid Summit on progression with Stage 1 from July 1990, as apart from anything else it gave EC members a valuable opportunity to experiment with the principles of EMU without loss of sovereignty. Moreover, it continued policies of convergence already illustrated in recent years as well as voluntary restrictions on the scope of decision-making implicit in the way countries have tied their currencies to the Deutschmark. However, equally, it was decided that the EC should not proceed further until Stage 1 was adopted. The UK and Germany had misgivings about proposals for Stages 2 and 3, especially the prospects for a centralized bureaucratic system outside the control of national governments, and the time-scale for progress.

The UK initially expressed reservations about the 'escalator' principle underlying the Delors Report, notably that, having embarked on Stage 1, there is a necessary commitment to the successive stages on the journey to union. Particular concern has been expressed that the Delors proposals would mean that control of monetary policy was taken away from national governments, while leaving them answerable to their electorates, and handed over to a non-elected and unaccountable central body. Only a European government and finance ministry can effectively balance the power of the ESCB, and member states have not agreed to such a change. The UK government also believes that binding rules on the size of budget deficits are unnecessary. Fixed exchange rate systems have operated without these in the past, and differing national deficits are not incompatible with sound monetary policies.

In November 1989 the UK Chancellor Nigel Lawson proposed a more 'market-based', gradualist and evolutionary approach to EMU outlining the way forward beyond Stage 1. Countries would compete on policies so that Europe would converge on the countries that produced the best record, notably on inflation. The features included a competing, multi-currency system with EC currencies as legal tender throughout Europe, but with the soundest EC currency eventually establishing itself as the dominant one. This competition is seen as leading to convergence of inflation rates at lower levels than would otherwise be the case. Monetary policy would remain in the hands of national authorities and there would be no major institutional changes. Over time this approach could evolve into a system of fixed exchange rates, but that was not something to be decided in Stage 1.

Following from this approach, a refined UK proposal was put forward in May 1990 by the British Invisible Exports Council under the chairmanship of Sir Michael Butler. The Butler proposal was quickly endorsed by the then Chancellor John Major and involved evolutionary steps to promote convergence, low inflation and stability, but with emphasis on the development of the ECU as the common currency. The Major plan focused around the creation of the new 'hard' ECU as opposed to the existing 'soft' ECU, which is so named because it is based on a basket made up of weaker as well as stronger currencies. The new 'hard' ECU would be a parallel, common, yet real currency to exist alongside the 12 national ones. The core of the plan was that it would never be devalued against any other European currency, and thus, as the strongest, would have the attractions the Deutschmark has now. Ultimately the preferences of users would determine whether it became dominant enough to develop as the EC's single currency. The ECU would thus cease to be a basket currency and instead would be given a trading life of its own so that its value can fluctuate independently of the other European currencies. A proposed European Monetary Fund (EMF) would act as a lender of last resort and manage the ECU by open-market operations. It would issue ECU deposits or notes in exchange for national currencies and would set interest rates on hard ECUs. Initially it would do this by setting rates on the interest-bearing deposits it took, expected to be mainly from commercial banks. Later, as the private market developed, the EMF could move to setting rates by normal central banking techniques of market operations.

For Germany, Karl-Otto Pohl, then Bundesbank president, argued for monetary cooperation before moves to redraft the Treaty. In spite of substantial progress towards convergence in anti-inflation policy, deep-seated divergences still exist as reflected, for example, in national budgets and external balances of the UK, Portugal, Greece, Italy and Spain. These divergences reflect long-standing institutional structures, economic orientation and attitudes, and consequently an early irrevocable fixing of exchange rates and transfer of monetary powers to Community institutions would threaten monetary stability. The Bundesbank especially wants central banks to make their monetary growth targets explicit and comparable so as to encourage monetary virtue.

Without adequate convergence and communality of policies, the Germans warned of the prospect of a 'two-speed' Europe, whereby possibly France, Germany and the Benelux nations will form a 'hard-core' economic and monetary union, with other nations following on later. The Germans fear a transitional period where only some of the final conditions are imposed upon members and argue that the Central Bank should be established only in the final phase of union. The Bundesbank president has long been against the setting up of a shadow central bank in Stage 2, which has no substantive role until the single currency exists. Thus, in essence the Germans approach implies merging Stages 1 and 2 and delaying the major jump to union until after 1997, by which time member states should have progressed to price stability, narrowed budget deficits and reduced interest rate differences. Any move towards Stage 3 would require the unanimous vote of member governments, but members unwilling or unable to accede to full union could temporarily opt out. Indeed, during 1991 the Dutch formally promoted the concept of a 'two-speed' Europe, whereby if 6 of the 12 members meet stringent economic criteria they should proceed to the final stage of monetary union, namely the adoption of a single currency, leaving the others to catch up later. The British government welcomed the Dutch proposals in so far as they effectively imply that members can choose whether or not to embark on Stage 3, but many 'southern' states were critical for fear of being left behind.

2.3.4 The Maastricht agreement on EMU

Such differing perspectives furthered the debate on EMU, but were as much concerned with the timing of the process as with the principle of union. The December 1990 IGC on EMU had led to recommendations for Treaty amendments necessary to implement full-scale EMU, with locked exchange rates, a single monetary policy and the potential for a single currency. Thus, the subsequent approval in December 1991 at Maastricht of the draft 'Treaty on European Union' by EC heads of state or government gave new impetus to the monetary integration process. The Treaty was formally signed in February 1992 to take effect from January 1993, subject to ratification within the member nations involved.

The Maastricht agreement on EMU is associated with visions of a politically united Europe, as discussed at a parallel IGC on political union and manifested in the strengthening of the European Parliament. It was agreed at Maastricht that Stage 2 of EMU would begin in January 1994, and would be a transitional and technical phase to enhance economic convergence beyond Stage 1. It would include the establishment of the major institution, a European Monetary Institute (EMI), to assume the functions of the Committee of Governors of Central Banks and the EMCF until such time as the European Central Bank was operational (see Chapter 5). Stage 3 should begin by January 1999 for those members deemed able to participate, but could start as early as 1997 if the pre-conditions are met and a qualified majority of members' heads of state and government so agree. The key features of this stage will be largely according to the Delors Report; the irrevocable fixing of exchange rates and the assumption by the ESCB/ECB of their full powers. They will conduct monetary policy and in due course issue the single currency which will replace national ones.

In reality, the decision on irrevocable entry to the final stage of EMU is not expected until 1996. The process is such that four convergence criteria must be met before eligibility for Stage 3 will be considered: (1) the *rate of inflation*, as measured by the consumer price index, is not to exceed that of, at most, the three best performing members by more than $1\frac{1}{2}$ per cent; (2) the *budget deficit* must not be excessive, e.g. not more than 3 per cent GDP at market prices; (3) *membership of the ERM narrow band* must have been maintained for at least two years without severe tensions or a devaluation; and (4) *long-term interest rate* gaps relative to the three best performing countries should not amount to more than 2 per cent. If these criteria are met together with other indicators (e.g. market integration, compatibility between national legislation and the Treaty provisions relating to the independence of the ECB and national central banks, and convergence in labour costs), then the Council, in conjunction with the Commission, EMI and finance ministers and after consultation with Parliament, will set the date for Stage 3. This will occur on a set date only if a majority of member states meet these convergence criteria by December 1996. If not, Stage 3 will begin on 1 January 1999. For this latter start date no such majority of member states will be needed; but, whenever the move to Stage 3 begins, only states satisfying the entry criteria will be eligible.

Thus, the Dutch concept of a 'two-speed' Europe is a distinct possibility, especially after the September 1992 currency crisis, although which nations would be the forerunners remains to be seen. Denmark reserved the right to make entry to Stage 3 conditional on the outcome of a referendum in June 1992, the result of which failed narrowly to ratify the Treaty; and at the time of writing the French have just voted in favour, although the narrow margin of victory has added to concern over the detail of the Treaty. The UK, in an additional protocol to the Treaty, has been granted the option of making its entry to the final stage conditional upon an explicit positive vote by Parliament nearer the time. While committed to Stage 2, the UK government has argued that the costs and benefits of a single monetary policy and currency cannot be adequately assessed as yet (Bank of England 1992a). Thus, although the UK must notify the ECOFIN Council before 1996 of its intention regarding Stage 3, the interim leaves aside the sensitive issue of central bank independence, and provides extra scope in terms of the convergence criteria.

2.3.5 A common or single European currency? Hard or harder ECU or . . .?

Proposals for future European money cover a spectrum: competing currencies; convertible and inconvertible hard ECUs; commodity-basket ECUs. Crudely, the underlying approaches may be split into those who advocate a single currency administered by a European Central Bank; and those who prefer national currencies operating under increasingly competitive conditions.

British proposals on the ECU fudge key issues: pro-Europeans see that if the hard ECU wins public approval it could eventually replace national currencies; anti-Europeans are kept at bay during monetary union negotiations by the possibility that the hard ECU will never materialize into a single currency. German criticisms focus on inflationary dangers, although safeguards could include obligations on members to repurchase their own currencies from the EMF for hard ECUs or strong currencies. The combined effect of the Fund's own money creation, through the issue of hard ECU liabilities and its influence on money creation by national banks, would thus not be inflationary. Convertibility into ECUs could also be suspended for persistent offenders, thus forcing a devaluation with the currency risk resting with the central bank concerned.

While British 'hard ECU' proposals have received little support from other EC members, the acceptance of an independent EMF was seen as a major breakthrough in terms of Stage 2, and there was implicit recognition that it could eventually evolve into a European Central Bank. Moreover, there is widespread agreement on the need to strengthen the ECU. The Spanish government, for example, has argued that the current ECU, as a basket of member currencies, should be retained, strengthened and elevated into a fully parallel currency— and *not* replaced by a new ECU. It also dismissed the competitive role which would 'crowd out' national currencies. Indeed, among the debate the issue has arisen as to whether it is better to set aside the current ECU and start again with a new currency unit.

In an effort to bridge the differences, EC commissioner, Sir Leon Brittan, suggested that the UK's aims could be met by developing the existing ECU in two ways. Firstly, the existing currency amounts comprising the ECU basket should be frozen, giving added certainty to the markets. Secondly, at the start of Stage 2 in 1994 all member states should make a formal commitment to avoid realignments. All countries would retain the legal power to adjust their national parities within the EMS, and there would be scope for movement within set bands. The ECU's contribution to the development of a stable low-inflation currency for Europe could then be based on existing contracts and markets. There would be no confusion over the type of ECU in circulation as there would be if the hard ECU existed, and the use of the ECU as a common currency would be market-driven. Thus, the UK's objectives in formulating the hard ECU would be achieved without any practical difference between the two forms of ECU. However, Sir Leon contends that differences would be narrowed even more if the UK accepted the progression from Stage 2 to Stage 3, and that the 'hard ECU' or 'harder ECU' would ultimately become Europe's single currency.

Discussion of the future role of the ECU, in whatever form, begs the question of its general acceptability as a single currency, compared with, say, the Deutschmark which has effectively held the EMS together as a currency bloc since 1979. An awkward feature of the ECU is that it might be less well managed than existing currencies. A currency that is a sort of average of the hard Deutschmark, the soft peseta, lira or drachma, etc., would be a poorer monetary standard than the Deutschmark itself. Would the German people agree to a monetary regime that offered the average rate of inflation rather than the German one? The hard ECU offers a solution by means of the built-in guarantees that in any realignment it would always move with the strongest currencies. However, even so, it might seem more logical to use the Deutschmark rather than invent a new currency for which rules are invented to make it as good as the Deutschmark! In reality, the sole use of the Deutschmark is politically unacceptable; besides, the Bundesbank's unwillingness to bear the responsibilities placed upon it for managing Europe's anchor currency during the September 1992 currency crisis bodes ill for the use of the Deutschmark as the European currency. Thus, one interim scenario to salvage the ERM might be a new 'franco-mark' currency covering Germany, France and Benelux, against which other currencies might float until such time as they could meet conditions similar to those in the Maastricht agreement.

In terms of acceptability, to date the ECU has had a chequered history. Within the EMS intra-marginal intervention has predominated, with little recourse to official ECU-denominated credit facilities. However, the private use of the ECU has expanded. Private ECUs are defined using the same basket as those official ECUs but are completely separated, created by private rather than central banks, and are bought/sold on the foreign exchange markets. This link is vital for the development of the market ECU to ensure the unity and marketability of present and future ECU-denominated instruments.

In theory, the ECU can be used like other international currencies as a medium of exchange, unit of account or store of value, but it has particular attractions in the latter role through its stability. For companies its benefits may be perceived in various areas, for example protection against exchange rate volatility; reduced Treasury transaction costs; the opportunity for wider financing choices; opportunities for internal accounting, invoicing and performance measurement among European subsidiaries; and the preparation of price lists without the need for constant updates. However, widespread use of the ECU depends largely on its promotion by the European banking fraternity. The main UK clearing banks now offer ECU facilities in terms of spot and forward exchange, deposits and loans, bonds, certificates of deposit and travellers' cheques. An ECU Banking Association (EBA) was established in 1985 to promote the ECU and, more significantly, to provide a clearing system. The latter began operating in 1985 based on a SWIFT (Society for Worldwide Interbank Telecommunication) system that nets ECU payment orders between banks. Settlement is by borrowing operations in ECUs between members, and thus a money market for ECUs is created. The Bank for International Settlements (BIS) is the EBA's agent and acts as banker to the clearing-bank members.

The private ECU has grown most significantly in terms of capital market transactions, notably the issue of ECU-denominated bonds. From the first offer in 1981, the market expanded rapidly in the 1980s and in 1989 was the fifth most popular currency for new issues, raising ECU11 billion in 113 deals. A factor behind this growth was that major issuing nations such as France and Italy did not impose exchange restrictions on the European institutions issuing ECUs as they did for their own currencies. While this advantage has disappeared with the ending of exchange controls, the issue of ECUs has benefited since March 1991 from the greater usage made by government borrowers, notably the Italian, Greek and French authorities. In March 1989 the UK launched an ECU800 million Treasury bill programme.

In addition to ECU bonds and government securities, ECU-related futures and option contracts have developed, thus giving the ECU market depth as investors can hedge their risks. In March 1991 the London International Financial Futures Exchange (LIFFE) launched futures on ECU bonds, which in essence promise the future delivery of a range of global issues. MATIF, the Paris futures exchange, already trades these derivatives (see Chapter 8). Elsewhere there has been a surge in the growth of interest and currency swaps involving ECUs. Further use could be stimulated by the establishment of the European Bank for Reconstruction and Development (EBRD) in 1991 with an initial capital of ECU10 billion (see Chapter 10).

With such developments, the ECU would appear to be more generally acceptable among financial sectors, industries and governments. However, this is somewhat misleading, since the central banks vary on its use domestically: it is widely accepted in the Benelux nations, is used for trading in Italy, Greece and Ireland, but is not legal tender in the UK and Germany. More significantly, the ECU is still rarely used in commercial transactions accounting for less than

10 per cent of intra-EC trade, in spite of the attractions, mentioned earlier. Lack of operational familiarity has been an obstacle, especially for smaller firms without Treasury functions, which are essentially unaware of the ECU, its uses and benefits, and are dependent upon their banks' advice. However, most constraints have tended to be political, such as UK membership of the ERM, the absence of a last-resort monetary authority or central bank, and controversy over EMU itself.

CONCLUSIONS

In the quest for European Monetary Union, the 1990s have started more promisingly than previous decades. The Werner Plan envisaged union by 1980 but foundered in the aftermath of the dollar crisis which encouraged currencies to float. In the early 1980s the embryonic EMS struggled to cope with the impact of the 1979 oil crisis, members' trade deficits and numerous realignments of the franc and Deutschmark. In recent years, notwithstanding the events of September 1992, the EMS has generally been more successful in reducing exchange rate fluctuations, intra-EC trade has burgeoned, and there is more political will for unity. Moreover, the necessary machinery is starting to be put in place: the Single European Act of 1986; the Delors Report of 1989; the Intergovernmental conference in 1990; and the 1992 Maastricht Treaty.

Monetary union is still a long way off, however, as many countries express concern at the means rather than the end. For the UK, the loss of sovereignty of independent action and the replacement of market forces by a central authority are still bitter pills to swallow. For Germany, there is concern over the control of inflation given the burden of unification and the varying degrees of convergence among member nations. Danish and French experiences of the referendum process have generated doubts over the Treaty as a whole. Indeed, the original dates set place very heavy demands upon member states to bring their economic, social and fiscal policies into line and to create the institutional changes necessary for Stage 3 entry.

Moreover, the convergence criteria for EMU membership are not without criticism. Wood and Coleman (1992) suggest that the requirements for fiscal convergence are both unnecessary and potentially counter-productive. Their premiss is that national government debts have no adverse effects on taxpayers elsewhere in the monetary union. For example, excessive national borrowing may raise interest rates and attract capital from elsewhere in the union, hence generating fears of 'crowding-out' investment, but the compensation is a higher rate of return, paid for by the taxpayers of the nation concerned. The argument that one nation running a large deficit will encourage high interest rates elsewhere in the union is inconsistent with the federal USA, where state debt varies according to differing credit ratings. Wood and Coleman also suggest that the Treaty budgetary restrictions may be counter-productive to nations wishing to borrow for temporary deficits caused by fluctuating tax receipts. Elsewhere, concerns exist over the wider Treaty implications, for example the fiscal transfers associated with regional and social policy, the relationship between the ECB and ECOFIN, and banking supervision, aspects covered in subsequent chapters.

Central to the concept of EMU is that of the single currency. For many this represents the ultimate recognition of the loss of national identity and sovereignty, and subjugation into the European culture. France, however, sees it as a means to avoid the nationalist frictions so harmful to the history of twentieth-century Western Europe. For others, the single currency is the inevitable and welcome conclusion to the removal of trade barriers and the Single-Market ideal. Volatile separate currencies may be seen as obstacles to trade, whereas a single one would facilitate price comparisons across borders, encourage investment and eliminate the risk of devaluations on profits. EMU would also mitigate the impact of external shocks on specific national economies and would provide a store of value and a medium of exchange outside the Community. However, debate continues as to the form of the potential currency, especially in the wake of the September 1992 crisis. Examples have included the UK's proposal for a 'hard ECU', namely a *common*, parallel currency in competition with national ones, whereas other possibilities include 'hardening' the existing ECU as a *single* currency, or even creating a new *'franco-mark'* currency. The conceptual acceptability of such options would be enhanced if business and finance made greater use of the existing ECU, rather than merely relying on political moves. This would encourage the idea of a single currency and its acceptability at the individual level, and thus would be a major step to our being truly European.

FURTHER READING

A comprehensive survey of European monetary integration from EMS to EMU is given in Gros and Thygesen (1992). For a literature review of the ERM see Bank of England (1991a) and on the operation and performance of the EMS see Barrell (1992) or Artis and Taylor (1988). For EMU, see the Delors Report (EC Commission 1989), and on Maastricht refer to Bank of England (1992a) and Deutsche Bundesbank (1992a). The Walters critique is expounded in Walters (1990).

FINANCE AND THE GOVERNMENT SECTOR

THREE

PUBLIC-SECTOR FUNDING: A QUESTION OF PHILOSOPHY?

A fundamental issue in modern economics is the acceptable and appropriate level of government influence. In Western Europe this is paramount, both in the context of the 'mixed economies' of individual nations, and in the debate over the form and structure of a federal European community and the associated powers vested in the decision-making bodies. The Treaty of Rome envisaged welfare gains and economic growth arising from free competition within a common market, an emphasis rekindled in the Single European Act, where a large, competitive market would in theory optimize resource allocation and economies of scale and would stimulate productivity, income and employment, along the lines of the Cecchini Report findings (see Chapter 1). Within the Treaty of Rome the role of government was seen in terms of the adoption of common policies (e.g. taxation, agriculture, regional policy), with the emphasis on maintenance of public goods, price and supply stability and competitive forces.

However, for much of the period between the 1957 Treaty of Rome and the 1986 Single European Act, the prevailing philosophy favoured state intervention. The concept of the welfare state was widely accepted, and the 'mixed economy' was perceived as a means of overcoming extremist political interests which had been so damaging to early twentieth-century Europe. The Treaty of Rome had been conceived in a period when Keynesian demand management policies were initially appearing successful at boosting postwar growth, so theorists advocated regulated markets, as opposed to extreme centrally planned or free market economies. Yet in terms of Community development, the 1960s and 1970s are now considered periods of stagnation. Nationalistic interests prevailed in the context of the Community budget and the transfer of decision-making powers, giving the impression of ineptitude at the supranational level. Furthermore, oil shocks and subsequent 'stagflation', i.e. combined inflation and stagnation, created an uninspiring climate for progress and favoured protectionism and national support for key domestic industry.

Indeed, excessive government intervention was increasingly blamed by many economists and politicians for the problems of the 1970s and early 1980s. The welfare state appeared unable to cope with mass unemployment and slow growth, as these seemed to increase government expenditure, reduce income and require higher levels of taxation at times when incomes and profits were depressed. Keynesian demand management policies were seen as ineffective in combating perceived supply-side rigidities in raw material and labour markets, especially as domestic industries became increasingly exposed to competitive forces in world markets. This increased internationalization also frustrated the abilities of national governments to enact 'stop–go' policies, with the result that their increasing deficits were financed rather than cured. While the causation may be debated, i.e. whether excessive government expenditure and involvement was a cause or an effect of the economic downturns, the philosophical shift has been evident, with a strong revival in free-market principles and a much reduced role for the government and public finance, features reinforced by the demise of centrally planned economies in the Eastern bloc.

The current challenge at the *national* level is to ensure that an appropriate balance of government influence is maintained, especially in finance. Among European nations considerable differences occur: the UK embraced 'Thatcherite economics', yet intense debates persist over funding for transport, health and education; in France supply-side measures have been enacted, but the government retains a strong influence on economic affairs. At the *European Community* level policy harmonization and economic convergence represent major challenges, especially as market-based integration is hampered by marked regional disparities created by the southward extension of the EC. Without economic convergence, the continued existence of such inequalities will naturally promote demands for protectionism and state funding.

3.1 UK PUBLIC-SECTOR FUNDING AND THATCHERITE ECONOMICS

As with most European nations, the UK experienced a postwar rise in the share of public expenditure relative to GDP, averaging over 40 per cent in the mid-1970s (Table 3.1). While the UK position was not unusual—indeed, if anything its rate of growth of public expenditure was relatively slow in the 1950s and 1960s—a large proportion of the increased expenditure reflected the growth of social payments and transfers rather than public investment in the capital stock. Moreover, the increase took place against a backcloth of declining UK economic

Table 3.1 Government expenditure as a percentage of GDP,[a] EC members, 1961–1990

	Bel.	Den.	Ger.	Gre.	Spa.	Fra.	Ire.	Ita.	Lux.	Neth.	Port.	UK	EC9	EC12
1961–70 ave.,	33.2	32.1	37.1	—	—	38.3	33.5	32.5	33.7	40.3	—	36.6	36.3	—
1971–80 ave.,	46.3	47.8	45.6	—	26.2	42.1	43.0	36.3	45.4	50.7	—	40.8	42.3	—
1981–90 ave.,	54.7	59.5	47.2	46.9	39.8	50.7	50.6	49.6	53.2	59.6	43.4	41.9	48.6	47.7
of which:														
1981	57.6	59.8	49.2	39.9	35.6	48.6	51.8	45.4	58.5	59.3	41.7	44.1	48.4	47.0
1982	57.6	61.2	49.4	39.7	37.5	50.3	54.6	47.4	55.8	61.3	43.8	44.6	49.5	48.2
1983	57.2	61.6	48.4	41.5	38.8	51.4	54.2	48.6	55.1	62.0	46.1	44.7	49.7	48.6
1984	56.1	60.3	48.0	44.3	39.3	51.9	52.3	49.3	51.8	60.7	46.6	45.4	49.9	48.8
1985	55.8	59.3	47.5	48.1	42.1	52.1	53.7	50.8	51.1	59.6	43.5	44.1	49.8	49.0
1986	55.1	56.0	46.9	47.5	41.7	51.5	53.5	50.9	51.7	59.7	44.6	42.8	49.1	48.4
1987	53.5	58.3	47.0	50.0	40.9	51.3	51.7	50.7	54.3	61.2	43.0	41.2	48.7	48.0
1988	52.4	60.3	46.6	50.7	40.5	50.2	47.9	50.8	52.2	59.1	42.2	38.4	47.7	47.0
1989	51.2	59.9	45.1	53.9	40.7	49.8	44.3	51.2	51.1	56.9	41.7	37.1	46.8	46.3
1990	50.2	58.5	44.1	53.8	40.8	49.4	41.7	51.1	50.3	56.6	41.3	36.6	46.3	45.8

[a] At market prices.

performance, rising tax and social security burdens and growing government indebtedness.

Hadjimatheou (1987) identifies periods of very rapid growth of public expenditure following electoral victories by the Labour Party in 1964–67 and 1974–75, and also periods when attempts were made to reverse the upward trend: 1967–70 following the devaluation of sterling, and 1976-77 following an inflationary crisis, a steep rise in spending and IMF pressure conditional upon the granting of borrowing facilities. Such occasions reinforced the 'stop–go' nature of the economy characteristic of postwar UK development. Attempts to stimulate the economy led to an influx of imports and balance of payments crises followed by the inevitable deflation, a situation that became progressively worse as the economy became more open to international influences. By the late 1970s Bacon and Eltis (1978) were arguing that the poor performance of the economy directly reflected excessive public expenditure growth, partly via a 'crowding-out' effect on productive market-sector investment and exports by non-productive, non-market-sector absorption. While controversial in its theoretical base and findings, this perspective was typical of concern about public finance.

In 1978–79 rising unemployment was met by increased public expenditure and attempts to curb wages, leading to the 'Winter of discontent'. Industrial relations reached a low ebb and the economic crisis was exacerbated by a second major oil price rise. Against this background, a new government under Margaret Thatcher was elected based on a manifesto of improving incentives to work and reducing personal taxation. However, commitments to raise public servants pay, VAT and nationalized industry prices initially fuelled inflation and government spending rose as a proportion of GDP. Thereafter, the new administration, by virtue of a large parliamentary majority, was able to introduce wide-ranging reforms and to extend these after subsequent elections in 1983 and 1987. Consensus politics and mixed-economy policies were to be abandoned along with Keynesian demand management, state subsidies and budget deficits. Instead, attention was paid to encouraging market forces and the supply side. The cornerstone of the new philosophy was the Medium-Term Financial Strategy.

3.1.1 The Medium-Term Financial Strategy (MTFS)

The new administration drew philosophical support from monetarist ideas that inflation is caused by excessive monetary growth and that enterprise and markets rather than governments create economic growth and wealth. The monetarist premiss was that to control inflation it is necessary and sufficient to control the rate of growth of the money supply over a number of years. While unemployment would rise and output fall in the short term, the sooner the public, unions and business revised their inflation expectations, the lower would be the cost in lost jobs and output. Thus, if anti-inflation objectives are to be taken seriously and built into expectations of pay negotiators, clearly defined medium-term targets need to be set and attained. As Greenaway and Shaw (1983) argue, this implies that agents form their expectations about inflation rationally, and therefore the pre-announcement of policy would allow them to revise their inflation expectations quickly and accurately.

The Medium-Term Financial Strategy (MTFS) was launched in the 1980 Budget and set out objectives 'to create the conditions in which growth could occur, largely through reduction in the rate of inflation. The strategy would involve a steady fall in the rate of growth of the money supply secured by requisite fiscal policy' (HM Treasury 1980). The macroeconomic, anti-inflation, 'monetarist' elements thus involved a commitment to monetary targets, namely £M3, and a progressive reduction in the public-sector borrowing requirement, both absolutely and as a percentage of GDP (Table 3.2). The other strand to the 'Thatcher experiment' was a set of microeconomic policy reforms designed to improve the supply side of the economy and remove impediments preventing people and firms from responding to changing conditions and market demands. These included tax concessions, incentives for self-employment, revisions to labour laws, abolition of foreign exchange, hire purchase and bank lending controls, and privatization.

The MTFS was not novel in its use of monetary and fiscal policy to fight inflation, but it was innovative in the adoption of monetarist orthodoxy, and, above all, in its adherence to a set of anti-inflation targets designed to influence inflationary expectations. The importance of the medium term was that the government was prepared to wait several years to see the benefits of its strategy, a radical departure from fine-tuning, 'stop–go' policies characteristic of the post-war UK.

The strategy centred on two target variables, £M3 and the PSBR, and provided an explicit acceptance of the interdependence of monetary and fiscal policy, and the need for a government budget restraint. The monetary side, the original heart of the strategy, proved problematic from the start, with £M3 rising by over 20 per cent between February 1980 and March 1981 and thereafter persistently overshooting its target ranges (Table 3.3). Moreover, while there appeared a reasonable relationship between £M3 and inflation prior to 1982, thereafter they moved in opposite directions as sharp cuts in inflation were recorded. Various attempts were made in the 1980s to introduce other targets, including broad (PSL2, M4) and narrow aggregates (M1, M0), as it became evident that no single measure could fully describe monetary conditions (see Bank of England 1990). In essence, the authorities had begun their monetary control by interest rate policy rather than by monetary base contraction. This implied controlling the demand for credit and estimating the level of interest rates required to hit a given target, in turn allowing interest rates to reach very high levels. However, difficulties arose from changes to the financial sector. The appearance of a wide range of substitutable monetary assets led institutions and individuals to switch between assets, a process aided by competition between banks and building societies, with the result that increased holdings

Table 3.2 The Medium-Term Financial Strategy: original proposals

	1978–79	1979–80	1980–81	1981–82	1982–83	1983–84
Ranges for growth of the money stock (£M3) (% change during year)			7–11	6–10	5–9	4–8
Public-sector borrowing (£billions at 1978–79 prices)						
Total expenditure	74	74.5	74.5	73	71.5	70.5
Total receipts	–65	–66	–67.5	–67.5	–69.5	–71
Implied fiscal adjustment	—	—	—	—	2.5	3
General government borrowing requirement	9	8	7	5	4	3
Public-sector borrowing requirement (PSBR)	9.3	8	6	5	3.5	2.5
PSBR as % of GDP at market prices	5.5	4.5	3.5	3	2.5	1.5

Source: HM Treasury (1980).

Table 3.3 UK monetary target experience, 1980–1987

Period	Aggregate	Target growth rate (%p.a.)	Result (%p.a.)	Comments
Feb. 1980 – Apr. 1981	£M3	7–11	19.4	Overshot—leading to rise in liquidity preference and move from building society deposits to bank time deposits as banks enter mortgage market
Feb. 1981 – Apr. 1982	£M3	6–10	13.1	Overshot—uncertainty re: inflation, jobs; rise in precautionary demand for money
Feb. 1982 – Apr. 1983	£M3	8–12	11.4	Broadly met—greater use of gilt sales to take out liquidity ('overfunding')
	M1	8–12	12.0	
	PSL2	8–12	11.1	
Feb. 1983 – Apr. 1984	£M3	7–11	10.2	Broadly met
	M1	7–11	11.1	
	PSL2	7–11	12.3	
Feb. 1984 – Apr. 1985	£M3	6–10	11.6	£M3 overshot—ahead of British Telecom sale liquid balances built up; PSBR ahead of target
	M0	4–8	5.5	
Feb. 1985 – Apr. 1986	£M3	5–9	14.8	Overshot—'overfunding' ends and raises £M3; M0 on target
	M0	3–7	3.5	
Feb. 1986 – Apr. 1987[a]	£M3	11–15	20.0	Overshot—official reservations on the use of targets; no further target set for £M3
	M0	2–6	2.0	

[a] In May 1987 £M3 was renamed M3; a new M4 was designated (M3 + private-sector holdings of building society shares and deposits and CDs, less building society holdings of bank deposits and bank CDs and notes and coin); and PSL2 was renamed M5.

were kept in interest-bearing deposit accounts, while banks entered the mortgage market allowing borrowers access to greater funds for house purchase.

Eventually, increasing attention was paid to targeting the exchange rate. The numerous revisions to the money supply target ranges, the lack of precision in the targets and regular overshooting had meant that monetary targeting had proved unworkable as a means of influencing expectations, and had seriously undermined the MTFS. Ultimately, UK membership of the ERM arguably spelled the death-knell for British 'monetarism', although not for the MTFS. Indeed, with the demise of the monetary targeting, the Thatcher and Major governments, not surprisingly, placed more emphasis on the other anti-inflationary element, the public-sector borrowing requirement (PSBR) target.

The PSBR is the balance of borrowing required by government after taking account of expenditure and receipts. It is a flow concept, an annual addition to the total amount of public debt. It is, strictly speaking, part of fiscal policy, but it had a high profile in the monetary-policy-dominated MTFS. Firstly, its control would require an effective curb on public expenditure, which the government had argued was at the heart of the UK's economic problems. Moreover, government philosophy and commitments led to a shift in the 'fiscal triangle', since previously budget deficits had implied that any shortfall in receipts compared with expenditure was met by borrowing as a residual element. Under the MTFS targets were set for reduced borrowing and expenditure with taxation as the residual. However, an electoral commitment to lower taxation meant that in reality shortfalls were to be effected by reduced expenditure.

Secondly, although the PSBR was seen as a counterpart to the rate of growth of the money supply, it was one aspect over which the government had some control. An excess of government spending over receipts tends to add to the volume of bank deposits as recipients of the government cheques pay these into their bank accounts. In turn, the banks may find themselves holding excess cash and can expand their lending operations; thus the deposit multiplier is stimulated and also the money supply. However, more significant in this context is the financing of any deficit, namely the method of borrowing used (Fig. 3.1).

Borrowing from the non-bank private sector can take place via the issue of securities such as National Savings products. Payment is via cheques payable to the Bank of England drawn on bank accounts; hence, *ceteris paribus*, bank deposits will fall and a brake will be applied to monetary expansion. However, if as expected the government spends the money raised, the latter will return eventually to the banks and the overall money supply impact may be broadly neutral. The main impact may be felt in terms of the higher interest rates needed to attract non-bank private-sector borrowers in the first place. The higher interest payable will add to the PSBR.

Borrowing from the banking sector involves 'residual financing' in a situation where the non-bank private sector is unwilling to purchase all the securities the government wishes to sell. The increase in government expenditure will need to be financed directly by the Bank of England. As the funds are spent,

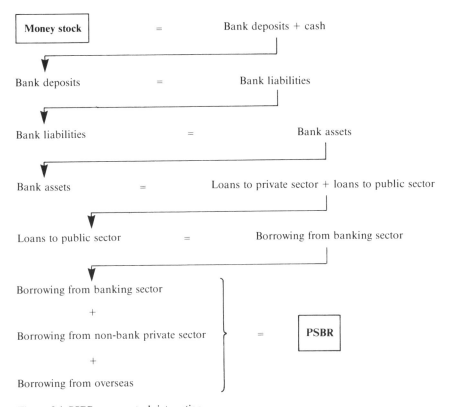

Figure 3.1 PSBR–money stock interaction

the government cheques are deposited with commercial banks, increasing their liabilities. In turn, their deposits with the Bank of England rise. Thus, the cash base of the banking system will increase and the surplus cash may be used to add to assets such as call loans to the discount houses and loans to the personal and corporate sectors. Loans to the latter will further raise bank assets and, following the multiplier effect, bank deposits until the additional holdings of government securities have matched the rise in PSBR. Thus, the money supply will have risen without a rise in interest rates. Partington (1989) suggests that, where a government deliberately chooses to sell securities to the central bank, the expansionary effect on the banking system and money stock is seen as the modern equivalent of its predecessors' resorting to the printing press to meet their monetary needs.

Borrowing from the overseas sector is more complex in its outcome. At a simple level, it represents an unfavourable outflow of national income in terms of debt service and is likely to require a rise in interest rates to encourage overseas demand for UK government securities. To purchase the securities foreigners must buy sterling, which thus expands the foreign exchange reserves of the Bank of England, and also the money supply. Thus, the rise in government expenditure causes bank deposits to rise while the higher interest rates cause deposits to fall, although this is offset partly by the influx of foreign exchange. The net effect is an increase in the money supply. However, there may be further complex and uncertain effects as the increased demand for sterling pushes up its value and impacts on the trade balance and future currency expectations, and the demand for UK securities alters with changes in foreign interest rates.

The Thatcher government argued that, given these borrowing alternatives, there was no wholly satisfactory method of financing the PSBR. Moreover, it also contended that as the PSBR rose so would interest rates. Hence, while Thatcherite fiscal policy focused on regulating the methods of PSBR funding to ensure non-expansion of the money supply, above all it sought to reduce the underlying causes of public-sector borrowing. The initial MTFS projections foresaw the PSBR falling from $4\frac{1}{2}$ to $1\frac{1}{2}$ per cent of GDP from 1979/80 to 1983/84, whereas later targets envisaged a zero absolute PSBR consistent with a balanced-budget philosophy. The impact of this on the UK public sector was significant, as seen by reference to UK flow-of-funds data.

3.1.2   UK public-sector finance: a flow-of-funds approach

'The impact of changes in financial variables on the real sector and inflation are major issues in monetary economics' (Barr and Cuthbertson 1989). Flow-of-funds accounting is an offshoot of National Income accounting, whereby the financial flows of each sector of the economy (persons, companies, government, financial institutions and overseas) represent the funding of a deficit or deployment of a surplus generated by activities in the real economy (income and expenditure).

Thus, flow-of-funds data set out financial transactions between sectors. The principal links are that those who receive income are not necessarily those who spend it: spending can also come from past saving or borrowing. Conversely, those who save are not necessarily those that invest. In theory, the resultant surpluses or deficits should sum to zero, since changes in one sector's assets relate to those in another's liabilities. In practice, it is rare for data on the real economy to be matched exactly by the financial transactions of the sectors. Errors or balancing items may be substantial, associated with recording difficulties, and particulary notable with the company and personal sectors from which few National Income data are directly obtained. Nevertheless, flow-of-funds accounts give insights not possible with National Income accounts, notably that changes in economic policy can be traced through sectoral flows to changes in spending decisions.

Table 3.4 summarizes total sector flows in the 1980s. The traditional pattern was a marked public-sector financial deficit offset by a personal-sector surplus, implying that personal-sector 'savings' would be channelled to fund essential government services. Elsewhere balances would reflect the state of the economy

Table 3.4 Financial sector flows in the 1980s (£millions)

Sector surplus/deficit	1980	1981	1982	1983	1984	1985	1986	1987	1988	1989	1990
Personal sector	11 803	12 141	9505	6294	9 362	8085	3457	-3103	-13 659	-4 247	8 008
Industrial/commercial companies	-106	1 593	3074	5027	5 126	2985	1025	67	-7 928	-23 404	-25 436
Financial companies and institutions	39	-1 365	-1374	2039	431	2211	3941	4487	407	2 056	2 927
Overseas sector	2 843	-6 748	-4649	-3765	-1 811	-2878	-187	4159	15 520	20 404	14 380
Central government	-5 171	-6 544	-7571	-8307	-10 220	-8319	-7672	-4308	6 012	7 422	-3 674
Public corporations	-2 603	-1 175	-898	-319	-346	-53	1324	1354	1 898	573	4 284
Local authorities	-2 669	-161	710	-1830	-2 617	-1743	-1398	-1306	-734	-1 359	29
Total	1 550	2 259	1203	861	75	-288	-490	1355	-1 516	-1 445	-518
Residual error[a]	-1 550	-2 259	-1203	-861	-75	288	490	1355	1 516	1 445	518

[a] Residual error is the difference between the expenditure-based and the income-based estimates of GDP.

Source: CSO 'Blue Book', *UK National Accounts*, 1991.

and prevailing levels of interest rates but would be relatively smaller. Over time sectoral flows have exhibited more diversity and imbalances have grown markedly during inflationary periods, features apparent with the corporate and overseas sectors where the latter equates to the growth in the UK balance of payments deficit. The most noticeable change, however, is the reversal of the personal-sector surplus and public-sector deficit.

A decline in the savings ratio from 13 per cent of GDP in 1979 to 5 per cent in 1988, the lowest proportion for 30 years, together with a noticeable 'consumer boom', widened the savings–investment gap and sent the personal sector into deficit. The savings decline was spurred by falling inflation in the mid-1980s which reduced the erosion of accumulated wealth and the need to top up savings with additional amounts. Interest rates were also relatively low, and the nature of exogenous savings had changed with a greater preference for liquidity. Contractual savings showed a significant rise, with greater awareness of risk encouraging flows into pension funds and insurance companies. The corollary, the 'consumer boom', was encouraged by rising incomes, financial deregulation and, above all, borrowing for asset acquisition, notably house purchase.

The fortunes of the personal sector stand in marked contrast to the public sector, where the effects of Thatcherite economics ultimately transformed the financial deficits into surpluses. For accounting purposes the public sector is considered both as a whole and in terms of its principal components: central government (all bodies for whose activities a minister of the Crown appointee is responsible to Parliament), local authorities (subject to the Local Authorities Acts), and public corporations (essentially public trading bodies). These are very distinctive, yet as we have seen they are traditionally considered as a whole in the formulation of financial policy and borrowing (PSBR). Moreover, their capital expenditure is subject to a high degree of centralized influence.

Public expenditure is the sum of expenditure on current and capital account of the public sector but excluding the appropriation and capital account activities of the public corporations and transfers within the public sector such as grants paid by central government to local authorities. The expenditure total includes current account consumption and capital account investment, which represent the public sector's claim on the real resources of the economy, and subsidies, current grants and capital transfers, which represent transfer payments between economic groups. By far the bulk of the expenditure is conducted by central government, most of which is on 'supply' services voted by Parliament such as defence and education. The major exclusion is social security, which comes from the National Insurance Fund.

The growing significance of public expenditure as a percentage GDP at the end of the 1970s was of great concern to the new Thatcher government. Partington (1989) estimates that the annual average percentage growth of general government expenditure (central government and local authorities) was around 18 per cent in the 1970s compared with 9 per cent in the 1980s. However, this belies the significance for economic resource absorption. Within public expenditure, claims on real resources (goods and services) have grown less rapidly than the rate of growth of transfer payments. Brown and Jackson (1990) cite transfer spending as accounting for 29.5 per cent of public spending in 1970 compared with 38.4 per cent in 1987. Among functions, the share of resources going to defence, law and order and social security expanded relative to that going to transport and housing.

These trends reflect the state of the economy as well as government attempts to curb central public expenditure. Prior to 1985 high unemployment meant there was a burden on demand-determined expenditure early in the MTFS, and, in spite of falls in 1986–88, pressures from an ageing population increased transfer payments. In terms of central government expenditure, the brunt of cutbacks has fallen on capital expenditure programmes via downgrading of existing proposals and non-approval of new projects, especially transport developments. Moreover, after 1976 cash rather than volume limits were applied and covered some 60 per cent of public expenditure, the rest being demand-determined, such as social security payments. Yet it was not until 1987/88 that the ratio of general government expenditure to GDP fell below the 1979 level.

That the central government financial deficit (CGFD) eventually managed to fall in the late 1980s (see Table 3.4) reflected the buoyancy of government revenue as well as the squeeze on central expenditure. In spite of commitments to reduce taxation, the UK tax burden as a percentage of GDP was persistently around 37–39 per cent in the 1980s compared with about 33 per cent in the late 1970s, and this reflected 'fiscal drag', whereby rising incomes generated higher income and VAT revenue. However, the government's desire was to shift the incidence of taxation from a direct to an indirect basis, which ministers perceived would stimulate entrepreneurial activity and reduce tax avoidance, although greater National Insurance burdens have been encountered by employers and employees. A similar policy was applied to corporation tax, where the effective tax rate was progressively reduced from 52 per cent to 34 per cent, with lower rates for smaller companies, yet rising company profits in the mid-1980s enabled the tax yield from this source to grow significantly.

The UK public-sector financial deficit/surplus (PSFD/S) also includes the deficits/surpluses of the local authorities (LAFD/S) and the public corporations (PCFD/S). While traditionally contributing less to the PSFD than the CGFD, they illustrate particularly well the influence of Thatcher government thinking on public finance. Local government in the UK is statute-bound by central government laws. Under a two-tier organization most local authority spending is conducted at the level of county or metropolitan district council, where responsibility is held for services such as education and policing, while at the local level environmental services and housing are funded. Local government current expenditure has been increasingly subjected to market forces, for example as a result of the introduction of competitive tendering from August 1989, whereby under the Local Government Act 1988 some 2000 service contracts with a value of around £2.7 billion are subject to competition from private contractors (Parker and Hartley 1990). These services include refuse collection, cleaning, catering, maintenance of vehicles and leisure management. Capital expenditure has been particularly hit by cash limits and greater central government control over budgets, as seen, for example, in the context of new building work in educational and health services establishments.

Local government's traditional principal sources of current revenue are central government grants; these increased significantly in relative importance in the 1970s, especially the rate support grant, designed to provide acceptable minimum levels of service, to share taxable resources between local governments and to reduce the burden of local tax on the domestic ratepayer. However, the Thatcher government wished to reduce this burden on central government finance and replaced the rate support grant with a unitary grant. The local tax base for local authority finance has usually been property, and until the introduction of the community charge in 1990 (1989 in Scotland), rates levied on the notional rental value of property were used to compute the rate poundage or target income required by the local authorities.

The 1979 Conservative government was already committed to abolishing domestic rates, given that rapidly rising property values would raise them to unacceptably high levels. In 1986 the Green Paper *Paying for Local Government* provided the basis for introducing a separate uniform business rate (UBR) and the community charge (CC), the latter a lump sum levied uniformly on all adults within a local authority for the services provided. In theory, any increase in local authority spending would be paid for by local residents out of an increase in the CC, as the UBR could not be changed.

Both the CC and domestic rates have defects. In particular, they are essentially regressive, being unrelated to income, and neither has much relation to local services since both are subject to central government capping. While rates are easy to collect, this has not proved true of the CC which is spread over twice as many people as properties. Secondly, the CC should be seen in the wider politico-economic context of the control of public finance. According to the 1981 Green Paper *Alternatives to Domestic Rates*, replacing rates with the CC would lower the retail price index since rates had been rising faster than prices and incomes thus fuelling inflation. Moreover, perversely, the more unpopular the CC, the greater the incentive for local authorities to keep it low. Since the CC is only about 25 per cent of local government revenue yet bears the weight of any expenditure increase, there is a gearing effect whereby a 5 per cent overrun in local government expenditure will raise the CC by 25 per cent.

Within a year of its full implementation, the government announced that the CC would be phased out in favour of a banded property tax based on the value of properties. The CC was particularly unpopular as it favoured those with large houses and/or small family units. One rationale for a local housing tax is that, if all expenditure except housing (and food) is taxed, then economic decisions are distorted, especially given the existence of mortgage interest relief.

The dispute over local taxes in whatever form will continue; it also begs the question of whether a separate local tax is appropriate at all within a highly mobile society. Burton (1991) argues that many users of locally delivered and publicly financed or subsidized services are visitors, and that, moreover, among residents the common reaction to high-cost/poor-quality local services is exit rather than voice. He contends that local government services that provide separate private benefits should be financed by fees or charges; all other government expenditure should be centrally provided and funded by consumption taxes, possibly via a component of VAT.

Notwithstanding the problems of local authority revenue, the impact of government pressure is manifested in the overall downward trend of the LAFD from its 1984 peak. More remarkable, however, is the turnaround in the financial position of the public corporations reflecting the changes in UK industrial policy. The Labour government of the mid-1970s had extended nationalization, set up the National Enterprise Board and attempted indicative planning on French lines by creating a planning forum with industry and the unions. The criticisms of state intervention mentioned earlier were thus fundamental to the Thatcher government's new privatization policy.

In terms of public finance, privatization had involved over 30 companies and raised £38.2 billion by 1991. Moreover, the level of state spending had been cut from 4 per cent of GDP in 1975 to 1.5 per cent of GDP in 1991 (Stone 1991). The policy was to run the public corporations as regular trading organizations, self-sufficient entities controlled by target rates of return, cash limits and market exposure. Their ability to contribute to their own financing varied; the utilities and Post Office proved more successful than the coal industry or railways.

Table 3.4 shows the improvement in the public corporations' financial position as a whole, but aggregate figures understate the impact of privatization, which is shown not as a method of financing but rather as a means of reducing the PSBR (i.e. negative public spending). Although one might argue that there is no real difference in terms of a lower PSBR between raising revenue via taxation or selling public-sector assets, the accounting treatment varies, with the former seen as an increase in general government receipts, thus reducing the PSFD, and the latter as a reduction in net lending to other sectors by general government. However, Howells and Bain (1990) argue that the economic effects may differ, since a tax increase may deflate the economy adversely, affecting unemployment and inflation, whereas when British Telecom was privatized in 1984 its shares were exchanged for other financial assets (e.g. building society accounts), with little direct effect on domestic demand for goods and services. For this reason, the PSFD may be a better guide to the effects of budgetary policy on the real economy than the PSBR.

Table 3.5 shows this link between the PSFD and the PSBR. The former is computed on an accruals basis so there is a delay, for example, before actual tax revenue payments. Within an accounting period borrowing may be necessary

Table 3.5 Financing the PSBR, 1980–1990 (£millions)

	1980	1982	1984	1986	1987	1988	1989	1990
Financial deficit/surplus								
Central government	−5 171	−7571	−10 220	−7672	−4303	6 012	7422	−3674
Local authorities	−2 669	710	−2 617	−1398	−1306	−734	−1359	29
Public corporations	−2 603	−898	−346	−1324	1354	1 898	573	4284
Total PSFD	−10 443	−7759	−13 183	−7746	−4255	7 176	6636	639
Accruals adjustments	469	402	1 709	257	930	985	1527	−227
Other financial transactions (net)	874	−3293	−4 592	−5504	−6619	−5 677	−4167	−1207
PSBR	11 786	4868	10 300	2499	−1434	−11 868	−9276	−2073
Financed by:								
Banks and building societies	2 558	−2141	956	−5259	−3928	−5 005	−4259	1579
Overseas sector	756	439	755	611	−5764	−823	4272	−4525
Non-bank private sector	8 472	6570	8 589	7147	8258	−6 040	−9289	873

Source: CSO 'Blue Book', *UK National Accounts*, 1991, tables 11.13, 11.14.

to cover the delay ('accruals adjustment'). Since central government acts as an intermediary in making loans or acquiring securities, the amount it borrows rises relative to its own deficit. Conversely, asset disposal or loan repayment reduces its borrowing needs. 'Other financial transactions' include National Insurance Fund receipts and payments relating to state pension schemes. Thus, government efforts to shift the burden of pension contributions by phasing out SERPS (State Earnings Related Pension Scheme) and introducing personal pensions from July 1988 were further attempts to reduce the pressure on public-sector finance (see Terry 1988).

The marked decline in the PSBR in the late 1980s is consistent with the original MTFS and Thatcherite philosophy. Indeed, by 1987/88 a public-sector surplus, the public-sector debt repayment (PSDR), of £3.6 billion existed, rising by 1988/89 to £14.3 billion or 3 per cent of GDP. This reflected buoyant tax receipts from the 'consumer boom' as well as continued public asset sales. However, as the 1990s began, government spending pressures became more intense; by 1989/90 the PSDR was down to £8 billion and by 1990/91 it was merely £0.46 billion, although this was complicated by Gulf War expenditure and money spent to soften the impact of the community charge. The financial position continued to deteriorate further as the deepening recession cut severely into tax revenues and raised benefit payments. By November 1991 the forecast 1991/92 PSDR of £3 billion was revised to an expected PSBR of £12 billion, although the subsequent out-turn was worse—a PSBR of £13.77 billion, some £11.75 billion of which was government borrowing on its own account (Bank of England 1992d). By late 1992 a PSBR of £37 billion (6.25 per cent of GDP) was forecast for 1992–93, and £44 billion (7 per cent of GDP) for the following year, the highest total since 1976 when the UK was forced to seek IMF support. This massive increase reflects the costs of the recession and the Treasury's decision to resist higher taxes.

Thus the PSBR (PSDR) has fluctuated widely since 1987 and the 1991/92 out-turn was similar to levels experienced in the early 1980s. However, then such deficits were deemed unacceptable to the Thatcher administration, whereas the volatility since 1987 partly reflects changed views on the relationship between monetary and fiscal policy. In the original MTFS the PSBR was seen as a major influence on monetary growth (£M3), unless government debt could be sold to the non-bank private sector. Hence, as Table 3.5 shows, the bulk of the 1980s public-sector finance was in this form. Indeed, overfunding was common, whereby sales of marketable debt (e.g. gilts) and non-marketable debt (e.g. national savings) exceeded the borrowing requirement. The downside of this approach was the potential upward impact on interest rates to attract investors, a feature that further encouraged the government to plan for a substantial reduction in the PSBR. More specifically, however, product and marketing innovations were made to gilts and National Savings, such as using convertibles, partly paid stocks and index-linked features which reduced the interest payable yet maintained their attractiveness.

Any direct link between fiscal and monetary policy was broken when specific targets for broad money were abandoned. Instead, the emphasis switched to debt management policy *per se* and a balanced budget. The fears were that on the one hand large budgets would grow explosively if government was not prepared to raise taxes to cover the additional interest payments; on the other hand, if there were large deficits government might encourage inflation to reduce the real burden of the debt. Thus, towards the end of the 1980s the PSDR was encouraged via the repayment of large issues of gilts and National Savings, allowing also the reorganization of the maturity and interest profile of the debt. This and further privatization proceeds in 1991 from the sale of the Water and Electricity utilities and the second tranche of British Telecom initially accounted for a more relaxed approach to the announcement of an expected return to a PSBR in 1991/92. However, the large size of the actual 1991/92 PSBR has generated a mixed reaction. In the 1980s a £14 billion borrowing requirement might have been met by severe expenditure curbs, notably on capital items in areas such as transport, education, and housing. However, with much of the deficit derived from recession-induced current expenditure, many people now advocate the need for significant investment-oriented capital expenditure to boost growth and jobs. In view of the commitment to curb inflation the government has sought ways to meet the above requirements while assuring the financial markets that any additional public expenditure is not feckless. These include encouraging more private finance of traditional public-sector infrastructure projects, curbing public-sector pay deals, and raising further privatization proceeds. The latter includes the auction of part of the government debt holdings in British Telecom and the privatized electricity companies. However, this approach shows perhaps implicit recognition that the financial and political gains from future privatizations are limited, especially in view of the controversy surrounding proposals for the coal and rail industries.

The failure of monetary targeting and the marked fluctuations in the PSBR, the two key elements of the MTFS, thus undermined its credibility. Subsequently, the government has introduced the concepts of a New Control Target (NCT) whereby government departments are set firm targets for approximately 85 per cent of their expenditure three years in advance. If a department's expenditure rises in one area, it must make suitable cuts elsewhere. The NCT will be set three years in advance in the new annual December budget covering both taxation and expenditure. However, this does not constitute part of a new MTFS, indeed, in the aftermath of the exit from the ERM, government macroeconomic policy has remained unclear and susceptible to the 'fine-tuning' the MTFS was geared to end.

3.2   PUBLIC-SECTOR FUNDING AMONG EC MEMBER STATES

The UK was by no means alone among EC nations in its attempts to curb public expenditure and borrowing in the 1980s, although, as Table 3.1 illustrates, the results were mixed, and within individual nations the philosophical justification for cutbacks in public-sector spending varied.

3.2.1   Federal Republic of Germany

The FRG has been preoccupied since the 1950s with the external value of the Deutschmark and the control of inflation, and thus its economic changes in the early 1980s were moderate compared with those of the UK. The Bundesbank was sceptical of UK attempts to link monetary growth and public-sector borrowing requirements. In any event, budget deficits were seen as damaging to the external value of the Deutschmark more through the impact on business confidence than via interest rates or 'crowding-out' effects. However, in common with the UK, there was a move towards supply-side policies and the introduction from 1982 of a medium-term approach to financial strategy.

The initial phase of this policy gave priority to reducing the public-sector deficit in order to ease pressure on the credit markets, improve the climate for private investment and generate growth on the supply side. Significant cutbacks were enacted by not increasing public-sector salaries and cash benefits in line with inflation, limiting educational assistance (e.g. conversion of student grants to loans) and reducing non-statutory, especially capital, expenditure by central, regional and local authorities. Given successful fiscal consolidation, a second phase began in 1986 directed at restructuring taxation to invoke a cumulative net reduction in direct taxes of DM48 billion by 1980, yet conditional upon continued expenditure restraint.

Considerable success was achieved in containing the rise in spending to an average of 3.2 per cent p.a. between 1985 and 1989, compared with 8 per cent p.a. from 1978 to 1981 (Deutsche Bundesbank 1990b). Favourable economic aspects, including relative price stability, moderate public-sector wage increases and low interest rates, assisted the process. The slowdown in the rise of expenditure was apparent in all levels of government. Between 1986 and 1989 federal expenditure rose by an annual average of 3.1 per cent, that of the *Länder* governments by 3.7 per cent and of the local authorities by 4.5 per cent. However, such figures mask divergencies at the local and *Länder* level, with in general the big cities, especially those in structurally weak regions such as Bremen, being more indebted than smaller municipalities. In terms of revenue, the effect of the tax reforms has been to decrease the proportion of direct taxes relative to indirect ones, but the strength of the economy maintained tax receipts. *Länder* tax revenue rose on average by 5.5 per cent from 1986 to 1989 (Deutsche Bundesbank 1990a).

The above trends meant that the growth of public-sector debt was contained in the late 1980s. The borrowing ratio (i.e. net borrowing to expenditure) averaged 9 per cent from 1985 to 1989 for the federal government compared with 13.5 per cent from 1981 to 1985, 6 per cent for the *Länder* (previously 10.5 per cent) and under 1 per cent for local authorities (previously 3 per cent), although again there were marked regional variations, e.g. Saarland 17 per cent against Bavaria 2.5 per cent (Deutsche Bundesbank 1991b). The financing of the public-sector debt has generally shifted in favour of securities, and the central authorities have made available a wide range of marketable paper to encourage direct borrowing from the public, as in the UK. Moreover, the appreciation of the Deutschmark and the abolition of the coupon tax for non-residents encouraged foreign holdings of German debt to rise from 15 to 22 per cent, although the banks still remained the main creditors with 57 per cent. The slower growth of borrowing is obscured by the growing value of refinancing (DM105 billion in 1989).

This pattern of controlled management of public-sector debt was altered by the unification of East and West Germany in October 1990. The deep-rooted restructuring problems of former East Germany have required massive fiscal transfers, estimated at 5.5 per cent of West German GNP. New funds have been established to finance the cost of unification: the German Unity Fund and the Debt Processing Fund. The former is to receive transfers totalling DM115 million from the federal and old *Länder* budgets and in turn will transfer these monies to the five new *Länder* and their municipalities to compensate for their low tax-generating capabilities. The Debt Processing Fund combines existing debt liabilities of the old GDR as an interim measure. Eventually this will be transferred to the Treuhandanstalt, the public institution responsible for organizing privatization, to be redeemed if possible against asset sales. The likely residual debt will be shared among the federal and *Länder* governments. Such budget deficits and heavy consequent borrowing may be tolerated in the short term given the extraordinary circumstances of unification. However, in the longer term they are seen as threats to economic growth and integration itself. Accordingly, financial plans issued in July 1991 envisaged a cut in the federal budget to DM50 billion in 1992 and DM26 billion by 1995 (Deutsche Bundesbank 1991a). Further consideration of German unification is given in Chapter 10.

3.2.2 France

France has a long tradition of significant state involvement in its economy, and centralized government influence remains in spite of moves to embrace free-market principles common elsewhere in the European Community. A major policy change occurred in 1983 following two years of reflation at a time when other nations were deflating their economies in the wake of the second oil crisis. The resultant growth brought with it foreign exchange pressures which endangered the ERM and necessitated tightened public expenditure and stricter foreign exchange controls.

Recognition that increasing state involvement was limiting the economy led the socialist government to place greater emphasis on supply-side policies. Industrial subsidies were progressively phased out, deregulation applied to financial markets, the emphasis on the traditional system of 'indicative planning' reduced and privatization introduced (see Sec. 3.3.3). From the mid-1980s, budgetary policy was aimed at stimulating the economy by lowering tax and social security contributions while curbing spending. As Table 3.1 illustrates, public expenditure as a percentage of GDP fell from 52.1 per cent in 1985 to 49.4 per cent in 1990 and the PSBR fell from 2.9 per cent GDP to 1.1 per cent in the same period.

Public spending cutbacks have affected most areas apart from education, legal administration, civil research and public-sector housing. The first three continue to be favoured, possibly as a result of the bureaucratic tradition of the French public sector and close ties between the civil service and higher education. The recovery in the economy boosted corporate tax receipts and allowed the effective tax rate to fall from 50 to 42 per cent (to 37 per cent on undistributed profits). Personal taxation is complicated by local levies. Although the system is progressive, the overall tax take, including high social security payments, is high by European standards. Thomson (1991) suggests that without reform of the social security system extra financing of around FF10 billion per annum will be needed until 1993, owing to an ageing population and the associated high costs of pensions and health care.

3.2.3 High or growing public-sector debt nations

In Table 3.1 several EC nations may be identified where general government expenditure either remains high or has continued to rise as a percentage of GDP, thus posing problems for the convergence criteria of EMU. In Belgium some slow progress has been made to reduce the high absolute levels, mainly through expenditure cutbacks; while in the Netherlands the levels have stabilized from enhanced revenue offsetting expenditure increases. The situation in Italy and Greece is of more concern, since in the former public expenditure has continued to rise rapidly in the 1980s and requires heavy tax increases to fund it. In Greece net government borrowing was estimated at 18.4 per cent of GDP in 1990 and interest payments at 11 per cent, a significant burden (Van den Bempt 1991). In Spain, in contrast to the other EC countries, the adoption of free-market principles has gone hand in hand with the determined expansion of the public sector. Table 3.1 shows that public expenditure rose from 35.6 per cent of GDP in 1981 to 40.8 per cent in 1990. The public-sector deficit reached a peak of 7 per cent GDP in 1985 and then fell to 2.4 per cent GDP in 1990. These moderate levels by EC standards have been achieved in an era of political and economic transition, culminating in EC membership in 1986.

Until the late 1970s, Spain under Franco's dictatorship had a small but highly interventionist public sector, lacking developed welfare functions common elsewhere in the EC. From 1977 public expenditure rose, largely as a result of transfer payments to the increasing numbers of unemployed resulting from the oil-crisis-related depression. By 1992 there was a large budget deficit and an evident need for fiscal reform, especially to overcome tax evasion. The new socialist government introduced a medium-term economic programme including restrictive wage and monetary policies and public-sector reforms, including the restructuring of nationalized firms, balancing the social security budget and decentralizing public income and expenditure (Garcia Crespo 1991). These measures have been fairly successful at a time when industry as a whole is being restructured along market-oriented lines to meet the needs of the European market. Nevertheless, state support for industry remains high, in spite of privatization programmes (see Sec. 3.3.5), notably for health and education (and possibly to the detriment of infrastructure and welfare services). These are relatively underdeveloped by EC standards and pose a threat to the country's further economic growth.

It would appear from the above that significant differences in public-sector debt policies occur between these countries. These cannot be explained simply as responses to different temporary 'shocks' experienced by national economies, but reflect differing political and economic philosophies.

In a wide-ranging empirical survey of public-sector debt policies and political and monetary institutions among OECD nations, Grilli *et al.* (1991) found that large public-sector debts are concentrated among countries that have representative democracies and fractional party systems encouraging short-lived governments, of which Italy is the prime example. In terms of the relationship between fiscal policy and inflation, their findings suggest that over time changes in government expenditure appear strongly positively correlated with changes in the tax rate, but not with inflation, either across countries or over time.

Moreover, whereas countries that rely heavily on seignorage (revenues from printing money) tend to have high public debt levels (e.g. Greece, Italy, Spain), the converse does not follow. The general conclusions are that in most OECD nations public debt policy has not been a major determinant of monetary stability in the postwar period.

3.3 PRIVATIZATION AND EC MEMBER STATES

3.3.1 The UK

Central to the Thatcherite philosophy was the creation of a more flexible and enterprise-based UK economic environment and the promotion of as much private-sector involvement in the economy as possible. This was epitomized in the privatization programme, the financial effects of which have been alluded to in

Sec. 3.1.2, in the context of the turnaround of the public corporations' finances. However, the policy is worthy of further consideration. In the first place, the term involves more than the denationalization of unprofitable state enterprises and is loosely used to cover various means of changing the relationship between government and the private sector. Kay and Thompson (1986) suggest that these include *denationalization* (the sale of publicly owned assets), *deregulation* or *liberalization* (the introduction of competition into statutory monopolies), and *contracting out* (the franchising to private firms of the production of state-financed goods and services). Secondly, what started as a means to an end, namely economic motives such as reducing the burden on public expenditure, or political goals in reducing union power, later became an end in itself through the promotion of efficiency and popular capitalism. Indeed, by the Conservative government's second term of office, privatization was a key economic objective.

Liberalization has affected many former 'artificial monopolies' in transport (e.g. deregulation of bus services), telecommunications (e.g. licensing of Mercury), electricity supply, optical services and civil aviation. Proponents of liberalization argue that insulation from competitive forces inevitably leads to inefficiency and failure to respond to consumer needs. Kay and Silberston (1984) cite deregulation as generating a wider range of coach services at lower fares and a more extensive range of British Telecom equipment at lower cost. However, critics contend that liberalization encourages the new competitors to select only profitable services, leaving the unprofitable ones to be provided by the former monopoly or not at all. This then raises issues of cross-subsidization whereby, say, rural bus services may be funded by users of express coach services or taxpayers as a whole. Another argument against liberalization is that many utilities are natural monopolies where competition is deemed wasteful.

In terms of the promotion of private provision, a whole spectrum of arrangements is feasible. In sectors where the state is the major provider, individual projects can be given over wholly to the private sector, e.g. the Channel Tunnel and the Dartford Bridge, as privately funded projects additional to existing transport facilities. Elsewhere private and public operations may co-exist, as in education and health. In addition, the state may retain the responsibility for provision financed through general taxation but may use private-sector expertise to provide the service. Compulsory competitive tendering has been widely introduced into local government and the NHS, whereby public-sector activities traditionally undertaken 'in-house' are subject to outside competition in areas such as catering, cleaning and vehicle maintenance (see Table 3.6 and Parker and Hartley 1990; Hulme 1990).

Notwithstanding the extensive development of deregulation and the encouragement of private provision, the main UK focus has been on ownership transfer via the sale of state assets, the strict definition of privatization. In 1979 nationalized industries accounted for 10 per cent of GDP and 14 per cent of fixed investment; they employed almost 2 million people and dominated basic industries, especially energy, steel, transport and communications (HM Treasury

1986). Yet they were characterized by low productivity and profitability, high labour costs, low consumer satisfaction and vulnerability to political interference. The introduction of target rates of return and internal controls failed to cope with the main problem perceived by the incoming government, namely insulation from market forces.

Since 1979 the policy has been, firstly, to introduce management principles aimed at boosting the efficiency of those industries still in public hands, and secondly, progressively to transfer to private ownership public corporations via a programme of flotations, placings, buyouts or pure sale. Table 3.6 shows that

Table 3.6 The scope of privatization in the UK

Form of privatization	Examples
Asset sales/transfers	
100% sales (public offer)	Amersham International (1982), Rolls-Royce (1987), British Gas (1986).
100% sales (public offer)	British Aerospace (1981 government offered 51.6%, 1985 offered 49.4%)
	BT (1984 government offered 50.2%, 1991 49.8%)
	Associated British Ports (1983 government offered 51.5%, 1985 49.4%)
	BP (various amounts offered 1979–83)
	Cable and Wireless (various amounts offered 1981–85)
Private part-asset sales	BR hotels (1983)
	Sealink (1984 to Sea Containers 60.6%)
	Inmos (1984 to Thorn–EMI 75%)
	Oil and gas exploration licences (various dates)
Sales to workforce/management	National Freight Corporation (1981)
	Shipyards (1986)
	Vospers, Vickers, Swan Hunter, Unipart (1987)
Contracting-out	Local government—cleaning, catering and maintenance
	Hospitals—cleaning, catering, laundry
	Testing/maintenance of public vehicles
Diluting public-sector influence/encouraging private-sector provision	Private health care and private funding of state colleges
	Enterprise zones, science and industrial parks
	Channel Tunnel, Dartford Bridge
Charging for service	NHS—spectacles, dentistry, prescriptions
Exit from provision	Pensions—(SERPS) phase-out
Deregulation of monopolies	Telecommunications, buses, postal services

privatization has also applied to the utilities and natural monopolies, although in order to prevent the replacement of a public monopoly by a private one, consumer interests have been represented by 'watchdog' bodies, such as OFGAS and OFTEL, and powers over future ownership and conduct have been retained via 'golden shareholdings'. These are made supposedly to secure national interests during the company's early years in the private sector.

The arguments for privatization are usually couched in terms of government revenue, efficiency and wider share ownership. As we saw in Sec. 3.1.2, the financial benefit appears significant, although much depends on the accounting treatment applied. Kay and Silberston (1984) point to the arbitrary nature of what borrowing is included/excluded in the PSBR concept. J. R. Shackleton (1984) argued that the transfer of assets from public to private sector is likely to have only a marginal effect on the 'real economy' in the short term. Moreover, the temptation to raise revenue from asset sales may jeopardize the other objectives of privatization. He cited continuing monopolies for British Telecom and British Airways as boosting their price in advance of privatization. Overall privatization revenue has come mainly from the large number of shares involved rather than from their issue price. Although most issues have opened at a healthy premium providing windfall gains for speculators, critics argue that the pricing has undervalued the companies involved, thus raising vitriolic accusations of selling off the nation's assets too cheaply.

In terms of efficiency, the government contends that privatization benefits customers via lower prices, improved choice and better service. Employees gain from working in an environment with objectives and salary incentives. The economy benefits from higher profitability and improved flexibility via productivity gains (HM Treasury 1990). Thus, operating efficiencies are based on removing political influence and opening firms to market forces, notably the rigours of the capital market and the threat of takeover. Parker (1991) argues that it is difficult to reconcile the takeover threat as a spur to managerial efficiency with the state retention of a 'golden share', introduced specifically to prevent foreign control of strategic industries such as British Aerospace. He cites the removal of the 'golden share' leading to Ford's takeover of Jaguar as government recognition of this contradiction. In reality, few privatizations have been associated with greater competition, and areas such as telecommunications and the utilities remain dominated by the former public corporations.

Towards the end of the 1980s, the government stressed the concept of popular capitalism via wider share ownership as a major gain from privatization. It pointed to a threefold rise in share ownership, the growth of employee shareholders in privatized companies, and priority in share allocation for the small investor. However, while 11 million people now own shares and 6 million hold shares in privatized companies, the vast majority have holdings in only one company and merely 17 per cent in four or more. Thus, privatization has done little to reverse institutional shareholder dominance.

Objective analysis of UK privatization is clouded by the rhetoric associated with the topic. Those that agree with the principle might question its implementation, especially given the impact on public finances and share ownership. Others might question the premiss that public-sector firms cannot be efficient. Competition is widely cited as a key feature in boosting operating efficiency, yet, despite overtures in this direction, most utilities will remain monopoly suppliers. What is evident is that the UK privatization experience has encouraged similar experiments elsewhere in Europe.

3.3.2   Federal Republic of Germany

By UK standards, the Germans adopted a far more cautious approach to privatization, notwithstanding the presence of a centre–right government throughout the 1980s. The scope was more limited in that relatively few large state enterprises existed; moreover, where there was government involvement, it was often at regional or local authority level, not federal level.

Nevertheless, the federal government committed itself to developing a privatization programme in 1983, and the following year reduced its stake in VEBA (Vereinigte Elekrizitaets- und Bergwerks AG), the country's largest industrial holding group, from 43 to 30 per cent. The programme developed slowly, but losses by some state entities pressured the finance minister, Gerhard Stoltenberg, to produce a list of 11 candidates for privatization (Bruce 1984). Table 3.7 shows that VEBA, Volkswagen AG and VIAG (an energy, chemicals and aluminium state holding company) were completely disposed of between 1984 and 1988. By December 1989 the number of companies in which the federal government had direct or indirect stakes had fallen from 808 to 132 (Hawkins 1991).

The 1980s privatization of central government holdings was not paralleled at the regional and local levels. The *Länder* have wide-ranging investments in regional banks (*Landesbanken*), utilities, transport, trade fairs and promotional

Table 3.7   Major German privatizations in the 1980s

Company	Date of sale	Government holding (%)		Revenue (DM millions)
		Before disposal	After disposal	
VEBA I	January 1984	43.75	30	760
VEBA II	March 1987	25.6	0	2500
VIAG I	May 1986	100	60	745
VIAG II	May 1988	60	0	1460
IVG	October 1986	100	55	163
VW	March 1988	16	0	1100
DVKR	March 1988	100	75.1	58
Lufthansa	September 1986	74.3	55	84
Salzgitter	October 1989	100	0	2000
				8870

firms, as well as in industrial companies which are important as regional employers. Buhl (1989) cites as examples the governments of Saarland (26 per cent shareholding in Saabergwerke AG), and Schleswig-Holstein (25.1 per cent in Howaldstwerke-Deutsche Werft AG). While some *Länder* have reduced their equity holdings, there is still little evidence of major privatization at the regional level. Indeed, Buhl suggests the converse, with further investment to ensure that regional needs are met. At the local level there is great scope for privatization to meet social service needs, and it is expected that contracting-out (e.g. refuse disposal) will grow as it has done in the UK.

Thus, in contrast to the UK, German privatization in the 1980s did not follow from a need to improve national economic performance or extend share ownership. While the benefit of market forces was favoured, the ability to raise funds from asset disposals was persuasive. There exists considerable scope for further privatization in the new Germany; and, the failure of centrally planned economies and state intervention in the east is likely to give it a further boost, especially at the local level.

3.3.3 France

In terms of the debate over public or private ownership of productive assets, France has undergone remarkable changes since 1980. For example, in 1982 the controversial Nationalization Act 82–155 took 500 companies, 18 listed banks, 21 unlisted banks and 2 financial companies into state control (see Dupont-Fauville 1983). Four years later the new conservative government set about reversing the process, even creating the post of 'minister for finance, the economy and privatization'. It pledged that within five years it would denationalize banks, insurance companies, media companies and the five major industrial groups, including Saint Gobain and Matra. However, unlike the UK, privatization was aimed not at public service providers, but rather at that element of the state sector involved in areas normally open to competition in other countries.

In common with Britain, the arguments put forward in favour of privatization were those relating to efficiency and funding, although critics of the programme pointed to political appointments in the new enterprises. By 1988 much of the programme had been enacted and it was then halted, leaving an ideological vacuum of neither privatization nor nationalization. However, since then the public sector has been given more freedom, and Thomson (1991) cites Renault's transformation into a state-controlled limited company to allow it to link with Volvo.

3.3.4 Italy and Spain

There would appear to be substantial opportunity for privatization in Italy, given the long tradition of state involvement. However, the industrial policy applied in the 1980s aimed to revitalize the loss-making state holding companies ENI

(Ente Nazionale Indrocarburi) and INI (Instituto per la Ricostruzione Industriale). Privatization has been restricted mainly to smaller companies, although state holdings in Alitalia (airline), Sirti (telecommunications), Banca Commerciale Italia (banking) and Alfa Romeo (cars) have been affected. Where applied, the policy has focused on efficiency gains and lowering the burden of public-sector debt. However, political constraints, notably disagreements among the various coalition governments, have hampered the process and the state enterprise sector still accounts for over 30 per cent of GDP.

Spanish industrial policy for much of the 1980s aimed at developing the industrial base rather than changing its ownership. In parallel with Italy, a restructuring of the state holding company INI (Instituto Nacional de Industria) was invoked. A 'Restructuring and Re-industrialization' Law of 1984 targeted the mature industrial sectors in order to bring their competitive capacities into line with other EC nations. A privatization policy has been encouraged, a notable feature of which was the sale of the government's majority stake in the car manufacturer, SEAT, to Volkswagen in 1986.

CONCLUSIONS

Throughout the EC, public-sector funding plays an important role in shaping overall economic policy. The distinctive philosophy of UK Conservative governments since 1979 has viewed public-sector expenditure unfavourably and sought to curb excesses while reducing the financing burden on the taxpayer. The MTFS, with its targets for the PSBR, provided a novel alternative to earlier fiscal 'stop–go' policies, while substantive changes were introduced to the component elements of public-sector financing, most notably at the local authority and public corporation level. The UK approach has often been mirrored elsewhere in Europe, especially in the context of privatization.

A major rationale for the philosophy was the perceived link between excessive public expenditure and inflation. However, evidence suggests that this is not clear-cut, and this has led to suggestions that fiscal convergence and implied EC rules on national budgets may not be necessary for monetary stability. Yet as we have seen, budgetary discipline may be in the interest of members, since debt accumulation can curtail the room for manoeuvre when high interest and capital payments 'crowd out' investment and restrict the quality of public service provision. The private sector is affected in so far as public procurement is reduced and high nominal interest rates are experienced. Moreover, a deteriorating debt position may adversely impact upon the external balance, at least in the short term. Thus, it would seem that the credibility of EMU would at least be strengthened by some degree of fiscal harmonization.

Within the framework of EMU, the first stage calls for coordinated action and ECOFIN surveillance of fiscal policies, especially as the monetary framework is similar to that of the EMS and requires special emphasis on fiscal policy.

Coordination will be necessary to cope with external shocks imposed upon EMU. Van den Bempt (1991) cites the financial consequences of German unity, where the high financing needs of the new Germany and the desire to avoid fuelling inflation lead to upward pressure on EC interest rates at a time of reduced economic activity. Thus, correction of the German fiscal deficit is of benefit to the whole Community. Indeed, such a scenario can be related to the European currency crisis described in Chapter 2. By 1992 fiscal transfers to eastern *Länder* had not been matched by a rise in output, hence prices had risen and inflation approached 5 per cent in March. This is a relatively acceptable level for most European nations, but not for Germany and the Bundesbank, with its medium-term inflationary goal of 2 per cent. Hence a high interest rate policy was followed, with rates reaching a peak in July when the Lombard rate rose to 9.75 per cent as monetary growth averaged 8.6 per cent. Other EC nations were then forced to keep their interest rates high, to persuade investors to hold their currencies rather than switch into Deutschmarks.

In the institutional Stage 2 the ESCB will begin to define a Community monetary policy, so there will be less scope for countervailing fiscal fine-tuning; moreover, the ESCB will influence the size of public deficits and thus strengthen budgetary discipline. By Stage 3 the irreversible fixing of exchange rates means there will be no recourse to the external value of a currency to offset domestic problems. The advent of a Community monetary policy, with no monetary financing of budget deficits, with controls over foreign borrowing and the discipline of market forces, will by then permit much less reliance upon fiscal policy coordination. Rational budgetary discipline would therefore seem to be a necessary condition for transition to Stage 2 of EMU; hence the fiscal guidelines in the convergence criteria, and the need for planned budgetary deficits to be advised to ECOFIN in advance.

FURTHER READING

A general coverage of the monetarist experiment is given in Smith (1987) with the economic and financial aspects also covered in Partington (1989) and Begg *et al.* (1991). Flow-of-funds data is available in the CEO 'Blue Book', *UK National Accounts* and *Financial Statistics*, and in *Bank of England Quarterly Bulletins* (February 1990 and 1991). Heald (1987) and Brown and Jackson (1990) provide thorough appraisals of various public expenditure issues, while Parker (1991) gives an analysis of privatization. In the context of other EC nations, see Grilli *et al.* (1991); Boltho (1990); Deutsche Bundesbank (1991c) and Thomson (1991).

FOUR

THE EUROPEAN COMMUNITY BUDGET

The Community budget is central to any discussion of European finance, let alone the public sector. From an administrative perspective, a central budgetary mechanism is necessary to cater for the costs of operating Community institutions (Parliament, Commission, etc.), for allocating expenditures to common policies, and for receiving and distributing revenues arising from the workings of the customs union. However, the budget persists as a major source of conflict within the Community; long-standing disputes have existed over the gains from economic integration, specifically the high costs of agricultural policy and the perceived inequality in budget contributions. The budget is also a focus for the 'federalist' versus 'nationalist' debate common to many Community activities. While the budget approximates to fiscal federalism, this has not prevented considerable rancour among the Council of Ministers, the European Parliament and national governments.

The EC budget differs in various respects from those of national budgets. Firstly, the Treaty of Rome stipulated that in principle the budget should balance current revenue and expenditure, with borrowing occurring only in exceptional circumstances for essentially capital items. Consequently, in a fiscal policy sense the budget to date has had no role as a macroeconomic management 'fine-tuning' tool. In any event, the 1988 reforms placed an upper limit of 1.2 per cent of GNP on 'own-resource' funding. Although this figure may be raised to 1.37 per cent of GNP under the 1992 Delors II 'financial perspective' package and is a large absolute figure, it is too small for macroeconomic stabilization purposes. Thus, the relatively modest level of funding reflects its function: to operate Community common policies.

A second difference is that expenditure dominates the budget to the extent that traditionally, once spending decisions are made, the required revenue contributions are assessed. Moreover, Community expenditure has significant economic impacts in certain areas, notably agricultural activity; yet spending allocations between policies are made largely independently of each other. In addition, the budget is constructed on a dual basis of committed expenditure and actual payments for the year in question. Thus, commitments made earlier may restrict actual payments in the year they are realized. An added complication is that a common accounting unit is required while various national currencies exist. Since 1980 the ECU has been used, but this necessitates exchange rate adjustments to the transactions involved. For these reasons, especially the separation of responsibility for revenue and expenditure, there have often been serious rifts among member governments over the spending allocations.

Finally, the budgetary authorization procedure allocates responsibility between the European Parliament and the Council of Ministers, which has made the budget a highly political source of tension as Parliament has sought more power. For many years its powers were limited since any modifications suggested by it could be rejected by a qualified majority of the Council of Ministers. In 1975, however, Parliament was given more power as expenditure was divided into 'compulsory' and 'non-compulsory' elements. The former relates to obligations under the Treaty of Rome, mainly agricultural expenditure and overseas aid; the latter include the structural funds. Parliament was given power to amend the latter 'non-compulsory' items; moreover, in 1977 final approval of the budget was transferred from the president of the Council of Ministers to the president of the Parliament, giving the latter the right to reject the budget at its second reading. The current procedure is set out in Table 4.1.

Since the early 1980s, as Parliament has extended its influence over the budget, it has sought to increase both the size of the cake and the share going to non-compulsory spending. In contrast, member states via the Council have wished to reduce their contributions and to curb what they see as Parliament's excesses. Consequently there have been disputes, notably as early as the 1980 budget when Parliament increased overall funding and reduced the Common Agricultural Policy (CAP) allocation, then rejected the budget when the Council failed to act on these points. Increased support for regional funds finally led to the late adoption of the budget in July 1980.

4.1 COMMUNITY EXPENDITURE

The growth of non-compulsory expenditure reflects the extent of Parliamentary influence and also the attempted diversification away from agriculture. However, Table 4.2 shows that agricultural expenditure still dominates, accounting for almost 60 per cent of direct spending—indeed, more, given that a large proportion of regional assistance is directed to rural areas. By the 1980s it was evident

Table 4.1 EC budget formulation

Appropriations for commitments (Operations)	Selected figures from 1990 budget expenditures to show changes as budget progresses (ECU millions)					
	Preliminary draft budget[a] (e.g. Jan.)	Council first reading[b] (e.g. July)	Parliament first reading[c] (e.g. Sept.)	Council second reading[d] (e.g. Nov.)	Parliament second reading[e]—adoption (e.g. Dec.)	Difference between draft and final budget
Agricultural market guarantee	26 788	26 452	26 733	26 452	26 452	−336
Guidance (agricultural structures)	2 056	2 077	2 095	2 082	2 095	+39
Regional developments/transport	5 970	5 940	6 028	5 960	5 978	+8

Source: EC (1990).

[a] Economic forecasts used to prepare expenditure estimates; Budget Committee considers draft.

[b] Council of Ministers discuss budget in July and revise/approve proposals to go to Parliament.

[c] Parliament must see budget by start of October. Debate leads to adoption (rare), proposed modifications to company expenditure (e.g. CAP) or proposed changes to non-compulsory element (e.g. structural funds).

[d] Council may approve/reject by qualified majority modifications to compulsory expenditure made by Parliament. For non-compulsory expenditure Council may alter the amendments adopted by Parliament.

[e] Budget now reconsidered by Parliament with respect to non-compulsory expenditure only. Parliament may amend (increase) non-compulsory expenditure, subject to a 'maximum rate of increase' in related inflation and growth rates.

Table 4.2 The general budget of the European Community (ECU millions)

	1992ᵃ	1991	1990	1989	1988	1987	1986	1985	1984	1983	1982
Expenditure											
EAGGF guarantee	36 022	32 419	25 069	26 741	27 500	22 961	22 112	19 955	18 333	15 811	13 671
Agricultural structures	600	583	259	1 522	1 222	943	802	688	675	653	774
Fisheries	425	346	296	389	281	197	190	112	112	84	88
Regional policy	16 546	13 283	9 835	4 331	3 201	2 738	2 578	1 698	1 489	2 383	2 948
Social policy	519	377	272	3 269	2 845	2 737	2 654	1 626	1 429	1 495	1 022
Research and energy	2 165	1 735	1 448	1 461	1 154	958	759	707	719	1 387	436
Developing countries	2 274	2 639	1 242	1 032	871	1 109	1 172	1 044	897	992	817
Administration	1 873	1 719	1 510	2 153	1 967	1 740	1 603	1 333	1 237	1 162	1 103
Miscellaneous	1 349	2 014	2 761	3 942	4 779	2 805	3 304	1 270	2 357	1 094	1 125
Total expenditure	61 773	55 115	42 692	44 840	43 820	36 188	35 174	28 433	27 248	25 061	21 984
Revenue											
Customs duties	12 889	13 278	11 428	11 459	10 345	8 937	8 173	8 310	7 961	6 989	6 815
Agricultural levies	1 353	1 262	1 173	1 283	1 505	1 626	1 176	1 122	1 260	1 347	1 522
Sugar levies	1 236	1 288	911	1 382	1 391	1 472	1 112	1 057	1 176	948	706
VAT	34 232	30 256	27 440	27 099	24 312	23 104	22 600	15 331	14 260	13 512	11 924
GNP-based resource	14 281	8 408	4 695	4 514	4 446						
Financial contributions (accession)	—	—	—	—	211	211	210	261	233	218	197
Miscellaneous (net)	-1 163	1 593	822	163	-367	433	396	2 004	1 172	1 752	969
Total revenue	62 828	56 085	46 469	45 900	41 843	35 783	22 667	28 085	26 052	24 766	21 427
Surplus/deficit	1 055	970	3 777	1 060	-1 977	-405	-1 507	-348	-1 196	-295	-557

ᵃ Provisional.
Source: EC: The Community Budget, 'The Facts in Figures', 3rd edn., (1990) for 1982–1989; Official Journal of the EC, 3.2.92 for 1990–1992.

that continued expansion of agricultural expenditure would severely restrict other policies being enacted.

4.1.1 Agricultural expenditure

Agriculture has long been perceived as a special case for government intervention in various countries, but also a source of tension, especially between the EC and the USA. EC enlargement and rapidly growing agricultural output, together with the impact of a previously strong dollar on US farmers' competitive position, have fuelled disputes over the high degree of protectionism afforded EC agriculture and its massive surpluses dumped at subsidized prices on world markets. Since 1947 there have been several rounds of negotiations on international trade liberalization under the guise of GATT, but agriculture has tended to be excluded; hence while tariff barriers have come down on many traded goods, agricultural protectionism has intensified, especially in the OECD nations. The result is significant trade distortion, with adverse consequences for food exporters in developing nations who have been displaced from world markets such as those for dairy products, vegetable oils and temperate cereals. The demand for change from the USA and the 'Cairns Group' of agricultural producers (Argentina, Australia, Brazil, Canada, Chile, Colombia, Fiji, Hungary, Indonesia, Malaysia, Philippines, New Zealand, Thailand and Uruguay) is such that agricultural trade dominated the recent Uruguay Round of GATT talks and within the EC gave an impetus to a review of existing agricultural policy.

Agricultural protectionism in the EC has radically altered the industry. Established to replace national policies and provide industry-wide support rather than assistance to individual units, the CAP was justified by the fact that in 1960 15.2 million people, or over 20 per cent of the workforce, were employed in the Community of Six on 6.4 million farms, and provided 10 per cent of Community GDP. The specific economic problems of agriculture are reflected in the two main elements of the CAP: short-run price support (guarantees) and long-run structural change (guidance). The former is required because agricultural demand tends to be price-inelastic, supply is volatile owing to climatic factors, disease and pestilence, and there is a long lead-time between decision-taking (planting, breeding of animals) and output realization (harvesting and marketing).

Economic theory illustrates this in the context of the 'cobweb' theorem (Fig. 4.1), which depicts the supply lag, often over a year, which leads to higher prices in the short term and an over-exaggerated response from future producers. From an equilibrium position P_0Q_0, a supply shortage of, say, wheat of Q_1, brought about by, say, inclement weather, brings forth a price P_1. Since supply cannot be increased in the short term, prices will remain high and will encourage farmers to plant for a supply Q_2 which matches this high price. However, when this output comes to market it will now exceed the relatively inelastic demand $(SQ_2 > DQ_2)$, and so prices will fall to P_2. At this price farmers will lower their

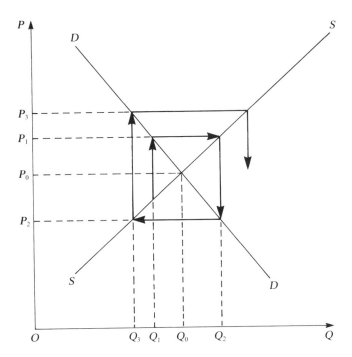

Figure 4.1 The cobweb theorem and EC agriculture

expected output the following year to Q_3, which leads to a price rise of P_3. This volatility means that equilibrium is never reached and markets swing between surplus and shortage.

In the long run there is the problem of a secular decline in agricultural prices and incomes, and yet overproduction. Figure 4.2 illustrates that demand for agricultural produce has risen, but by a relatively marginal amount (DD–$D'D'$), as a result of population growth and to a limited extent better incomes. However, although individual products may vary in fashion, the income elasticity of demand for foodstuffs in general is low: people do not eat more because they are wealthier. Thus, the industry cannot expand its income by raising output in line with economic trends, even though, as the supply curves (SS and $S'S'$) indicate, in the long run there has been a significant shift in output.

Agricultural productivity has grown dramatically this century with the application of technology, fertilizers, pesticides, drainage, crop development, etc., and the resulting abundance of food has furthered the downward price trend. Consequently, many farm incomes have fallen, encouraging rural unemployment or underemployment and long-term migration from the land. As Nevin (1990) observes, in the late 1950s the farming community was large and poor, a combination to be neglected by elected politicians only at their peril. The

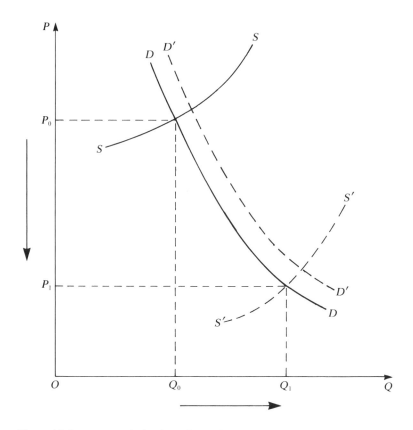

Figure 4.2 Long-term agricultural supply and demand

industry was thus in need of both short-term price support and long-term restructuring.

The establishment of the European Community in 1957 took place against wide disparities in agriculture among member states. The farming population represented 33 per cent of the workforce in Italy, 25 per cent in France and 10 per cent in Belgium. Holdings of under 5 hectares encompassed 85 per cent of farms in Italy, 55 per cent in Germany and 35 per cent in France. Agriculture accounted for 36 per cent of goods produced in Italy, 30 per cent in France and 15 per cent in Germany (EC 1989). Thus, creating a common market in farming was more difficult than for other sectors, especially given the aforementioned volatility in prices which mitigated against simple tariffs and encouraged complex national support schemes. Yet a common market would necessitate a Community-wide support mechanism to allow nations with large farming sectors to reap the benefits of trade in the same way as the more industrial countries. As Ardagh (1990) observes, France was starting with the lowest wholesale prices and largest production of the member states, hence would benefit most from any realignment of prices and dismantling of trade barriers. Moreover, the French saw their potential gains in agricultural trade as a counterweight to the risks from German industrial strength, and had agreed to the initial EEC Treaty on this basis. However, neither French industry nor German agriculture could be seriously disadvantaged by policies if the Treaty was to endure. Thus, as Pinder (1991) observes, the CAP may be seen as the product of national interest secured by bargaining power.

The objectives of the CAP, as set out in Art. 39 of the Treaty of Rome, are to raise agricultural productivity, to ensure a fair standard of living for the farming community, to stabilize markets, and to ensure that supplies are available to consumers at reasonable prices. In 1958 the Stresa Conference set out the principles of the CAP: a Single Market in agricultural products throughout the Community, implying common prices; Community preference with protection for the internal market against cheap imports and world price fluctuations; and financial solidarity, so that the costs of the policy should be shared by all concerned. To this end the European Agricultural Guidance and Guarantee Fund (EAGGF) was set up in 1962 to finance expenditure on the CAP.

Within the CAP the price support mechanism (guarantees) dominates, traditionally accounting for over 95 per cent of the EAGGF. In essence, a Community levy is charged on imports into the EC and is redistributed to farmers via price supports and export subsidies. This protectionist mechanism aims to encourage self-sufficiency, maintain farm incomes and promote integration by means of a unified market in a key area of the economy. The fixing of prices varies among products but is essentially a politically determined exercise by the Council of Ministers responding to their farmers' lobbying. Given the diversity of European agriculture, it is not possible to set prices that reflect differing levels of farm productivity and income, let alone equate supply and demand. Thus, the traditional method employed is to price at the highest level obtainable rather than the average. Hence, if wheat was cheapest in France and dearest in Germany, the latter price would prevail. This mechanism merely encourages overproduction and expensive stockpiling in the form of 'wine lakes', 'butter mountains' or the export of surpluses. The latter are often 'dumped' at a world price that is below the EC one and so exporters must be compensated by export restitution payments.

The principle of price-setting can be seen in Fig. 4.3 using wheat as an example. Three prices are used as the main instruments for agricultural support. The EC *target price* P_1 limits the upper end of the range within which producer prices may fluctuate, and is the price to which it is hoped the market price will move. In the case of wheat, it is fixed by the Council of Ministers based on wholesale grain prices at Duisburg, Germany, the place where demand exceeds supply by the greatest amount and hence where prices are dearest.

The *threshold price* P_2 sets the lowest internal price for imports and is based on a variable import levy (P_2-P_w) added to the world price P_w by port

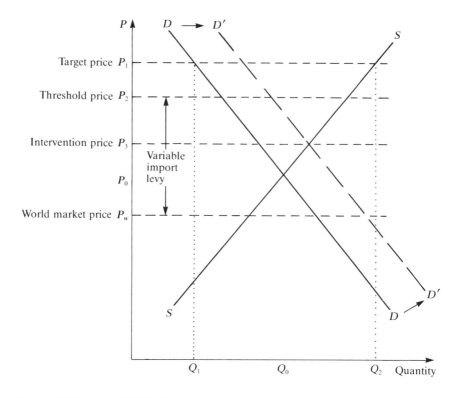

Figure 4.3 Principles of CAP price-setting

authorities. The levy goes up when world prices fall and vice versa. The difference between the target and threshold prices is the estimated transport and administration costs involved in delivering imported wheat from the main port at Rotterdam to Duisburg.

The *intervention or guarantee price* is the theoretical minimum price for wheat in the EC and is set below the threshold price to fully protect domestic producers from competing imports. Intervention occurs when wheat is withdrawn from the EC market via stockpiling or dumping overseas. As the wheat is purchased the demand curve shifts from DD to $D'D'$ and prices rise from P_0 to P_3, the intervention price, at which farmers are encouraged to produce more, notwithstanding the already excess supply!

The long-run structural reform (guidance) element of the EAGGF has been less significant. Early recognition was made that higher prices may enable the marginal farmer to survive, but pricing alone cannot rectify land deficiencies, poor training, lack of marketing, etc. Thus, migration of labour out of farming was initially encouraged by the 1968 Mansholt Plan, but recession in the 1970s and lack of alternative employment reduced its impact and incomes remained depressed. Farming expenditure also must be seen in the context of regional policy, but until recently there has never been a coherent policy for long-term structural reform of agriculture.

Within the Treaty of Rome there was an assumption that the CAP would be self-financing. Intervention would require funds when market prices were below target prices, but these would be recovered as surpluses were disposed of when market prices rose above target. Structural funds would derive from import levy proceeds. Not surprisingly, these assumptions were not realized. Farm prices initially varied too much among member states and were significantly above world prices. Members could not sanction substantial cuts in prices received by their farmers so that the target prices equated with the highest prices prevailing, often two or three times world levels. This situation has created inevitable excess supply, which has to be financed and disposed of. In the initial years expenditure rose, with the transfer of spending operations from national budgets to the EC budget and in the 1970s with the accession of the UK, Denmark and Ireland. Since 1975 spending has grown at approximately 7.5 per cent p.a. (in constant terms), three and a half times the rate of growth of the Community's GDP (EC 1989). Indeed, costs escalated in the 1980s with the greater expenditure on intervention, storage and disposal of stocks, and the 'southern enlargement'. By 1992 the total budget was ECU61.8 billion, of which EAGGF committed expenditure was ECU36.6 billion (59 per cent), including ECU36.0 billion (98 per cent) on the guarantee section. This compares with a total budget of ECU18.4 billion in 1981 (ECU12.1 billion on the EAGGF) (Table 4.2).

Financial problems with the CAP have been compounded by exchange rates. To minimize these distortions to prices, a system of monetary compensation amounts (MCAs) was introduced in 1969, although modified later. Gupta *et al.* (1989) suggest that MCAs are equivalent to a system of import levies and export subsidies for countries with appreciating currencies (positive MCAs) and export levies and import subsidies for those with depreciating currencies (negative MCAs). In reality, the MCA system made a mockery of the idea of a common price throughout the EC. In 1978 UK farm prices were 30 per cent below the Community average and German farm prices 10 per cent above, leading to huge variations in prices paid. The budgetary implications were severe, with MCAs taking up to 10 per cent of the EAGGF budget. Eventually they were to be phased out as the EMS developed, but they illustrate the underlying need for economic stability if the CAP is to operate effectively.

The CAP may be judged against its original objectives. In terms of *productivity*, any evaluation must take into account the tremendous advances in world agricultural technology since the 1950s as cited in the context of Fig. 4.2. Nevertheless, labour productivity in EC agriculture has increased more than that of total labour productivity, encouraged by mechanization, restructuring in favour of larger farms, the application of chemicals and the declining workforce. The numbers employed in agriculture have halved since 1960, notwithstanding the doubling of the Community nations to include the 'southern extension' with their large agricultural workforces. Thus, the CAP appears to have been successful in raising agricultural productivity, although this has compounded the problems of dealing with surpluses.

A second objective was to *raise agricultural incomes*, but, in spite of the above productivity gains and price supports, producer prices have fallen relative to general EC prices, and farm incomes as a whole have worsened. Since farm incomes depend on output, the CAP encourages large-scale production. Hitiris (1991) suggests that 75 per cent of CAP support goes to the richest 25 per cent of farmers, a fact inconsistent with the objective of raising living standards throughout the EC farming community. Proponents of the CAP argue that it has generated higher incomes than would have occurred if farmers had received no protection, but this denies alternative forms of support.

In terms of *market stability* within the EC, the CAP appears successful. Although agricultural prices have risen continuously, the increases have been moderate relative to the Community's inflation rate. Nevertheless, the CAP has arguably disrupted markets outside of the EC. Excess production has diverted trade by restricting cheap imports and replacing them with high-cost domestic output. Moreover, EC subsidies for the export of surplus production have led to the dumping of produce on the world market, further depressing prices.

The CAP would seem to have achieved its fourth objective, namely to *guarantee supply availability*. Self-sufficiency has been attained in the principal farm products; indeed, massive overproduction is the norm. However, given the climatic diversity of member nations, imbalances persist. Moreover, despite publicized 'butter mountains' and 'wine lakes', the Community remains a major world food importer of products such as tea, coffee, fruit, rice and animal feedstock, notably soya products.

The final objective was to *ensure reasonable prices for the consumer*; yet EC agricultural prices have normally far exceeded those prevailing on world markets, and consumer prices have been significantly above producer ones. These trends imply welfare losses, with the high prices outweighing the benefits of price stability and supply availability. Since the CAP subsidizes agriculture via the price mechanism rather than by direct public expenditure, the burden of support falls on the consumer. Given that people on low incomes spend a greater proportion of their finances on food than those better off, the CAP may be seen as regressive in transferring wealth from the poorest consumers to the richest farmers and landowners.

Demekas *et al.* (1988) have surveyed empirical studies of the total impact of the CAP. Partial-equilibrium approaches estimate welfare losses ranging from 0.27 to 1.3 per cent of EC GDP with the higher levels associated with more sophisticated models (see Tyers and Anderson 1986—1.3 per cent; Tyers 1985—1.1 per cent). General equilibrium approaches add non-agricultural sectors, labour and capital markets and macroeconomic considerations. Burniaux and Waelbroeck (1985) used a model which implied that abandoning the CAP would have generated a real income gain of 2.7 per cent of EC GDP in 1995, based on implied falling international commodity prices.

Evidence also suggests a significant redistributive effect on income within the EC nations. Buckwell *et al.* (1982), Spencer (1986) and Breckling *et al.* (1987) all imply that the UK, Germany and Italy are the main losers from the CAP with Ireland, Denmark and the Netherlands the main beneficiaries. Harvey and Thompson (1985) estimated that the British and Germans were each paying out ECU6 billion more than their farmers were gaining in 1984. In sum, British agriculture has benefited from the CAP to the extent that it is a small, relatively efficient sector with a high proportion of large, modern farms. However, British consumers have suffered because domestic demand exceeds supply and therefore output has had to be supplemented from expensive Community sources. This suggests a resource transfer greater than that implied in the budget alone (Barnes and Preston 1988).

The performance of the CAP is thus mixed. Huge production gains have secured food supplies, increased choice and stabilized prices and in many areas farming has been transformed from a backward, traditional occupation into a modern industry. However, the economic, social and political costs are high: expanding stockpiles, falling real incomes, disquiet on world markets and, above all, an escalating drain on the EC budget, which in turn has stunted the growth of key Community regional and industrial policies, encouraged political crises over the budget and discouraged integration. Not surprisingly, there have been calls for reform of the CAP both from within and outside the EC.

The process of reform has met stiff resistance. Among obstacles Lintner and Mazey (1991) cite: vested interests among the main beneficiary nations such as France and Ireland; the large and efficient agricultural units throughout the EC; farming lobbies; the bureaucratic decision-making process in the EC, especially the use made of the veto; and fear of change. Early attempts at reform focused on the 1968 Mansholt Plan, which advocated price restraint to eliminate surplus production together with substantive structural adjustment to enhance efficiency. Moyer and Josling (1990) argue that the plan was unique in its focus on developing the agricultural sector, as nearly all subsequent reforms concentrated on saving the CAP. However, political wrangling meant that the final version was inevitably 'watered-down'.

The momentum for reform gathered pace in the early 1980s in the face of financial strains on the budget, the pending 'southern enlargement' and the unacceptably high stockpiles of wheat, butter and milk. By 1984 budgetary funds were decimated and the CAP was faced with imminent financial collapse. The British would not agree to extra funding unless CAP spending was curbed. Agreement was made to move towards less generous support with an enhanced role for market forces and structural measures to reduce the need for support. Specific actions included: stricter use of quotas to lower production, notably milk quotas given that dairy products accounted for 25 per cent of EAGGF spending; a penal 'co-responsibility' levy on milk production beyond quota; the gradual elimination of MCAs; and the introduction of price cuts averaging 3.5 per cent in real terms (EC 1989).

However, the quota system was ineffective in that levels were set above self-sufficiency, thus encouraging surpluses to continue. By 1988 agricultural spending was 30 per cent up on 1984 levels, exacerbated by the membership of Greece, Spain and Portugal. It was evident that a fundamental stab at reform was needed to break the link between prices and politics. The CAP pricing mechanism encouraged overproduction, and while politicians advocated austerity in general, national interests meant they looked after their own farming lobbies.

In February 1988 a major reform package was agreed at the Brussels European Council meeting. The purpose was to provide a financial framework which would give a stable outlook for agricultural institutions and member states. This involved three elements: the containment of expenditure under rules imposing budgetary discipline; the provision of adequate, stable and guaranteed resources; and a closer link between contributions and ability to pay. Specifically, CAP expenditure was to be limited to 74 per cent of the Community's GNP in the previous year. Thus, at last the size of the budget would determine CAP spending and not vice versa. Moreover, control was to be effected by the use of 'stabilizers', providing price cuts when agreed quotas were reached and applying to the vast majority of agricultural products. The basic intention here was to provide a means by which the budget is not committed to ensuring an unlimited financial guarantee for agricultural production (M. Shackleton 1990). In addition, structural measures were at last applied, notably encouraging farmers to set land aside, and receive income support related to need.

While this package represented a serious effort to control agricultural expenditure, long-standing weaknesses have remained. Among these are the reality that consumers still bear the burden of prices, stockpiles have continued, and structural polices that have focused on farm income support alleviate but do not cure the industry's ills. Indeed, given that there is a relatively inelastic supply of agricultural land, theory would suggest that income support might be seen to manifest itself through ultimately higher returns to factor owners, both of labour and of land, the latter including absentee landlords. Arguably, an increase in farm income might also retain more people in the industry, even attract some to it. This might conflict with other measures such as fund allocation to encourage out-migration and retraining which are possibly more appropriate structural policies. Moreover, at the macro level problems have remained from the fact that agricultural spending decisions are made by ministers who are not responsible for raising the revenue, and at times the expense of the CAP has undermined the financial stability of the Community.

However, perhaps the most significant issue has been the failure of the policy to open EC markets to international competition. Conflicts between the EC, the USA and the 'Cairns Group' over liberalizing agricultural trade threatened to undermine the 1990–93 Uruguay Round of GATT trade talks and precipitate retaliatory protectionism in a range of traded products worldwide. A danger exists that world trade might become dominated by regional power blocs such as the enlarged EC (or EEA: see Chapter 10) and the newly formed North American Free Trade Area (NAFTA), with GATT powerless. With this scenario the indirect macroeconomic burden would far surpass the costs of protectionism. The USA, supported by major agricultural exporters, sought substantive cuts in EC farm export subsidies with commitments to reduce internal price supports and tariffs. The EC originally offered to cut internal assistance by 10–30 per cent over a 10-year period based on 1986 levels, which would reduce the differential between EC and world prices but leave a margin for Community preference. However, the absence of EC agreements on lowering export subsidies and allowing greater market access led to the breakdown of talks in December 1990 (see Junz and Boonekamp 1991; Corbet 1991).

In an effort to salvage the negotiations, Arthur Dunkel, director-general of GATT, produced a compromise package for the period 1993–99 calling for: a 36 per cent cut in agricultural export subsidies; a 24 per cent fall in their volume; a 20 per cent cut in income support grants; and the conversion of import quotas and variable levies into tariffs ('tariffication') and their lowering by 36 per cent. Although the EC resisted some of these measures, notably the cut in income support grants, the GATT talks have given added importance to the implementation of the EC's own 1991 proposals for reform of farm policy (the 'MacSharry Plan').

After much debate and amendment, this plan was finally approved by the Agriculture Council in May 1992. It includes the following main market-based proposals:

- Price reductions, including a 29 per cent cut in cereals and 15 per cent in beef and poultry over three years starting in 1993/94
- Compensation to be granted to farmers but not directly linked to the quantities produced, and budgetary resources to be geared to supporting farmers' incomes rather than promoting the stockpile of excess production
- Measures to limit production to market needs, including limits on the number of animals per hectare and quotas, and the setting aside of 15 per cent of arable land

Supplementary measures include the establishment of early-retirement schemes for farm personnel, the promotion of land for forestry, ecological or recreational purposes, and aid for environmental and resource protection (see EC 1992b). The package aims to provide a long-term framework of policy and market stability; to separate pricing policy from incomes policy; and, via price cuts, to lessen the incentive to overproduce. The abolition of unrealistic subsidies is seen as helping to stabilize international markets and going some way to meet the objections of the USA which blocked the conclusion of the GATT talks. For consumers there should be cheaper food, although gains are likely to be redistributed via taxation to finance compensation payments to farmers.

The proposals have been criticized as bureaucratic, with a potential for fraud as farmers seek compensation for setting aside land and reducing stocks. Moreover, the earlier comments on income supports apply as they slow down capacity adjustment in the industry. Environmentalists fear the set-aside land will be rotated and thus will delay the development of wildlife habitats (EIS 1992). The 29 per cent cut in prices for cereal production is paid irrespective of farm size and discriminates against the profitable and efficient larger-scale farm units.

Thus, the CAP has come under more and more pressure for reform; yet its track record suggests that only small parts of such plans reach fruition, especially as national governments can partially offset cuts in EC-level subsidies. Nevertheless, there is now more impetus for changes that combine price reductions and volume cuts with measures to promote employment outside the sector. An old-style CAP which 30 years ago catered for over 20 per cent of the working population is no longer tenable when less than 7 per cent of the population are now so employed and the sector contributes only 3 per cent to Community GDP. The major shift away from high price supports towards greater emphasis on structural reform and trade liberalization appears long overdue.

4.1.2   Non-agricultural expenditure

The 1988 Brussels Agreement was significant not only for at last limiting the growth of agricultural expenditure, and creating a new income resource based on GNP (see Sec. 4.2), but also for introducing a 'financial perspective' of a medium-term strategy for expenditure planning and control covering the period 1988–92 (Delors I). The argument was that the Community would acquire enhanced resources only if members could see more effective control over their allocation. Further budgetary expansion was to be mainly for the structural funds, whose allocations were to double, based on a rise from ECU7.2 billion in 1987 to ECU14.5 billion in 1993 (all at 1988 prices) (see Table 4.4). Thus, with agricultural expenditure contained, the share of the total budget devoted to non-compulsory expenditure was expected to rise to over 30 per cent by 1993. In order to effect this massive increase in non-compulsory expenditure, an Inter-institutional Agreement had to be reached between Parliament and the Council of Ministers, such that Parliament would accept the funding for the structural funds and Council would not allocate monies to agricultural support in excess of those agreed in the 'financial perspective'.

The presumption was that the structural funds needed considerable enhancement. However, there had been concern over previous increases in the regional fund without clear purpose, and M. Shackleton (1990) cites the House of Commons Select Committee criticism that these were essentially political transfers. This stems from the nature of the European Regional Development Fund (ERDF), set up in 1975 as the main organ of regional policy.

The ERDF was founded to support national regional policies, allocating funds on a quota basis, rather than as a means of implementing a Community-wide regional policy. From 1975 to 1984 it operated in this mainly redistributive role in spite of disputes over what constituted a region eligible for assistance, and changes to the quota system to include a 'non-quota' element of funding for regions adversely affected by Community policies. By the early 1980s it was apparent that the ERDF was ineffective. It accounted for only 7–8 per cent of the budget and was spreading its resources too thinly. Over 90 per cent of the fund was being allocated on a national quota basis, mostly to infrastructure projects in specific countries, some of which were well able to afford their own regional aid, i.e. France, Germany and the Benelux nations. Very little was being spent on employment-generating integrated development.

Reforms were instigated in 1984 with a view to coordinating national regional policies within a Community framework. The ERDF was to participate in the development and 'structural adjustment' of regions whose development is backward or subject to industrial decline. Emphasis was placed on job creation as opposed to infrastructure projects, and the distinction between the quota and non-quota sections of the ERDF was replaced by flexible quotas or minimum and maximum ranges for each country (Table 4.3).

Thus, requests for support would be judged against Community-wide criteria and approximately 11–12 per cent of the Fund would be left for Community programmes involving more than one region or nation-state instigated at the initiative of the Commission. In addition, in 1985 several six-year Integrated Mediterranean Programmes (IMPs) were launched as specific regional projects to aid the mainly rural areas of Greece, Italy and southern France. Ironically, part of the rationale was to allow these regions to adjust to the entry of Spain and Portugal, countries that include some of the poorest areas of this nature (see Chapter 10).

The other major structural fund (apart from the guidance section of the EAGGF) is the European Social Fund (ESF), which mirrors the relatively narrow focus of social policy since the Treaty of Rome; namely, primary concern with employment. During the 1960s the ESF played a minor role within the Community, assisting national governments with retraining and improving labour mobility. It was reformed in 1972, with the priority tasks of reducing structural unemployment in declining regions and overcoming labour market imbalances. Funding was to be from the general budget and the annual average

Table 4.3 ERDF quotas, 1992

Country	Quota (%)	Country	Quota (%)
Italy	21.59–28.79	Ireland	3.81–4.61
Spain	17.95–23.93	Germany	2.55–3.40
UK	14.48–19.31	Netherlands	0.68–0.91
Portugal	10.65–14.20	Belgium	0.61–0.82
Greece	8.35–10.64	Denmark	0.34–0.46
France	7.47–9.96	Luxembourg	0.04–0.06

allocation to be over ECU80 million. However, growing Community unemployment towards the start of the 1980s led to a second major reform in 1984: a further 40 per cent increase in resources, with as specific target problems the young unemployed and the poorest regions. Since then 75 per cent of its funds have been directed to the training or employment of people aged 25 or under and there has been much greater regional concentration of resources, notably in low-income 'absolute priority' regions: Italy, Ireland, Greece, Portugal and Spain.

In spite of these periodic resource increases, for much of its history the ESF, in common with the ERDF, has been limited in its impact, tending to augment projects in specific countries rather than operate an integrated Community policy. M. Shackleton (1990) cites 3841 Community investment projects in 1988 totalling ECU3.8 billion. The 1988 Brussels Agreement to double the structural fund resources, and the requirements of the Single European Act calling for greater 'economic and social cohesion', gave an impetus to move away from such detailed projects towards wider integrated programmes. The Delors Report (EC Commission 1989) in particular was concerned that economic, and ultimately political, union could be jeopardized and talked of 'narrowing regional and structural disparities and promoting balanced development throughout the Community'.

Consequently, since 1989 the IMPs have become a fourth structural fund, and, together with the ESF, ERDF and the guidance sector of the EAGGF, provide coordinated roles in regional and social development. Five specific objectives were set under Delors I for structural support: (1) to promote development in backward regions (Greece, Ireland, Portugal, the Mezzogiorno and parts of Spain); (2) to provide support for areas suffering industrial decline, notably the UK, Spain and France, where the rate of unemployment was consistently above the Community average; (3) and (4) to combat long-term unemployment and youth unemployment; and (5) to monitor the impact of the reform of the CAP in terms of (a) adjustment of farming areas and (b) rural development.

A second package of structural and financial measures (Delors II) was adopted in March 1992 covering the 'financial perspective' 1993–97, and in the wake of the Maastricht Treaty (EC 1992a). These proposals build upon the 1988 package, which in essence laid the financial foundation for the completion of the internal market. The new framework has two roles: to support Stage 2 of EMU, and to translate into financial terms the outcome of European union in respect of the new Community powers. Expenditure is to be concentrated on three areas: economic and social cohesion; maximizing the effectiveness of the internal market; and external action relating to the Community's overseas obligations.

Table 4.4 indicates the proposed expenditure commitments and an overall limit of ECU 87.5 billion by 1997. Spending on the CAP as a whole is scheduled to rise overall in line with the guideline of 74 per cent of GNP growth. The major focus for expenditure growth is therefore the structural funds. Objective

**Table 4.4 Financial perspective of the EC budget, 1992–1997
(ECU millions, 1992 prices)**

	1992	1993	1994	1995	1996	1997
Commitment appropriations						
Common agricultural policy	35 348	35 340	37 480	38 150	38 840	39 600
Structural operations	18 559	21 270	22 740	24 930	27 120	29 300
Structural Funds	17 965	19 770	20 990	22 930	24 870	26 800
Cohesion Funds (IMPs/Pedip)	594	1 500	1 750	2 000	2 250	2 500
Internal policies	3 991	4 500	5 035	5 610	6 230	6 900
External action	3 645	4 070	4 540	5 060	5 650	6 300
Administrative expenditure of the institutions	4 049	3 310	3 465	3 720	3 850	4 000
Staff and administration						
Commission	1 696	1 760	1 825	1 890	1 960	2 035
Other institutions	895	930	960	1 000	1 040	1 070
Pensions (all institutions)	249	290	325	380	400	445
Buildings	287	330	355	450	450	450
(Repayments)	922					
Reserves	1 000	1 500	1 600	1 200	1 300	1 400
Monetary reserve	1 000	1 000	1 000	500	500	500
Exceptional expenditure		500	600	700	800	900
Total	66 592	69 880	74 860	78 670	82 990	87 500
Payment appropriations required	63 241	67 005	71 650	75 110	79 060	83 200
Payment appropriations (% GNP)	1.15	1.19	1.24	1.27	1.30	1.34
Margin for revision (% GNP)	0.05	0.03	0.03	0.03	0.03	0.03
Own resources (% GNP)	1.20	1.22	1.27	1.30	1.33	1.37

Source: EC *Bulletin*, no. 3, 1992.

(1) regions have been redesignated to include the five new German *Länder*, even though the bulk of the reconstruction there will be borne by Germany itself, and in total will receive 67 per cent of available resources. Greece, Ireland, Spain and Portugal also qualify for assistance under the new *Cohesion Fund*, such that by 1997 they will receive double the amount gained in 1992 under objective (1). The process of converting regions affected by industrial decline is still incomplete and here the focus is on job creation schemes. Objectives (3) and (4) are to be redefined with more emphasis on training and occupational redeployment with regard to industrial and technological change. Co-financed operations under objective (5a) represent a major element of agricultural adaptation and modernization, while objective (5b) is likely to assume more significance with the exodus from the land. A new objective (6) has been established to cater specifically for structural measures associated with the fishing industry.

The *internal* expenditure policy in Table 4.4. is geared mainly to improving industry competitiveness and features technological emphasis, a reflection of the perceived low level of EC R&D expenditure (2.1 per cent of GDP in 1991) compared with Japan (3.5 per cent) and the USA (2.8 per cent). Other internal expenditure relates to trans-European developments in transport, telecommunications and energy, and environmental policies to enhance integration. The *external* action mainly covers existing aid and financial assistance to third nations, but excludes exceptional items, such as humanitarian aid, for which reserves are set aside.

The impact of these measures remains to be seen, but reservations exist as to the amount of Community expenditure necessary for regional convergence and social cohesion. Padua-Schioppa *et al.* (1987) estimated that capital investment of ECU55–76 billion was necessary to raise GDP by 1 per cent in the less favoured regions. Mair (1991) argues that it is thus most important that the Community's contribution is additional to that of the member states and is not swallowed up by their national expenditure. There thus appears to be a much greater emphasis and sense of urgency about EC regional policy, especially in view of the unification of Germany. Indeed, further widening of the Community to encompass EFTA or former Eastern bloc nations will exacerbate regional and social policy problems and expenditure, an issue to which we will return in Chapter 10.

4.2   COMMUNITY REVENUE

As we have seen, Community expenditure decisions have tended to precede the means of financing. Consequently, given that budget deficits are not allowed in principle, as expenditure on the CAP has grown, so newer sources of revenue have had to be found. From 1958 to 1970 funding came from member nations' contributions, mainly in line with ability to pay, although influenced by political bargaining and modified by non-EC trade. However, Jean Monnet was very influential in establishing the Treaty of Rome, and he foresaw that the Community would be hampered in its development if it merely depended upon contributions from members who might renege on their contributions. Hence, incorporated into the philosophy underlying the Treaty of Rome was the principle of *fiscal federalism*, namely that the Community should match its expenditure with its own sources of revenue.

Following the Treaty of Luxembourg in 1970, a system of 'own resources' was introduced the following year, based on, firstly, all customs duties on products emanating from outside the EC and subject to the Common External Tariff (CET), and, secondly, variable agricultural and sugar levies on products from outside the EC. It was argued that these 'traditional resources' could be collected at the point of entry to the Community and could be destined for any member country, and thus are justifiably a Community resource. However, by the 1970s CAP expenditure was outstripping these 'traditional resources' and so a third resource, a share of VAT receipts levied by members, became payable. This was phased in from 1974 and amounted to 1 per cent of the total value of sales, a complex calculation given the lack of VAT harmonization among members. It was envisaged that by 1978 the Community would be funded entirely by 'own resources', but growing expenditure and delays in the introduction of VAT meant that members continued making national contributions until 1980 (Table 4.2).

By 1983 the budget was running desperately short of funds and pressure was placed upon the variable element, the VAT contribution. After lengthy debate, agreement was reached at the 1984 Fontainebleau summit to raise the VAT base to 1.4 per cent from January 1986 in exchange for refunds from Britain (see Sec. 4.2.1) and undertakings to restrict CAP expenditure. In 1984 and 1985 funds were made available by intergovernmental agreements; thus, the new 1.4 per cent limit was fully taken up on introduction in 1986. There followed a further crisis in 1987 when the implied VAT rate required would have been 1.9 per cent had it not been for 'creative accounting' in deferring CAP expenditure, and emergency intergovernmental funding agreements.

At the 1988 Brussels Summit proposals to raise the VAT base to 1.6 per cent were rejected; indeed, 'capping' was introduced whereby the assessment base for VAT should not exceed 55 per cent of the gross GNP (market prices) in any country. Instead, a new fourth resource was agreed, an extra contribution based on the difference between the GNP of a country and its VAT assessment. The level was set to be sufficient to bridge the gap between Community expenditure and the yield of the other three sources. Revenue would be linked more to members' ability to pay and hence to Community economic performance. However, it was agreed that the total revenue raised should be such as to limit expenditure to 1.2 per cent GNP by 1992, reached via interim ceilings starting at 1.15 per cent in 1988. Thus, while the VAT limit was to be maintained at 1.4 per cent, this 'fourth resource' was seen as providing an element of security, and as a kind of income tax, a more equitable source of finance.

The initial experience with the new system has been favourable, eased by the aforementioned shifts in expenditure and the greater-than-anticipated growth of Community GNP. For example, in 1990 the 'own resources' were 0.98 per cent of GNP as compared with the 1988 envisaged ceiling for 1990 of 1.18 per cent, and reflect the buoyancy of VAT receipts. Thus, although the reform of 1988 has been reasonably successful and enhanced the fiscal federalist nature of the budget, redistribution issues still arise, both from the varying incidence of the Community policies and from member contributions.

The Delors II package envisages raising the 'own resources' ceiling from 1.2 to 1.37 per cent of Community GNP by 1997, and thus makes the 'fourth resource' the major component of funding. Of this, 0.03 per cent is seen as a contingency element for revision and external policy purposes. In contrast, the VAT appropriation rate is to be lowered from 1.4 to 1.0 per cent and the assessment base from 55 to 50 per cent of gross GNP in a member country. The proposed increase in the GNP-based resource has not been universally welcomed in view of the current economic recession in Western Europe. Most members wish to hold Community expenditure to 1.2 per cent of GNP until 1994 and extend the budget perspective until 1999. The EC argues that the shift of resource funding away from VAT is necessary because of its regressive nature and its being a source of financing distortions, given that the less prosperous nations devote a larger proportion of their GNP to consumption.

Moreover, difficulties have existed so far in the framework of the Single Market in devising suitable methods of collecting VAT, and also in harmonizing rates levied in individual nations. Technically, from 1993 there should be no difference between a domestic and intra-Community sale for VAT purposes. Under the Commission's proposals exporters would charge VAT on sales on both goods and services for the home and 'export' markets, and 'importers' would reclaim this. To allocate revenue between members and avoid distortion, a 'clearing house' has been proposed with members aggregating the VAT charged and accounting to the Commission. However, this 'origin' system potentially involves considerable paperwork for companies, a task made harder by the dilatory nature of some nations, such as Italy, Belgium and Portugal, in putting the changes on to their statute books. The VAT return forms are not harmonized, with different EC member countries asking for distinctive information. New Euro-VAT numbers are needed, but as late as September 1992 major member countries, such as France and Germany, had not issued them. In view of such problems the changeover from the existing 'destination' system (goods taxed where imported) to the 'origin' system (tax levied at factory gate) has been deferred with a five-year transitional period. Thus a VAT-registered business will pay VAT on delivery but individuals or businesses not VAT-registered will pay it in the exporting country. Small companies may be forced to hire tax consultants or accountants specifically to ensure compliance with the new tax laws, whereas large companies face problems with three-way trade. If the Belgian branch of a company orders goods from the UK for delivery in France, the buyer must choose where to register for VAT or risk double taxation. The major current distortion, however, arises from differing VAT rates, providing a potential for 'tax-based shopping' across neighbouring countries with large differentials. The Community's proposal for a minimum rate of VAT of 15 per cent has met considerable resistance in the UK, where a unique set of zero-rated items has existed, including children's clothes, books, transport, domestic gas and electricity. In the event, the Community's directive allowed for a concession for Britain on zero-rating, but British objections have gone further to the very loss of sovereignty over setting tax rates, even though the government has agreed that it will not lower the current basic rate of VAT of 17.5 per cent to below the EC minimum of 15 per cent.

4.2.1 Budgetary incidence, equity and the UK

Given the aforementioned problems of escalating expenditure and increasing demands on members for revenue, it is not surprising that as a redistributive mechanism the budget has been a source of dissatisfaction among member states. Long-standing disputes over its perceived regressive financing from a narrow range of taxes, and the vast sums spent on one economic sector—agriculture—have plagued the budget. It is, of course, inconsistent with Community ideals that contributions between nations should be equal given the diversity of wealth involved. However, it is equally apparent that often budgetary incidence has been unjust and encouraged national self-interest.

In part, the issue is exacerbated by the failure of the Community in the past to calculate accurately the national incidence of the budget. Among various studies, Ardy (1988) suggested that the main determinant is the incidence of the CAP, so naturally major beneficiaries from the CAP are the major net recipients from the budget. Consequently, he saw Denmark, Greece, Ireland, the Netherlands and to some extent France as net beneficiaries, with net costs imposed upon Belgium, Luxembourg, Germany, Italy and the UK, a pattern reflected in the economic wealth of these nations.

In theory, inequity also occurs on the contribution side. Revenues from customs duties and agricultural levies are a function of non-EC imports. However, a 'Rotterdam effect' may arise whereby major ports handle a share of EC imports destined for other member countries. Thus, import duties recorded at the port of entry may be paid for by consumers elsewhere. This complicates the calculation of contributions. Agricultural levies may fall harder on nations with small agricultural sectors who are net importers of food, unrelated to GDP. However, much of the concern over contributions has focused on the dynamic element, the VAT base, and here incidence relates to consumption patterns, so that poorer countries which spend a higher proportion of disposable income face a proportionally heavier burden, a situation compounded if the expenditure is on imports. Nevin (1988) analysed member nations' VAT contributions for 1980–84 against what would have been the case based on ability to pay (national incomes converted at purchasing power parity). His findings suggest a relatively small differential, yet the overall perception remains that the VAT system is unfair and regressive.

The major manifestation of the issue of budgetary incidence has been the 'British problem', which dominated UK–EC relations between 1975 and 1988. In essence, the UK has been a major contributor to the budget despite a poor growth record and low level of income. In terms of revenue, the UK imported large amounts from the Commonwealth and other non-EC nations, and thus was subject to heavy 'traditional own-resource' levies and import duties. Moreover, the UK's high marginal propensity to consume meant that relatively little expenditure went on VAT-exempt goods such as investment and exports compared with 'consumer' items subject to VAT. Thus, the UK's gross contribution (20 per cent) is higher than its share of Community GNP (16 per cent) (HM Treasury 1991). In terms of expenditure, the small efficient agricultural sector meant that less benefit would accrue to the UK from price supports than to the larger agricultural sectors in other EC nations.

These problems were recognized at the time of the UK's accession, and agreement was reached that a solution would be sought if the burden was unacceptable. Moreover, a transitional period was agreed to 1980 before the EC budgetary system would apply in full to the UK, and by when it was hoped the agricultural share of the EC budget would have fallen. The incoming Labour government in 1974 set about renegotiating the terms of entry and budgetary contributions, and at the Dublin Summit in 1975 the EC Council of Ministers agreed to a 'corrective mechanism' designed to limit financial burdens and refund excess contributions. However, the mechanism was conditional and complex, given the difficulties of calculating precise payments and receipts, and never came into effect. Renegotiation of the budget issue was thus taken up in earnest by the new Conservative government under Mrs Thatcher in 1979, and eventually it was agreed that the UK would receive fixed refunds of two-thirds of its non-adjusted net contributions. However, these were granted on an *ad hoc* basis negotiated acrimoniously each year over the period 1980–84, and took the form of both direct rebates and extra EC spending on projects in the UK.

The period from 1975 to 1984 was one of considerable hostility within the Community over the incidence of budget contributions, the seemingly uncontrollable expansion of agricultural expenditure, the complicated decision-making process and the lack of forward planning. As Pinder (1991) remarks, the British government was prepared to stall Community development until its budgetary demands were met, an attitude that discouraged a favourable response from other nations.

The impending financial collapse of the CAP triggered a solution at the Fontainebleau Summit in 1984, whereby a complex abatement mechanism was agreed. A refund of ECU1 billion for 1984 was to be followed in subsequent years by a rebate equal to two-thirds of the difference between the percentage share of the UK's VAT payments and its share of Community expenditure. The rebate was to be made up by higher VAT payments by other members. Table 4.5 shows the UK's contributions and the impact of the Fontainebleau abatement, which established the principle of corrective adjustment for member states carrying an excessive budgetary burden relative to their economic circumstances. Although complex, the mechanism was not upset by the 1988 Brussels reforms featuring the GNP-related fourth resource. Compensatory rebates related to the GNP-related as well as VAT payments, although the British refund is not agreed beyond 1993.

4.3 THE EC BUDGET IN THE 1990s

As it develops, the budget performs greater integrative and redistributive roles. It does not merely coordinate national expenditure and revenue, but rather funds common policies, thus allowing consideration of expenditure that national governments might not sanction otherwise, while maintaining control of the

Table 4.5 UK contributions to and receipts from the EC budget, 1980–1991 (£billions)

	1980	1981	1982	1983	1984	1985	1986	1987	1988	1989	1990	1991
UK gross contributions	1.8	2.2	2.9	3.0	3.2	3.9	4.5	5.2	5.1	5.6	6.4	6.3
UK receipts	-1.0	-1.1	-1.3	-2.0	-2.0	-1.9	-2.2	-2.3	-2.2	-2.1	-2.2	-2.8
Negotiated refund	-0.1	-0.7	-1.0	-0.5	-0.5	-0.1	n.a.	n.a.	n.a.	n.a.	n.a.	n.a.
Fontainebleau abatement	n.a.	n.a.	n.a.	n.a.	n.a.	-0.2	-1.7	-1.2	-1.6	-1.1	-1.7	-2.4
Net contributions												
Cash terms	0.7	0.4	0.6	0.7	0.7	1.8	0.6	1.7	1.4	2.3	2.5	1.2
Real terms (1980 prices)	0.7	0.4	0.5	0.5	0.5	1.0	0.7	1.2	0.8	1.3	1.4	0.6

common pool of funds. Moreover, the budget redistributes from the fortunate to those less well-endowed rather than merely allocating on efficiency grounds. This has become apparent with increased structural spending. As such the budget is evolving on the basis of fiscal federalism, whereby a central (Community) body obtains resources from lower-tier (member) governments and spends these via grants on redistribution-based projects. Fiscal federalism implies that redistribution creates externalities which need intervention by the central authority via transfer payments or a change of responsibility for redistribution from lower-tier authorities to the centre (see Oates 1972, 1977; Musgrave 1969).

Wilsadin (1990) suggests that fiscal federalism leads to a difference between real and perceived benefits from EC grants, since regions in receipt of Community support may receive less domestic aid. For example, reduced UK budget contributions have been linked formerly to greater EC structural fund expenditure on deprived UK regions. If EC-fostered policies represent significant projects in member states, then interchange between structural fund cash flows will make the costs and benefits difficult to assess. Member nations are concerned that, as integration and redistribution needs intensify, the spread of redistributive expenditures may be uneven, to their individual cost. Padua-Schioppa *et al.* (1987) suggest that the linkage between the expenditure and revenue sides of the budget makes it vital to ascertain *net* member contributions to ensure equity of incidence.

Thus, implicit in the development of the EC budget are the issues of which functions should be transferred to central control and when, concerns that will assume greater significance as the impact of the Single Market and the EMU take effect. To date the Community budget has serviced a narrow range of functions, with national budgets the main instruments of policy for influencing public expenditure on health, education, defence, etc. However, with the advent of the Single Market, labour mobility will intensify and with it incomes will converge, which Wilsadin (1990) suggests will reduce redistribution at the national level in favour of increased pressure for EC-level intervention. Greater competition and the pursuit of common policies will require more central coordination and redistribution to offset the adverse effects of integration on specific regions.

However, the Treaty of Rome provides for a balanced budget, so amendments would be required if a macroeconomic policy role is to be undertaken. More significantly, the EC budget would require substantial enlargement to function as an economic stabilizer. Pinder (1991) estimated that EC expenditure accounted for only 1 per cent of EC GDP and 4 per cent of total public expenditure in the Community in 1990, and for 1993 amounts to only ECU70 billion (Table 4.4), equivalent to the GDP of Switzerland—relatively insignificant amounts in macroeconomic terms. The MacDougall Report (EC Commission 1977) envisaged a public finance union with expenditure amounting to the 5–10 per cent of GDP deemed necessary for effective redistribution purposes. The extra funding was to come from adjusted VAT contributions such that the richer nations paid progressively more. An effective redistribution function within the Community requires substantial funding on at least this scale, but the sanction of such resources is a thorny political issue. The MacDougall Report rapidly became dated, given the 'southern enlargement' and the widespread aversion to enhanced public expenditure noted in Chapter 3. However, a stronger role for the Community is now recognized in the wake of the aforementioned integrative trends; indeed, the debate on future financing prior to the 1988 Brussels European Council showed that member states were attracted to the ideas of strengthening Community institutions at the expense of national ones.

CONCLUSIONS

The 1988 Brussels reforms ameliorated short-term tensions and laid the framework for a medium-term perspective for budgetary planning. Significant shifts were made to subsequent patterns of expenditure with limitations placed upon agricultural price support and greater spending on the structural funds; while in terms of revenue the additional fourth resource has given greater flexibility in funding. The solution to the British issue was seen to be in the interests of the whole Community in order to prevent countries with below-average GNPs making disproportionate contributions.

Nevertheless, member states will be wary lest familiar problems that have beset the budget in the past reappear. The Inter-institutional Agreement has enhanced the influence of Parliament over the compulsory expenditure. Indeed, the distinction between compulsory and non-compulsory expenditure would seem unnecessary given the agreed longer-term financial perspective on spending. This division has been weakened further by the Council's insistence on a difference between 'privileged' and 'non-privileged' non-compulsory expenditure. The former covers the structural funds whose annual budgetary increases are guaranteed, whereas the latter is subject to a 'maximum rate of increase' agreed by Council. Parliament contested that this was not in the Treaty and expressed concern lest its attempts to strengthen its budgetary powers were undermined. Moreover, as the 'non-privileged' non-compulsory expenditure covers sensitive areas such as the environment, energy, and transport, there is potential for conflict in future. Community economic and political integration requires transport improvements, and, for example, various state railways have sought Community finance for developing interlinked high-speed networks. Arguably, assistance for eastern and central European nations, many of which aspire to EC membership, may be better spent on such infrastructure than on straight financial transfers. In reality, the Inter-institutional Agreement ensures Parliament's position regarding non-compulsory expenditure, but the issue is indicative of the problems of agreement over the content and control of the budget.

On the revenue side, disputes over the need for significantly enhanced funding have been temporarily shelved by the creation of a fourth resource. However, this is inherently contrary to the Treaty in that it is not an 'own resource' but a contribution from member states. Further substantive demands for financial resources will therefore require Parliament and the Council to prove unequivocally that the Community budget can efficiently and equitably re-distribute funds to members for the good of the Community as a whole.

FURTHER READING

M. Shackleton (1990) provides an insight into the budgetary process, and for budget facts and figures refer to the *Official Journal of the EC (OJ)* or the *Bulletin of the EC*. Demekas *et al.* (1988) provide a literature survey of the CAP, while Moyer and Josling (1990) compare EC and US policies with respect to protectionism and reform. Corbet (1991) discusses the Uruguay Round. The principles of tax harmonization are covered in Guien and Bonnet (1987) and Cnossen (1987).

FIVE

EUROPEAN CENTRAL BANKING: INDEPENDENCE ISSUES

If progress towards EMU as proposed by the Delors Plan has been complicated by issues such as a single- or two-speed Europe and a single or common currency, dispute has also arisen as to the nature of central banking under monetary union. A fundamental feature of the original Delors Plan was the establishment in Stage 2 of new Community institutions including a European System of Central Banks (ESCB), to pave the way for the creation of a new European Central Bank (ECB) in Stage 3. However, discussion of the nature of such an institutional development begs consideration of the role of modern central banks, their powers and their relations with government.

5.1 THEORETICAL PERSPECTIVES

Central banks are by no means homogeneous throughout the world. They differ in the range of their activities, their powers, the techniques at their disposal and their legal and constitutional position. The German central bank, the Deutsche Bundesbank, is often cited as being independent of government, but, as we shall see it is nevertheless constrained by legal and constitutional requirements. The US Federal Reserve Bank has autonomy in the management of monetary policy, while the Bank of England has some statutory responsibilities but in financial policy is the agent of government, as also is the Banque de France. Thus, to define a central bank as the bank entrusted with the duty of regulating the volume of currency and credit in the country is to reflect the Deutsche Bundesbank position, whereas Sayers' (1967) traditional definition would relate more closely to the Bank of England:

> the central bank is the organ of government that undertakes the financial operations of government and by its conduct of these operations and by other means, influences the behaviour of financial institutions so as to support the economic policy of the government.

However, in its 1991 Annual Report, the Bank of England (1992b) defines its current core purposes as 'to maintain the value of the currency and integrity of the financial system and to promote efficiency of financial markets', an operational definition more akin to that of the Deutsche Bundesbank.

In spite of these definitional nuances, a common feature of central banks seems to be the provision of banking services to the banking system and government. As such they play key roles in carrying out monetary policy, both domestically in their economies and collectively in influencing world markets. Nevertheless, it is questionable whether some of their functions might be performed more beneficially by other institutions.

The general responsibilities of central banks to other domestic banks, the government and individuals would seem to include functions eminently suitable for private banks or other institutions. The provision of accounts for daily settlement of the clearing between commercial banks could be undertaken by an entity such as a clearing houses' association or a designated bank, possibly without the need for the commercial banks to maintain the high operational balances on non-interest-bearing accounts, which currently form a major source of income for some central banks. In the UK all major banks are required to hold 0.4 per cent of their sterling deposit base on non-interest-bearing deposit with the Bank of England. The official government accounts such as (in the UK) the Exchequer, the National Loans Fund and the Paymaster General could be shared among various private banks, possibly on a tender basis and subject to agreed disclosure requirements. Responsibility for the note issue and management of foreign exchange might be seen as more contentious aspects; yet even here a Treasury, possibly working through the major commercial banks, could take over such tasks. Mullineux (1985) cites the case of Hong Kong, where the note issue has been handled by the two major banks in the absence of a recognizable central bank, and where foreign exchange intervention is devolved partly to relieve the market of the sensitivity caused by central bank intervention.

Central banks have traditionally held important roles in smoothing the functioning of the money markets through 'lender-of-last-resort' functions. However, in a competitive, market-oriented system liquidity should be available for commercial banks without recourse to a central intermediary. Moreover, even if such an intermediary is required, a designated bank could in theory act in this capacity.

In many countries the development and maintenance of a sound and stable financial system is seen as the major central bank function and hence supervisory legislation has developed to match this view, e.g. via the 1979 and 1987 UK

Banking Acts. Arguably, central banks have a wealth of data, experience and expertise in dealing with the financial system and are ideally placed as regulators. Frequently, however, these supervisory duties are shared with others, notably the Treasury and other government agencies, and extend beyond their mainstream banking roles. The Bank of England has played a leading role in guiding the securities industry through a period of unprecedented change in the mid-1980s. However, it is not a prerequisite that the regulatory agency should be the central bank, any more than it should be a government department or independent agency. Indeed, given recent problems in the UK such as the Johnson Matthey and BCCI affairs, it is questionable whether a central bank can reasonably act as both supervisor and sponsor of the financial system.

If such observations are valid, then with the extensive deregulation of the financial system why is it that the central banks retain such wide-ranging functions? One simple answer is that central banking is profitable. In the year ended February 1992 the Bank of England made an operating profit of £166.2 million (£161.8 million in 1990/91), enabling it to make a payment in lieu of dividend to the Treasury of £67.2 million (£87.5 million in 1990/91). A second answer is that many central banks operate as agents in functions that might otherwise be undertaken by other public-sector bodies.

This begs the question of how independent central banks should be, given that they might be vulnerable to political manipulation, especially in pre-election periods. The issue of central bank independence is a key one in a European context. The introduction of EC banking and investment directives with their 'passport principles', allowing institutions regulated in one nation to operate elsewhere, and the convergence of policies under the EMS have already reduced central bank independence. However, these issues become even more significant in the context of a European Central Bank.

5.2 OPERATIONAL ASPECTS

5.2.1 The Bank of England

Founded in 1694, the Bank of England has been a role model for many central banks worldwide, even though many of its powers, functions and responsibilities have developed from practice and precedent rather than statute, a feature relatively unique among modern central banks.

It started as a commercial bank, having been given a Charter of Incorporation with joint stock status in return for helping the government fund the Nine Years War with France. Thereafter it operated as a large private banking business, even issuing banknotes, but its resources from its ability to issue stock meant that it increasingly became the banker to the government. In due course the duties of financial adviser, registrar and agent in the foreign exchange and money markets were added. The development of the Bill of Exchange drawn on London and its long-standing role in discounting bills offered by the discount houses gave it an important role as an agent of government in implementing monetary policy, and also gave it much supervisory experience. Thus, since the mid-nineteenth century the Bank has behaved as a public institution, although it has also evolved as a banker to the banking community by virtue of holding the settlement accounts for clearing.

These tasks were not enforced by legislation when the Bank took them over, and indeed, until recently there has been little significant legislation affecting its operations. The 1844 Bank Charter Act gave it a monopoly over the note issue in England and Wales and stipulated that the profits so derived were attributable to the government, and the 1946 Bank of England Act led to its nationalization after 252 years as a privately owned institution but did not drastically alter its operations. In recent years the 1979 and 1987 Banking Acts have given the Bank powers over the financial system; but, these supervisory aspects apart, it is not dependent upon legislation for many of its roles.

The Bank of England follows a highly centralized structure based on the Threadneedle Street head office, notwithstanding the presence of regional branches in the major cities. The policy-making body is the Court of Directors, all of whom are appointed by the Queen and are mainly non-executive directors. They are also chairmen or chief executives of important industrial and commercial firms, for example GKN, Redland, Warburgs, Thorn-EMI and Prudential Assurance, thus representing a cross-section of industry and City interests. The four full-time executive directors are responsible with the governor and deputy governor for the daily operations of the Bank. Appointments are usually for five years for governors and four for directors, although both terms are renewable, as is the case with the present governor who was first appointed in 1983. The organizational structure reflects its operational responsibilities, which may be broadly classified as banking relations and information provision, financial policy and market operations, and supervision.

The Bank has three important groups of customers: the commercial banks, the government, and overseas central banks. Banking services to the other banks include the provision of accounts for the settlement of daily interbank indebtedness or clearing. The Bank also supplies banknotes to the commercial banks, is an information and dialogue intermediary between the government and the financial sector, and acts as a 'lender-of-last-resort' to the banking system in time of need. For the government, the Bank holds accounts which allow public departments to transact payments, borrow or repay debt. The Bank also arranges new issues of government securities, debt redemption and the payment of interest. Any surplus funds are applied to the short-term money markets or debt repayment. The Bank also manages the country's external account, the Exchange Equalization Account, which represents the nation's reserves of gold and foreign currency. In addition, other central banks maintain accounts to conduct foreign exchange business, namely obtaining sterling in exchange for foreign currency deposits.

The provision of the above services to the banking community and government also forms the base for implementing financial policy. Although the Treasury is ultimately responsible for policy, the Bank will have considerable influence on its formation and execution, especially in view of its heavy involvement in the foreign exchange and money markets. Inasmuch as one of the Bank's core purposes is to safeguard the value of the currency, monetary policy is now enacted largely through interest rate policy. The Bank's influence over short-term rates derives from its role in the money market, where it smooths imbalances in the flow of liquid funds between banks and government. If excess money flows to the banks from government the market will be in surplus, which will be absorbed by selling short-term assets (commercial and Treasury bills) to the market operators. However, the pattern of government and bank operations usually creates the opposite flow and a shortage of cash, which the Bank relieves. This is the key to short-term interest rate control; the Bank chooses the rate at which this shortage is alleviated by buying bills (re-discounting) or by adopting a higher profile and announcing the rate at which it has lent to the market.

In conducting these operations the Bank has traditionally used the discount houses as intermediaries, although from 1988 other eligible institutions have been involved. Originally bill-brokers, these now specialist principals hold large quantities of first-class commercial bills and cash from the commercial banks. They service the latter's needs for an independent market in certificates of deposit, and provide a source of liquid assets for the banks since loans to the discount houses are callable at very short notice. In the event of an unrelieved cash shortage, the discount houses would seek funds to repay the banks that are calling in their loans. If the whole system is unable to provide cash loans to the discount houses, the result would be rising interest rates. In the context of monetary policy, a desired rise in interest rates can be engineered by a persistent shortage of cash in the market, alleviated at increasingly penal interest rates, in turn raising rates on various short-term assets (commercial bills, certificates of deposit (CDs), Treasury bills) and then on bank loans and deposits in general.

Since 1981, the Bank's intended management of the money market has placed more emphasis on open-market operations, namely buying and selling bills, than on direct lending to the discount houses at announced rates (lender-of-last-resort) to relieve shortages. Shaw (1990) notes that the Bank aimed to intervene primarily in very short-term bills of Band 1 (1–14 days' maturity), leaving interest rates in higher bands (Band 2, 15–33 days; Band 3, 34–63 days; Band 4, 64–91 days) to be market-led. However, substantial unexpected cash shortages necessitated active dealing and interest rate determination in all four bands. This in turn meant that bill and market rates sometimes diverged and encouraged arbitrage, i.e. companies borrowing via bill finance and redepositing, thus raising both lending and deposit rates.

These cash shortages partly reflected the policy of overfunding at the start of the 1980s. Table 5.1 shows that this involved the sale of gilt-edged stock

Table 5.1 Overfunding and redemption: the PSBR and PSDR, 1980–1990 (£millions)

	1980	1981	1982	1983	1984	1985	1986	1987	1988	1989	1990
PSBR/PSDR	11 786	10 507	4 868	11 574	10 300	7 445	2 499	–1 434	–11 868	–9 276	–2 073
of which, financed by:											
Non-bank private sector	8 472	8 888	6 570	11 073	8 598	8 547	7 147	8 258	–6 040	–9 289	873
of which:											
UK government securities	6 755	6 904	4 724	7 111	6 657	6 272	4 776	2 113	–4 090	–11 904	–1 147
National savings	1 377	4 185	3 643	2 988	3 386	2 491	2 612	2 541	1 482	–1 515	819
Issue dept.'s transactions in bills	–368	–2 185	–3 097	718	–1 875	–1 162	–469	3 710	–1 273	3 034	–554

Source: CSO 'Blue Book' *UK National Accounts* 1991 edn. T.11.14.

and national savings products to the non-bank private sector in excess of the public-sector financial deficit (PSFD) and public-sector borrowing requirement (PSBR) as a policy decision to neutralize the impact on the growth of the money supply of substantial bank lending. Bank lending was at the time insensitive to interest rates and the resultant overfunding created money-market cash short- ages. To relieve these, the Bank bought substantial quantities of commercial bills ('bill mountain'). The gradual reduction in the PSFD and the PSBR, the shift to a full funding policy with neutral monetary impact and the disillusion with money supply targeting eliminated the need for overfunding—but not the perception that the Bank, rather than the market, determines interest rates. Part- ington (1989) observes that the Bank's intention is to keep short-term interest rates within an unpublished band and not to preset dealing rates, although, as above, changes in short-term rates can be effected by manipulating the terms on which the Bank deals with the discount houses.

Through its operations in gilt-edged securities, the Bank also influences longer-term rates. The gilt-edged market enables government securities to be marketed with the Bank operating as issuer, redeemer and daily trader. As indic- ated above, the main concern in the early 1980s was to fund public-sector needs without inflationary consequences, and so experiments were conducted with index-linked, variable-rate, partly paid and convertible stocks. To further the market influence auctions were used for new issues. However, as the decade wore on the Bank encouraged the re-emergence of the corporate bond market to discourage the inflationary effects of company borrowing from banks. This, together with reduced public-sector borrowing and the Bank's concentration on shorter dated stocks, helped to reduce longer-maturity interest rates. By 1988 the PSBR had become a PSDR (public-sector debt repayment) and the Bank was a net redeemer of stock via 'reverse auctions', with holders selling through competitive offers.

These gilt market changes have occurred against a backcloth of structural reforms following deregulation. Prior to 'Big Bang' the Bank sold gilts through its broker to only two jobbers: Ackroyd and Smithers and Wedd Durlacher, who both operated a small but profitable cartel. After October 1986 the market became fiercely competitive, with 27 gilt-edged market-makers (GEMMs) and 6 inter-dealer brokers (IDBs). The GEMMs were intended to bring liquidity and widen out the market by quoting continuous buying and selling prices at which they were prepared to deal. The IDBs were to enable the GEMMs to obtain or dispose of stock arising from their market-making operations. In reality, the market has proved unprofitable relative to the large required capital outlays and several firms have withdrawn, including Lloyds Bank and Prudential Baache; thus market concentration has reappeared, with most business undertaken by a limited number of GEMMs.

Since the 1930s the Bank has operated in the foreign currency market through its Exchange Equalization Account (EEA), a government account holding the UK's foreign currency reserves. This is normally used to stabilize exchange rates within the context of the ERM; and any balance of payments deficit, say from an increase in imports, would be met by the EEA supplying foreign currency to meet UK residents' needs and taking up the sterling they offer in return via their banks. The supply of foreign currency and absorption of the excess sterling stabilizes the rate. However, official currency reserves will have fallen, the EEA will hold additional sterling which will be transferred by the Bank into the Consolidated Fund, and UK residents' sterling deposits will have fallen, with *ceteris paribus*, a contracting effect on the money supply. The opposite situation arises with a balance of payments surplus, as the sale of sterling to avoid appreciation will help fuel the money supply. Where balance of payments pressures are not perceived as temporary, the operational onus thus falls again on interest rates as the main instrument of Bank policy.

Operational policy in recent years has been increasingly influenced by the exchange rate, especially during the period of the UK's membership of the ERM. In January 1985 the minimum lending rate was reintroduced in response to a sterling crisis, and by 1987 monetary conditions were being assessed by reference to the exchange rate as well as movements in narrow and broad money. By joining the ERM in October 1990, intervention on the foreign exchanges to maintain the value of sterling became a major function of the Bank.

A prime example of such support occurred in the first week of September 1992, when the Bank of England, acting on behalf of the Treasury, borrowed the currency equivalent of ECU10 billion (£7.27 billion). Half of these funds were immediate Deutschmark borrowings, the rest a mixture of currencies over successive weeks, and all were to be sold for sterling, thus supporting the pound which had been trading perilously close to its ERM floor. The UK government wished to avoid any devaluation of sterling from its DM2.95 parity in the ERM and also hoped the borrowing would negate the need for a further damaging rise in UK interest rates should the French vote 'no' in their referendum on Maastricht later in the month. The Treasury and Bank of England argued that such borrowing was acceptable in view of the UK's relatively strong foreign exchange reserves (£44.5 billion in August) and its firm monetary stance. The sterling proceeds of the borrowing programme were also to be used to help finance the PSBR estimated at over £28 billion for the financial year.

The mechanics of the operation involved an ECU5 billion multi-currency revolving credit facility, drawn in Deutschmarks, at an interest rate of 3/32 over LIBOR (the London Inter-Bank Offered Rate), arranged by the 'Big Four' UK clearing banks and running for three years. The zero risk weighting of the government debt did not necessitate a rise in their capital bases, hence allowing a fair return for the banks. The remaining ECU5 billion consisted of a variety of bill and note issues. If, as expected, the borrowed funds were converted into sterling while the pound was weak and repaid when it was stronger, then there would be some benefit to offset the borrowing cost. The downside risk was that a continued strengthening of the Deutschmark and lack of sterling recovery would lead to a need for devaluation within the ERM, or indeed suspension from, or the collapse of, the ERM itself, all of which would push up the cost of repayment. In the event sterling could not be held by such intervention, as we discussed in Chapter 2.

5.2.2 Deutsche Bundesbank

The German central bank has institutional characteristics distinctive from those of many other central banks including the Bank of England and Banque de France. The German attachment to federalism extends to the Deutsche Bundesbank, whose organization and powers reflect the rule of law or Rechstaat and whose operating practice centres on a basic norm: protecting the currency against inflation. However, given the leading role of Germany in the world economy and the anchor role of the Deutschmark in the ERM, the Deutsche Bundesbank is an anachronism, a national institution struggling to manage international pressures without sacrificing its own institutional identity, yet in reality no longer a purely national entity.

The distinctive philosophy of the Deutsche Bundesbank is a refusal to compromise on inflation. Currency stability is seen as the precondition of a functioning market economy and economic growth, and Bundesbank President Otto Pohl's statement to commemorate the fortieth anniversary of the 1948 currency reform stressed the Bank's achievements in this respect 'forty years of economic success with an average inflation rate of 2.7 per cent . . .' (Pohl 1988). This preoccupation arises from the devastating effects of two runaway inflations on German political and social history this century (whereas in 1914 the dollar had been worth approximately 4 marks, by 1923 it was worth over 4 billion marks!)

Following the Second World War, Allied occupation and the German basic law, the Grundgesetz, had the objective of creating decentralized, federal structures in a distinctive split with the previous unitary state tradition. Thus, in the banking sector in 1949, *Landeszentralbanken* (*Länder* central banks) were set up in the occupied zone together with a coordinating body, the Bank deutscher-Länder (BdL), whose structure and powers closely resembled those of the present Deutsche Bundesbank, save that the occupying powers could veto its policies, although in reality they never did. The BdL was succeeded in 1957 by the Deutsche Bundesbank.

The administrative structure follows the federalist pattern established in the Grundgesetz. Together with a head office in Frankfurt, 11 *Länder* central banks (LCBs) were established, and when German Economic, Monetary and Social Union (GEMSU) came into force in 1990, 15 additional provisional Deutsche Bundesbank offices were created throughout the former GDR together with an administrative office in Berlin. While rationalization will occur with the closure of smaller LCBs and greater emphasis on Frankfurt, the federalist nature will remain. The ultimate policy-making body is the Central Bank Council (Zentralbankrat) which determines monetary and credit policy. It is democratically organized on a one person, one vote principle, and hence the institutional position of the president may appear out of all proportion to his or her international standing among economic decision-makers. The president's power to commit the Deutsche Bundesbank at G-10 meetings depends on the persuasion of Zentralbankrat colleagues before and after a summit.

The daily administrative body is the Frankfurt Directorate which, with a staff of 15 000, provides a range of operational and analytical tasks including the issue of banknotes. The main divisions in the present organization of the Deutsche Bundesbank are:

- Treasury, buildings, administration and personnel
- Statistics and national economy
- International and foreign divisions
- Organization and bookkeeping
- Banking, minimum reserve and the Berlin (*E. Länder*) administrative divisions
- Credit
- Press and public relations
- Legal and supervision

A certain tension exists between the Directorate and the presidents of the *Land* central banks. As members of the Zentralbankrat, these bank presidents often exhibit disdain towards Directorate staff charged with the execution of their policies. As the Deutsche Bundesbank open-market operations and responsibilities within the EMS have increased, the daily operations of the Frankfurt Directorate have expanded and widened the scope for conflict. Deutsche Bundesbank dealings with the *Länder* governments and transactions with local banks are restricted by law and tradition to the *Länder* central banks and their branches. The LCBs vary in organization but act as the main administrative branches of the Deutsche Bundesbank, having credit, banking, economic, foreign currency and bond divisions as well as personnel, accounting, premises and legal divisions common to most bureaucratic organizations. They also provide a mechanism whereby they disseminate Deutsche Bundesbank policy and gather reactions to it. They have managing boards responsible for running the LCBs on a daily basis and advisory boards made up of local business, banking and labour interests.

The extensive organization of the Bundesbank has been criticized as outdated, too big and too expensive, and the LCB presidents as too powerful. If the federal structure is to be retained, then many advocate a more streamlined organization while retaining a mechanism for representing the economic interests of the *Länder* in the Zentralbankrat.

Stability of the currency and maintenance of the payments system are the major objectives of monetary policy, and all the normal banking functions (note issue, banker's bank, etc.) are subordinate to these needs. However, while the purpose is clear, the means have often been debated, notably in terms of (1) the internal versus external value of the Deutschmark; and (2) the relationship between monetary and wider economic policy.

The internal–external currency value debate now centres mainly on the risks of imported inflation under fixed or semi-fixed exchange rates whenever other countries' inflation rates are higher than domestic ones. From time to time differing opinions occur between government and bank over the impact of exchange rate movements, as in May 1989 when, with the strong US dollar trading above DM1.90 (Plaza Agreement ceiling), the government called for a fall in the dollar but a week later the Deutsche Bundesbank president argued that the German economy was not strong enough to cope with any rise in the Deutschmark. Thus the Bank is compromised by its international commitments, such as the Louvre and Plaza Agreements, to buy dollars when the dollar falls below the bottom of its range. However, this raises the domestic money supply even though the Deutschmarks created might be neutralized elsewhere and a strong Deutschmark can limit inflationary pressures. Such interventions can thus fuel domestic inflation and upset the EMS, yet the international significance of the Deutschmark and dollar restricts the Bank's flexibility. Hence the Deutsche Bundesbank argues that currency intervention without money supply control and other domestic fiscal measures is ineffective, a stance that applies equally to the maintenance of parities within the ERM. The Deutsche Bundesbank has tended to suggest that Germany's trading partners maintain low inflation rates and balanced economies, tracking the German standard and allowing internal price stability at a constant Deutschmark rate.

The second area of conflict is increasingly more difficult; fitting monetary management into wider economic policy. Critics of the Deutsche Bundesbank advocate a more active role for it in directing the economy, especially as unification is likely to produce more growth, inflation and social pressures. However, the combination of legal obligations and responsibility for growth, employment and external balance place it in a difficult position. The constant repetition of the ills of inflation masks complex thinking in the Deutsche Bundesbank on the need for growth in the economy.

In order to defeat inflation, four basic instruments are used: the discount rate for loans to banks; the Lombard rate for overnight money; open-market operations; and a minimum reserve asset policy. The policy shift has been towards a more market-oriented approach with greater use of open-market instruments, and indirect use of liquidity instruments geared to influence longer-term interest and market movements. In reality, short-term transactions have been increasingly favoured by the Deutsche Bundesbank, implying that it has been forced into the task of market management. The use of short-term bonds of one week's to two months' duration as 'fine-tuning' devices together with the sales of Treasury bills, repurchase agreements, and currency swaps offer flexibility but also risk the danger of being misread by the international markets. In late 1987 the rise in interest rates on short-term bonds, designed to give a domestic signal, was acted upon internationally as a sign of weakness in the US economy and arguably was one of the factors that precipitated the 'crash' of October 1987.

In spite of these conflicts, the core elements of the Deutsche Bundesbank ethos remain. Indeed, the success of the German economy and the Deutschmark within the EMS arguably stem from the Bank's loyalty to its central goal.

5.2.3 Banque de France

The French financial system is heavily influenced by state intervention at various levels, in keeping with the concepts of indicative planning and *dirigisme* that have characterized the economy as a whole. Direct control has been established in ownership, close specification of eligible activities, representation on and influence over supervisory committees, and civil servant appointments at very senior levels in many financial institutions. For most of the postwar period the French financial sector was governed by regulations adopted in 1945 which encouraged specialization and a strict separation of function between banks and a wide variety of credit institutions. This division was itself a legacy of a private banking system dating back to Napoleonic times. Indeed, the central bank, the Banque de France, was established as a private bank in 1800 and, although having state involvement, was not nationalized until 1945 along with the 'Big Three' commercial banks. During the 1960s banks were encouraged to extend their operations in the maturity of their lending and scope of activities undertaken along the lines of the 'universal banking' model, and also at the expense of the credit institutions.

Thus, by the 1980s the country was over-banked. The newly elected Socialist government felt that the sector ought to play a greater role in stimulating the economy, so it nationalized a further 36 banks and various ancillary financial institutions. The 1982–83 nationalization proved unsuccessful and a privatization programme enacted in 1986–87 reversed the process. The rationale behind the latter move was the pressure of competition, the need for credit institutions to raise their capital bases to maintain their credit standing following the onset of the Third World debt crisis, and technological advances which were heavily capital-intensive. However, the shifts in ownership have not lessened the grip of the monetary authorities on the financial sector, enacted through direct operational influences on the volume and price of credit.

The main monetary authorities are the Banque de France and the Treasury Department of the Ministry of Finance. The central bank, headquartered in Paris but with an extensive branch network, is involved in the formulation and enactment of monetary policy, although the Ministry of Finance retains overall control of the financial system. Prior to the 1984 Banking Act the distinction between banks and other credit institutions was maintained in dealings with the monetary authorities. The Banque de France operated with banks via the Association Française des Banques (AFB), the Commission de Contrôle des Banques (CCB) and the Conseil Nationale du Crédit (CNC). These covered barely half of French banking activity, with other financial intermediaries, mainly credit institutions, directly controlled by the Treasury. All banks operating in France were required to join the French bankers' association (AFB) which transmits directives from the regulatory authorities to the banks. The CCB acted as a supervisory vehicle to ensure that banks complied with banking regulations, while the CNC's role was to oversee the operation of the financial system in respect of credit policy.

The 1984 Banking Act attempted to introduce more consistency into the supervision of financial institutions, but it has not reduced the bureaucracy involved. It provides a broad definition of banking to allow the Banque de France to incorporate a range of banking and credit institutions under its orbit. Consequently, fewer entities are now under the direct control of the Treasury than previously. The Banque de France now operates via three committees: the Comité des Éstablissements de Crédit (CEC), chaired by the Banque's governor and responsible for the authorization of specific institutions; the Comité de la Réglementation Bancaire, responsible for devising new and amending existing regulations, and chaired by the Minister of Finance; and the Commission Bancaire (CB), which replaced the CCB, is chaired by the Banque's governor and supervises compliance with the Banking Act and other regulations. The CNC's role is now reduced to an advisory capacity. In recent years the Ministry of Finance has delegated more powers to the Banque de France but it still plays the major role in policy formulation and regulation via these committees, most of whose members are appointed by decree of the Minister of Finance.

The Banque de France provides the usual range of central banking functions. It is the sole bank sanctioned to issue and distribute notes, and it remains the government and bankers' bank. Its main functions mirror those of the other central banks mentioned, namely to protect the external value of the franc and to regulate the supply of credit and money in circulation.

French monetary policy has had to adapt to a more liberal banking environment, as evidenced in terms of securitization, more varied instruments and maturities, and above all more internationalism following the dismantling of exchange controls and emphasis on market forces. Thus, monetary policy has shifted in focus from a credit-related policy based largely on volume via credit limits to one more dominated by price via interest rates, with changes in reserve requirements as necessary. This reflects the growth of disintermediation which rendered credit ceilings ineffective.

Monetary targets have remained, notwithstanding disaffection with them in, say, the UK and Germany. The selection of the target has reflected the inflation estimates and has shown similar problems to those encountered in other nations as a result of financial innovation and disintermediation. A relatively narrow aggregate M2 is targeted, based essentially on notes and coin and on sight deposits, both interest- and non-interest-bearing, although broader aggregates are monitored. The requirements of the ERM necessitate currency-oriented intervention which impinges upon the monetary base and hence on interest rate determination. While allowing more market determination of rates than in the past, the Banque de France will intervene to raise or lower money-market rates to alleviate currency tensions.

Banks operate under restrictive conditions which affect their profitability. They are subject to minimum capital, liquidity and lending limits, and must hold non-interest-bearing deposits with the Banque de France as compulsory reserves, in a similar fashion to the Supplementary Special Deposits scheme ('Corset') operated by the Bank of England in the 1970s, which was unpopular with the clearing banks. Moreover, these reserves are on both sight (5 per cent) and time deposits (2.5 per cent). They provide funding for the Banque de France and also ensure that the banking sector is forced to borrow from the Banque, giving it greater control over interest rates. Money required by banks is supplied increasingly via open-market operations in first-class bills or notes in the money market.

5.3 THE CASE FOR INDEPENDENCE

The case for central bank independence revolves around differing time-horizons and conflicting interests. An independent institution is perceived to be able to devote itself to attaining long-run price stability without being deflected from this goal by competing economic, social and political influences. By contrast, elected politicians are subject to shorter-term pressures from the electoral cycle and the need to reconcile often competing macroeconomic objectives, such as growth, unemployment and the external balance as well as inflation. Such pressures can undermine the credibility of any pre-announced anti-inflationary policy, and can lead to uncertainty and higher nominal interest rates. Once an anti-inflation objective is set by an independent central bank and is widely known, expectations will adjust as the policy incentives take hold. Hence in the inflation–unemployment trade-off unemployment will rise in the short term with reduced demand. However, with low or zero inflation established as a goal, expectations and wage demands may adjust quickly, reducing the policy costs in unemployment terms. Such a scenario would be less likely where elected politicians can revoke pledges made in pre-election periods.

However, the concept of unelected and unaccountable central bankers in control of major economic policy remains unacceptable to many, and was the crux of Mrs Thatcher's early objections to the creation of a European Central Bank to administer a single currency. Of more fundamental concern is whether independent central banks do in fact promote better anti-inflationary performance. The experience of Germany might suggest that they do, yet France has shown financial restraint through its ERM commitments, notwithstanding heavy government involvement. This raises the question of what level of independence is appropriate to conduct monetary policy? While the general perception is that independence does strengthen the credibility of monetary policy, the actual level will reflect country-specific factors; Castello-Branco and Swinburne (1992) cite the history of inflation, existing controls in the political system, the level of public economic awareness and debate, and the state of development of financial markets.

Healey and Levine (1992) imply that political and economic independence must prevail. The former is established via senior appointments to central bank boards. These should be for a term that exceeds the short-term political cycle and should not involve mandatory government representatives on the decision-making body. Economic independence should exist such that the bank can operate monetary policy without disruption by government actions, notably excessive borrowing.

Lack of independence in these contexts is well illustrated by the Banque de France, both in the composition of its banking committees and in its banking relationship with the government. The latter uses the central bank as its sole banker and has an overdraft facility which, according to Raymond (1990), was originally set at FF20.5 billion, of which approximately half did not bear interest. The amount now varies according to exchange gains or losses on the value of foreign exchange reserves.

Since the Bank of England is owned by the Treasury, it is ultimately an agent of government. The relationship was formalized in the 1946 Bank of England Act when the Bank's capital was nationalized and the Treasury was given powers to issue directives to the Bank. Thus, in the final analysis, the Bank of England must conform to the wishes of government and its policies. However, the Bank is also an adviser to government and derives power from its pivotal role in the banking system and in money and foreign exchange markets. Thus, it is able to express its views in such a way that it might be difficult for government to ignore it. Moreover, public confidence might suffer if both entities were seen openly to dispute policy. Consequently, although government can ultimately force the Bank to meet its objectives, these are likely to have been discussed with reference to the Bank.

Nevertheless, the question of a new independent Bank of England has been raised. In terms of monetary policy, reference is made to the success of the independent Deutsche Bundesbank in curbing inflation. In the UK the Bank of England has a function to preserve the value of the currency, yet there is no statutory responsibility for it to do so: it does not have the duty or the means to do so as it does not formulate monetary policy. Secondly, in terms of supervision much criticism has been levied at the Bank in the wake of the BCCI affair, with suggestions that the resignation of the Governor might be sought to relieve pressure on the government. Supervision is enacted through the Banking Acts which make the Bank directly accountable to Parliament, but these limit the extent to which it can use influence rather than legislation. Thirdly, undue political influence is seen as a feature of interdependence. For example, in September 1991 a speech by the Governor was widely described as 'partisan' and supportive of the government in the run-up to the election, implying that the economy was coming out of the recession when shortly before less positive forecasts had emanated from the Bank.

Such problems for the Bank of England do not occur for the Deutsche Bundesbank, as the Bundesbank Law of 1957 assigns responsibility for economic policy to the federal government, and for monetary policy to the Deutsche Bundesbank. Monetary sovereignty is established by the statutory definition as 'protector of the currency' and by the creation of the Deutsche Bundesbank as a unique entity not subordinate to government. However, the Bundesbank Law also bestows upon the government authority to determine general economic policy and binds the Deutsche Bundesbank to support it. So, while the Bundesbank is independent of government, the latter is responsible for the bank's monetary policy in so far as it is responsible for economic policy! Thus, claims to independence occur within a politicized environment of economic policy-making in both a domestic and an international context.

Directors of the Bundesbank are appointed by the federal president on the recommendation of government which has a potential veto over Bundesbank policy in the sense that decisions can be delayed. Technically the Bundesbank is obliged to advise the government on matters of monetary policy and to supply information as it is needed, such as over currency values in the EMS (often a bone of contention) which are under the authority of the finance minister. However, while the Bundesbank has no authority over federal government economic policy, it must be consulted on major changes planned, a feature that can give it political clout. Its real power lies in its ability to make monetary policy decisions which have an immediate impact through the instruments at its disposal.

In recent years it is in the international arena that Bundesbank policy-makers have felt their independence of action really threatened, most notably in September 1992 in the face of political and economic pressures to lower German interest rates as the weaker European currencies struggled to stay within their ERM bands. Talk abounded of a 'U-turn' by the Bundesbank and of its being forced to bow to political pressure. Less than two months after raising its discount rate to 8.75 per cent and Lombard rate to 9.75 per cent in a reaffirmation of its anti-inflationary commitment, the Bundesbank cut these rates by 0.5 and 0.25 per cent respectively on 14 September 1992, barely a few days after publicly stating that there was no case for relaxing its stance. Significantly, the announcement of the cut was made on Sunday 13 September by European finance ministers prior to an extraordinary meeting of the Bundesbank Zentralbankrat the following morning, the first such meeting for 12 years and at which the cut was ratified.

While Helmut Schlesinger, the Bundesbank president, admitted that foreign pressure was behind the move, he argued that monetary concerns were paramount and thus that the Bundesbank's independence was not compromised. The Bundesbank had spent some DM24 billion the previous week in supporting the lira and other weak currencies, and such an operation was both unsustainable and was undermining the purpose of a high interest rate policy by boosting the Deutschmark money supply. The Bundesbank called for a devaluation of the lira but to achieve this had to concede a relaxation in German interest rates. The decision was seen internally as a sovereign one of the Bundesbank itself, and as the price necessary to regain control of German monetary policy. In reality, the 'international independence' of the Bundesbank had been affected many years earlier by the 1987 Basle–Nyborg agreement which introduced intra-marginal intervention into the ERM. This required the Bundesbank to finance the sort of intervention seen above with the lira to stop it or other weak currencies from breaching their lower ERM limits. By buying the threatened currency in exchange for the sale of Deutschmarks the Bundesbank inflates the German money supply, thus conflicting with its statutory obligation to safeguard the value of the Deutschmark. More recently, in July 1990, its 'domestic independence' was compromised by the political decision that GEMSU should occur on the principle of a generous conversion rate of two ostmarks to one Deutschmark (see Chapter 10).

5.4   TOWARDS A EUROPEAN CENTRAL BANK

The above independence issues together with the actual circumstances of the three major European central banks have been central to discussions concerning the constitution of a future European Central Bank (ECB). The Delors Report on EMU envisaged the establishment of a European System of Central Banks (ESCB) in Stage 2, the transitional stage. The ESCB lies at the heart of the Delors Plan, as the vehicle for creating monetary union and a single currency. It would be organized on a federal basis, consisting of a central institution and national central banks. It would absorb the present EMCF, the committee of central bank governors and its sub-committees, and the permanent secretariat. During Stage 2 the difficult transition of decision-making power from national authorities to the new institution would be completed, and in Stage 3 the ESCB would be fully operational. The ESCB would be autonomous and independent of instructions from national and community authorities but could dictate to national central banks, whose role would diminish over time.

As with the concept of EMU and the stages towards it, the ideas for the establishment of the ESCB were not universally welcomed by the member states. The Germans were initially against the establishment of any new institution until a single currency is in place and members can cede monetary power to it. The British alternative Major Plan of May 1990 (see Sec. 2.3.3) envisaged the 'hard ecu' managed by the European Monetary Fund (EMF). The argument was that there would be no guarantee that an independent ESCB could deliver successful anti-inflationary policies, whereas under the Major Plan the ESCB would be set up to include the EMF. The EC Council of Economic and Finance Ministers (ECOFIN) would remain responsible for coordinating macroeconomic and fiscal policy and deciding on exchange rate policy, the latter being implemented by the ESCB. ECOFIN and the EMF would exercise surveillance and sanctions over policies. The French too have favoured development of the EMF and see a major role for ECOFIN rather than the ESCB in policy-making.

Some advocates of EMU may feel there should be an early move to establish a European Central Bank. However, while national currencies remain there is considerable flexibility of operational policy for national governments and central banks, notwithstanding moves towards economic convergence. Indeed, in Stages 1 and 2 a European Central Bank is not vital. Arguably, a large expansion of reserves in the EC central banks arising from the exchange of currencies could be supplemented by market operations to stabilize exchange rates. This would leave central banks and currencies at the centre of the system and presupposes a parallel- rather than a single-currency development. However, Stage 3 implies the move to a single currency and thus to one issuer of money and one monetary policy, features that necessitate a European Central Bank.

In spite of such differing views, by November 1990 central bank governors had agreed the draft statutes for the ESCB. The Bank's articles of association will oblige it to have an overriding aim of price stability and independence of political control. Its functions are likely to mirror traditional central bank tasks: to ensure the smooth functioning of the payments system; to undertake foreign exchange operations; to conduct monetary policy; and to participate in the formulation, coordination and execution of policies relating to prudential supervision. The system will consist of two tiers: the European Central Bank (ECB), and the national central banks that will be its shareholders. Under the agreement the national central banks will be independent of their governments and their governors would form the ESCB council, together with a president, vice-president and four others appointed by EC finance ministers.

This structure has been dubbed 'Eurofed', an analogy with the US Federal Reserve system which has 12 member reserve banks and is decentralized. Harden (1990) suggests that this accords with the EC principle of 'subsidiarity', whereby decision-making powers are exercised by member states as far as is possible and Community institutions intervene only where they can do so more effectively than member states. However, while the Delors Report encompassed this principle, the reality of monetary union implies a central decision-making body, and the weaker member states may find that they have limited influence over their own affairs.

An independent ECB implies a Community institution which might report to the European Parliament or Commission or the Council of Ministers, but will not be subject to their control. Indeed, just which of these it will report to is another issue, given the debate over their relative powers. The statutes tend to favour Parliament, but there is a lobby for strengthening the Council of Ministers which is accountable nationally. Independence also implies that the ESCB will be outside the influence of individual member states, a feature easier to achieve if existing national banks were independent now. In the UK there has been a shift in stance in this respect. Former Chancellor Nigel Lawson's plan for an independent Bank of England was vetoed by Margaret Thatcher, who was firmly opposed to any transfer of monetary sovereignty, but by September 1991 the UK government had accepted the concept that any 'Eurofed' should have operational independence.

While constitutional statutes and strict reporting requirements, plans and objectives can provide the accountability consistent with independence, they will not legitimize it. Essentially, the ECB will in theory represent an unelected body with substantive economic policy powers and as such will be open to political attack. Moreover, some of these powers are questionable, since for example the ECB was originally to have an advisory and operational responsibility but not to determine exchange rate policy. D. F. Lomax (1991) argues that this would undermine the ECB's monetary independence as it would either concentrate on keeping inflation down (as its Articles stipulate) or manage exchange rate policy, but not both.

This issue was addressed by the October 1991 Dutch draft treaty on EMU, which suggested that the Council of Ministers should determine the policy following consultations with the ECB to reach a consensus consistent with the objective of price stability. The Dutch draft also allowed for 'temporary exemption' for countries unable or unwilling to proceed in 1997 to Stage 3 and the irrevocable fixing of their currencies. While this suited the British stance it angered the Germans, who are concerned for a unified approach to EMU. In terms of the ESCB, it circumvented the issue of whether the ECB would be established in Stage 2 and if not, when, and proposed the creation of a European Monetary Institute (EMI) to coordinate monetary policy in the interim.

Thus, prior to the Dutch proposals for the Maastricht Treaty, the expectation was that the Delors Plan would prevail, i.e. that there would be a gradual transfer of monetary control to the ECB and that the ESCB with the ECB at its head would begin work in Stage 2. While the Delors Report influenced the pre-Maastricht debate on EMU and the Treaty followed from it, there were important differences. The Maastricht Treaty put dates on the development of EMU and spelt out the 'convergence criteria' required; moreover, it ended the above expectation regarding the ECB.

Thus, the Treaty text signed by the heads of government incorporated the statutes of two new monetary institutions: a European Central Bank (ECB), which would manage the eventual single currency; and a European Monetary Institute (EMI), which would absorb the roles of the present Committee of European Central Bank Governors and the board of the EMCF, and prepare for the ECB.

The EMI, which is planned to come into effect in January 1994, will also administer the EMS and aid national monetary policy coordination efforts in the interim before it is replaced by the ECB at the very beginning of Stage 3. The EMI's role reflects member nations' concerns that monetary authority should remain in their hands until the full transfer to the European level in Stage 3. As a temporary institution it has the advantage of being a learning mechanism, in that operational details and mistakes can be effected and cured before the ECB comes into force. The presence of all the central bank governors on the EMI Council reflects its limited, consultative role, even though Stage 3 policy formulation will inevitably occur. The EMI president will be appointed for a three-year term by the European Parliament and will hold a position similar to that of the Bundesbank president in its Zentralbankrat. The location of the EMI, and probably the ECB too, is at the time of writing undecided. One significant aspect of the EMI statute is that its independence is stipulated; that is, Council members must not take or seek instructions from Community institutions or national governments. Gros and Thygesen (1992) suggest these features; the appointment of an external president, the move to a permanent location and the independence of the EMI Council give credence to its role in preparing for Stage 3.

The EMI gives an insight into the future ECB and the characteristic of independence in particular is mirrored in the constitution of the ECB. This is akin to that of the Bundesbank; indeed, if anything it is geared to making the ECB more independent and price-stability-conscious than the German central bank. The proposed control of monetary policy and exchange rate commitments places the ECB in a more powerful role in order to effect its objectives. The requirements on the independence of executives, appointed with lengthy terms of office exceeding five years, should ensure freedom from overt political pressures.

CONCLUSIONS

The individual European central banks vary considerably as do their financial systems. Their functions encompass a broad range, including printing money, acting as lenders-of-last-resort, providing economic data and advice, supervising, offering normal banking facilities and maintaining the external accounts. Many of these represent inherited functions from the distant past, and not all of them need to be undertaken by a central bank. A common feature has been the relationship with the national government through the provision of banking services to it and the conduct of monetary policy. It is the very nature of this relationship which has fuelled debate on the future ECB. The success of the relatively 'independent' Bundesbank has proved pervasive compared with the government-influenced Banque de France or, to a lesser extent, the Bank of England.

Proponents of independence argue that the proposed ECB will avoid political involvement and policy commitments from the European Commission which might undermine its monetary objectives. Opponents of independence fear its lack of accountability to elected bodies. In reality, while the principles have been debated and the draft statutes agreed, there will be a considerable transition period required from the current freedom of action of present central banks. The advent of a common monetary policy and possible single currency will severely curtail the activities of these national banks to those of departments or regional offices of the ECB. On the assumption that progression is made towards EMU, the next few years will be particularly difficult as governments and central banks come to terms with the potential loss of their autonomy.

FURTHER READING

On the need for central banks see Mullineux (1985). Kennedy (1991) provides an insight into the Bundesbank philosophy and de Boisseau (1990) examines recent developments in France. The Delors Report (EC Commission 1989) and Maastricht Treaty (EC Commission 1992b) provide the basis for EMU, the EMI and ECB. The UK approach is covered in HM Treasury (1989). Gros and Thygesen (1992) give a comprehensive review of the wider framework of monetary integration.

EUROPEAN CENTRAL BANKING: SUPERVISION ISSUES

Banking history is littered with individual bank failures and banking crises. In the 1920s and 1930s thousands of banks were suspended during the hyperinflation of Germany and the depression in the USA. Thereafter the problem appeared to diminish, but since the early 1970s there have been some notable collapses. In 1974 there was the 'Secondary Banking Crisis' in the UK involving 'fringe banks' such as London and County Securities, while in Germany Bankhaus I. D. Herstatt and in the USA Franklin National Bank failed. In 1984 Johnson Matthey Bankers in the UK and Continental Illinois in the USA collapsed. However, two most dramatic events have occurred more recently still: the US savings and loans associations crisis, and the demise of the Bank of Credit and Commerce International (BCCI).

Such events have rekindled concern about the effectiveness of banking supervision with its twin aims of protecting depositors and preserving stability in financial systems. Bank depositors find themselves at risk from two basic types of bankers: fraudulent operators with no intention to repay, and incompetent risk-takers who mismatch currencies and maturities, hold insufficient liquid reserves and lend badly. The extent to which these risks become excessive and are passed on to customers depends on the bank's capital structure. However, national banking regulators have tended to define acceptable balance sheet structures to such an extent that deposits have been widely believed by the public to be relatively risk-free. Thus, although deposit protection schemes are in operation, the main focus of regulation has been to stabilize the financial system against systematic risks brought on by the failure of individual banks. In this chapter we consider the nature of banking supervision and depositor protection with specific reference to BCCI.

6.1 THEORY OF BANKING SUPERVISION

Banking instability can clearly arise from either bad loans or heavy deposit withdrawals or some combination thereof. In addition, as financial systems have evolved from bank-dominated to strongly market-oriented ones, fuelled by deregulation, competition and product/market innovations, greater risks have followed the search for higher returns. Moreover, increased exchange and interest rate volatility have raised uncertainty in the macroeconomic environment of banking.

In economic terms, banking regulation is justifiable if adverse externalities occur which evidence market failure. Fama (1980) argued that, if banks only provided basic services such as money transmission or portfolio management, there would be no special need for regulation. However, the classic bank intermediation function involves 'borrowing short and lending long', i.e. taking in liquid short-term deposits and transforming them into illiquid, longer-term loans. This creates a source of instability and thus risk in the absence of a perceived guarantee of deposit safety. As Dermine (1990) states, various triggers might occur, such as bad news about the value of bank assets which creates a crisis of confidence and precipitates a deposit withdrawal 'run' on the bank. In these circumstances market failure occurs because a cooperative solution among depositors is difficult to enforce. Each individual wants to be first in line to withdraw his or her deposit at face value, even though there is an economic cost in that illiquid assets may have to be sold at a loss.

Market failure also occurs with contagion, whereby the insolvency of one bank is seen as symptomatic of wider problems which leads to a crisis via runs on other banks. Here imperfect information means that depositors are unable to distinguish whether the problem is specific or systematic and so tend to follow the crowd rather than assess individual banks. Immediate withdrawal of funds thus appears rational and reinforces the crisis. Lewis and Davis (1987) argue that bank runs involve substantial social costs beyond the inevitable losses to depositors, shareholders and creditors. Borrowers find their businesses disrupted by the need to make earlier loan repayments or replace them, possibly under unfavourable conditions. Indeed, the banker–customer relationship may be destroyed and this may make it harder to obtain facilities elsewhere. The taxpayer may often have to bear the brunt of any payout by the regulatory authorities. In the case of the savings and loans fiasco, Seiffert (1991) cites the cost to the US taxpayer to be over $500 billion over the next 30 years.

The demise of the savings and loans (S&L) industry in the USA stemmed largely from these firms' rigid and antiquated regulatory systems and the high interest rate environment, but above all from the mismatch of their assets and liabilities. The S&Ls had to specialize in relatively long-term home construction loans funded by savings deposits withdrawable at short notice. Once interest rates climbed above 20 per cent at the end of 1980, low-interest, fixed-rate mortgages had to be refinanced by high-interest savings deposits. The government attempted to deregulate the industry by widening its scope for investments and funding, lowering the minimum equity–capital ratio and raising the limit of insured deposits from $40 000 to $100 000. However, as Seiffert (1991) indicates, this fuelled the crisis as S&L owners embarked on high-risk strategies and depositors benefited from high returns yet felt secure because of the deposit insurance. In the event, the S&L deposit insurance body FSLIC (Federal Savings and Loans Insurance Corporation) was unable to cope with the losses and resultant insolvencies.

Market failure arising from imperfect competition also occurs when the uninformed investor is subjected to incompetence, fraud or negligence. Financial markets are prone to information problems because financial services rely on network effects, namely established contacts, and thus the quality of services is often difficult to evaluate. Individuals delegate the responsibility for monitoring and evaluating borrowers to institutions and thus free-ride on the information collected. It would seem that the potential for false trust and misinformation is more prevalent in institutions dealing with private individuals (investment management firms, deposit-taking banks) than in those transacting with other companies or institutions which have screening capabilities.

In theory, there are various methods of protecting depositors and stabilizing the financial system against systematic risk. Clearly, one method is for banks themselves to limit their exposure to risk by maintaining adequate capital, holding reserves of liquid assets and diversifying their loans. While prudent for normal risks, additional insurance against contingencies might be seen as unduly unprofitable. However, one insurance for crisis situations is to suspend deposit redemption on demand, a policy commonly used by banks confronted by runs in the 1930s (Diamond and Dybvig 1983). Costs are imposed on individual depositors by the loss of liquidity, but if the returns from maintaining funds exceed those of crisis withdrawal the incentive to join the crowd is reduced.

A radical alternative approach is to rely on bank reforms to overcome the basic transformation risk of holding short-term deposits against illiquid, risky assets. An extreme would be for banks to hold, say, 100 per cent cash backing for deposits. This would severely curtail their operations, turning them into virtual depositories and forcing them to rely on transactions services for income. Separation of function would therefore occur within the system, in contrast to modern trends towards the creation of 'universal banks'.

Neither of these approaches appears satisfactory in a modern risk-bearing financial system and so the favoured method tends to focus upon deposit insurance or prudential regulation. Deposit insurance can be provided by a voluntary contributory scheme run by the industry or a private agency or compulsory government-run scheme. Voluntary schemes suffer from difficulties in the formulation and enforcement of rules and in obtaining total commitment. Lewis and Davis (1987) argue that setting a premium structure that entices all potential contributors to join is a major problem, as is the impossibility of insuring against complete systematic failure of the industry. Premia considerations mean that only certain levels of risk will be covered, leaving the scheme vulnerable if claims exceed a bank's net worth. Government-sponsored schemes aim not so much to recompense people after deposit losses as to maintain confidence in banks so that they may continue as normal.

Table 6.1 indicates that deposit schemes have been created in many European countries, but vary considerably in size, coverage and premia and generally lack harmonization. Indeed, it is not clear what objectives lie behind these schemes, since Dale (1984) argues that few provide either the 'protection against system panic' or the social/political objective of protecting individual depositors. Moreover, the public is generally ill-informed of the existence of the schemes, which normally protect depositors only for small amounts or percentages. Bourke (1988) suggests that existing deposit insurance has become inequitable between large and small depositors and large and small banks because it is universally priced on a flat-rate basis.

As banks assume more risk than their balance sheets should ideally allow, inevitably the mechanism left to deal with bank runs is direct intervention via the lender-of-last-resort function to rescue the entire bank or bail out depositors. Baltensperger and Dermine (1990) suggest that this meets the objective of financial stability, while the private incentives for risk remain because the timing and extent of intervention are unknown. The authorities have traditionally limited their exposure by an array of ancillary measures such as liquidity constraints, restricted entry to banking via licensing, restrictions on the type of investment undertaken, informal dialogue and the ability to replace management. An examination of banking supervision in the UK and Germany illustrates the range of such controls imposed by European regulatory bodies.

6.2 THE UK EXPERIENCE

Until the 1979 Banking Act, the use of formal regulation was very limited in the control of UK banking, and self-regulation meant that the sector effectively carried its own supervisory costs. The 'Secondary Banking Crisis' in 1973–75 helped to change attitudes. It was sparked by a tight monetary policy culminating in a doubling of nominal interest rates in 1973 and fuelling a collapse of property prices in 1974. Imprudent banking was thus exposed—funding at variable rates, lending at fixed rates and over-dependence on property loans, and over-reliance on wholesale money-market funds. Following the crisis more attention was paid to supervision, notably via tighter reporting requirements, but it was evident that a major statutory reform was necessary, especially to conform with the EC First Banking Coordination Directive.

Table 6.1 Coverage of European deposit protection schemes

Country	Set up	Membership	Amount covered (£ equivalent)[a]	Foreign currency	Deposits at domestic branches of foreign banks	Deposits at foreign branches of domestic banks	Premium rates (% of total deposits)
Belgium	1985	Voluntary	£8 591	No	Yes	Yes	0.02
Denmark	1987	Compulsory	£22 951	Yes	Yes	Yes	0.2 (max.)
France	1980	Compulsory	£41 808	No	Yes	No	Variable
Germany	1966	Voluntary	'30% of the liable capital'[b]	Yes	Yes	Yes	0.03
Greece	—	No scheme	—	—	—	—	—
Ireland	1989	Compulsory	£9 403 (staggered scale)[c]	No	Yes	No	0.2
Italy	1987	Voluntary	£392 707 (staggered scale)[c]	Yes	Yes	Yes	Variable
Netherlands	1979	Compulsory	£12 550	Yes	Yes	No	Variable
Portugal	—	No scheme	—	—	—	—	—
Spain	1977	Voluntary	£8 315	Yes	Yes	No	0.2
UK	1982	Compulsory	£15 000 (or 75% if <£20 000)	No	Yes	No	0.3 (max.)
Japan	1971	Compulsory	£40 568	No	No	No	0.012
USA	1933	Compulsory	£51 894	Yes	Yes	No	0.195
Switzerland	1984	Voluntary	£11 823	No	Yes	No	Variable

[a] Average spot middle rates on 10 August 1992.

[b] Implies full coverage for most investors.

[c] Staggered scales: Irish punt: 80% coverage up to IR£5000, 70% for IR£5000 to IR£10 000, thereafter 50% to IR£15 000; Italian lira: 100% for first L200 million, thereafter 50% to IR£5000 to IR£15 000; Italian lira: 100% for first L200 million, 80% for next L800 million.

Source: Deutsche Bundesbank (1992b).

The focus of the 1979 Banking Act was authorization, whereby institutions were deemed either recognized banks or licensed deposit-takers, depending on the services that they provided and their reputation in the financial world. To qualify for authorization, banks and licensed deposit-takers had to satisfy management, capital adequacy, liquidity, currency exposure and bad/doubtful debt provision criteria. Another feature of the Act was the creation of a Deposit Protection Scheme which originally guaranteed 75 per cent of the first £10 000 (later raised to £20 000 under the 1987 Act) of sterling deposits of under five years' maturity made by non-bank customers with institutions covered by the Act. To fund this, institutions had to pay levies related to their deposit bases.

A subsequent Banking Act was introduced in 1987, mainly in response to the collapse of Johnson Matthey Bankers (JMB) in 1984, which required a Bank-of-England-led rescue. The collapse raised the classic dilemma of whether to preserve the stability of the financial system or risk resource misuse and welfare losses from intervention. Hall (1987) argues that failure to act over JMB might have created a crisis of confidence among other banks, seriously undermined the London 'Gold Ring' and damaged London's invisible earnings. JMB exposed weaknesses in existing authorization procedures through the apparent incompetence of its management in areas such as loan diversification, credit monitoring, amount of security demanded and assessment of provisions. It also understated its two largest exposures and failed to report others; in its 1985 Annual Report, the Bank of England claimed that in June 1984 the reported figures were 38 and 34 per cent for the two largest exposures, compared with the 'real' figures of 76 and 39 per cent. JMB's auditors Arthur Young were also criticized—indeed, sued—for negligence.

The resultant 1987 Banking Act thus addressed issues directly arising out of the JMB affair. The two-tier authorization process was replaced by a single authorization to take deposits, and the minimum criteria were stiffened. The latter are set out in Schedule 3 of the Act (Bank of England 1988b) and include requirements for a bank to conduct its business in a prudent manner; to exercise caution on the composition of its board of Directors; to carry out its operations with 'integrity and skill'; to maintain a minimum asset level; and to ensure that directors, controllers and managers are 'fit and proper' persons.

'Prudent conduct' is essentially interpreted in terms of the internal strategy, systems and controls applied, with key considerations in terms of capital adequacy to sustain losses. In terms of the board composition, UK incorporated institutions should have as many non-executive directors as the Bank of England considers appropriate and these should play an important role as members of the institution's audit committee. High ethical standards are implied in the criteria relating to 'integrity' and are designed to protect the public against loss due to incompetence, dishonesty or malpractice. 'Skills' relate to the appropriate competitiveness of banks in conducting their business. The minimum asset level required by an institution on authorization will be £1 million (or equivalent in foreign currency or part sterling/foreign currency), and, although this requirement does not apply after authorization, institutions have to meet stringent capital adequacy requirements. The 'fit and proper' requirements are wide-ranging with regard to the skills, knowledge and judgemental capabilities of the individual in relation to the requirements of the position involved.

In deciding whether or not to grant authorization, the Bank will consider the above criteria, the likelihood of its receiving adequate, accurate information flows from the institution involved, and the institution's track record. Applicants not supported by an established deposit-taking organization have found it difficult to obtain authorization. Depositor interests are deemed to be a priority in all considerations.

For non-UK-based institutions, the Bank under Sec. 9(3) may be satisfied that the above criteria have been fulfilled if:

1. The banking supervisory authority in the country where most of the business is conducted informs the Bank that it is satisfied with respect to the prudent management and overall financial soundness of the institution.
2. The Bank is satisfied as to the nature and scope of the supervision exercised by that authority.

Even though some reliance is placed upon assurances from overseas supervisors, the bank examines the planned business of the UK branch, its liquidity, systems, controls and expertise. In the event of concerns, authorization is withheld. However, once authorization is confirmed, then supervision is the joint responsibility of the Bank and the home supervisor.

Other issues raised by the JMB affair were addressed in the Act, including stricter requirements for reporting accountants and auditors to carry out independent reviews of accounting and other records, systems and returns, and the encouragement of the appointment of audit committees. Notification of large exposures to individual customers or groups in excess of 10 per cent of a bank's capital base and prior notification of exposures in excess of 25 per cent were also required. Furthermore a Board of Banking Supervision was established to provide the bank with advice on supervisory matters. The Deposit Protection Scheme was enhanced as indicated above.

Thus, the 1987 Banking Act provides a statutory framework for supervision supplemented by notices and consultative papers from the Banking Supervision Division of the Bank of England. However, the Bank argues that it adopts a flexible approach, with much emphasis placed upon visits and discussions with the supervised banks. Additional statutory support is given by the 1986 Financial Services Act covering the regulation of all investment businesses.

6.3   THE GERMAN EXPERIENCE

Regulatory control in Germany is exercised by two bodies: the Bundesbank and the Federal Banking Supervisory Board. The impact of the former is manifest in operational areas, namely: limits for individual banks for which it will redis-count letters of credit or grant short-term Lombard loans; minimum reserve requirements; and statistical information needs. However, the main thrust of regulation comes from the Federal Banking Supervisory Board, an independent federal institution with ultimate responsibility to the Ministry of Finance. The Board's functions include deposit protection and safeguarding the orderly func-tioning of the banking system and, in turn, the economy from adverse banking developments. Its operational role is to approve banking licences, issue regula-tions on capital, liquidity and audit requirements, approve the appointment of senior staff, request information, conduct investigations and intervene as necessary.

The Board's operations are enshrined in the 1961 Banking Act (Kreditwesengesetz) and subsequent amendments. These have mainly been reac-tions to political pressures in the face of apparent faults in the banking system. Changes in 1976 followed the collapse of Bankhaus I. D. Herstatt and brought stricter rules on large exposures and disclosure requirements. Substantive changes with regard to consolidation of banking groups followed in 1985 after the rescue of Schroeder, Münchmeyer, Hengst and Co.

The Banking Act defines requirements for full authorization including capit-alization and prescribes structural rules on equity and liquidity, limitations on investments, large loans, related borrowers and information needs, such as audit, reporting and statements. The structural requirements include a set of principles relating to capital and liquidity. Principle I stipulates that a bank's volume of loans and investments should not exceed 18 times its equity capital, with loans weighted according to risk groups. Principle Ia sets out limits on commodity and foreign exchange exposure. Both of these principles were amended in 1990 to reflect the growth in off-balance-sheet transactions in swaps, options and similar 'risk assets' (see Deutsche Bundesbank 1990d). Principle II seeks to ensure suitable matching of long-term assets and liabilities. Principle III aims to guarantee funding of assets that are neither long term nor easily liquid; it also details rules on lending limits and procedures for the reporting and approval of loans, on consolidation of group activity, and on reporting and auditing activities.

Deposit protection schemes in Germany are voluntary, established by the various banking associations. Although the credit cooperatives set up support in the aftermath of the 1920s depression, it was not until 1966 that the private banking industry established a joint fund. In the aftermath of the Herstatt col-lapse, a comprehensive approach to protection was adopted by the commercial banks. The current scheme guarantees all sight, time and savings deposits of non-banks up to 30 per cent of the liable capital of the bank concerned per depositor. Deposit protection covers the entire member institution including its branches abroad with coverage for both domestic and foreign depositors. Although deposit protection schemes are widespread, membership is technically not a prerequisite for obtaining a banking licence. However, consultation between the Federal Banking Supervisory Board and the appropriate banking association occurs before licences are granted to prevent, as far as possible, deposit-taking institutions being established without a corresponding protection scheme. To finance the commercial banks fund, member banks have to pay an annual fee of 0.03 per mille of the balance sheet item, 'Liabilities to other creditors arising from banking business' (see Deutsche Bundesbank 1992b).

6.4   BANKING SUPERVISION AND INTERNATIONAL HARMONIZATION

As Baltensperger and Dermine (1987) argue, two main areas form the focus for the harmonization of international banking supervision. Firstly, should the responsibility of the domestic lender of last resort and deposit insurance systems extend to branches overseas? Should they cover branches and subsidiaries of foreign banks operating domestically? Secondly, should domestic regulation apply to all banks operating in the country (national treatment principle)? Should it apply to overseas branches of domestic banks operating abroad (home-country principle)?

The collapse of Bankhaus I. D. Herstatt in 1974 through foreign exchange speculation losses encouraged the formation of a Committee on Banking Regulations and Supervisory Practices under the direction of the Bank for International Settlements (BIS). Its recommendations became known as the *Basle Concordat* and broadly argued for joint supervisory responsibility, although supervision of liquidity was deemed to be the remit of the host country since foreign establishments generally have to conform to local practices for their liquidity management. Where a bank's liquidity could not be judged in isolation from the whole bank, it was seen to be subject to the source authority's monitoring. The supervision of solvency was essentially to be covered by the parent authority.

A revised Concordat in 1983 stemmed from the failure of Banco Ambrosiano, an Italian multinational group with a complex structure whose Luxembourg-based holding company had routed dubious loans via Latin American subsidiaries to Panamanian companies. Responsibility for lender-of-last-resort functions was deemed outside of its remit, but the new Concordat does cover 'consolidated supervision' with emphasis on the need for close cooperation among supervisors. The parent authority is to be responsible for ensuring the worldwide supervision of its domestic banks, but the host country is required to inform the parent where it feels unable to effect adequate supervision.

In the mid-1980s the BIS launched a new initiative in the area of bank

capital adequacy to raise standards to an acceptable level and encourage convergence of regulation among the G10 major industrialized nations. The Basle
Supervisors Committee, chaired by Peter Cooke, eventually set out recommendations with regard to the definition of bank capital and a timetable for the
attainment of minimum international standards. The Cooke initiative took place
in parallel with EC proposals relating to banking and solvency directives for all
credit institutions, not just banks.

In terms of capital adequacy, a 'tiered approach' was proposed to provide
a common framework into which various systems could fit and be compared.
Five tiers of capital may be defined, built up from the strictest (Tier 1) to the
broadest (Tier 5). Tier 1, or 'core' capital, includes ordinary shareholders' funds
and non-redeemable preference shares, and at least 50 per cent of capital should
include such 'core' elements; Tier 2 represents Tier 1 plus undisclosed reserves;
Tier 3 is Tier 2 plus asset revaluation reserves; Tier 4 is Tier 3 plus general
provisions; and Tier 5 is Tier 4 plus subordinated debt (up to a maximum of
50 per cent of Tiers 1–4). Risk-weights are applied to this framework ranging
from 0 per cent for cash to 100 per cent for commercial lending. The eventual
consensus in 1988 produced a minimum core capital adequacy ratio of 4 per
cent and a total capital ratio of 8 per cent to be achieved by end-1992 (Cooke
1990).

Harmonization of banking supervision is a concept consistent with European Community philosophy. However, in practice the common banking market
has still not fully evolved, and progress towards harmonization really began
only with the 1977 First Banking Coordination Directive. This established the
principle of 'home-country control', whereby effective supervision would shift
from the host to the parent supervisory authority, a move not entirely consistent
with the later Basle Concordat. In recent years the major supervisory initiatives
stemming from the EC have related to the completion of the internal market by
1992. The Single European Act in the context of banking calls for a single
banking licence, home-country control and mutual recognition, principles
incorporated into the 1988 Second Banking Directive. This establishes the 'passport principle', that authorization in one's home country is sufficient to allow
credit institutions to operate throughout the EC without further authorization.
Home-country regulation of solvency and large exposure will exist, but host-
country control will apply for monetary policy. Other directives on solvency
ratios and 'own' funds have followed, the former providing a minimum measure
of capital to be used by EC supervisors, the latter concerned with deriving a
uniform risk-weighting system in line with the Basle guidelines and the agreed
8 per cent minimum risk ratio.

The EC Commission also argued that deposit protection schemes should
exist in all member states. However, in spite of a 1986 'Recommendation' to
this effect, Table 6.1 shows that Portugal and Greece still lack such schemes.
Accordingly, and in the wake of the BCCI collapse, in May 1992 the Commission adopted a proposal for a directive to enshrine in law the need for such

schemes (EC Commission 1992a). Under this directive, all credit institutions will have to belong to one of these schemes which are intended to protect all depositors and hence safeguard the stability of the financial system.

Deposits will be refunded up to an amount of ECU15 000 if the financial situation of the credit institution holding them, or one of its branches in any member state, is such that the deposits are unavailable for 10 consecutive days. The amount stipulated is the minimum cover and is set in such a way that some element of risk occurs for individual depositors yet the vast majority of deposits will be covered. The minimum amount may be modified such that only a percentage of deposits may be refunded, the intention being to transfer some responsibility to the depositor for the safety of his or her deposits and the selection of suitable banks or credit institutions. Member states are also free to maintain higher guarantee ceilings, which would seem to be necessary given the relatively low level of prescribed cover.

With regard to depositor protection for branches of credit institutions from other member states, the draft directive follows the principle of deposit protection being provided by the deposit guarantee scheme of the home country. However, if the host-country scheme offers more comprehensive investor protection, then these branches must be allowed, on competitive grounds, to join the scheme. Thus, the proposal adds to the safety net established by the directives relating to solvency and the single banking licence, and to the Basle guidelines on capital adequacy.

Nevertheless, some issues have remained outstanding in recent years. Hall (1989) argues that national, especially UK-based, regulation lacks any explicit cost–benefit analysis to validate the supervisors' approaches. Lewis and Davis (1987) suggest that secrecy laws in offshore centres inhibit the application of consolidated supervision, and that some institutions escape regulation by being deemed non-banks. Moreover, efforts by one authority to tighten regulation may encourage relocation to less restrictive centres. Bourke (1988) implies that the Basle Concordat has missed the opportunity to provide international guidelines on areas such as financial reporting, information disclosure and the role of auditors. Some of these very issues have come to the fore in the context of BCCI (below) and are now the subject of current legislation.

6.5 IMPLICATIONS OF THE BCCI FAILURE

The collapse in July 1991 of the Bank of Credit and Commerce International (BCCI), referred to as the 'Bank of Crooks and Criminals International' by the Governor of the Bank of England, has been widely described in the press as the 'largest banking fraud in financial history' (Financial Times 1991). It may also be one of the longest-running, stretching back as far as the mid-1970s (see Appendix B).

The emerging picture is a complex web of shell companies, false loans, unrecorded deposits, concealed losses, phantom accounts and widespread fraud by senior managers. For example, a suspected fictitious person, A. R. Khalil, is shown in the accounts as having received US$150 million without any signed agreements or correspondence. Elsewhere BCCI's Treasury operation lost over US$850 million between 1977 and 1985, mainly through taking large positions in the futures markets. Moreover, there have been many allegations concerning BCCI's involvement with covert political, military, terrorist and drug-related groups worldwide. Some of these links have led to US convictions, such as in 1990 when BCCI executives were convicted of conspiracy to launder US$32 million of cocaine profits for Colombian drug barons. Elsewhere in the USA stories abound of fees paid to Washington legal firms, of bribes to African and Latin American leaders and of donations to win political favours.

It seems that BCCI was ultimately caught in a vicious circle of fraud. Covert operations aside, it ostensibly offered banking services to many developing countries considered excessively risky by Western banks and, not surprisingly, sustained substantial doubtful debts in the process. Various methods were used to conceal these and the above-mentioned Treasury losses, but eventually unrecorded deposits and loans had to be repaid, and funds diverted had to be replenished. Thus further deposits, loans and funds were necessary. It appears that BCCI was never truly profitable and eventually was unable to pay its debts as they fell due; and its assets were less than its liabilities—the two key tests of insolvency.

Such revelations by Price Waterhouse to the Bank of England precipitated the July 1991 winding-up petition, in which eight grounds were cited: fraudulent and dishonest management; concealment of those fraudulent activities and their consequences from the Bank of England and other regulators; concealment of the financial position of the company; unsatisfactory accounting records; inadequate systems and controls; lack of management integrity and skill; loss of Bank of England confidence in BCCI's senior management; insolvency. Given such a comprehensive indictment, many issues derive from the case, although here the focus is on supervision and compensation.

6.5.1 Supervisory issues

To state the obvious, it seems that there was grossly inadequate international supervision of BCCI. Although the bank had more regulators than many other banks, shared supervision in reality meant little or no supervision. Through an intricate control mechanism (Fig. 6.1), BCCI, registered in Luxembourg, owned by Middle East interests, run from London by Pakistanis, yet operating in offshore tax havens such as the Cayman Islands, was able to play its regulators off against each other.

With limited resources, neither the Luxembourg nor Cayman Islands' authorities, the main ones responsible for overseeing BCCI, were able to uncover the illicit operations. The Luxembourg authorities admitted their inability to

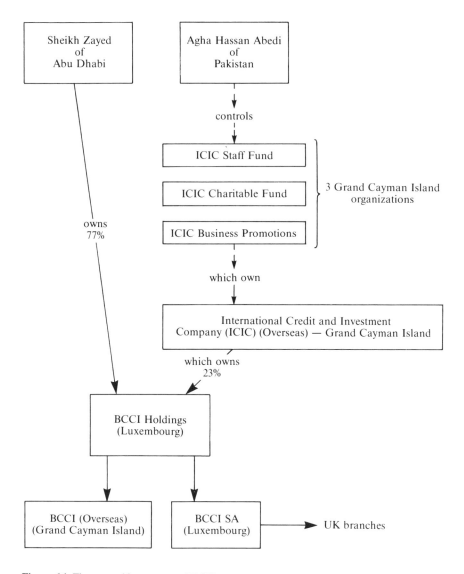

Figure 6.1 The ownership structure of BCCI

deal effectively with BCCI SA, and attempted unsuccessfully to get the bank incorporated elsewhere. Hall (1991a) alleges that BCCI offered to incorporate its branches and other operations in the UK in the mid-1980s but the Bank of England refused. Indeed, at the Bank's insistence the BCCI SA operating headquarters in London was transferred to Abu Dhabi in 1990. While it is clear that BCCI was an extraordinarily complex organization covering many jurisdictions, there is also the suspicion that regulators are more concerned to shift the burden of supervision than to consult with each other or take actions to expose a banking group.

The obsession with secrecy among central banks and regulators bodes ill for coordinated international regulation. The Bank of England might well be questioned for licensing BCCI a decade ago, when it had already been excluded from Saudi Arabia and New York. The Saudis distrusted the Pakistani background of BCCI, while, more poignantly, the New York authorities realized that BCCI had no primary regulator and could manipulate funds through tax havens without the Americans' knowledge. By granting BCCI a deposit-taking licence, the Bank of England gave it a measure of respectability, enabling it to open up elsewhere.

However, perhaps the most severe indictment of international attempts at supervision was the failure of the 'college of regulators', established in 1987 precisely to ensure effective coordinated supervision of BCCI. While the participants (Luxembourg, Cayman Islands, UK, UAE, France, Spain, Switzerland and Hong Kong) did agree on the shareholders' restructuring and capital proposals with incorporation in London, nevertheless, disagreements over responsibilities and action dissipated their effectiveness. Thus the Basle Concordat's ruling on consolidated supervision, which determines supervisory responsibilities among international regulators, appears to have been a marked failure in the case of BCCI. While, clearly, well orchestrated fraud may be hard to regulate and protect against, the international banking community cannot afford to be undermined by regulatory loopholes such as BCCI exploited.

For Europe this is of particular concern with the advent of the Single Market. Inherent in the 'passport principle' is the idea that host-country regulators will be dependent upon their European colleagues for the effective supervision of foreign branches operating within their territory. However, the EC has responded to the BCCI scandal with a proposal to make a bank's home country responsible for failures wherever they occur within the community. If this plan had been in force earlier, Luxembourg would have had to recompense BCCI depositors in the UK since BCCI SA, registered in Luxembourg, owned the UK business. The potential cost of such a scheme is seen as an incentive to improve supervision. The EC is also keen to improve the flow of information between regulators, to improve consolidated supervision and to outlaw BCCI-type banking structures. However, while further directives may be forthcoming, there is still a need to harmonize the resources and experience of supervisors throughout the EC.

At home, the domestic supervisory role of the Bank of England has come under criticism, namely that, with the evident long-standing concerns over BCCI, the Bank was dilatory in closing it down, although others, notably the shareholders in Abu Dhabi, complain that the actual closure was too hastily executed. Back in 1978 the Bank of England, concerned at BCCI's growth, limited its branches to 45 and refused it a full banking licence. Since then the

Bank has been aware of BCCI's drugs money laundering activities, its accounts held for terrorist groups and its flouting of international banking regulations, while offering unusually high interest rates and favourable credit terms. However, the Bank contends it had insufficient grounds for action until the Price Waterhouse report in June 1991.

In essence, supervisory authorities may close a bank, firstly, if deposits are threatened (BCCI had frequent, sizeable capital injections from its Middle East shareholders), and secondly, if the persons in charge are deemed not 'fit and proper'. On the latter grounds, the evidence found by Price Waterhouse allowed for closure. Moreover, the Bank had requested 10 reports from Price Waterhouse since they had taken over as sole auditors in 1987, and it appears that two of these, in April and October 1990, provided written evidence of fraud. Such reluctance to take action is consistent with the Bank's view that it should preserve banking institutions wherever possible for the sake of depositors.

However, this contrasts with the abrupt actual closure two days after the Abu Dhabi shareholders had submitted their latest plans for a restructuring of BCCI. The Bank of England argues that the evidence of fraud was too overwhelming, but existing depositors' interests may have been more harmed by that action than if the restructuring had gone ahead. Timewell (1991) implies that the Bank acted to avoid accusations of incompetence, knowing that the US authorities were building a case against BCCI leading to indictments on 29 July 1991.

In terms of available legislation, the Banking Act gives the Bank of England substantive powers, even though in discharging these it relies on auditors and overseas supervisors. However, more discretion and influence in the use of these powers might be beneficial. The Bank claimed it was unable to express its concerns publicly, and, more significantly, was prevented from handing material it held on BCCI to the American authorities in their action against BCCI.

The auditors Price Waterhouse have also been criticized for their work on BCCI, their apparent conflict of loyalties and their inability to uncover fraud or take action until their tenth report to the Bank of England. Clearly, depositors can have little confidence in bank audits if concerns are expressed solely in the form of short notes in the 'language of audit', or if auditors are prepared to sign off accounts, ignoring transactions they themselves have seriously queried. In part, Price Waterhouse's willingness to sign off the 1989 and 1990 accounts might have been a response to the accountancy industry's belief that its prime responsibility is to shareholders, and they did so on the condition that the major shareholders injected more funding into BCCI. However, this 'duty' later appears to have conflicted with that of advisor to the Bank of England. As sole auditors, Price Waterhouse were better placed to uncover the fraud and had a right to advise the Bank—but unfortunately, not a duty—under the Banking Act. A 'duty' might have encouraged them to probe more deeply and sooner.

Many of these criticisms have been highlighted by the influential, non-statutory Treasury inquiry under Lord Justice Bingham, set up firstly, to consider the supervision of BCCI under the 1987 Banking Act and the action taken by the authorities. The detailed findings (Bingham Report 1992) implied that: the Bank of England did not pursue the truth about BCCI with the vigour that BCCI's reputation and the information accruing to the Bank warranted; the Bank was 'timid' in its use of the powers at its disposal; it relied excessively on the auditors Price Waterhouse; and internal communications and structures within the Bank of England were inadequate to deal competently with the problems involved.

The second role of the Bingham inquiry was to recommend changes. With regard to UK banking supervision the report recognized this ultimately relies on the 'skill, alertness, experience and vigour' of the supervisors but saw scope for operational improvements. These include, firstly, the establishment of a trained and qualified special investigations unit within the supervision division to consider all evidence and suspicions of fraud and malpractice and ensure that they are investigated thoroughly. Secondly, the Bank's legal unit should be strengthened to ensure supervisors are fully cognizant with their legal powers. Thirdly, that procedures should be undertaken to strengthen internal communications, and fourthly, changes to the 1987 Banking Act should be made, if deemed necessary, to strengthen the Bank's powers to refuse or revoke authorization of licences of banks whose structures cannot be properly supervised. In response to these recommendations the Bank immediately established a Special Investigations and Legal Unit staffed by professional experts, and strengthened its capacity to conduct more extensive examination of banks on their own premises. It has also sought to improve the training of bank supervisors and enhance the effectiveness of the Board of Banking Supervision, the senior staff whose role was undermined by the inadequate information they received about BCCI.

With regard to EC and international supervision the Bingham Report recommended that the Second Banking Coordination Directive should confer on EC states the right to refuse or withdraw authorization in the case of structures deemed inappropriate for entities undertaking banking activities. Moroever, Bingham felt that the EC's proposal, that a bank's place of incorporation should be its home and that head offices should be in the same state as registered offices, should be incorporated formally into the directive. The report also suggested the need for international monitoring of supervisory standards, possibly under the auspices of the BIS. The findings were less critical of Price Waterhouse, but argued that auditors should have a legal duty to report information relevant for supervisory purposes to the Bank of England, a feature to be incorporated into amendments to the 1987 Banking Act. Moreover, the Bank should have the power to require a separate audit of banks domiciled outside the EC.

6.5.2 Compensation issues

Earlier criticism was made of deposit insurance schemes in terms of their coverage, harmonization and inequality. These comments appear substantiated in the aftermath of BCCI as the maximum payout of £15 000 per customer in the UK is dwarfed by the scale of support (£250 million) needed to refund BCCI's 120 000 UK customers, and by the payouts elsewhere in Europe. Defenders of the UK scheme might argue that it belies what depositors actually receive because liquidators often get back a proportion of bank assets for distribution to depositors. Moreover, too much depositor protection has played a role in the demise of US savings and loans banks. Neither of these points was any comfort to BCCI depositors who contended they were too heavily exposed. Moreover, protection is available only for sterling deposits, whereas many UK-based Asian customers of BCCI had dollar accounts. An added complication is that large numbers of 'offset' deals operated, whereby BCCI customers were given financial facilities in the UK against collateral overseas in India, Pakistan and East Africa. If forced to repay loans, they might have to realize these overseas assets and bring the funds to the UK, which could lead to further tax liabilities.

Concerted action through depositor support groups has been directed towards pressurizing the UK authorities into providing compensation. In turn, the High Street banks have been levied to subscribe around £100 million to restore the depleted Deposit Protection Fund, but in turn they are requiring amendments to it. Current quotas are related to the size of the sterling deposit base of each bank, irrespective of profitability. The banks want regulators in the home country of a failed bank to pay deposit protection, in line with the EC proposals, rather than in accordance with the current host-country scheme. There is also a clear need for a European minimum level, given the disparity of protection among nations. The Bingham inquiry also recommended that the EC directive should impose a deposit guarantee obligation in respect of qualifying liabilities in member states other than the bank's home state.

BCCI creditors in the UK may have recourse through the courts if they can prove negligence on the part of the auditors or the Bank of England, and the Bingham Report findings may encourage some test cases. However, a US$1.7 billion compensation package has been devised by the liquidators and the Abu Dhabi shareholders, which is generally expected to be accepted and compensation payments should begin in 1993. Realizable BCCI assets were put at US$1.15 billion, compared with liabilities of US$10.6 billion (Hall 1992a).

Other avenues of legal action considered were against the money brokers and investment advisers who deposited customer funds with BCCI. Some 50–60 local authorities are thought to have had money on deposit with the failed bank. They argue that their money brokers had a duty to inform them that the bank was in difficulty; whereas the money brokers defend their position, saying they are subject to the Bank of England 'Grey Paper' (*The Regulation of the Wholesale Markets in Sterling Foreign Exchange and Bullion*) and the London Code of Conduct. These guidelines, which exempt money brokers from the provisions of the 1986 Financial Services Act and put them under direct control of the Bank, place ultimate responsibility for investment decisions with local authority Treasurers.

6.5.3 'Caveat emptor'

The BCCI closure has dealt bitter blows to large numbers of its customers ranging from Asian entrepreneurs to major local authorities. Many argue that they are innocent victims of fraud on a global scale, lured into the false belief that BCCI was a safe bank with which to do business. As we have seen, much of their anger and frustration has been directed towards the regulatory authorities. However, the scandal also reminds us that the dictum *caveat emptor* is particularly appropriate, and that customers might therefore improve their lot by remembering some basic principles about international finance.

The modern banking environment may be viewed as highly competitive, innovative and global. There is over-capacity, falling profits, a plethora of new products and services; and there are many fringe operators, often with their roots outside of banking, such as retailers offering financial services. Market forces are impeded by regulation and government reluctance to allow bank failures, sometimes through the mechanism of state control of enterprises that would otherwise go under. Yet as we noted, government protection is patchy and loopholes do occur. If this scenario is accurate, then the principle of the trade-off between risk and return will apply.

As we have seen, BCCI's reputation for dubious activities stretches back to 1978; and, with the more recent convictions over drugs money laundering, warning bells should have sounded for many depositors. In the wholesale money markets, in order to attract deposits BCCI offered money brokers higher commissions to encourage them to seek depositors. For their part, the depositors were attracted by the unusually high returns, although one local authority— York City Council—claimed that one of its money brokers offered no alternative to investing with BCCI. At the retail level BCCI also offered higher returns on deposits; so clearly, one basic lesson in a competitive financial world is that, if an organization is offering abnormally better rates to attract deposits, there may well be a corresponding risk.

Moreover, whatever the bank or financial institution, the risk–return trade-off should indicate the need to diversify or spread risks. Some 30 local authorities face losses of more than £1 million each, with the Western Isles having had £23 million on deposit with BCCI. Notwithstanding their arguments that BCCI was on an 'approved' Bank of England list of banks licensed under the 1987 Banking Act, it would seem highly imprudent of professionally qualified, public-sector employees to risk placing so many funds with one institution.

The nature of BCCI's banking operations should also have alerted those borrowing from the bank or financing their trade through it; yet again, the lure of cheaper loans and the bank's willingness to do business that others would not proved enticing. For example, BCCI was active in the documentary credit business, including back-to-back credits frowned upon by many Western banks which enabled cargoes to be routed between unfriendly countries via a third country. Here two letters of credit would be involved, where a second or outward credit is opened on the strength of a first or prime (inward) one. However, the two credits operate independently, and should the terms and conditions of the second credit not be fulfilled, the bank issuing it may not get recompensed. BCCI also dealt with many high-risk countries; for example, it handled the finance of the vast bulk of trade to Bangladesh, and for a time was the only bank confirming letters of credit to Nigeria. It was also the first international bank into China.

There are various other pointers for customers seeking evidence of bank safety. If it has a spread of profitable activities, is a component of a diversified, regulated, banking system, or is publicly or mutually owned, then its chances of survival would seem better. Other indices are its share price, its rating with credit agencies and banking analysts, and the flow of information it provides from reports and accounts and from returns to the banking authorities. While BCCI was not highly specialized, as were the US savings and loans banks, it certainly contrived to mislead in the context of information and regulation, doing its best not to be associated with any strongly supervised locality. Indeed, in this context its demise warns of the dangers of poorly regulated offshore banking centres and 'fringe banks'. Banking centres offering secrecy, such as Liechtenstein and Switzerland, will be adversely affected by the BCCI affair, as will banks from the developing world, especially in the Middle East and Asia. Although the systematic risks to banking communities from BCCI's closure would appear to be limited given the uniqueness of its situation, nevertheless, there has been some 'flight to quality' with the switching of deposits.

CONCLUSIONS

With the advent of the European Financial Common Market, the collapse of BCCI is a timely reminder of the need for competent banking supervision and adequate investor protection. Banking supervision has tended to focus on the overall stability of the sector to prevent individual bank 'runs' causing contagion. Hence guidelines on domestic operations permitted, and capital requirements have received, high priority. Deposit protection has been given secondary consideration, possibly a function of the view that a properly regulated system does not require it. However, the rapid growth and internationalization of banking in the 1980s, encouraged by market liberalization, offered new innovations, opportunities and risks. It would seem that regulation has struggled to keep pace with the changes, especially as pressures for deregulation exist in many areas of financial services and 'interference' by authorities has not been popular.

The complexity of the BCCI structure and the lengths the group took to mislead the authorities point to the need for greater harmonization of procedures. The collapse highlights weaknesses in crucial areas of overlapping supervision, international coordination, the timing of action, information disclosure, audit responsibilities and deposit insurance, as well as instances of depositor irresponsibility.

Although there is no guarantee against fraud or illegal behaviour, recognition has been made of the need to improve collective supervisory responsibility. Specifically, the July 1992 revisions to the Basle Concordat aim to close the very loopholes that BCCI exposed. They are designed to ensure that no bank may establish branches abroad without the whole group being subject to effective supervision. The core features are, firstly, that all international banking groups must be supervised by a home-country authority capable of performing effective consolidated supervision; this establishes the need for a lead regulator with sufficient power to stop the establishment of banking structures that prevent effective supervision. Secondly, banks establishing branches outside the home country require the consent of both the home-country and host-country regulators. Thirdly, supervisors should possess the right to gather information from the cross-border banking establishments of the banks or banking groups for which they are the home-country supervisor. Fourthly, host-country supervisors should have the power to prevent a bank setting up under their jurisdiction or should take other restrictive measures deemed necessary.

These measures, together with the Bank of England responses to the Bingham Report and the EC directive on formalizing the establishment of deposit protection schemes, go some way to rectifying the weaknesses BCCI exposed. Meanwhile the financial environment becomes more complicated, especially with the growth of 'Bancassurance' and other links between financial and non-financial entities. In an EC context, the 'single-licence' concept does not ease the supervisory problem, nor does the prospect of an enlarged Community, especially with members whose regulatory regimes are suspect.

FURTHER READING

On bank failures see Hall (1989), and for the theory of banking supervision see Diamond and Dybvig (1983) and Baltensperger and Dermine (1987). For deposit insurance see Dale (1984). The Basle Concordats are covered by Cooke (1990). For the background to BCCI see Financial Times (1991), and for the regulatory and supervisory issues see the Bingham Report (1992). The whole BCCI affair is reviewed by Hall in a series of articles (Hall 1991a,b,c, and 1992a,b).

THREE

FINANCE AND THE PRIVATE SECTOR

FINANCIAL INSTITUTIONS: STRATEGIC ISSUES FOR THE 1990s

7.1 CHANGE AND THE FINANCIAL SYSTEM

The lifetime of the EC has been one of unprecedented change for most financial institutions, in marked contrast to the gradual evolution characteristic of the previous two hundred years. For much of the eighteenth and nineteenth centuries financial activities were dominated by trading centres such as London and Paris, whose institutions served wide areas of the world as effectively 'colonial outposts'. Gradually, domestic institutions grew with the establishment of national central banks, and the typical emergent pattern was of a specialized yet relatively inert system and one that Sayers (1967) argued did not easily cross national frontiers.

The binding forces were those of established custom and practice, concentration via mergers and economies of scale, and protectionism. In the UK the latter stemmed from the Bank of England's desire to curb fears of inadequate investor protection and systematic risk by encouraging oligopolistic, self-regulating clubs such as the Acceptance Houses Committee (AHC), the Committee of London and Scottish Clearing Banks (CLSCB), and the Building Societies Association (BSA). For members benefits arose from restricted access and control of competition, largely through interest rate agreements, as in the case of the clearing banks, which fixed borrowing and lending rates by collective agreement and by 1955 held three times the deposits of the building societies.

This relatively stable pattern was interrupted by a series of interconnected developments, including the growth of wholesale banking, the internationalization of operations, product innovation and technical developments, deregulation, intensified competition, and a shift from the focus on institutions to that on markets. In the 1960s the emergence of wholesale banking was spurred by the growth of the Eurocurrency markets and the entry of US banks, especially into the UK market. The traditional demarcations between markets and institutions began to be eroded as the latter competed for a wider range of activities. Whereas most banks had relied on short-term deposits to fund their essentially short-term lending portfolios, the new money and interbank markets enabled liability management with banks bidding for funds as required (see Harrington 1990). This reduced dependence upon the slowly growing deposit base and traditional liquidity needs. Bank assets in cash and liquid Treasury bills fell in favour of short-term money-market loans, while bank liabilities in the form of funds from the wholesale markets rapidly increased. This advantage of raising liquid funds was transmitted into increased lending, but greater reliance on the markets also brought disadvantages, notably mismatches in maturities, currencies and interest rates.

During the 1970s the pace of change quickened in an era of deregulation and competition which transformed the financial system and spawned significant financial innovations. Perhaps more significant was the '*internationalization*' of European banking as 1960s American entrants to the Eurodollar market were joined by Japanese and European banks. The recycling of oil revenues in the form of large-scale 'sovereign loans' to developing countries became a feature of the 1970s, but equally, European deposit banks were keen to circumvent domestic lending restrictions and raise their international profile. Consequently overseas lending rose substantially but was not matched by traditional sources of supply, so that the role of the markets was strengthened further. Financial innovations began to emerge to cope with increased interest rate volatility. Among these measures, the use of LIBOR-linked floating-rate (as opposed to fixed-rate) contracts, roll-over credits, money-market funds, swaps and offshore centres was significant, as were associated developments in computing and telecommunications to effect and speed up transactions.

In general, banks became more growth- and profit-oriented and thus more aggressively competitive. In international markets, the absence of formal controls over Eurocurrency operations meant that regulation was by the price mechanism, and as new entrants swelled the market, not surprisingly margins fell, thus further spurring the drive for innovation and efficiency. The competitive search for profit was also manifest in domestic operations. In the UK the first real phase of deregulation had occurred in 1971 with the abolition of credit controls and the interest rate cartel under Competition and Credit Control (CCC). Thereafter lending expanded, notably to the corporate sector, which needed to supplement internal funding with longer-term bank finance. There was a marked shift away from fixed-interest debentures in favour of floating-rate term loans in an effort to cope with declining rates of return, volatile inflation and interest rates. For personal customers retail banks offered little by way of interest-bearing accounts in spite of high nominal interest rates; thus, increasingly funds found their way to other institutions—life assurance and pension funds, unit trusts and building societies, the latter of which grew on the strength of the housing boom in the late 1970s and generous tax concessions.

The events of the 1970s were significant but not sufficient to break the dominant oligopolistic 'club' structures characteristic of many national financial systems. Indeed, in the UK a series of mergers had produced the 'Big Four' clearing banks and to some extent had reinforced the pattern. However, a second phase of deregulation began in 1979 with the abolition of exchange controls and this coincided with the election of the pro-market Thatcher government. The resultant surge in overseas investment undermined the effectiveness of the supplementary special deposits 'Corset' and this was abolished in 1980 as were consumer instalment credit controls in 1982. Thereafter competition between financial institutions intensified as the banks returned to the retail deposit market to fund their lending. Free of 'Corset' restrictions, the clearing banks attacked the mortgage market while the building societies remained subject to restrictive legislation until 1986. Ultimately the building societies were able to seek whole-sale market funding and change their orientation as with the transfer of Abbey National to plc status. Thus their liability structure became more akin to that of the banks. The intensively competitive environment in the UK was mirrored elsewhere in Europe as savings and commercial banks began to compete more actively for similar business.

The greater attention paid to domestic retail markets was in part a reaction to changes in the international environment. Whereas during the inflationary period of the 1970s syndicated Eurocurrency lending dominated bank expansion, the advent of the 1982 debt crisis reduced the attractiveness of such loans. The prospect of bank failure thus encouraged a switch in lending towards OECD borrowers, but bank responses to the crisis also included increased provisions and rights issues to augment their capital bases. However, the most significant feature, with far-ranging implications for financial systems, was the growth of '*securitization*', whereby securities trading replaced bank lending. For banks securitization offered opportunities to earn fee income, to alter asset portfolios by trading securities rather than waiting for loans to mature and thus overcome maturity mismatches, and to shift risk in so far as non-bank investors were willing to hold the traded securities. For corporate borrowers, security issues were often cheaper than bank borrowing; they offered a wider range of funding, and the risks attached to being locked into unfavourable rates or terms could be alleviated by refinancing or swapping interest obligations.

Securitization assisted by technological innovation spawned new instruments. Long-term straight and floating-rate bond issues grew in significance and were joined by note issuance facilities (NIFs), revolving underwriting facilities (RUFs) and later Eurocommercial paper (ECP). Essentially, these allowed borrowers to obtain term funding against the issue of renewable short-term notes. Initially banks underwrote these (NIFs, RUFs) but later they provided informal standby facilities (ECP). Traditional syndicated loans were securitized by trading sub-participations, whereas OECD corporate customers began to issue hybrid securities often in the form of preference shares, convertible loan stock and debt with warrants. Such developments thus implied the exchange of traditional corporate lending for newer, riskier investment banking activities. Thus, banks had to improve their risk management and pricing capabilities in the face of the debt crisis, yet raise profits under fiercely competitive conditions. Off-balance-sheet operations, notably guarantees, were therefore favoured as alternative income sources, and risks could be hedged in the emergent futures and options markets. The ability to cover risks encouraged the use of interest rate guarantees and currency swaps, and so served to bring domestic and international financial markets closer together.

Such financial innovations and market integration have been assisted by technological advances speeding up payments and communications, so that reference is often made to the '*globalization*' of finance and the concept of 24-hour financial trading based on the three key centres of London, Tokyo and New York. However, securitization has not eased the position of traditional banking institutions in the 1980s and 1990s. Financial innovations have driven down the profit on wholesale business and securitization has brought forth new competitors. By the mid-1980s investment and merchant banks, securities brokers and dealers had all become significant operators in the new international financial system, leaving deposit banks the choice of reallocating resources to these new areas or retreating into domestic markets (Metais 1990).

The above trends have influenced the developing character of European financial systems, and with the completion of the internal market the process of change will continue apace. However, international and technological developments affect national financial sectors in differing ways, and this begs the question of which patterns and competitive strengths are likely to dominate the Europe of the 1990s and how these will affect the economies involved.

7.2 THE FUNCTION OF THE FINANCIAL SYSTEM

At its simplest level, the financial system consists of those institutions and markets that enable funds to be transferred from those who save to those who invest. This is traditionally associated with the financial intermediation role seen in the context of retail deposit banks who open accounts for savers (ultimate lenders) and channel these deposits via advances to the ultimate borrowers. However, financial intermediation involves more than merely passing on funds, since the provision of investible funds involves the creation of financial assets or claims by financial institutions themselves. The bank will hold a financial claim (asset) on the ultimate borrower to repay the loan (liability to borrower), while ultimate lenders deposit their funds (assets) in bank accounts and hold financial claims against the bank (liabilities to bank).

The outputs of the financial system are a varied range of services and advice. The core functions relating to savings include operating payments mechanisms (e.g. banks); maturity transformation (e.g. short-term building society deposits used to fund long-term mortgages); aggregation of long-term savings to optimize return and lower costs (e.g. institutional investors); facilities for direct marketable asset purchase (e.g. company rights issues to existing shareholders) and financial security (most institutions). In addition, the financial system provides other services: advice, disintermediation (e.g. the inter-company market for direct company borrowing), valuation via share quotation, and liquidity through money markets allowing short-term portfolio management. Arguably the most significant function of a developed financial system, however, is its role in enabling the economy to carry risk, an activity central to the spread of innovation and growth.

Financial innovation involves risk-pooling and transformation, while modern markets are often specifically geared to risk-hedging, as witnessed by the growth of futures and options markets. Risk-pooling advantages derive from economies of scale, whereby institutions know that the statistical probability of claims on the deposits they hold or defaults on the loans they grant is small relative to the funds involved. In the absence of such advantages depositors, as ultimate lenders, would be reluctant to lend directly to ultimate borrowers for fear of loss. Risk transformation arises when intermediaries create assets that are more liquid than those they themselves hold. For example, bank deposits, largely repayable on demand, represent highly liquid assets to depositors who benefit from access, convenience, security, etc. However, the deposited funds are used by the banks for lending often over several years. Given that most individual ultimate lenders wish to lend relatively small amounts for short periods for a secure return, and most borrowers wish to borrow for as long as possible, banks, building societies and similar intermediaries offer 'contracts' to both parties which resolve these opposing needs, and differ in content from what would have been the case had there been a direct lending operation between lender and borrower.

The extent of intermediation derives from the risk-return optimization of financial institutions within the constraints of market organization, regulation and costs. Rybcynski (1984, 1985) suggests that the structural evolution of the financial system may be related to its risk-carrying capacity and that it develops in a three-phase process: initially bank intermediation dominates; then market orientation; and finally securitized or strong market orientation. The advent of industrialization requires that reliance upon retained earnings and direct lending to firms by wealthy entrepreneurs is supplemented by external, institutional funding. Banks, in particular, dominate the provision of working capital, whereas in the early phase of industrialization risk capital is provided by the owner–managers of the firm. The main function of the financial system is one of intermediation, that is the provision of new capital channelled from ultimate savers to borrowers via loans. In general, capital markets are limited and underdeveloped. Market orientation is associated with the growth of capital and credit markets which channel savers' funds more directly to industry. They price the risk–reward trade-off, provide a mechanism for borrowers and lenders to diversify their risk, and facilitate the divorce of ownership from control and the use of professional management. Financial intermediaries themselves also make use of markets in this phase in order to fund their operations.

Ultimately the function of the financial system expands with advanced technological progress, the internationalization and deregulation of financial services, and the move towards post-industrial societies and market economies. The nature and integration of financial markets grows with demands for venture capital funds, hedging facilities and securitized asset trading. Banks, building societies and other intermediaries raise more of their funds in the wholesale money and capital markets. Consumer debt increases, and their savings are institutionalized via pension funds and insurance companies rather than channelled directly to borrowers.

The evolution into a securitized financial system in theory enhances the economy's ability to carry risk. In the first place, markets become more significant for channelling larger volumes of savings, yet offer a wide variety of innovative financial instruments offering different risk–reward trade-offs. Secondly, the ownership of resources encompasses institutional investors whereas control is in the hands of appointed professional managers; thus, performance evaluation and monitoring is more widespread and competition aids the use of resources. Enhanced risk-carrying capacity therefore assists capital formation, savings and economic growth.

However, the evolutionary process is modified by the existing regulatory framework. If this imposes obstacles to charging market prices for savings, hinders financial innovation or restricts the operations of institutions, change will be hampered. The prevailing regulatory framework is a complex function determined by a wide variety of political and economic influences. Deregulation is currently popular with governments of varying political persuasion, prompted by underlying shifts towards greater emphasis on market forces. In terms of specific economic influences, Stigler (1986) cites the abolition of interest rate ceilings, minimum commissions and the growth of non-bank financial intermediaries in the USA as responses to inflation, high interest rates, institutional investment and computerization rather than revulsion against public regulation. In the UK in the early 1980s, institutional pressures over commission rates and external competition threatened to undermine stock exchange business, hence hastening reform. In Europe recent policy efforts have favoured the evolution of financial systems and thus have encouraged deregulation, notwithstanding problems of seeking a philosophical and practical balance between disproportionate intervention or liberalization. The need for safeguards arises to prevent users of funds assuming risks that savers would deem excessive, hence re-regulation is often a more appropriate concept—for example the 1986 Financial Services Act in the UK with its system of self-regulatory organizations.

The Rybcynski model provides intuitive appeal and a convenient framework for evaluating the relative development of financial systems in Europe, especially for contrasting strongly bank-oriented and market-oriented ones. However, it should be borne in mind that financial systems evolve in differing timescales and not necessarily in the same prescriptive stages postulated in the model. Rapid 'marketization' of many European systems has occurred since the mid-1980s, and in some instances, notably France and Germany, strongly bank-dominated systems are developing sophisticated derivative, risk-hedging markets without having developed capital market systems, thus effectively missing phase 2. Moreover, it is easy to assume from the model that strongly market-oriented systems will lead to less risk and better growth than bank-dominated ones. But securitized systems have been far from immune from exposure to risk, as can be seen in the context of insider dealing scandals in the UK and USA and the worldwide stock market crash of October 1987. In terms of economic performance, bank-dominated systems have existed within very advanced economies such as Germany. However, they have evolved to promote wider 'universal' roles for banks, including the provision of risk capital as well as basic intermediation. Thus it is appropriate to consider institutional and market developments separately, in order to assess the financial system as a whole. European financial markets are considered in Chapter 8.

7.3 FINANCIAL INSTITUTIONS IN THE UK, GERMANY AND FRANCE

7.3.1 The UK

Within a European Community context, the UK has the most developed, open, diverse and strongly market-oriented financial system. Coexistent with established capital, risk-hedging markets and money markets is a formidable array of domestic and international institutions concerned with bank and non-bank financial intermediation (BFI and NBFI). Thus, the functional classification in Table 7.1 provides a convenient breakdown of UK financial institutions but is not without ambiguity, as a glance at the annual report of any one of the UK banking groups or major insurance companies shows. For example, Lloyds Bank plc has subsidiaries and associate companies operating in leasing, credit factoring and insurance (Lloyds Abbey Life).

Primary retail banking sector   As with any financial system, the main institutional players in the UK are the banks, notwithstanding the uniquely important position of the building societies and institutional investors. The UK banking sector is often classified into retail (primary) and wholesale (secondary) banks, which, although useful for analysis, belies the diverse range of activities operated by banks in both groups. Howcoft and Lavis (1986) define retail banking

Table 7.1 UK financial institutions

Sector/institution	Examples
Primary retail banking sector (21)[a]	English, Scottish and Northern Ireland clearing banks (e.g. Barclays, Lloyds, Midland, Natwest)
	Girobank plc
	TSB plc
	Bank of England Banking Department
	Abbey National plc
	Discount houses (8)[a]
Secondary banking sector	British merchant banks (33)[a]
	Other British banks (136)[a,b]
	Overseas and consortium banks (273)[c]
Other deposit-taking institutions	Building societies
	National savings
Miscellaneous financial institutions	Insurance companies
	Pension funds
	Investment trusts
	Unit trusts

[a] Number of institutions included in Bank of England classification of banks as at 31 December 1991. For full listing see Bank of England (1992b).

[b] Includes finance companies.

[c] Includes 38 American and 32 Japanese banks.

in terms of branch-based activity focused on the personal sector, but further suggest that it should incorporate institutions providing a range of related services: money transmission, deposit and credit services and some forms of financial advice. Lewis and Davis (1987) define it in terms of services to individuals and small businesses where large-volume, low-value business is involved, whereas wholesale banking encompasses customers who tend to be large corporate or government entities and the transactions small in volume and high in value.

Although the Bank of England lists 21 retail banks in the UK, in common with concentration elsewhere in Europe the system is dominated by the 'Big Four'; Barclays, National Westminster (NatWest), Midland and Lloyds, known, together with the TSB and Co-operative banks, as the London clearing banks' (LCBs). This title is somewhat misleading in that, firstly, responsibility for payments and clearings is now vested in a wider grouping, the Association for Payment Clearing Services (APACS), and, secondly, through their extensive branch networks these institutions have a national and international distribution. The high degree of industry concentration reflects largely the economies of scale inherent in a relatively standardized business such as retail banking. The clearing system is expensive to maintain, so further expansion by adding deposits needs to be accompanied by a less-than-proportionate cost increase, a rationale for economies in data processing which helped prompt the 1968 merger between National Provincial and Westminster Banks. Size also confers stability in terms of deposit withdrawals relative to total assets, and, with the large branch network allowing for internal cash transfers, both aspects enable economies to be made in the amount of liquid assets held. Moreover, size and geographical diversity permit risks to be spread among many different regions, borrowers and industries (Gilbody 1988).

The 1980s was a difficult decade for the UK retail banks in which their traditional functions, structures and profitability altered markedly. The forces of concentration and competition encouraged diversification into wholesale banking and capital and securities markets operations. Consequently, one major issue has been to integrate corporate cultures and styles within appropriate organizational frameworks. Traditional clearing bank hierarchical structures contained a high degree of integration in which branch networks and regional geographical organization were emphasized. Any new services and technological developments, such as cash management, were geared to support existing frameworks, with non-mainstream activities loosely coordinated via separate subsidiaries. However, diversification into areas such as securities market operations has rendered many of these structures inflexible and inefficient, and has encouraged a more profit-centred approach in which management responsibility has been pushed increasingly down the hierarchy and greater attention has been paid to branch profitability and alternative delivery mechanisms.

In terms of retail banking functions, Table 7.2 shows that the traditional intermediation role of recycling personal-sector deposits into business loans has altered in favour of greater lending to the personal sector and recycling business deposits to the corporate sector. The major areas of expansion have been, firstly, mortgage lending, and secondly, loans to and from the wholesale financial markets. As Johnson (1988) comments, home ownership and the City have been the twin poles of banking growth.

These changes are associated with a shift in bank emphasis from asset to liability management. Traditionally, retail banks took the supply of deposits as a given function of their money transmission service and were able to enjoy the benefits of essentially 'free' capital and the endowment effect: namely, paying minimal non-market-related interest on deposits while lending at cartel-determined base rates plus a margin. Returns thus reflected the ability to manage assets and lend profitably. However, rising interest rates, reduced savings growth, aggressive competition for those savings from the building societies and the rising costs of operating the money transmission service and banking network have meant that retail deposits have become more expensive and moreover have not matched the banks' asset growth. Personal-sector savers have been more selective in their choice of institution and the returns they offer. By 1980 building societies held 54 per cent of personal deposits compared with 30 per

Table 7.2 Selected transactions with UK financial institutions, 1980–1990 (£millions)

	1980	1982	1984	1986	1988	1990
Personal sector						
£ sight deposits	711	2 302	3 212	7 266	8 605	8 574
£ time deposits	5 530	1 343	−252	910	8 152	7 031
Foreign currency deposits	364	143	358	31	292	538
Deposits with building societies	7 175	10 294	13 269	11 856	20 237	17 964
Bank borrowing (non-housing)						
Sterling	−2 814	−4 794	−4 169	−5 168	−12 636	−7 726
Foreign currency	−151	−195	−5	−22	−292	−360
Loans for house purchase						
Building societies	−5 715	−8 133	−14 530	−19 427	−23 720	−24 103
Banks	−500	−5 078	−2 043	−5 196	−10 909	−7 186
Other institutions	−1 153	−917	−468	−2 363	−5 414	−2 500
Life assurance/pension funds	−12 845	15 557	19 292	21 342	24 834	37 138
Industrial and commercial customers						
£ sight deposits	−324	359	1 359	3 552	1 734	1 595
£ time deposits	2 519	114	1 132	4 807	3 066	894
Foreign currency	760	1 096	−1 171	3 011	427	4 214
Banks						
£ sight deposits	−676	−4 362	−7 682	−14 457	−12 758	−12 840
£ time deposits	−12 516	−7 634	−8 675	−16 314	−39 980	−30 726
Foreign currency	−31 804	−21 025	−19 782	−66 079	−23 774	−44 837
Bank lending (£)	11 892	12 363	15 996	26 808	49 061	37 537

cent among the retail banks, and during the next decade building society deposits grew at 15 per cent p.a., compared with 11 per cent p.a. for the banks, so that by 1990 the banks' share was below 25 per cent. This trend has prompted greater liability management as the shortfall in the deposit base has had to be made up by wholesale deposits, whose cost is based on money-market rates, thereby raising funding costs. Thus, retail banks have become more cost-conscious as a whole, introducing charges on their money transmission services and rationalizing their branch overheads.

On the assets side, the long-term shift from corporate to personal borrowing partly reflects the greater variety in financing sources available to companies in recent years. However, retail banks have actively sought to compete with the building societies in mortgage lending, and by 1988 before the downturn in the housing market they supplied £10.9 billion (27 per cent) of house purchase loans compared with £23.7 billion (59 per cent) for the building societies. Equally significant has been the expansion in consumer credit, which swelled sterling bank lending to all sectors (apart from housing loans) to a massive £55 billion in 1990 in spite of high interest rates. Although banks themselves provide half of this lending, their involvement has increased through their credit-card subsidiaries and the credit they extend to retailers.

On top of these trends, the earlier mentioned securitization of the financial system has encouraged retail banks to enter newer, riskier, often off-balance-sheet business with more attention paid to fee income rather than interest spreads. This reflects pressures to retain corporate customers who will seek alternative and sophisticated funding sources. However, significant bad-debt provisions incurred by their international divisions on developing country debts compounded the difficulties of the 'Big Four' in the late 1980s, to which were added domestic bad debts in 1990 and 1991. Although their capital–asset ratios have in general met the Basle Concordat guidelines (see Chapter 6), bank balance sheets and profitability have been weakened, and have led to greater concern with cost control and capital maintenance.

In terms of income, the aforementioned competition for deposits in the late 1980s included the payment of current account interest, while competition for loans forced the banks to target low-margin mortgage and large corporate business, thus putting downward pressure on net interest margins. However, this differential was partly reversed as the recession developed and the glut of capital vanished. Service profitability was restored, but at the cost of deteriorating customer relations as charges leapt at a time when customers were forced to seek 'distress lending'.

Costs have continued to rise rapidly, averaging a growth rate of 8 per cent p.a. for the 'Big Four' in 1990 and 1991. The expense of maintaining the branch networks is manifestly high, although major cuts have been made in both branches and staff, especially since 1988. Early in 1991 Barclays announced a programme of job cuts totalling 15 000 to 1995, and that same year the 'Big Four' closed 520 branches. These reductions have been made possible by technological advances in data-processing and payments mechanisms which are capital-intensive. However, in addition to operating revenue and expenditure, bank profits are influenced by their own reporting procedures, notably in the context of bad-debt provisions.

Table 7.3 shows a deteriorating picture since 1987; indeed, the 1991 results were the worst since the 1930s. Between 1975 and 1986 the Big Four clearing banks made total provisions of £7.8 billion, but between 1987 and 1990 these rose to £15.3 billion or some 69 per cent of operating profits (Llewellyn 1992). In 1987 alone some £3.4 billion was specifically set aside against the risk of non-payment from LDCs out of provisions totalling £4.3 billion. However, by the end of 1989 exposure to and provisions for LDC debt had been significantly cut and were overtaken by non-LDC provisions as the domestic economy slumped. By 1991 record provisions of £5.2 billion were made, of which Nat-West contributed £1.88 billion including £1.2 billion offset against domestic lending, mainly defaulting personal borrowers and small and medium-sized enterprises (SMEs).

It should be borne in mind that these are provisions, not write-offs, hence

Table 7.3 UK clearing banks' results, 1986–1991

	1986	1987	1988	1989	1990	1991	% change 1991/1990
Pre-tax profits (losses) (£millions)							
Barclays	895	369	1391	692	760	533	−30
National Westminster	1011	704	1407	404	504	110	−78
Lloyds	700	(248)	952	(715)	591	645	+9
Midland	412	(505)	693	(261)	11	36	+227
Bad-debt provisions (£millions)							
Barclays	416	1072	301	1397	1233	1547	+25
National Westminster	373	759	266	1435	1153	1875	+63
Lloyds	215	1273	172	1763	778	918	+18
Midland	320	1246	201	307	703	903	+28
Capital ratios relative to Basle requirement of 8% by 1992 (%)							
Barclays			8.3	9	8.3	8.7	
National Westminster			9.8	9.1	9.1	9.6	
Lloyds			8.5	7.4	8.5	9.7	
Midland			9.8	10	9.8	10.3	

Source: Annual reports.

a proportion of the outstanding amount is likely to be recoverable. Nevertheless, the scale of the provisions is substantial. It is blamed on the recession, although a less charitable explanation would point to profligate lending in the highly competitive market-place of the late 1980s, which fuelled a consumer credit boom that was unsustainable in the underlying economic conditions. Public reaction has been understandably vitriolic, with increasing complaints levied against the banks' apparent tendency to make good their losses by raising charges and widening the interest spread on loans and deposits.

The recession and increasing prices have focused attention on the need to maintain bank capital. Colwell (1991) suggests that this underlies the emphasis on cost control, a greater questioning of whether business justifies the capital it requires, and diversification into less capital-intensive fee-earning areas such as insurance. Capital is affected by provisions because these are deducted from operating profit before arriving at pre-tax profits, and lower pre-tax profits affect the retained reserves (Tier 1 capital). The capital position is of concern if the general trend of provisions seen in the past five years continues. Retained earnings would seem too low to support expansion, and extra external equity (e.g. rights issues) may be difficult to acquire if the rate of return on equity remains low.

Building societies No examination of UK retail financial developments can omit reference to the building societies whose competitive position has already been alluded to. Originally established as mutual or friendly societies, they were designed to provide a social function by offering housing finance to their 'members' who lent to the societies by buying shares, effectively deposits. As there were no 'owners' as such, the societies' excess of funds over receipts was not distributed but retained as reserves. Before 1986 they were thus able to provide the simple yet profitable function of lending via mortgages and were effectively the monopoly suppliers of housing finance, borrowing virtually exclusively from the personal sector at rates determined by the prevailing cartel mechanism.

This lending long and borrowing short carries maturity risk and transformation needs. However, the building societies have maintained liquidity through the historical stability of retail funds, their holdings of liquid assets (mainly deposits with the banking system), regular inflows of mortgage interest and capital repayments, and the cash flow advantages of paying out interest on shares only once or twice yearly, much of which is credited to existing accounts. In addition, their operations are closely scrutinized by the chief registrar of Friendly Societies under the 1962 Building Societies Act.

Such long-term specialization would normally be vulnerable in the highly dynamic and competitive world of modern finance, but the societies have been remarkably successful in their field, as is indicated in Table 7.2 by the expansion of their business with the personal sector. Their past success reflects the long-term buoyancy and favourable treatment of their market. The demand for mortgages has derived from the underlying growth in home ownership, itself a factor of rising incomes, the desire to invest in real assets that have an inflation hedge, and favourable policy geared to its promotion. Various UK governments have supported home ownership, predominantly by tax concessions such as mortgage interest relief at source; the application of composite rate tax to interest paid to depositors thus slightly subsidizes the basic-rate taxpayer when, say, the composite rate was $25\frac{1}{4}$ per cent, the basic rate is 30 per cent, and there is no capital gains tax on the disposal of the householder's principal residence.

In addition, the building societies fuelled their own success. The existence of an interest rate cartel, together with the monetary controls placed upon the banks, effectively stifled the latter's threat and encouraged building society balance sheet growth. Unlike most interest rate cartels, it operated within the remit of the underlying social philosophy to promote home ownership and thus to keep prices down and limit interest rate competition between societies. The effects were to keep mortgage rates low and lagging behind upward movements in interest rates, to protect the smaller, less efficient societies, and to encourage non-price competition, notably the rapid expansion of the branch network, advertising, attention to customer service and flexible opening times. The cartel served the industry well in the 1960s and 1970s but came under strain following the Wilson Report criticism of its inefficiency and anti-competitive nature (Wilson Committee 1980). The Report suggested that abolition of the cartel would produce higher returns to shareholders and depositors and would enable societies to meet mortgage demand (Pawley *et al.* 1991).

The demise of the interest rate cartel in 1983 heralded a competitive and essentially more difficult era for the building societies, in which success was to depend more on their management ability than on a favourable tax and industry environment. The ending of the cartel stimulated price competition among the societies. Banks had already entered the market following the changes to monetary control in 1980, and the government was promoting National Savings products in order to fund its borrowing needs. In response, individual societies began to offer less homogeneous products, including high interest shares, contractual savings and ATM (automated teller machine) facilities, and to attempt market penetration by seeking new segments such as young adults, women and savers in lower socioeconomic groups. As the benevolent characteristics of the cartel disappeared depositors began to get better returns yet pay more for mortgages; above all, net margins narrowed. The societies lobbied for the right to extend their range of services and compete more directly with bank lending rather than remaining restricted to house purchase loans. Eventually the Building Societies Act 1986 allowed societies to provide an extended range of services including full banking and money transmission, currency and securities management. They are now allowed to engage in joint ventures, raise up to 40 per cent of their funds in the wholesale markets and, most significantly, be incorporated as public limited companies (plcs), thereby offering scope for further capital-raising capacity.

Given the dramatic growth of the building societies in recent years and the profound changes they faced in the 1980s, not surprisingly the industry is going through a phase of restructuring. Abbey National has transferred to bank and plc status, and the number of societies has continued to contract, from 456 in 1972 to 227 in 1982 and 126 in 1989. While the latter figure implies a competitive environment, it belies the high level of concentration and the Pareto principle prevalent among financial intermediaries everywhere, with the top 20 societies holding over 80 per cent of assets. Some rescue takeovers have been necessary, such as the assimilation of the Leamington Spa Building Society by the Bradford and Bingley and of Town and Country by the Woolwich, and the acquisition of Southdown by the Leeds Permanent. Formal mergers among the larger societies have been rarer, an exception being the link between the Alliance and Leicester in 1985. Other potential partnerships failed, including those between the Leeds Permanent and Leeds and Holbeck, and between the Yorkshire and the Bradford and Bingley. Nevertheless, this essentially one-product industry is likely to experience further rationalization in the future as competition and costs increase.

The secondary banking sector   The secondary or wholesale banking sector is a diversified group of deposit-taking institutions, which as Table 7.1 indicates can be broadly sub-classified into merchant banks (accepting houses), overseas banks with UK offices, consortium banks and miscellaneous British banks. Their collective characteristics are that they traditionally deal in large-scale deposits, often in foreign currencies, and have corporate customers that are engaged in domestic and international trade and often require term facilities. However, as with the UK banking sector as a whole, such a classification is indistinct, especially as a significant element of retail banking constitutes wholesale business, notably through the merchant banking arms or subsidiaries of the clearers.

The merchant banks derive from nineteenth-century merchant houses which promoted trade and its financing, mainly through the acceptance of bills of exchange issued by merchants, thus enhancing the marketability of such bills. For the core merchant banking group of 16 accepting houses, acceptances provided the bulk of their activity until the 1950s; thereafter a wider range of financing operations has been added, spurred by the growth of the Eurocurrency markets centred on London. They now take in large 'wholesale' sterling and currency deposits and lend in the form of medium-term corporate finance. In addition, they increasingly provide fee-based investment management, takeover and other advisory services and handle share and bond issues. They are active in the secondary money markets, notably the CD, Eurobond and interbank markets, using these to reinsure the risks attached to the mismatching in time and currency of their assets and liabilities.

However, the growth of their investment banking operations has not been without problems. The development of multiple banking relationships has undermined the traditional close rapport between the merchant banks and their customers. Gardener and Molyneux (1990) note the greater banking emphasis on the middle corporate market, where the clearing banks with their branch networks have dominated. In addition, the strong competition from overseas firms, notably the very large Japanese securities houses such as Nomura, has squeezed margins on international business and threatened the independence of the smaller UK merchant banks. Consequently, according to Timewell (1990) they have tended to develop into three broad categories: (1) those captured by other banks, such as County NatWest, Samuel Montagu (Midland), Barclays de Zoete Wedd (BZW) and Morgan Grenfell (Deutsche Bank); (2) major securities houses such as SG Warburg and Kleinwort Benson; and (3) old traditional firms which have remained largely advisory, such as Lazards, Schroder Wagg, Rothschilds and Barings.

The prevalent philosophy was that the merchant banks were too small to survive in the capital-intensive investment banking market following 'Big Bang' in 1986 (see Chapter 8), and that only large, integrated banks would prevail. Barclays followed this line when it acquired brokers de Zoete and Bevan and jobbers Wedd Durlacher, then united them into its merchant banking and investment arms to form BZW. In spite of erratic performance, with a £60 million loss stemming from the October 1987 crash (Hewitt 1988) and pre-tax profits of £54 million in 1989 but only £5 million in 1990, Barclays has consistently injected cash into BZW.

Among the second category, Kleinwort Benson followed the capital-intensive, integrated-securities-house route with mixed fortune. In preparation for 'Big Bang' it acquired stockbrokers Grieveson Grant and jobbers Charlesworth, and extended its banking services to include corporate finance, securities, bullion and fund management. It also raised its capital base and reorganized its management structure to shift decision-making from the bank to the new group. Indeed, although Kleinworts made a rights issue in 1987 of £148 million, it soon appeared over-capitalized and began buying back its capital, implying that size and capital are not always prerequisites for success. However, the import-ance of capital re-emerged as some of the new services proved unprofitable, notably share-dealing after 'Big Bang' and, more recently, the placing of oilfield stock just as Iraq invaded Kuwait. In 1990 Kleinworts suffered one of the heavi-est reversals of any merchant bank, with pre-tax losses of £68 million compared with profits of £83 million the previous year at the height of acquisition and merger activity. Much of the downfall was associated with bad debts on property lending.

For merchant banks following more traditional paths, human capital and low overheads are seen to be as important as financial muscle. Firms such as Lazards reaped the benefit of their active corporate finance advisory work as European mergers and takeovers reached record heights in 1989, only to see activity decline with the onset of the bear market in 1990. Hence, the 1990s herald uncertain times for British merchant banks, with the downturn in their staple activities of capital-raising, corporate financial advice and secondary mar-ket trading.

Among other secondary banks, significant inroads have been made by over-seas banks in the UK, notably the 32 Japanese and 38 US banks established during the 1960s and 1970s to serve their multinational firms located in Britain and also in response to the Euromarket developments. Not surprisingly, much of their activity is dominated by interbank operations, foreign currency transac-tions with resident banks and cross-border transactions with related offices and unrelated banks. Japanese banks in particular borrow actively from unrelated banks and then on-lend to their own offices in Japan (Lamb 1986). They are also prominent in 'securitized' lending and have displaced the US banks as the most significant foreign banking group in the UK. During the past decade Japanese banks have enjoyed the benefits of their booming domestic economy to invest overseas, normally (so far) by building up their own operations rather than buying into existing British firms.

Consortium banks form a small group of UK-registered entities owned jointly by other financial institutions, with at least one overseas-based share-holder and no individual shareholder having more than 50 per cent. They grew rapidly in the 1960s as a mechanism for their owners to gain access to the London markets. As the shareholders themselves have expanded, the relative significance of these institutions has fallen. Their operations are similar to mer-chant banks, especially the banking activities associated with long-term lending, and often are related to project finance.

The final category of the secondary banking sector is represented by a vari-ety of British banks, most of whom conduct business overseas, such as Standard

Chartered, and the overseas subsidiaries of the UK clearers. However, in addition there are banking arms of major retailers such as Marks and Spencer Financial Services, Harrods Bank Ltd and various authorized institutions now classified as banks, notably finance houses, whose primary business is the financing of consumer credit sales and instalment purchases.

UK institutional investors The major institutional investors are the classic intermediaries; they rely on a large scale of operation, on known probabilities associated with their liabilities, and on creating assets rather than merely passing on funds. They invest for their own account on behalf of their 'clients': policyholders (insurance companies), pensioners (pension funds), shareholders (investment trust companies) and unit-holders (unit trust companies). As such they enable individuals to participate in collective investments by pooling many individual contributions and purchasing diversified portfolios of financial and real assets to reduce the risk associated with direct investment.

Among institutional investors, the most significant are the insurance companies and pension funds, which provide the main mechanism for contractual savings but are also linked via their function of risk transfer. Insurance companies estimate the probability of event risk—death, fire, theft, etc.—and then spread these risks among the policy-holders. Not only is a significant amount of pension fund business conducted by insurance firms, but defined benefit pension schemes are a form of retirement insurance against factors such as social security cutbacks, investment risks, inflation and even longevity! Both types of institution face the problem that their future obligations will exceed the income received from policy-holders, hence their preoccupation with equity investment. Nevertheless, they both hold a mixture of government securities, local securities and corporate securities according to the prevailing market circumstances. As a group, the institutional investors play a significant and unique role in the provision of long-term funding for British industry and commerce. Insurance companies and pension funds alone account for over half the shares held in UK listed companies and are thus the principal 'owners' of UK industry; hence they face all the associated concerns over governance and short-termism, factors to which we return in Chapter 9.

Insurance company operations may be classified into long-term insurance, mainly life cover, and general insurance, involving risks such as fire, theft, accident, motor, marine and aviation. Both types provide insurance against financial loss in return for premium income determined by the risk involved. Life insurance has been growing at approximately 10 per cent per annum for the past decade, twice as much as general insurance; and, indeed, it has doubled its share of the personal savings market to 26 per cent in the period 1978–87 (Johnson 1989). Total UK life and general insurance premium income amounted to £49 billion in 1990 out of a worldwide flow of £66 billion. Of this UK amount, some 68 per cent came from life insurance business (ABI 1991). Table 7.4 shows the growth of long-term life insurance and premium business since 1986.

Table 7.4 UK insurance premium business, 1986–1990 (£millions)

	1986	1987	1988	1989	1990
Life insurance					
Income					
UK premium income	18 241	21 473	22 207	29 932	33 567
Overseas premium income	3 183	3 996	4 845	6 308	6 597
Investment income	9 972	10 906	12 397	15 166	17 406
Other income[a]	10 249	3 598	8 626	20 063	(14 239)
Total	41 645	39 973	48 075	71 469	43 331
Expenditure					
Death claims	1 345	1 514	1 707	1 889	2 180
Maturities	2 942	3 500	3 985	4 932	6 391
Surrenders	3 386	4 223	4 528	4 991	5 653
Other expenditure	11 222	9 355	13 358	16 483	17 940
Total	18 895	18 592	23 578	28 295	32 164
Balance	22 750	21 381	24 497	43 174	11 167
	41 645	39 973	48 075	71 469	43 331
General insurance					
Worldwide net premium income					
Fire and accident	11 835	12 114	13 331	15 296	15 373
Motor	5 566	6 231	7 039	8 308	8 549
Marine, aviation and transport	1 498	1 364	1 532	1 643	1 564
Total	18 899	19 709	21 902	25 247	25 486
Underwriting profit/loss for 1 year account basis: motor, fire and accident	−1 156	−956	−490	−1 421	−4 043
Transfer to P and L account for					
Other business	−257	−176	−77	−549	−908
Investment income	2 526	2 631	2 911	3 546	3 474
Overall trading profit	1 113	1 499	2 344	1 576	−1 477
Profit as % premium	5.9%	7.6%	10.7%	6.2%	−5.8%

[a] Includes revaluation of assets, realized investment gains/losses, transfers to/from special/general reserves and miscellaneous net income.

Source: Association of British Insurers (ABI), *Insurance Statistics 1986–90.*

Over the years, life insurance has become an important mechanism for contractual savings involving a long-term commitment for the saver. While premature repayment is feasible, penalties will be incurred and benefits lost. Thus, much life insurance business may be seen as part of the savings market, and so insurance companies compete with other savings intermediaries. Not surprisingly, the composition of life insurance assets reflects the long term, with the need to combat inflation, whereas the need for short-term liquid assets is low. Figure 7.1 illustrates its greater emphasis on equities, with a proportion in

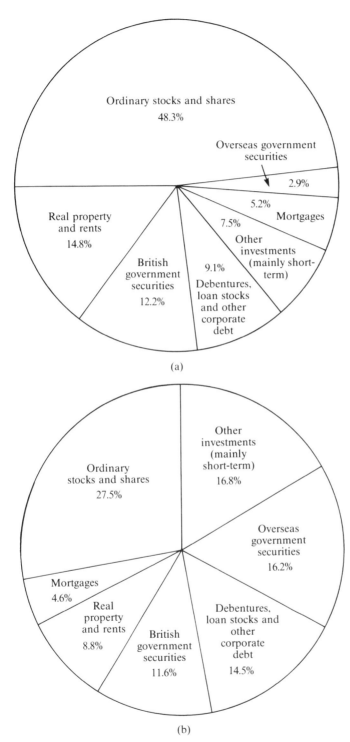

Figure 7.1 UK insurance investments, 1990 (a) Life insurance (b) General insurance

gilts to spread risk, and contrasts this with general insurance investments which pay greater attention to the short term to meet contingency needs.

In 1990, 60 per cent of all UK general business was non-motor, fire, theft and accident, 32 per cent was motor, and 8 per cent marine, aviation and transport. General insurance has tended to make underwriting losses in recent years, which implies that claims and expenses have exceeded premium income, although traditionally the relatively high rates of returns from company investments have kept insurers profitable. Clearly, any deterioration in margins could encourage general insurers to withdraw from the market or raise premiums further. Indeed, the late 1980s and early 1990s have been particularly difficult for the industry worldwide, and especially in the UK. Major adverse weather incidents, such as the 1990 January and February gales and floods which alone cost £2.3 billion; increased thefts, notably from cars, which rose from £222 million in 1987 to £432 million in 1990; and fire claims, which were up from £639 million in 1987 to £1008 million in 1990, have all undermined profits. This adversity is reflected in the performance of leading companies such as Commercial Union, which announced an overall 1991 pre-tax loss of £68.6 million (1990 profit of £1.4 million) in spite of a £114.3 million contribution from its life insurance operations. Elsewhere Royal Insurance and Sun Alliance have both lost heavily on mortgage guarantee insurance as the slump has encouraged repossessions and lenders have sold in a weak housing market. The Royal estimated that mortgage indemnity claims would cost it £400 million over the period 1991–93 (Durman 1991).

The UK insurance industry is relatively competitive, with no one company having more than 10 per cent of the market and the top ten having only just over 55 per cent. Within the life sector the UK industry is small, largely because of the significant role played by pension funds for contractual savings. However, the UK plays an important role in general insurance, where Lloyds of London has traditionally been the main general insurance market. Unfortunately, Lloyds' reputation has suffered of late with record £500 million losses on the underwriting account to 1991, a decline in membership and accusations of insider dealing scandals. Attempts at reform have tended to be frustrated by the relatively old-fashioned and fragmented organization of the market, in which unlimited personal liability exists, reserves are limited, accounts remain 'open' for several years without the ability of some syndicates to 'close' their positions and ascertain profits/losses, and restrictive practices persist in the channelling of business, thus reducing efficiency. Some signs of improvement are the greater use of computer technology and a shift away from the weaker US market. The advent of the Single Market offers a potential impetus, both to Lloyds' members and to the UK insurance industry as a whole, to break into the highly protected European market-place, but further reforms and repair of the Lloyds' image will be necessary.

The value of UK pension funds quadrupled to £220 billion in the 1980s, boosted by buoyant stock markets, the growth of occupational and personal pension schemes, tax concessions and government incentives to shift the burden of pensions away from the social security system and on to the private sector. Whereas in the public sector the government might be expected to raise taxation if necessary to meet its pension obligations, private firms may find their existing workforce too small to pay existing pensioners. Hence employers' and employees' contributions are made at rates that, with appropriate management, will meet known current and anticipated future obligations. Thus, pension funds benefit from regular contractual inflows and long-term liabilities based on actu-arial calculations with little liquidity risk. Consequently their investments are geared to high-yielding long-term assets, mainly UK shares, with other invest-ments sufficient to provide portfolio risk diversification. Davis (1991) suggests that the composition of UK pension fund portfolios has changed relatively little in the period 1970–88 save for a shift from fixed interest to real assets to reflect market conditions rather than objectives. UK pension funds have wide invest-ment powers, although from time to time these have led to criticism that the funds have been too willing to invest overseas or in 'non-ethical' investments.

Prospects for the 1990s are somewhat uncertain, given that the slump in the stock market in 1990 ate into their profits and new legislation has raised their operating costs. The 1990 Social Security Act requires pension schemes to raise pensions in line with inflation up to 5 per cent, and European Court rulings that men and women should be able to retire and receive pensions at the same age could prove expensive for schemes that currently do not provide for common retirement ages. However, in a European context there is a general reliance on pay-as-you-go state social security schemes, so UK pension funds should benefit from the opportunities to liberalize the provision of pensions across national borders.

7.3.2 Germany

In Germany the 4 000 banks dominate the financial system. Indeed, the country is essentially over-banked, especially as most of the business done by German credit institutions involves 'universal banking', whereby banks are not separated into commercial or investment banks as are the UK or US models, but are required (by German banking law) to offer a wide range of retail banking, investment and securities transactions in order to obtain a banking licence. How-ever, this does not preclude some degree of specialization based on historic or regional precedent or, indeed, on determined strategic orientation. Consequently the concept of a uniform universal bank is inappropriate, and Rudolph (1990) suggests that the term really applies only to the three large branch banks, various regional banks and the central institutions of the savings and cooperative banks. These offer the full range of services, often have a European presence via subsidiaries/affiliates, and exercise ownership and supervisory powers over non-bank companies; whereas other institutions loosely called 'universal banks', such as the savings banks, aspire to offer wider services in their own regions and outside, hence fuelling the fierce competition characteristic of the system.

As a group, Germany's banks are generally regarded as among the world's soundest. Jones (1988) cites solid capital–asset ratios, hidden reserves, limited Third World debt exposure and a cautious approach to balance sheet management. The volume of banking business in Germany grew at 7 per cent per annum throughout the 1980s, raising the numbers employed in the sector from 500 000 to 610 000 in the period 1978–90. In common with UK banks, traditional operations have broadened with increasing off-balance-sheet and overseas operations, creating changes to balance sheet structures. On the asset side, increased purchases of bank and public-sector bonds reflect the downward trend in interest rates for much of the decade, whereas lending fell in the mid-1980s as firms used liquid reserves to reduce their gearing. Moreover, borrowers replaced shorter-term obligations with longer-term fixed-rate loans. Maturities have also lengthened on the bank liabilities side with a growing significance of time deposits as insurance companies, acting as true financial intermediaries, recycled their savings inflows to the banking sector. In addition, banks have issued high-yielding savings bonds, thus promoting 'securitization'. These latter developments raised the cost of funding, and, by squeezing interest margins, reduced the growth rate of the banking groups' operating profit in the mid-1980s.

Operating profit recovered in 1990, increasing by 5.3 per cent as the net interest margin widened between borrowing and lending and there was an expansion of profitable short-term lending to trade and industry. The rise in interest rates boosted interest income received by 6.2 per cent (Table 7.5), but the continued trend in favour of non-interest business was reflected in a 13 per cent rise in net commissions received (Deutsche Bundesbank 1991b). However, this 1990 profit improvement belies growing pressures within the banking system. In addition to the slowdown in economic activity and the rising cost of funding, there has been a steady rise in administrative costs and in competition.

Administrative expenses rose by 8.3 per cent in 1990 partly as a result of the cost of extending operations to East Germany, but also as a result of the upward trend in pay settlements (6 per cent in 1990) in the sector. Competitive forces have been widespread, with all banks offering new product lines to customers which has served to blur the differentiation between institutions. Thus, although the number of banks has fallen, the 4000 currently in existence are still too many for the country and reflect the tradition of regional and local institutions, the large number of publicly owned as well as private banks, and the functional classification into savings, cooperative and special-function institutions. Figure 7.2 illustrates the institutional division of the banking system into universal and specialized entities, and according to whether or not they are registered in the Bundesbank statistics.

Commercial banks   The private commercial banks are dominated by the 'Big Three'—Deutsche Bank, Dresdner Bank, and Commerzbank—with their Berlin subsidiaries and extensive national branch networks. In recent years they have

Table 7.5 West German banks' results, 1986–1990 (DM millions)

	1986	1987	1988	1989	1990
All West German banks					
Net interest income	70 478	70 468	72 522	73 143	77 666
Non-interest income	12 072	11 828	12 948	15 024	16 977
Expenses	(61 256)	(62 846)	(63 595)	(69 028)	(74 493)
Pre-tax profit	21 294	19 450	21 875	19 139	20 150
Bad debt provisions	12 714	11 707	8 088	16 740	17 873
The 'Big' Three					
Net interest income	10 968	9 999	10 690	11 398	13 039
Non-interest income	3 807	3 671	4 187	4 812	5 118
Expenses	(11 137)	(11 252)	(10 908)	(11 663)	(13 485)
Pre-tax profit	3 638	2 418	3 969	4 547	4 672
Bad debt provisions	1 296	1 329	504	1 035	2 491
Savings banks					
Net interest income	23 354	23 586	24 443	24 314	24 968
Non-interest income	2 356	2 470	2 619	3 141	4 077
Expenses	(18 809)	(19 934)	(20 887)	(23 312)	(24 095)
Pre-tax profit	6 901	6 222	6 175	4 143	4 950
Bad debt provisions	3 142	3 205	2 420	5 850	5 662
Credit cooperatives					
Net interest income	13 301	13 693	14 045	14 749	15 757
Non-interest income	1 556	1 675	1 957	2 255	2 630
Expenses	(11 994)	(12 358)	(12 578)	(14 320)	(14 794)
Pre-tax profit	2 863	3 010	3 424	2 684	3 593
Bad debt provisions	1 408	1 295	755	3 216	2 377

Source: Deutsche Bundesbank (1991b).

all benefited from their strong position in short-term lending, but have lost market share in terms of savings deposits, and, in common with European retail banks as a whole, have increasingly supplemented their deposits on the interbank markets. The largest commercial banks have responded to the intensified competition by following the 'Allfinanz' strategy, i.e. the integrated provision of financial services in a form of 'one-stop' financial supermarket. For personal customers, traditional retail services are offered together with mortgages, life insurance and investment operations. For corporate customers there is the traditional corporate financing together with advisory services, property management, risk capital and hedging facilities, and insurance products.

The integration of banking and insurance reflects the shift in the character of the German savings market, with an increasing proportion of funds being channelled into life insurance and pensions products (44 per cent of savings in 1989, compared with 35 per cent in 1981). Deutsche Bank has responded to such trends by forming its own life company in 1989, Deutsche Bank Leben,

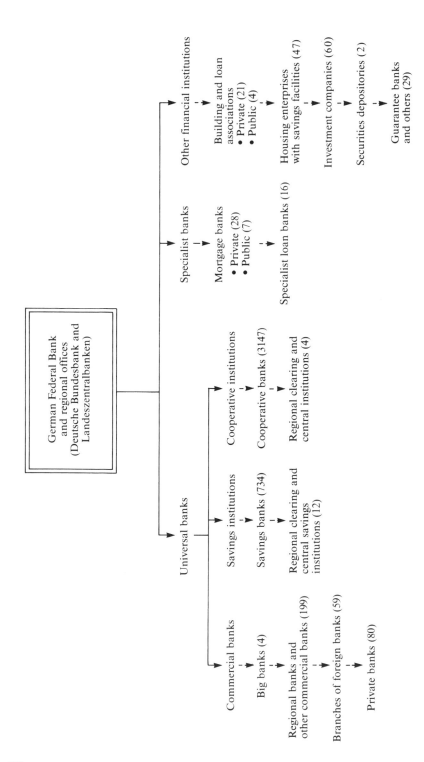

Figure 7.2 The German banking system (*Source:* Figures based on reporting banks as at 31 December 1991 (Deutsche Bundesbank 1992).)

which sold DM4 billion of life policies in its first year of operation drawing upon the established bank client base. In May 1991 Deutsche Bank formed a joint venture with Gerling, an industrial risks insurer, to sell employee benefits policies to small and medium-sized enterprises. Elsewhere, Commerzbank in 1989 acquired a 50 per cent stake in Deutsche Beamtenversicherung, a mutual insurance company specializing in the public employee sector, and 40 per cent of Leonberger Bausparkasse, Germany's fourth largest home finance operation. Dresdner Bank has sought smaller strategic participations in insurers throughout Germany, including Deutscher Herold, Victoria and Hamburger-Mannheimer in northern Germany.

International developments have tended to assume lower priorities for the 'Big Three' until recently. Deutsche Bank opened its first foreign office only in 1969, and then in Luxembourg. However, it began building an overseas operation in the 1980s with acquisitions in the Far East, Australasia and Europe. The latter included the acquisition of Bank of America Italian interests in 1988 and the British merchant bank, Morgan Grenfell, in 1989 for £950 million. The latter was acquired to add a presence in securities trading and fund management, and to set Deutsche Bank on a path to becoming a pan-European bank. Morgan Grenfell's equity market skills are seen to complement Deutsche Bank's bond and debt market activities, but above all the UK bank will be able to market its products via the German bank's huge client base. Commerzbank has expanded in Europe by linking with Banco di Roma (Italy), Banco Hispano Americano (Spain) and Crédit Lyonnais (France), collectively the 'Europartners Group'. These links were intended as reciprocal stakes; for example, Commerzbank secured 7 per cent of Crédit Lyonnais in return for a 10 per cent holding.

Since 1990 the attention of the major commercial banks has been deflected towards German unification. Deutsche Bank invested DM500 million in start-up costs for its own eastern branches and a joint venture with the former eastern state-owned Deutsche Kreditbank to form Deutsche Bank-Kreditbank, now the east's biggest commercial bank. Dresdner has also taken a stake in the Deutsche Kreditbank to form Dresdner Bank-Kreditbank, but Commerzbank decided to start anew by building its own branches. This avoided the need to guarantee the wages of state bank employees, as do the agreements covering Deutsche Bank, Dresdner Bank and the former state bank. In spite of heavy investment costs and the uncertain outcome of these ventures, the Big Three German banks maintained their profitability in 1990. As Table 7.5 shows, their net interest received rose by 14.4 per cent, although provisions more than doubled.

Among other commercial banks are a heterogeneous group of regional operators with often only a few branches, and the branches of foreign banks. The former have expanded but found it difficult to penetrate the over-banked retail market, and thus have concentrated upon investment banking, notably bond underwriting, and specific niches such as swaps and currency options. Acquisitions and joint ventures have helped, such as Lloyds Bank's purchase of Shroeder, Munchmeyer, Hengst, and Midland's 70 per cent holding in Trinkhaus and Burkhardt, but they remain fringe operators in West German banking.

Savings banks This sector comprises 575 municipal and regional banks (*Sparkassen*) coordinated by 11 central institutions (*Landesbanken-Girozentralen*) acting as regional clearing houses and state banks. The *Landesbanken* are public law entities owned by the state or the state savings bank association and traditionally have provided the savings banks with wholesale banking and, to a lesser extent, international functions, while the savings banks have concentrated on private clients and SMEs.

However, falling market shares and profitability in the face of fierce competition from the commercial and cooperative banks has created tension between the *Landesbanken* and the *Sparkassen*. The latter have traditionally financed their operations via savings deposits and the issue of bank savings bonds; but as more private savings have been channelled into life insurance and pensions, time deposits and high yield accounts, the savings banks have been forced to rely on borrowed bank funds. The smaller savings banks have also found customers going elsewhere for sophisticated off-balance-sheet and fee-generating services which traditionally were diverted to the regional *Landesbanken*. Accordingly, the *Landesbanken* blame their *Sparkassen* for failure to develop new products and route sufficient business their way, while the latter accuse the former of expensive foreign investment and unnecessary increases in charges.

The *Landesbanken* are thus under pressure as foreign banks enter the over-banked wholesale market, and for survival are faced with the prospect of rationalization or vertical integration with the *Sparkassen*. The former could produce one or two 'federal' entities, although as similar problems exist in savings banks elsewhere in Europe a pan-European central bank for savings banks has also been suggested (Jones 1989). Vertical integration between the *Sparkassen* and their regional *Landesbanken* is seen as a way of giving the *Sparkassen* control and creating a wide-scale financial group on 'Allfinanz' lines. One move in this direction was the 1990 acquisition by public savings banks in Hesse of the 50 per cent shareholding they did not already own in Hessiche Landesbank (Helaba), then the fourth largest *Landesbank*, and a similar stake in Hessen-Nassauische Versicherung, a state insurance entity.

Meanwhile the competitive pressures on the savings banks continue and rationalization would appear essential if most are to survive. Some have already sought economies of scale via mutual cooperation and merger, especially in order to benefit from technological innovations. However, their numbers fell only from 592 to 575 in the period 1983–90, of which less than half had assets in excess of DM1 billion, the accepted minimum level to operate in the post-'1992' single banking market. Given their local, public ownership, changes in structure or control are politically sensitive. Those *Sparkassen* best equipped to survive are the dozen or so large, urban, 'independent' ones subject to civil as opposed to German public law. These include the *Sparkassen* of Hamburg,

Stuttgart, Frankfurt and Bremen. The last-named was founded in 1825 by the citizens of Bremen, is not subject to direct government influence, nor obliged to finance public borrowing, and can provide a complete range of banking and related services throughout Germany. This contrasts with the *Regionalprinzip*, which restricts public-law savings banks to specific activities within a town or district region. In this way, 'Die Sparkasse in Bremen' is able to provide international banking services in addition to accounting for two-thirds of the Bremen domestic market.

Credit cooperatives   The final group of universal banks consists of the 3050 local credit cooperatives for trade (*Volksbanken*) and agriculture (*Raiffeissenkassen*), the five regional central clearing institutions, and a central body, the Deutsche Genossenschaftsbank, Germany's seventh largest bank. Thus, the sector exhibits some organizational and regional similarities to the savings banks in keeping with the federal nature of the *Länder*. However, the Deutsche Genossenschaftsbank (DG Bank) believes that this structure is uncompetitive and cumbersome, and in preparation for closer links with other European cooperative banks has sought to acquire the regional entities and form a two-tier structure, leaving the local cooperative banks intact. In the 1980s DG Bank began to assume the mantle of a full universal bank rather than, as before, acting largely as a lender-of-last-resort for the cooperative system. It now has operations in corporate finance, lending, equity and bond markets and is located in 13 countries. A full merger with all the proposed entities may prove difficult, however, given regional differences and concern over the growth of DG Bank.

As a group, the credit cooperatives increased their share of the savings deposit market at the expense of savings and commercial banks in the 1980s. With their large number of depositors (around 11 million) and the presence of similar organizations elsewhere in Europe, there would appear opportunities for collaborative ventures with the likes of Crédit Agricôle in France, Rabobank in the Netherlands and the Caja Rurales in Spain, rather than mergers or takeovers as have occurred within the larger individual commercial banks. Indeed, conceivably the establishment of a federal European cooperative bank, built on each nation's cooperative retail bank's central organizations, such as DG Bank, might harness their resources to compete with the commercial banks.

Miscellaneous financial institutions   Among other German financial institutions, the most significant are those involved with property financing, notably the mortgage banks (*Hypothetekenbanken*) and building/loan associations (*Bausparkassen*), and the insurance sector.

The mortgage market is tightly controlled, and the system of long-term fixed-rate loans funded by long-term savings has tended to keep house prices relatively stable. The mortgage banks rely on funding from their right to issue mortgage bonds (*Pfandbriefe*), which pay low returns but rank first among claims if the bank folds, and carry terms of up to 10 years. They include both public and private banks but have been limited in their operations by restrictions on overseas operations, which were not lifted until 1988. Their main rivals in housing finance are the *Bausparkassen*, effectively, mutual savings and mortgage associations which grant mortgages over a set period, usually 7–10 years, by which time savings will have reached approximately one-third of the required sum. They cater for younger borrowers eligible for tax advantages, and, since borrowing rates are low, they work on thin margins. In recent years competition has come from the 'Big Three' commercial banks who have set up their own subsidiaries or acquired stakes, as with Commerzbank's 40 per cent holding in Leonberger Sparkasse.

The attraction of the *Bausparkassen* lies in their ability to sell products, notably insurance-linked savings plans, via outside sales forces on a commission basis, thus opening the way for new customers and regular deposits. However, independent *Bausparkassen*, such as Wustenrot, currently face pressure to meet EC demands on 50 per cent risk–asset weighting on home loans and 100 per cent on commercial property, and thus are vulnerable to overtures from the larger banks. The home savings market in Germany is seen to have a good future, and Wustenrot has been opening about 10 new outlets a year in order to develop its market share in preparation for competition after '1992'. As a group, the *Bausparkassen* are pressing for deregulation along the lines of the UK building societies so as to offer a wider range of services, and, as with the German savings and cooperative banks, have flagged the concept of pan-European collaboration with similar institutions elsewhere in the EC.

The Germans invest heavily in insurance, and reference has already been made to the banking–insurance links engendered by the 'Allfinanz' concept. Although there are a large number of local insurance companies, the market exhibits the characteristics of a restrictive cartel with regulations governing charges, product features, market entry, etc. This reflects the legacy of many insurance company failures in previous years. As a result, the authorities have encouraged concentration, and less than 10 companies now control over half of the health and life insurance markets, with the largest company, Allianz, having approximately 15 per cent of the total market.

Allianz is Europe's largest insurer, having acquired stakes in Cornhill (UK), Riunione Adriatica di Sicurita (Italy) and Cie de Navigation Mixte (France), as well as capitalizing the East German state insurance monopoly Deutsche Versicherung. In addition, it has interests in Spain, the Netherlands and the USA. The international strategy of Allianz began in the early 1970s largely to satisfy its expansion plans, which were restricted at home because of its already large market share and the possible threat of monopoly action if this were increased. The acquisition of Cornhill in 1986 for £305 million gave Allianz a foothold in the important UK market, although Cornhill was ranked only eleventh in UK general insurance and its main business was personal and motor insurance, not commercial non-life activity which determines a major presence in the London market. The 1989 purchase of a 50 per cent stake in Cie dc

Navigation Mixte, 'La Mixte', an industrial holding company, gives it 3 per cent of the French market and is typical of recent agreements between big insurance companies in Europe. Whereas Deutsche Bank and other major German banks have followed the 'Allfinanz' route to offer various financial services, including insurance, under one roof, Allianz has concentrated on becoming an insurance conglomerate rather than developing reciprocal banking operations, notwithstanding minority holdings in various financial institutions including Hypobank. Instead, it has sought to balance its insurance product lines, and in particular to develop its private as opposed to industrial business.

This strategy has run into problems with the 1990 acquisitions in East Germany and the USA. Allianz spent DM270 million capitalizing Deutsche Versicherung (DV), a loss-making company operating in the difficult yet emerging East German market and where DV's 14 000 staff generated DM2 billion in premium income compared with DM10 billion by the 20 000 staff in West Germany (Lapper 1991). In contrast, the US acquisition of the Fireman's Fund was to satisfy Allianz's desire for an international presence but is a high-cost, industrial market operation in a competitive developed market. The aim is to provide international business to clients among the top 500 US companies, and, while the operation could benefit from Allianz's strength, the initial attempts at cost-cutting have proved difficult.

By European standards, German personal insurance is expensive, yielding high profit margins and offsetting competitive pricing on the industrial lines. With claim costs rising rapidly, companies have been losing money on their industrial risks business, so the opportunities for expansion into eastern Germany are welcomed. However, EC approval of insurance directives and deregulation of the domestic market will expose German insurers to intense price competition, notably from the UK; hence the rationale for Allianz's expansion strategy.

7.3.3 France

At first sight the French financial system appears to share certain common characteristics with that of Germany. It is still essentially a bank-oriented system, with a large number and range of financial institutions, yet dominated by three large 'universal' banks: Banque Nationale de Paris (BNP), Crédit Lyonnais, and Société Générale. Moreover, the market is similarly over-banked; indeed, according to Dixon (1991), 99 per cent of French adults have a bank account and they are served by 26 000 branches. However, such similarities are of relatively recent origin, stemming largely from the 1984 Banking Act which bought more uniformity to the French banking sector. Previously legislation introduced in the 1940s encouraged a strict specialization of credit and banking functions and allowed for heavy state involvement in the financial sector, both through ownership and through regulation. In its application of technology the French system is more akin to that of the UK, with emphasis on financial innovations, computerization and electronic payment systems, and a high usage of cheques, credit and debit cards and automated teller machines (ATMs).

The 1984 Banking Act offered French banking an opportunity to move away from strictly specialized spheres of operation by broadly defining institutions under its control. Credit institutions are deemed to provide at least one of the following banking operations: receiving deposits from the public; granting loans; managing the payments mechanisms. As they are all subject to similar liquidity constraints and capital adequacy rules, there is little incentive for, say, merely non-bank deposit-taking institutions to be formed. However, the Act does classify credit institutions into various groups: banks belonging to the Association Française des Banques (AFB), which are short-term deposit-takers; mutual and cooperative savings institutions; savings banks; and other financial entities. Nevertheless these institutions can choose to specialize or diversify without great hindrance.

Banks belonging to the AFB   Only BNP, Crédit Lyonnais and Société Générale may really be considered 'universal' banks out of the 400 AFB institutions. The majority are too small, too specialized or too regionally oriented to offer a comprehensive range of operations. In contrast, the 'Big Three' account for approximately half of total bank credit and deposits with commercial banks; they have large retail branch networks, investment and corporate banking arms and operate internationally.

However, their development in recent years has been affected by state involvement. All three were nationalized in 1945, but Société Générale was one of 65 industrial groups privatized in 1986–87. Thereafter, in the wake of the 1987 stock market crash and Mitterand's socialist political influence, the 'ni ni' policy of neither more nationalization nor more privatization has been followed. Accordingly, Crédit Lyonnais and BNP are still indirectly controlled by the government and have faced pressure to meet the Basle capital adequacy rules without recourse to the stock market and rights issues that Société Générale was allowed. Both BNP and Crédit Lyonnais have used the full range of non-voting certificates and loan stock issues, and so the government has had to provide alternative methods such as state-based capital injections and allowing share swaps, often via links with insurance companies creating so-called 'Bancassurance'.

As an example, Crédit Lyonnais received a direct subsidy in 1989 when state-managed Caisse des Dépôts invested FF1.3 billion and then exchanged voting shares for part of the state holdings in Rhône-Poulenc, and later Thomson-SCF. Through these share issues Crédit Lyonnais raised its capital by FF9.8 billion (Shreeve and Alexander 1991). BNP arranged a 10 per cent share exchange with Union des Assurances de Paris (UAP), a leading state-owned insurer, which boosted BNP's capital by FF2 billion. A similar link occurred when the troubled CIC banking group joined with the second largest insurance company, Group des Assurances Nationales (GAN) for a similar reason. Hence

Laurie (1989) suggests that 'Bancassurance' may be seen in a French context as a mechanism to hide the fact that 'banks are poor, insurance companies rich and the state is playing marriage broker'.

In terms of their current strategies, the 'Big Three' are moving along different routes. Crédit Lyonnais aims to be a global bank and is rapidly expanding its European bases via acquisition. In the Netherlands it is the fourth largest bank with over 100 branches, in Belgium it has 30 branches, in Italy 95, in the UK 40 and in Spain 110. Recent acquisitions have included 49 per cent of Credito Bergamasco (Italy) and Banco Comercial Espanol (Spain), although a proposed merger in 1991 with Commerzbank failed. Société Générale has instead concentrated on fund management and investment banking, taking control of Strauss Turnbull, the London brokers; while BNP has not only followed the 'Bancassurance' route but also gone for asset swaps including an 85-branch trade with Banco Bilbao Vizcaya in Spain.

Among other large banks, Banque Indosuez and Banque Paribas are international investment banks with limited branch networks, but are part of complex groups which contain the seeds of future pan-European operations. In recent years Banque Indosuez has focused on Europe to balance its presence in the Far East and to this end has taken a 25 per cent stake in Morgan Grenfell. The CIC group, Crédit Commercial de France (CCF) and Crédit du Nord are the other substantive AFB banks, although they are oriented more towards domestic retail banking and less towards international business than the other five.

Crédit du Nord has experienced a dramatic turnaround in its fortunes in recent years. For a long time under joint control of the state and the then nationalized bank Paribas, it was one of the worst performing French banks. By the mid-1980s it was making significant losses brought about by excessive costs, overmanning and inadequate bad-debt provisions, most notably for the collapsed Ribouel property development group, losses on which totalled FF500 million. A new 'kill or cure' regime was introduced in 1987, and now that the bank is 100 per cent owned by the privatized Paribas its fortunes appear to have revived. The workforce, which had fallen by 2800 since 1974, was trimmed by another 1500; 70 branches were closed, mainly in the group's homeland in northern France; investment was cut back, with budget and profit responsibility devolved down the organization. Indeed, decentralization and computerization were the two pillars on which the turnaround, a net profit of FF49 million in 1988, was built. The former was a reaction to a top-heavy central administration, the latter a need to service corporate treasury payments and enhance internal efficiency.

The privatized Crédit Commercial de France (CCF) has also improved its performance following a restructuring of its balance sheet and a strategic decision to pursue international expansion via corporate finance and securities operations. CCF ingeniously sold $500 million of its LDC debt exposure to an offshore trust (Finov) for $230 million and Finov issued $500 million of long-term secured notes subscribed for entirely by CCF. With the net proceeds Finov bought mainly short-term blue-chip investments, and in this way CCF's assets are thus easier to evaluate.

According to Henrot and Levy-Lang (1990), the above-mentioned eight largest French banks account for some 75 per cent of the AFB banks' business. They are also among the most innovative, expanding into new areas functionally and internationally, and are adapting to new technologies and structures. The other AFB banks are by no means universal or international in outlook, apart from the foreign-owned banks. Most are either regional retail banks or specialists in areas such as leasing or property finance.

Mutual and cooperative banks   The three mutual bank networks, Crédit Agricôle, Crédit Mutuel and Banques Populaire, account for 97 per cent of the deposits and savings sector. Historically these were directly controlled by the Treasury and enjoyed special privileges, some of which have been retained in spite of denationalization. All three share common features of a decentralized organization incorporating autonomous regional retail banks geared to the consumer and smaller businesses.

The largest mutual bank is Crédit Agricôle, one of the world's largest banks in terms of assets. It was known abroad as Caisse Nationale de Crédit Agricôle and ran international and capital market operations for the group's 94 regional cooperative banks (*caisses regionales*). On denationalization the *caisses regionales* purchased 90 per cent of the Caisse Nationale from the state; a further 7 per cent went to employees, and 3 per cent was retained by the state for future distribution to staff. This has reduced tension between the Caisse Nationale and the regions which stemmed from the influence over the former by civil servants while the boards of the regional banks were dominated by agri-businessmen. Crédit Agricôle is the leading lender to consumers, especially for property loans, a major force in retail savings and strongly represented in unit trust and life insurance operations. Future strategy aims to raise efficiency by increasing returns on assets by moving the simpler banking operations away from branches to intermediaries such as estate agents or car dealers, and focusing on higher value added work. As it depends on retail as opposed to wholesale deposits, Crédit Agricôle faces the growing cost of savings plus the fixed cost of the extensive branch network.

Crédit Mutuel differs in that it has no strong central authority to link its *caisses*. It is strongly represented in Alsace and Brittany but has a low market share in many areas of France, a result of quantitative ceilings imposed on lending in the 1970s which stifled its geographical expansion. Arguably, it could benefit most from deregulation allowing the payment of interest on deposits. Crédit Populaire consists of 36 regional cooperative Banques Populaire geared to small businesses. In the past they enjoyed privileges in the distribution of subsidized loans to this sector, although this is now less significant.

Savings banks   The caisses d'épargne are savings institutions run by locally elected boards, including local authority representatives. Traditionally they have offered regulated rates of interest on deposits and have had a monopoly with the postal savings banks over the tax-free Livret A (passbook), which enabled them to boost their deposit base. The collected funds are centralized by Caisse des Dépôts et Consignations (CDC), a public body, and various regional financing agencies owned equally by the CDC and the *caisses*. In turn, the monies have tended to be directed to finance low-cost rented housing and into local authority funding.

In 1987 the *caisses d'épargne* were allowed to start lending to small and medium-sized businesses and to individuals. Their local presence and underpricing of loans has gained them a substantial share of the consumer market, much to the chagrin of the commercial banks. However, their future is uncertain, since, although they play a key role in raising funds for the low-cost subsidized housing system, a politically sensitive area, their source of deposits via the tax-exempt passbook is suffering competition from other deregulated savings products. Moreover, the costs of transition from effective depositories to full banks is taking a toll. In 1983 there were 467 *caisses d'épargne*, but by mid-1990 this had fallen to barely 180. Indeed, the expectation is that some 40–50 regional rather than local banks will ultimately exist, none of them with less than FF11 billion in total assets (Blanden 1990).

Miscellaneous financial institutions   Among other significant institutions in the French financial system are various specialist credit and finance houses, and the insurance firms. The numerous *sociétés financières* cater for the consumer and small to medium-sized businesses in specialist areas such as hire purchase, operational leasing, property finance and factoring. As in the UK, many are subsidiaries of major banks, and, as their funding comes from the wholesale markets, their performance is interest-rate sensitive. Another group is the *institutions financières specialisées* (IFS), which operate specific duties in the public interest under the influence of a Treasury representative on their board. These include Crédit Foncier de France, Crédit Nationale and various *Sociétés de developpment regional*. Traditionally they have raised funds on the money markets for lending at subsidized rates as mortgages to households (Crédit Foncier) or to small businesses. Since the mid-1980s these subsidies have been reduced and they have competed directly with the banks and the finance houses. Henrot and Levy-Lang (1990) suggest that the IFSs will retain their importance, given their favourable image and use as a government vehicle for assisting specific sectors.

France has traditionally lagged behind other European nations in the areas of insurance and pension funds, the latter a reflection of the importance of the national compulsory pension system. However, in recent years households have become concerned about a potential decline in their living standards on retirement and there has been a marked upturn in funds channelled into life insurance and supplementary pension products. New savings devices have been stimulated by tax incentives, such as the *'Bons de Capitalisation'* (accumulation bonds with tax-free earnings after ten years), and *Plan d'Epargne Populaire* (PEP), a retirement savings plan started in 1990. Metais (1990) suggests that the life insurance and earnings accumulation schemes business sustained growth rates averaging 28.7 per cent in the period 1986–88 so that the French market now ranks third behind the UK and Germany. Moreover, it is insurance business as a whole that has burgeoned, and not just life cover, as French consumers and businesses have paid more attention to their non-life needs. Not surprisingly, this market expansion has favoured the insurance companies but has also encouraged strategic alliances and restructuring within financial services as a whole.

As late as 1987 there was a clear demarcation between private- and public-sector insurers. The three state-owned companies—Union des Assurances de Paris (UAP), Assurances Generales de France (AGF) and Groupe des Assurances Nationales —were far larger and more significant than the myriad of small and medium-sized private operators. By 1989 this situation had been reversed, with UAP the only state-owned company to remain in the top three, following partial privatization. Earlier reference was made to 'Bancassurance' for capital-raising purposes, but the complementary nature of the businesses, one of which brings in short-term deposits, the other long-term savings, is a strong attraction. One such example is the Cie Financière de Suez (Fig. 7.3), which, after a century of building and managing the Suez Canal, has turned itself into a diversified

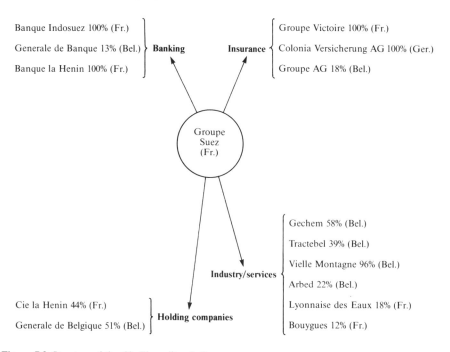

Figure 7.3 Structure of the Cie Financière de Suez

financial services group through the 1989 takeover of leading insurer Victoire, which in turn had earlier acquired the German insurer, Colonia.

Elsewhere French insurers have sought links both at home and overseas. In 1988 the AXA group allied with Cie du Midi in a defensive merger to defeat the acquisition intentions of Italy's Generali and to form the second largest French insurer behind UAP. The new group already has a presence in the UK through Equity and Law, the life insurance group bought in 1987 by Midi. Anglo-French links have included Commercial Union's Eurofil telephone sales subsidiary and Sturge Holdings, a leading Lloyds' agency which has opened a Paris branch. However, difficulties have arisen as shown by Eagle Star's sale of its French general insurance subsidiary, and Sun Life had problems with its link with UAP.

7.4 STRATEGIC CHOICES FOR THE 1990s

Central to the Single Market ideal referred to in Chapter 1 is the concept of the European Financial Common Market (EFCM), which provides for the free movement of money and capital for all citizens. Financial brokers and institutions may establish a presence anywhere in the Community without prior permission, and may offer their 'financial products' across borders without restriction. Hence EC citizens are able freely to invest their funds, open accounts and arrange loans and insurance wheresoever they desire within the EC. Banks and insurance companies can take full advantage of the internationalization of securities markets and fund management activities, and offer a wider product range.

In the field of insurance, the 1988 approval of the Second Directive for non-life insurance, liberated the market for commercial risks insurance, allowing medium-sized companies (above 500 employees and turnover in excess of ECU33 million) to purchase policies from insurers established in any member state. As we have seen, the 1989 Second Banking Directive essentially provides for a single passport or licence, home-country control and mutual recognition of national regulations. Similar provisions occur with the 1988 Investment Services Directive, the major differences being that substantial powers are given to host authorities in respect of business operations.

Thus, developments in the European financial system will open up an environment of opportunity for financial institutions in terms of new products, markets and alliances both within their specialized segments and across the wider definition of financial services activity. However, attainment of an effective EFCM is still distant, given that a common currency does not yet exist and that monetary policy is still controlled by national governments or central banks, which through exchange and interest rate policy influence money and capital markets. Moreover, the Single Market proposals will not remove the problems of differences in languages and culture and in legal and accounting principles, and varying traditions in supervision and investor protection. For many firms these are perceived as obstacles but not major threats to their operations. More difficult issues arise from competition, market concentration and merger controls, and capital adequacy needs. In terms of competition, most European financial systems are over-banked; this is especially true of bank-dominated ones as in France and Germany, but even in the UK competitive forces have led to shake-outs in terms of jobs and branch closures. Deregulation further stimulates this highly competitive environment in such a way that banking, insurance and investment firms know that any operational weaknesses will be fully exploited by the competition.

The issues of financial market concentration and merger control are complex in an EC context. Domestic restructuring and the creation of pan-European linkages could lead in smaller countries to the emergence of groups with huge domestic market shares. Ugeux (1989) cites French control via UAP of Belgian insurance companies, and earlier reference was made to the ostensibly defensive alliance of the French AXA group with Cie du Midi to create UAP's nearest rival. In the Netherlands the authorities have effectively allowed a 'free-for-all' in the financial sector, with mega-mergers such as that between Algemene Bank Nederland and Amsterdam-Rotterdam Bank to form ABN-Amro, which dominates the securities sector with an estimated 65 per cent of domestic business and 50 per cent of corporate sector activity (King 1991).

However, merger control and regulations in the EC are still far from effectively harmonized and they create uncertainty as well as an additional tier, rather than replacing national legislation. This was evident in the prelude to the rival '1992' bids by Lloyds Bank and the Hong Kong and Shanghai Banking Corporation (HSBC) for Midland Bank. Lloyds indicated that it would formally bid if its bid was put on a 'level playing field' by the EC and UK authorities, i.e. if the Monopolies and Mergers Commission (MMC) would examine both bids. HSBC was hoping that the Brussels merger authorities would scrutinize its offer and the MMC could be avoided; indeed, the Brussels authorities had begun a preliminary investigation. The Lloyds bid was more likely to be investigated in the UK because the combined group would have insufficient assets outside the UK to trigger a Brussels inquiry (Peston and Holberton 1992).

For many financial entities operating in the new European market, a major issue remains capital adequacy. Indeed, Llewellyn (1992) argues that this is the major strategic issue for banks in the 1990s. The availability and cost of capital ultimately determine the banks' lending capacity via the level of assets sustainable; accordingly, if a bank faces a capital shortage or its cost of capital is too high, it loses business to competitors. Given that the financial services industry provides services based on the public confidence in its ability to meet its commitments, specific regulations such as the Second Banking Directive and BIS capital adequacy rulings are vital. However, in recent years European banks have had their capital and reserves eroded by heavy provisions for bad and doubtful debts and significant cuts in operating profit as margins have been squeezed. With UK banks' provisions rising to almost 70 per cent of operating profit towards the end of the 1980s, it would seem that substantial provisions will remain for the foreseeable future. The intensity of banking competition continues to exert downward pressure on margins, and deregulation, coupled with the economic downturn, has encouraged, firstly over-zealous, then later distress lending by many institutions with the inevitable consequences for their loan portfolios.

It is clear that the current financial environment provides a host of opportunities and threats to EC institutions, making it imperative that due consideration be given to future strategy. Among the strategic decisions facing European financial firms are the following:

- Do we consolidate, restructure or expand? If we expand, where? Which customers—domestic or overseas? Wholesale or retail?
- What products—specialist/niche or 'universal'?
- How do we market—retail network or mobile teams?
- Delivery system—branch, agency or home-orientation?
- What level of technology—for payment or delivery?

Such issues will clearly create strategic resource implications in terms of capital and labour needs. For convenience we may consider these in terms of, firstly, the product-market focus or *strategic direction* involved, and secondly, market coverage, technology and structure, or the *strategic methods* employed.

7.4.1 Product-market alternatives

The strategic directions in which firms normally develop may be divided along consolidation and expansion paths. Currently external growth is perceived as a complement rather than a substitute for internal strength, and thus attention is often focused on supply-side policies geared to restructuring and consolidation. Abraham and Lierman (1991) contend that many firms are less concerned with launching new products, discovering new niches of profitable business or setting up new markets, but instead are adjusting their volume and resources to the deregulated, competitive European market.

Ironically, European integration encourages consolidation at home as the opportunity for oligopoly profits from a closed market is reduced in the face of outside competition, and hence companies are forced to restructure to improve domestic efficiency. Throughout Europe banks, building societies and insurance companies are making severe reductions in their labour forces, although cutting costs is a zero-sum game if they all do it. As productivity requirements increase, there is more pressure for effective management as well as financial controls and greater in-house training. In the past the larger banks have used retail profits to cross-subsidize other operations without accurately measuring the amount of capital involved or the operational profitability of specific activities. Lloyds Bank has shown the benefits of using capital to back only proven profitable business. In the 1980s it moved away from low-margin overseas lending and

Products Markets	Present	New
Present	Market penetration	Product development
New	Market development	Diversification

Figure 7.4 Ansoff's growth vector matrix

securities trading, unlike the other major UK clearers. Consequently it had a higher market share and City valuation than its rivals despite its smaller size.

However, while consolidation—indeed, retrenchment—is often one interim strategy, most financial institutions seek expansion opportunities. Indeed, Lloyds Bank may have withdrawn from securities operations in the late 1980s, but it was prepared to bid for Midland in 1992 to expand its domestic operation. The generic strategic alternatives may be seen in the growth vector model (Fig. 7.4).

Market penetration entails selling more of the same products to existing markets in order to build market share. In the financial services context the distinction between consolidation, as described above, and market penetration is indistinct. However, many of the building societies have followed the latter strategy as the banks have moved away from housing finance. Mike Blackburn (1989), chief executive of the Leeds Permanent Building Society, argued that cultural differences and the specific nature of operating systems in individual nations have made expansion into Europe unattractive for his company and also for other building societies. Consequently the Leeds has focused upon raising its share of the core house mortgage business. Product development, for example the launch of the Leeds' VISA card, is ultimately seen as complementary to this market penetration objective.

Market development involves selling existing products to new markets, and would appear to be the major opportunity offered by the Single Market. Leading companies in financial services will aim for a presence at least in the main European countries as part of a global rather than merely pan-European strategy.

However, Europe is by no means homogeneous, and for the majority of institutions certain locations will become more attractive than others. The 'Nordic' region in an enlarged EC–EFTA grouping would include the Scandinavian and Germanic-influenced areas, the latter covering Benelux, Austria and Switzerland. However, there are considerable differences between the currently unprofitable Scandinavian systems and those of Austria and Switzerland. The 'Latin' group includes southern nations with prospects of high profits but often at high cost because of operational inefficiency, for exmple in Spain, Greece and Portugal, and middle countries such as France and Italy, where market saturation, low prices and high costs reduce profit potential. On this basis the UK stands out as unique and pre-eminent in terms of the level of development and specialization of its financial services and its links, but opportunities for successful entry to the UK market would seem limited by the fierce competition.

The Second Banking Directive offers the opportunity for both product development and diversification. Banks will be able to offer a range of services throughout the EC and thus to assume the mantle of 'universal' banks providing a range of, often new, services to customers. In the Ansoff model 'product development' entails extending or modifying the product range. In retail banking the reduced efficiency of the branch network to raise deposits commensurate with rising costs has eroded profits and led to the search for new products to meet specific market segments and customer needs. Given the expensive, volatile and rate-sensitive nature of the deposit mix, it is not surprising that banks have introduced high-interest-bearing current accounts and management services aimed at higher net worth customers, not to mention technology-based transactions and savings accounts with savings accessed by ATMs. Further developments include 24-hour banking such as that offered by FirstDirect, a Midland Bank subsidiary, and the Bank of Scotland's PC-based HOBS product, geared to the business community. At a simple level, the latter saves telephone costs and allows customers to examine transactions on disk in their own dwellings, but sophisticated software also offers transaction analysis, reconciliation and planning, and a gateway to electronic data interchange in the future. Thus, such technology is seen as meeting customer needs and, notably in the case of FirstDirect, as reducing High Street branch overheads.

Retail banking epitomizes many of the dilemmas facing financial services firms in their strategic orientation in the 1990s. Banks have had to broaden their service range, maintain quality and yet price competitively. Consequently, many European banks are emphasizing 'relationship banking', with greater emphasis on marketing a range of services geared to specific customer needs using preferential pricing packages. These may include special rates on credit cards, consumer credit, mortgages, insurance, investment services and direct payment facilities. To develop such ranges of services, banks have followed diversification paths into other service sectors such as stockbroking, insurance broking, travel and estate agency work, and fund management, as well as placing more emphasis on business and personal financial advice.

Indeed, while in many cases the concept of a 'universal' bank may be more accurate, the term applied to such entities is often financial 'conglomerate'. This accords with the principle, implicit in the Ansoff matrix of diversification, of moving well away from the core activity, but conglomeration is often associated with products or services that are completely unrelated in terms of technology or market. Yet in a banking context the aim is often strategic marketing of a range of services, and hence bankers are quick to counter criticisms of conglomerates, notably lack of direction and questionable synergy, especially diseconomies of scale and uninspiring performance. Gardener (1990) cites operational advantages over specialist firms which include a stream of core retail deposits, a record in financial innovation, capital strength, large and diverse balance sheets and expertise in credit and risk management. However, many of these areas are precisely those that have come under scrutiny, especially in the light of the major UK banks' recent performance.

7.4.2 Market coverage, technology and structure

A major issue for many financial institutions is how to service their markets within the new Europe. The chosen methods will be influenced by integrated factors such as distribution and technology costs and the desired organizational structure. Ugeux (1989) suggests that financial market evolution is polarizing into retail and institutional foci. Retail-oriented organizations are geared to a close physical proximity to the customer, hence their traditionally heavy investment in branch networks with attendant large labour forces and computer operating systems. The institutional or corporate sector is seen as serviceable by small, specialist units or teams using state-of-the-art technology and remaining flexible in their location needs.

The position of branches is tenable so long as they are not superceded by more cost-effective or efficient delivery systems, and provided they meet the locational needs of their institutions. However, competitive pricing and the greater use of profit-centre-based accounting mean that individual branches must increasingly justify their performance. Moreover, whereas to date technology has supported the branch network, and even ATMs complement branch functions, the advent of home banking, plastic cards and EFT–POS (electronic funds transfer at point of sale) may be seen as competing alternatives. Thus, the branch network will be managed as part of a mix of delivery systems; moreover, its nature will change. Already most bank branches have undergone functional shifts from administrative to marketing centres, with accompanying changes in layout and image. Greater emphasis is placed upon 'open-plan' formats with enhanced customer-contact space, front-office terminals and ATMs inside and outside the banking hall, all in contrast to the traditional large areas devoted to clerical, data-processing operations.

The cost of such adaptation is high, however, and, as the branch network remains inherently inflexible, rationalization is currently more common than the opening of new outlets. Such branch restructuring places greater emphasis on efficient resource allocation and profitability, as a result of which segmentation is often apparent, with specific branches offering corporate banking services in industrialized centres, personal banking in predominantly residential zones, small-business advisory centres and transaction-only outlets. The traditional High Street branch providing a range of banking services will continue to exist, but by no means as ubiquitously as before.

Behind these substantive shifts in distribution mechanisms lie significant technological developments. Advanced technology is now commercially viable through the use of expert systems, document image processing and voice response systems. Information technology pervades each branch, providing customer account, bank, on-line economic and market information, enabling speedier and, ideally, higher-quality service.

Perhaps the most significant developments are in the changes to payments systems, the base on which original bank oligopolies were established throughout Europe, and which are still seen as the key to competing successfully in banking. Cash is the most elementary system, but it is labour-intensive; hence the heavy investment in ATM-type technology. This is now relatively mature and most machines can offer a broad range of account services such as balance enquiries, statement and cheque book orders, and the payment of bills and issue of transfers. Moreover, ATM locations have spread 'off-branch' to shopping precincts, hospitals, educational establishments and some industrial estates. As a delivery system, they supplement branch activities and allow the latter to process greater volumes of business and thus to concentrate on the customer service and marketing activities mentioned above. However, this type of technology affects the competitive balance by allowing market access to institutions without the need for a branch. If various plastic cards can be used in dispensers, the banks' domination of this payment mechanism is eroded. Howcroft and Lavis (1986) cite international groups such as Citibank, non-aligned insurance groups, data-processing companies and retailers as potentially offering financial services via such outlets. In Germany, Switzerland and the Benelux countries, the Eurocard/Eurocheque can be used in ATM networks and has effectively replaced personal cheques as a payment mechanism.

For paper-based payment systems—e.g. a cheque clearing system—to operate, they must be flexible, secure, acceptable and must involve cooperation between institutions. Cheques remain the dominant form of payment in France, Italy and the UK, their acceptability having risen with the advent of the cheque guarantee card. Fraudulent use of UK domestic cheques and cheque cards in Europe led to their abandonment and their integration with the development of European-wide cheque guarantee cards. Since traditionally two-thirds of most banks' staff work in payment processing, it is not surprising that bank marketing and applied technology efforts have been directed at this area. Technology has constantly been oriented to speed up the actual processing, including by cheque truncation, whereby it is the information on the cheques, rather than the cheque itself, that is transmitted by the branch into which it is paid. However, effort has also focused on cheque replacement by encouraging the use of plastic cards and electronic funds transfer.

Plastic cards are essentially tools for activating paper or electronic payments systems. In the UK credit cards were introduced in the mid-1960s and are generally widely acceptable. Customers benefit from the ease and convenience of using cards and the free credit period to settlement date. The major group cards (VISA, Mastercard) allow payments to preset prescribed limits, whereas charge cards (e.g. Diners Club, American Express) are settled monthly, and in-store retail cards (e.g. Marks and Spencers, Debenhams) combine credit and charge functions. As their name implies, debit cards activate automatic debits to a customer's account via an encoded magnetic strip which operates as the card is passed through ATMs or in-bank terminals. These functions are being incorporated increasingly into cheque guarantee cards, and thus debit cards are now more widely available.

Technological developments in the card usage area continue to focus in the first place on expanding international networks and terminal usage. Not surprisingly, the brand image associated with a credit card can be a powerful marketing tool. Barclays Bank, the largest bank-owned issuer of UK credit cards, is treating continental Europe as an extension of the home market and has invested in processing facilities in France, Spain and Germany to further its market share (Laurie 1989). Secondly, technology has concentrated on reducing fraudulent misuse of cards via the introduction of holograms, user photographs and by speeding up the identification of lost or stolen cards.

The most radical technological developments in modern payments systems relate to electronic methods, which overcome the vulnerability of cash and the fraud associated with cheques and plastic cards and, above all, cut the volume and cost of paper transactions. Of these, the most significant is electronic funds transfer at point of sale (EFT-POS), which normally involves a connection between the retailer's cash terminal and the bank to transmit electronic messages. Thus, there is no need for a paper transaction; moreover, administration of the payment is taken off-branch. France is the market leader, with over 65 000 terminals, most of which are bank-owned, whereas in most countries the extent of EFT-POS is largely experimental (Gardener and Molyneux 1990). In the UK considerable marketing is still required to convince retailers of the benefits of the system and persuade them to invest in the terminals. Enhanced customer usage will be more problematic, especially as long as free credit periods are associated with credit cards. France also leads Europe in futuristic home banking, although FirstDirect and the Bank of Scotland have launched UK telephone-based schemes. The concept is attractive, but a full range of services depends on the introduction of interactive viewdata systems, possibly via cable television.

Such technological advances further undermine the role of the branch network and open up opportunities for new market entrants, e.g. FirstDirect. The branch, therefore, is no longer a competitive *entry* barrier; indeed, the cost of physical transformation from processing to marketing centre and the high fixed overheads mean that branch networks are increasingly *exit* barriers in the industry. An added technological issue for banks in this context is that their back-office 'production' facilities often need renewal. Frequently information technology has been accepted reluctantly and data-processing and computer systems have proved vulnerable to changed economic conditions, financial innovations and security problems, e.g. viruses, access. Therefore internal restructuring is often needed to cater for decisions about electronic data processing, operating systems, networking and database management. Whereas personal computers have gradually penetrated the branch system, many of the above computing developments require capital-intensive, centralized processing centres in order to gain from economies of scale. The implication is thus that back-office tasks can be performed more efficiently by a smaller, specialist, staff conversant with the technology and located in a few central locations.

The changed focus of the branch from an administrative and data-processing role to marketing-oriented profit centre; the high costs of staffing, refurbishing and running branches, the heavy capital investment in banking technology, brand image and advertising needed in the current competitive environment—all present major problems which impinge upon the crucial strategic decision of how to establish a European presence and embrace the opportunities of the Single Market. Moreover, given the cost, uncertainty, need for local expertise and, above all, time involved in building a branch network overseas, these factors tend to favour external restructuring. Dixon (1991) cites a senior Barclays official as saying that to replicate the bank's UK network across Europe would involve establishing 12 000 additional branches and an investment of £12 billion, a prohibitive sum.

External restructuring may be split into acquisitions of total or majority holdings in financial institutions, and various types of strategic alliance. Earlier reference was made to insurance company acquisitions, such as those of Germany's Allianz group in the UK, Italy and France, and the French Cie du Midi purchase of UK's Equity and Law. Cross-border acquisition of smaller banks by large national banking groups has been common for Deutsche Bank (Germany), Banco Santander (Spain) and Crédit Lyonnais (France), notable predators, as they set out to establish a pan-European presence. The main rationale for such takeovers is often the possibility of ready access to a retail branch network while maintaining control. However, national governments through their central banks can complicate the takeover process in the interests of the national economy. The UK, German, Spanish and Italian authorities have all intervened in acquisitions affecting key parts of their financial services industry. More significantly, the Basle capital adequacy rules add constraints because of the need to inject new capital. Given such factors, plus the high financial costs often associated with hostile takeovers and the fear in profit- and cost-conscious financial institutions of having to subsidize unprofitable operations, many firms have recently favoured agreed mergers or cooperative ventures.

National mergers are apparent, for example the German *Landesbanken*, the Banco de Bilbao–Banco de Vizcaya (Spain) and Amro-ABN (Netherlands). The last-named indicates that not all of these are defensive, since the merged group now dominates the domestic market. Cross-border mergers and alliances tend to involve firms of similar size and market orientation, and to overcome national restrictions on takeovers. These invariably involve in the first instance cross-shareholdings, asset swaps or technology-sharing product distribution agreements rather than mergers *per se*. For example, equity swaps include 5 per cent between Banco Santander (Spain) and the Royal Bank of Scotland, and 2 per cent between Paribas (France) and Banca Commerciale Italiana (Italy). Cross-shareholdings often seek to combine entities with a strong regional presence and ambitions to increase their geographical scope without loss of identity. They can promote technological developments such as home-banking and can lead to product distribution agreements, for example the marketing of insurance or specialist products such as mortgages. As an example, Paribas (France) has linked with Hafnia, a Danish insurance company, while Abbey National has made several alliances, notably the acquisitions of Scottish Mutual (insurance) and Ficofrance (French mortgage lender), and joint ventures in Spain with the Cor group and a Swiss insurer and in Italy with Diner's Club.

Such external restructuring, together with diversification of functions encouraged by EC banking, investment and insurance directives, further the prospect of financial conglomerate growth. Crédit Lyonnais and Société Générale (France) and Dresdner and Deutsche Bank (Germany) epitomize this concept, especially the last-named, which is more than a domestic 'universal' bank offering securities trading, investment management and retail banking facilities. In recent years Deutsche Bank has acquired Morgan Grenfell (UK) and Bank of America's Italian operations, has taken holdings in Austrian, Portuguese, Spanish and Dutch banks, has opened a mortgage bank in Luxembourg and has established a German insurance company.

The major UK institutions have followed different conglomerate strategies in servicing the European market. For example, Barclays is essentially building on its brand name via its existing market presence and through cross-border promotion of its credit card operations, although it has acquired Européene de Crédit (France) and Merck, Finck and Co (Germany). NatWest is concentrating on specific zones, notably France, Spain and northern Italy, by developing a distribution network. To this end it has purchased control of two Spanish banks (Banco March and Banco d'Asturias) and a minority stake in Banca Credit West, and has acquired branches of Banque de L'Union Européene in France. In contrast to Barclays, NatWest see cross-border selling as having a limited role, hence the focus on specific countries. However, the corollary is that building a distribution network is expensive, and may be overtaken by technological events. Among merchant banks attempting a pan-European presence is Hambros, which has forged links with Banco Bilbao Vizcaya (Spain) and Sao Paulo Bank (Italy). UK merchant banks see opportunities in providing advisory and investment banking services to European industry, and in the expected growth in cross-border mergers, acquisitions and alliances after '1992'.

UK insurance companies have been reluctant to engage in European mergers and takeovers, tending instead to launch agencies and then convert to offices, such as Eagle Star in Greece, Netherlands and Portugal, or to link up with joint ventures, such as Commercial Union's marketing agreement with Credito Italiano. However, foreign inroads into the insurance market have been noted, e.g. the acquisition of Equity and Law by Cie du Midi and of Cornhill by Alliance. The latter is representative of 'Allfinanz' and 'Bancassurance' common on the Continent and shows that true financial conglomerates are emerging, offering a wide range of financial services. UK firms' preparations for the Single Market have followed this theme at home with related diversification and strategic alliances among domestic banks, building societies and insurers (Table 7.6).

The trend towards greater concentration and conglomerate growth in the financial system accords with economies of scale engendered by the Single Market and the EC directives, of which the Second Banking Directive is a role model for the all-embracing universal bank. However, various constraints exist, especially in the context of retail banking. The pace of technological innovation is rapid, the cost of delivery and payments is exorbitant, and the market-place is over-banked. For these reasons, many firms need to consolidate their domestic position, adjusting to economic forces at home before embarking on pan-European strategies. It is noticeable that universal banking has worked most successfully in relatively protected bank-dominated environments, such as Germany. There would still appear to be scope, therefore, for regional and specialist operators tailoring their products and services via local distribution systems. Indeed, in certain sectors such as housing finance differences in culture and operating systems make the local markets difficult to penetrate; and those entities with wider ambitions will need to have genuine pan-European products, such as credit cards, to be really successful.

Table 7.6 Strategic alliances between major UK financial institutions

Insurance company	Link[a]	Bank/building society
Barclays Life	Wholly owned subsidiary	Barclays Bank
Clerical Medical	NW Life, a JV owned 92.5% by	National Westminster Bank
Abbey Life	59% owned by	Lloyds Bank
Commercial Union	Midland Life, a JV owned 65% by	Midland Bank
Scottish Equitable	Royal Scottish Life, a JV 51% owned by	Royal Bank of Scotland
Standard Life	TA; also Halifax Standard Trust	
	Management (unit trusts), a JV	Halifax Building Society
Norwich Union	TA	Leeds Permanent Building Society
Sun Alliance	Woolwich Life, a JV owned 51% by	Woolwich Building Society
Scottish Amicable	TA	Alliance and Leicester Building Society

[a] JV = joint venture, TA = tied agent.

CONCLUSIONS

The forces of technological development and innovation, together with existing moves towards liberalization, are radically shaping European financial systems in such a way that markets are less segmented/more integrated, cover more risks and offer a wider range of products. New technology has allowed greater volumes of transactions to be undertaken, yet has promoted innovative risk-carrying and credit-creating instruments and trading procedures. Above all, it has promoted the quicker communication of developments and the wider dissemination of information, thus linking markets in varying time-zones.

Such market integration has been furthered by national desires for greater efficiency and access to international markets which have in turn prompted the reduction of price and quantity controls (e.g. easing of exchange controls) and the relaxation of restrictions on certain types of activity (e.g. the use of floating-rate notes in Germany). Indeed, Neven (1990) argues that the current EC directives represent a process of competitive deregulation that is more important than harmonization *per se*.

The basic functions of European financial systems remain those associated with their major traditional institutions, notably intermediation. However, as those systems have evolved to carry more risk in the face of liberalization, competition and changing customer demands, so too have their institutions. Within national boundaries a large amount of restructuring is apparent. The UK entities have traditionally been highly specialized in function, although operating in an open environment. In contrast, their counterparts in France and Germany have offered a wider range of services but within a relatively restricted domestic context.

Thus, European firms have faced important strategic choices as they position themselves in the new European market-place, in terms of both the direction involved and the methods employed. This process is still evolving, but the competitive demands of the modern financial European environment point to cooperative ventures, technological innovation and flexibility of delivery as key features for success.

FURTHER READING

See Chant (1992) and Rybcynski (1984, 1985) for perspectives on intermediation and financial system development. The role of UK financial institutions is covered by various writers including Buckle and Thompson (1992), Howells and Bain (1990), Partington (1989) and Pawley *et al*. (1991). For UK retail banking see Lewis and Davis (1987) and Howcroft and Lavis (1986), for building societies see Boleat (1986), and for insurance see Dodds (1987). European financial systems are covered by Mullineux (1987) and Gardener and Molyneux (1990). Dixon (1991) provides an introduction to banking in a Single Market context. Strategic and structural aspects are reviewed by Abraham and Liermann (1991) and Neven (1990).

FINANCIAL MARKETS: COOPERATION OR COMPETITION?

In the previous chapter the developing characteristics of modern European financial institutions were seen to be strongly influenced by the forces of product innovation, technology, deregulation and above all competition, which made firms increasingly profit- and cost-conscious in their strategic decisions. Such forces have also had an impact upon the other component parts of the financial system, the markets. Indeed, it was suggested that the evolution of the financial system is dependent upon its ability to carry risk, which is vital for the spread of innovation, capital formation, savings and growth. The evolution from a bank-dominated into a highly securitized market-oriented system is seen to enhance this risk-carrying capacity, mainly because markets can trade large volumes of savings yet offer a diverse range of assets with varying risk–reward profiles. As European economies have expanded in the past decade, there has been a rapid 'marketization' of their financial systems.

8.1 THE NATURE OF FINANCIAL CENTRES AND MARKETS

8.1.1 Financial centres

Many modern financial markets involve 'on-screen' trading and high-technology communications systems without necessarily having a physical market-place. Given the rapidity of technological advances, and the fact that financial services activity is spread throughout towns and cities in individual countries, one might assume that financial markets do not always need to be location-specific. However, in reality they have often tended to polarize in one main centre within a country. Moreover, in a European context these national centres appear to be competing to be *the* major European centre, or at least, to capture a significant share of European activity in a particular market. This leads to the following questions: How do financial centres develop? How do they sustain their advantage? What are the prospects for the major European centres in the Single Market?

Industrial location theory would suggest that basic influences on location decisions should include the availability of factor inputs (labour, materials, technology, etc.) and demand for the product or service produced. This leads inevitably to a consideration of relative transport costs in the final choice (Richardson 1978). But economies of scale may also be influential, both firm-specific from, say, its size of operation, and external economies from a common location with related organizations. Widening the analysis brings forth further factors, such as psychological influences related to the uncertain perception of different locations, the availability of reliable information on which to base the decision, and inertia. The latter derives from the often considerable 'sunk' costs of establishment in one specific location, which discourages a move.

Such a framework may be applied to financial centres. Factor inputs, notably a supply of available premises and labour, are important locational influences, but in the latter case technology may reduce the impact, e.g. with the decentralization of routine clerical or computer operations, such as registration activities. The move to 'on-screen' trading furthers this trend with the dispersion of dealing. On the demand side, the traditional importance of customer access has been discussed in banks' deliberations over their retail branch networks, although the advent of home-banking represents a departure from this viewpoint. In the context of wholesale financial markets, the growth of offshore financial centres would suggest that customer access is not necessarily a prime influence. Within financial firms there are internal economies to be gained from centralization of dealers, analysts and similar specialists; but, since most firms have more than one branch in a centre and branches in several centres, it may well be possible to make transfers in response to economic circumstances. The implication therefore is that financial institutions may not be as location-specific as formerly presumed.

If, however, we consider external economies of scale and 'sunk costs', a different scenario emerges. In essence, a body of expertise builds up over time and with it economies of information provision. This may derive from linkages with organized markets, or from the close proximity of trades and professions such as specialist lawyers, accountants and brokers geared to support financial institutions. Joint services are also important, such as clearing houses, research bodies, professional institutes and clubs which reinforce the information flow. Significantly, government officials and the head offices of major customers may be located in such centres to benefit from speedy access to their advisers, institutions and markets, thus strengthening the locational attraction. In terms of sunk costs, the start-up expenditure may be less important than for manufacturing, but the 'contact costs' arising from the business relationships that such centres generate will be more important. Hence withdrawal from the centre will not guarantee the continuance of these relationships and business opportunities.

In considering the continued development of major financial centres various general factors can be identified, notably a liberal business and trade environment which encourages entry and competition, the absence of capital controls, and political stability. However, growth ultimately develops from the dynamic aspects of the external economies mentioned above. Contacts and market participation increase with the number of firms involved, and as a reputation develops growth becomes self-sustaining, with new skills emerging and new firms being attracted. Modern technology can also polarize the growth of certain centres; indeed, with telecommunications advances and market integration, in theory continuous global market trading requires only one major centre in the United States, the Far East and Europe.

External economies are thus seen as key influences on the development of major financial centres, although their impact will vary according to the nature of the institutions involved. Certainly a pool of expertise, access to other financial institutions and business support services are central to international banks, while insurance firms would seem to benefit from proximity to organized insurance markets, brokers and legal firms. Yet in reality, the advent of information technology has meant that in the UK many insurance companies and building societies' headquarters are dispersed throughout the country. For markets, technology and contact needs are pervasive. Davis (1990) suggests that primary issuing trading (e.g. new equity, bonds, loan syndication) requires a greater need for personal contact and established relationships than does secondary trading, especially where there are commodity operations or homogeneous products (government bonds, foreign exchange). Here technology can aid the dispersion of securities trading although the attraction of centres with established reputations and international banking cannot be denied.

Significant benefits accrue to economies from developing international financial centres. Positive macroeconomic effects are invisible earnings for the balance of payments, employment and growth. The latter aspects stem from self-sustaining external economies. These benefits are seen to outweigh costs associated with diseconomies of agglomeration, such as transport congestion, housing availability and pricing, regional dislocation and de-industrialization, although arguably some of these will occur in major cities anyway. In a European context, the Single Market may prove an impetus to self-sustaining growth for a pre-eminent centre or centres with specific 'prizes', such as the location of the EMI and ECB. Not surprisingly, most European centres are actively competing for such business.

8.1.2 Financial markets

An insight into the prospects for European financial centres can be gained from an examination of their markets. On the one hand, the aforementioned external economies might imply that groups of markets may be so closely interrelated that they can operate effectively in only one location. This would reinforce the growth of one or two major centres at the expense of the 'minnows'. Conversely, markets might be considered more footloose than firms, especially with the advent of technological advances in communications and the fact that many market functions involve secondary trading. Moreover, in theory, the deregulation associated with the Single Market could allow a more widespread location for financial services, possibly with the emergence of specialized niche markets. What is apparent is that past changes in markets' locations have had an important influence on institutions' location decisions, as seen in the influx of foreign banks to London in the 1960s following the establishment of the Euromarkets. Clearly, no centre will wish to risk losing existing markets and so all will be keen to minimize diseconomies such as congestion or high office costs, and to ensure that the markets' operations instil confidence in participants.

Financial markets vary in their function and nature but they are not always easy to classify. This can be illustrated by reference to the UK. One common distinction is that between maturity with markets for long-term instruments (capital markets) and those for very short-term instruments (money markets). Gilbody (1988) and Howells and Bain (1990) broadly follow this classification, with the last-named including the bond, equities and mortgage markets in the former category and the discount, interbank, CD, local authority and Eurocurrency markets in the latter. Most authors agree that market interdependence is increasing, thus blurring the distinctions between markets on a maturity basis. Such a classification omits the important UK insurance, foreign exchange and derivative markets which cover a range of maturities, although here a common feature is risk management.

Alternative methods of classification focus on the operational nature of the markets. Physical markets are now less common than 'screen-based' ones, although paradoxically the newer derivative markets often have physical market places, whereas the older share and bond markets have moved 'off-floor'. Within stock markets an important distinction can be made between the primary new issues, and secondary valuation and trading market.

In examining the relative opportunities for different European centres and their markets, our attention will focus on the major equity and derivative markets. There are four reasons for this. Firstly, the markets for retail banking services, and to a lesser extent insurance, have been examined through the institutional context of the previous chapter. Related to this, most financial systems, whether bank-dominated or not, have short-term money markets, essentially serving domestic banks' liquidity needs, and not by themselves sufficient to compete for business with their foreign counterparts.

Secondly, in international banking and bonds, insurance and foreign exchange, London has a pre-eminent role in Europe (Table 8.1). This position is considered further in Sec. 8.6, but it seems unlikely that this dominance will be seriously challenged by other centres, notwithstanding their growth and problems in London with Lloyds insurance market.

Thirdly, the development of capital and derivative markets marks the transition to a securitized financial system, especially when accompanied by deregulation and exposure to competitive forces. Indeed, the series of 'Big and Little Bangs' affecting European stock markets (UK 1986, France and Spain 1989, Italy 1991) was prompted in part by the need to enhance local capital-raising capabilities, but in part by the fear that companies would move elsewhere to raise funds, thus undermining the domestic financial system.

Fourthly, in recent years capital and derivative markets have experienced rapid growth and innovation in terms of both the products traded and the technology applied. This in turn has spurred competition between these markets while at the same time bringing them closer together. Thus, competition or cooperation are recurrent tensions in their development.

Notwithstanding technical considerations, financial markets operate largely on the basis of confidence. The market mood is liable to change if confronted with a sudden reversal in economic activity, but even more so if the market's reputation itself is tarnished. Hence for effective operation financial markets, especially those relating to equities and derivatives, need to satisfy certain prerequisites, i.e. adequate yet not restrictive supervision, technological competence and efficiency. Changes in the first two areas impinge upon the third.

In recent years European capital markets have paid considerable attention to the modernization of their regulatory and technical frameworks. Supervisory changes have tended to focus on deregulating heavily restricted markets, hence 'Big Bang' and 'Little Bang'. Within individual countries liberalization has followed one of two paths: either a relaxation of price or quantity controls, as with exchange controls in France, or an easing of limitations on certain activities, such as futures trading in Germany. In addition, at the EC level in preparation for the Single Market various directives have focused upon capital move-

Table 8.1 Market shares, major European financial centres

Index	UK	France	Germany	Italy	Netherlands	Switzerland
Banking[a]	20	7	4	2	3	6
Foreign exchange[b]	32	—	—	—	—	10
Stock markets[c]	38	25	12	5	10	10
Derivative markets[d]	37	30	8	—	10	8

[a] Gross lending as a % share of total market as at end-1989.
[b] % shares of turnover of major global foreign exchange centres as at end-1989.
[c] % shares of total market capitalization of above centres as at end-1990.
[d] % shares of all European options and futures contracts traded as at end-1990.

ments, harmonization of key prudential standards and mutual recognition of the way those standards are applied. However, such changes bring forth the issue of the extent to which self-regulation or intervention is appropriate in individual markets. This debate is manifest in the UK, where competition has encouraged deregulation of self-imposed cartel rules, yet the 1986 Financial Services Act imposes stringent and far-reaching legislation on a wide range of industry activities based on functional rather than institutional criteria. It is practitioner-based self-regulation within a statutory framework. The fundamental issue was the need to modernize the UK's segmented markets while denying access to unsuitable practitioners. However, the shift in the regulatory framework shows that deregulation is often more about the reorganization of controls than about their elimination (Henderson 1989).

Attempts at European coordination of market activity are concerned with guarding against a systematic crisis in securities markets, rather than with regulation *per se*. Here attention is being directed to agreements on common capital adequacy standards for securities firms and at upgrading settlement systems. A major concern is that markets should be technically competent, yet not be driven by technology to unnecessary strain. The 1987 worldwide stock market crash had various underlying causes, but arguably advances in communications and computer technology, such as programmed trading, exacerbated the crisis. Pre-arranged 'sell' orders were executed when stock prices fell to particular levels, thus adding to a falling market. The converse use of technology to place limits on programme trading, or the use of 'circuit-breakers' to close markets at times of high variability, offer no guarantees against contagion, and moreover, by preventing trading, create market inefficiency. Markets may or may not behave differently when they are executed by computer-based systems as opposed to open-outcry, physical markets; but as Crystal (1992) notes, modern technology now integrates markets so closely that stresses are transmitted quickly and regulators thus have less control over their domestic markets.

Market efficiency is central to any consideration of capital markets since the main functions of these markets are normally to raise funds for investment, spread risk, and accurately price and trade financial assets. The secondary functions of a securities market are not directly involved in fund allocation for the finance of firms; but, by estimating the level of risk and pricing securities, the secondary market gives information signals to primary issuers and also to traders in that market. Hence market efficiency implies that security prices fully reflect all available information that could affect the price of a security, and the interpretations of that information. Moreover, the assumption is that new information received will lead to a rapid and unbiased adjustment in price. In this way, an efficient market establishes security prices as true indicators of the value of a security, and investors will not be consistently disadvantaged, or make abnormal returns compared with other market participants.

However, the above *Efficient Markets Hypothesis* (EMH), i.e. that prices 'immediately and fully reflect all available and relevant information', will suffer imperfections if, for example, not all investors are able to interpret the market information, if the information is partial or inaccurate, and if transaction costs, market operations or regulations distort prices. Information efficiency has been tested by various studies to determine whether future prices are predictable, including tests of the effectiveness of trading rules to produce profits above what a 'buy and hold' strategy would generate. These studies have tended to follow from a threefold classification of financial market efficiency: weak form, semi-strong form, and strong form (Fama 1980).

With the weak-form EMH and associated tests, the market is considered efficient if current security prices fully and instantaneously reflect all past information. Thus, future price changes are independent of past movements, implying that past prices provide no clues about the future, and that therefore there are no mechanical trading rules based on historical price patterns that will yield excess profits; the market is deemed to have no memory, and prices follow a 'random walk' without any serial correlation with past movements. The vast bulk of evidence appears overwhelmingly to support the 'random walk' approach and implies that markets are efficient in a weak-form sense. However, this has not daunted 'chartists', who use technical analysis of past patterns to predict future trends. In spite of proof that the practice does not consistently produce superior results, it continues, partly, as Griffiths (1991) suggests, because of human desire to foretell the future and the strength of anecdotal argument.

The semi-strong form EMH holds that prices adjust instantaneously and fully to all new publicly available information. By implication, the market absorbs the information and dealers adjust their prices accordingly, with, *ceteris paribus*, good news leading to a rise in prices, bad news to a fall. Tests have tended to focus on the speed of adjustment and price response to specific information, notably accounting data. If the market is inefficient in this sense, then it may be worth undertaking fundamental analysis of company reports, accounting statements and other information to detect discrepancies between the share's market price and its intrinsic worth. The general consensus of research is that the market appears to compound new information quickly; indeed, in the case of annual reports, most of the 'news' is anticipated and incorporated before their publication. Thus markets seem to be efficient in a semi-strong sense, and intensive fundamental analysis will not consistently generate excess returns. However, the existence of such activity paradoxically helps to enhance efficiency as it adds to the information set available.

The strong-form test of the EMH judges market efficiency by observing the adjustment of share prices to all available information, whether publicly available or privy to insiders. By implication, if strong efficiency exists then share prices will always reflect their intrinsic worth, and thus 'insiders' holding 'privileged' information will be unable to benefit from it. The evidence in this regard is inconclusive, partly because identification of non-public information is difficult. Tests have focused upon examining the investment behaviour of individuals likely to be insiders, and on the performance of large institutional investors. Essentially, any individual may become an insider if he or she deals for gain on the basis of unpublished, price-sensitive information. In the 1980s there were several notable cases, such as Boesky in the USA and Collier in the UK, which suggest that the strong form of the EMH does not hold. In any case, insider dealing is an illegal activity. Institutional investors, on the other hand, spend considerable resources on assessing companies in which they have investments, and much of the information is privately, but not illegally, obtained. However, these institutions do not necessarily earn excessive returns when their research costs are taken into account. So in the context of the EMH, the general consensus seems to be that capital markets exhibit weak- and semi-strong forms of informational efficiency, but are not necessarily strongly efficient.

The foregoing assumes that the EMH is a valid framework for interpreting share price behaviour. Under the EMH the share price equates with its fundamental or intrinsic value. An alternative perspective is that share prices are also affected by bouts of optimism and pessimism which create 'noise', in this context perceived as opposed to actual information. Consequently share prices may experience 'speculative bubbles', whereby the actual price diverges from that warranted on fundamental grounds, the direction depending upon the balance of optimism and pessimism. When expectations are not realized a sharp price adjustment may occur. Such a feature is one explanation for the sudden 30 per cent fall in UK share prices associated with the October 1987 'crash'.

Overall, between 1980 and September 1987 UK share prices rose on average fivefold, with earnings per share (e.p.s.) and price/earnings (P/E) ratios doubling. However, Table 8.2 indicates that the rate of growth of e.p.s. had slowed from 1986 even though share prices had accelerated, to such an extent that P/E ratios had risen to disproportionately high levels. These could be sustained only if future earnings growth was expected to be faster than in the past, which was not the case. Throughout the 1980s a fairly steady relationship had been maintained between earnings yields on shares and gilts yields, as investors switched portfolios between both to equalize their returns. However, in 1987 the earnings yield on shares fell to 7 per cent while the gilt yield was over 9 per cent; so for the earnings yield to rise in line with gilts a 30 per cent fall in share prices was needed. When this occurred share price levels again reflected their fundamental values. This sharp fall in share prices appears inconsistent with a price-efficient market, although an alternative interpretation is that the market exhibits long-run efficiency combined with temporary self-correcting anomalies. Indeed, on this basis, the correction itself is evidence of efficiency.

The other forms of efficiency to be considered are allocative and operational efficiency. The former relates to the services that financial markets provide for the economy as a whole, notably the financing of real investment, and implies that funds will be directed to those firms with the best investment opportunities. However, given their volume of activity, it is arguable that the capital markets have relatively little to do with the direct financing of real investment, or with

Table 8.2 The stock market 'crash' of October 1987 and P/E ratios

	Growth rate (% change p.a.)			Yields (% average)			
	Share prices[a]	Dividends[b]	Earnings[c]	Gilts[d]	Dividends[e]	Earnings[e]	P/E ratios
1981	13.3	2.9	−11.8	14.7	6.0	14.7	6.9
1982	15.9	5.8	−1.6	12.9	5.5	12.3	8.1
1983	27.1	6.9	4.4	10.8	4.6	10.1	9.9
1984	19.1	15.2	24.4	10.7	4.5	10.6	9.5
1985	23.6	21.4	21.9	10.6	4.4	10.4	9.6
1986	24.1	11.2	9.3	9.9	3.9	9.2	10.9
1987	38.0	12.7	5.9	9.3	3.2	7.3	13.8

[a] FT-Actuaries index of 500 industrial, oil shares (nominal value).
[b] FT-Actuaries index × gross yield.
[c] FT-Actuaries index × earnings yield (net) on full payment basis.
[d] 20-year gilt.
[e] FT-Actuaries index: average yield.

the translation of savings into corporate business investment (see Tobin 1984). This impinges on contentious issues concerning short-termism and industry–institution relations, to be examined in Chapter 9.

Operational efficiency exists when the transaction costs and difficulties of buying and selling market securities are minimized. This implies that under competitive conditions market-makers and brokers earn only normal profits as rewards for supplying investors with marketability, information and intermediary functions. If, in contrast, there are fixed commission rates or barriers to entry to the agency or market-making function, and if the research and information services provided about the traded securities are inaccurate, then the market involved would be deemed operationally inefficient. It would also misallocate resources and lead to inefficient pricing of assets. Such issues were central to the operational changes made to many major markets in the 1970s and 1980s.

In most markets membership has widened, capital resources have increased, and negotiated commission scales have replaced fixed ones. In a competitive market it seems fair to assume that transaction costs will fall as the number and liquidity of market-makers increases, especially when their profits come from both dealing and taking positions in specific stocks. Nevertheless, some sources of operational inefficiency will be hard to eliminate, notably investors' ignorance and failure to investigate the merits of their proposed investments, or their inability to question management actions and use of funds raised.

It can be seen that, although market efficiency is often equated with informational efficiency, both allocative and operational efficiency are also prerequisites for successful capital market operations. The significance of an efficient market is that all levels of investor have confidence that the prices paid are a fair reflection of the value of a firm. In turn, that the share price will reflect the company's ability to raise capital, and managers will know that the decisions they take will add to, or reduce, the value of the firm, and thus be mirrored in the share price. As European countries overhaul their stock markets, therefore, they seek efficiency gains lest their companies move to alternative financial centres to raise capital.

8.2 THE UK

8.2.1 The International Stock Exchange of the UK and the Republic of Ireland (ISE)

The International Stock Exchange in London is Europe's biggest equity market by capitalization (Table 8.3). It is essentially a capital market, where government and industry can raise long-term capital and investors can buy and sell securities. The former, primary issue, function covers gilts, corporate bonds and equities; the latter, secondary, function is the trading of these and selected foreign stocks and shares. Around this market function have been built the Exchange's operations: its membership, dealing and settlement rules, its listing requirements for companies seeking quotation, and its advisory services.

From modest beginnings as one of several late-eighteenth-century voluntary groups meeting in a London coffee house, the Stock Exchange in London emerged as the leading private exchange by means of attrition or assimilation of its competitors. This private 'club' membership foundation survived until recently, notwithstanding fundamental operating changes inflicted by 'Big Bang' in October 1986. Supervision has been a mixture of self-regulation and government scrutiny with greater emphasis on the former. Thus, as a 'private' bourse the ISE contrasts with the 'bankers' bourses common in Germanic-based and Scandinavian financial systems, and with the 'public' bourses operated under government authority in the more Latin-based European countries such as France, Spain and Italy.

Before October 1986 the Stock Exchange's 4582 members were organized into 192 broking and 17 jobbing firms along strict functional separation lines. Under 'single capacity', stockbrokers ('brokers') acted as *agents* for the investing public, earning commissions on deals negotiated with jobbers, managing portfolios and providing investment advice. The stockjobbers ('jobbers'), as *principals*, acted as wholesalers in stocks and shares, making profits on the differences at which they bought and sold. They traded securities on a competing market-maker basis but could deal only with brokers, not with the public direct. To reinforce the position of the jobbers and make the market wider and more liquid, the Stock Exchange insisted that all deals be channelled through jobbers rather than between brokers. To avoid broker discontent at this in the event of their being able to deal more cheaply between themselves, the Stock Exchange required that minimum fixed commissions be paid to brokers. Investing clients

Table 8.3 Major European equity markets, December 1990

	Market capitalization (£bn)			Total market turnover (£bn)	Shares traded	
	Bond	Equity	Total		Domestic	Foreign
Belgium	66	34	100	4.3	293	178
Denmark	100	22	122	5.6	329	14
France	252	159	411	65.3	892	278
Germany	n.a.	194	194	450.3	776	616
Italy	1	85	86	14.7	334	0
Luxembourg	n.a.	5	5	0.9	61	199
Netherlands	82	77	159	22.2	347	309
UK	191	445	636	643.8	2081	742
Portugal	n.a.	n.a.	n.a.	n.a.	n.a.	n.a.
Spain	29	64	93	22.3	427	2
Greece	13	8	21	2.8	229	0

were charged 1.65 per cent on the first £7000 of deal values, 0.55 per cent on the next £8000, 0.5 per cent on the next £115 000, 0.4 per cent on the next £17 000, 0.3 per cent on the next £600 000, 0.2 per cent on the next £1 million and 0.125 per cent thereafter.

These commission scales undoubtedly raised the cost of dealing and were a restraint on trade, but single capacity was favoured by the Exchange as it had built-in protection for investors. Brokers were committed to deal at best for their clients and to offer impartial advice. Jobbers dealt in their own interest but competed with each other so as to maintain a continuous market and price securities in line with supply and demand. For members there were limited capital needs. Brokers were merely agents, whereas jobbers handled large volumes with modest sums because of order-flow concentration; that is, brokers fed orders to relatively few jobbers. For the Exchange, single capacity made supervision relatively easy as it reduced the potential for conflicts of interest. As Goodhart (1987) comments, where operators are both agents and principals there is a temptation to offload unwanted securities on clients, or to push through unnecessarily frequent deals ('churning'), or to place new issues in portfolios managed for clients, or simply to act illegally by fraud or insider dealing.

Pressure for reform of this self-regulating, oligopolistic, price-fixing club arose in the late 1970s and early 1980s from various commercial sources. Institutional investors had become increasingly more significant in securities trading. In seeking to diversify and 'internationalize' their portfolios, they were attracted to efficient markets where they could trade large volumes of stock and benefit from economies of scale in transaction costs. Their importance was mirrored by the decline in influence of the private client. This resultant change in investor structure and rise in average transaction size put pressure on the jobbers, whose numbers fell from 100 in 1970 to 17 in 1986, of which only 5 were substantial.

Larger-size orders meant the need to pool resources but reduced the potential competitiveness and efficiency of the market.

Another feature was the greater internationalization of securities trading, made manifest in terms of technological developments which allowed for information dissemination, market integration and the growth of 'securitization'. These aspects fuelled the need for UK reforms in several ways. Firstly, deregulation of the New York market in 1975 enabled it to gain business from London, notably large deals involving trading in the major 20 equities. On the London Stock Exchange equity transactions attracted stamp duty (2 per cent until 1984), which could be avoided with transfers of UK securities in the USA. There, deals traditionally took the form of transfers of American depository receipts (ADRs) rather than the equities themselves. ADRs were issued by US depository banks once the registered shares that they represented were lodged at a bank overseas. Hence dealings in major UK stocks on US markets became significantly cheaper than on the London Stock Exchange.

Secondly, although overseas firms were increasingly attracted to London, this was not necessarily to participate in the Stock Exchange but rather to exploit the City's location and expertise. Moreover, the greater sophistication of corporate treasurers in their financing methods had promoted securitization, and in particular expansion of the international Eurobond market based in London. This provided a competitive alternative to domestic equity and bond financing, especially with the advent of swaps, options and futures, and, above all, the abolition of exchange control.

In addition to such external factors, internal rules threatened the competitiveness of the market. Restrictions on Stock Exchange membership left member firms undercapitalized, technologically backward and uncompetitive *vis à vis* competing exchanges in the USA and Japan. Outside institutions could retain only a maximum 10 per cent shareholding (imposed in 1971 and raised to 29.9 per cent in 1982), so that membership of wider corporate bodies was effectively curtailed. This prevented the capital injections needed for effective and efficient market-making.

The most significant pressure for greater operational efficiency came from the need to reform the minimum commission scale. Indeed, arguably the proximate cause of 'Big Bang' was criticism of this membership and commission structure by the Office of Fair Trading, which identified procedures contrary to the 1956 Restrictive Practices Act and, moreover, proposed legal action. In June 1983 agreement was reached between the Secretary of State for Trade and Industry and the Stock Exchange whereby the government would exempt the Stock Exchange from legal action provided it abolished its minimum fixed commission scales by the end of 1986. This led the way for sweeping reforms, since, with negotiated commissions, greater competition and capital needs, single capacity was no longer tenable.

The new structure was effected during 1986. A 'Little Bang' occurred on 1 March when the Stock Exchange Council relaxed the rules on ownership of participating firms so that limited-liability membership was permitted and outsiders were now able to fully own member firms, and establish new firms from scratch. By October 1986, out of 209 original member firms, mainly partnerships, more than half had become part of larger groupings or had otherwise lost their identity. Moreover, by January 1987 new entrants had boosted membership to 360, although this included separately capitalized subsidiaries of some firms, such as those operating in the gilt-edged market (Ingram 1987). Such changes were needed to bring capital and liquidity to the market in the wake of the abandonment of fixed commissions and, inevitably, single capacity. With the prospect of lower commissions, brokers would be forced to diversify into securities trading, a high-risk, capital-intensive business in the new technological environment. Hence the attraction of alliances with banks and overseas investment firms which were keen to diversify into UK securities trading and could supply the necessary financial muscle.

The main reforms took place on 27 October 1986 in a swift changeover, hence 'Big Bang'. Fixed commissions and single capacity were replaced by a 'dual-capacity, quote-driven market-maker system'. Stock Exchange member firms would henceforth have to be separately capitalized entities of their parent financial groups. However, all are regarded as dual-capacity broker-dealers, acting either as principals (buying from and selling to clients in direct deals from their own book), or as agents (arranging deals for clients through other broker/dealers for a negotiated commission). Members are obliged to inform their clients of the capacity in which they operate, and cannot act in both capacities simultaneously. If firms wish to deal on a permanent basis, they must register as market-makers, which implies quoting firm prices and maintaining an active, continuous and liquid market in specified stocks (the counterpart of the old jobber function).

The emergence of the dual-capacity structure and the elimination of fixed-commission scales changed the basis of charging fees. For private-client, agency work firms charge separate commissions as before, but the rate varies as to the security, amount and whether the service provided is 'execution-only' (dealing) or whether advice or portfolio management is involved. Thus, rates vary considerably between and within firms according to the services required.

The new system depends totally on technological innovation. Sophisticated electronic information, dealing and settlement facilities have been devised to cater for the increased volume of activity and the required speed and reliability of data transmission. Dealing has changed from face-to-face contact on the Stock Exchange floor to 'on-screen', computerized market-making with bargains completed by telephone. Central to dealing is the computerized price display system SEAQ (Stock Exchange Automated Quotations), which provides 'real-time' bid and offer prices for over 3 500 securities. This information is relayed via TOPIC, a videotext information system, to members or investing subscribers in diverse locations. Users of SEAQ can see on-screen details of market-makers' trading prices and the volume of shares to which a particular trade relates. All equity transactions must be transmitted to SEAQ within three minutes by the market-maker concerned, so that the information can feed back into SEAQ to update prices and maintain price efficiency, and also to be recorded as part of the market surveillance process. Hence trading is more visible and independent than in the days of the old trading floor.

The gilt-edged securities market was restructured in parallel with the equity market changes under 'Big Bang'. Dual-capacity gilt-edged market-makers (GEMMs) replaced existing jobbers and brokers, and screen-based trading displaced on-floor operations. Other market participants include inter-dealer brokers (IDBs) whose role is to allow market-makers to take up or unwind positions, and money brokers, who act as intermediaries in borrowing or lending stock and cash. Far from being a deregulated activity, however, gilt-edged market operations are supervised by the Bank of England through the government broker. The overall policy is to encourage a broad, liquid and competitive market which satisfies the financing needs of government and, where necessary, assists monetary control, notably the reduction of money supply growth via gilt sales.

At the time of 'Big Bang' 27 GEMMs registered, including nine new operators from overseas. All firms were separately capitalized, and collectively they brought much needed liquidity to the market. However, the intensely competitive operating conditions reduced numbers to 22 by 1989, with Lloyds Bank, Morgan Grenfell and Citicorp Scrimgeour Vickers all having withdrawn. Moreover, the traditional government PSBR had been replaced by a PSDR, thus reducing the scale of new market operations as maturing debt was redeemed. Accordingly, during 1987 and 1988 GEMMs made heavy losses in spite of increases in turnover compared with pre-'Big Bang'. Much of the commission income in the market had disappeared with most deals struck at net prices. At the private-client end, a wide range of rates prevail, and for small bargains charges rose rapidly after 1986. Not surprisingly, most small investors tend to trade more cheaply and conveniently by using the National Savings Stock Register via post offices.

Between October 1988 and January 1991 there were no new gilt issues, but during 1991 new issues totalling £13.9 billion were launched (Bank of England 1992c). Various issuing techniques have been adopted, including minimum price tenders, direct placings with the Bank of England to sell 'on tap' to the GEMMs in the secondary market, and auctions. The latter were first used in May 1987 and have proved successful with active bidding. The Bank of England feels that the market is entering a period of stability, as indicated by the return to profitability of the GEMMs and a resurgence of investor interest after three years of market contraction. However, given that the top six firms undertake 63 per cent of retail turnover, further withdrawals cannot be discounted, even though Deutsche Bank's recent entry to the market means there are now 19 GEMMs.

The ISE consists of two formal equity markets covering 2000 shares: the Official List, and the Unlisted Securities Market. The latter caters for smaller, growth firms and is less demanding in its listing requirements. Stocks quoted on SEAQ are classified into 12 normal market size (NMS) bands ranging from 500 to 200 000 shares calculated on the basis of turnover in the previous year of trading. These are normally used as, firstly, the minimum quote size (MQS), i.e. namely the minimum number of shares in which market-makers are obliged to display prices on SEAQ for securities in which they are registered; secondly, to calculate the maximum on-line publication level (MPL), normally three times NMS, which is the maximum bargain size in each security published on SEAQ following trade reporting; and thirdly, the maximum SAEF size (MSS), the maximum bargain size in each SEAQ security that can be transacted via SAEF (SEAQ automatic execution facility). After much delay, SAEF was introduced in 1989 and is further evidence of the increasing role of technology in the London market. It is designed to simplify low-value share dealing and allows members to transact deals by computer link rather than telephone, providing a faster, more efficient service, with an 'audit trail' to monitor deals if required. In this way, small-order information is fed into SEAQ along with details of quotations and deals executed. The orders are automatically matched against the best possible price and the bargain reported.

One area where the ISE has lagged in technological upgrading is in its settlement facilities. TALISMAN, the transaction clearing system, was introduced in 1979 to automate the transfer and registration of security ownership by putting all shares sold into a computerized temporary nominee, SEPON. It replaced a labour-intensive, inefficient and expensive system which had existed for about a century and which Griffiths (1991) estimates cost £100 million per annum amd employed 5000 people. However, TALISMAN failed to modernize the whole settlement system, leaving many operations dependent upon the physical movement of stock; this has frequently resulted in backlogs of orders, especially in the aftermath of 'Big Bang'. To overcome this problem a fully computerized system for paperless share settlement is being introduced: TAURUS (Transfer and Automated Registration of Uncertificated Stock). Investors will continue to receive dividends and company reports, but share certificates will be replaced by regular statements showing their holdings, together with a confidential investor authorization code for use when selling.

TAURUS was originally planned to operate from October 1991, but it has been dogged by delays and at the time of writing is not expected to start much before mid-1993. The delays stem from technical problems but also from concerns voiced by the Law Society to the DTI over regulations governing the ownership of shares under the new system. The original cost estimates of between £45 and £50 million spread over a five-year period have now virtually doubled. Many stockbrokers are critical of the changes, arguing that TAURUS may deter individual investors from dealing and is far from paperless, creating new share statements instead of certificates. Moreover, private-client brokers face additional expenditures resulting from the changeover, and bemoan the accompanying introduction of rolling settlement to replace the traditional fortnightly account: instead of paying for shares ten days after the end of the two weeks in which the investor bought them, he or she will have to pay for them in a ten-day period after purchase. The Stock Exchange aims to reduce this to five and eventually three days, arguing that rolling settlement will reduce the incidence of backlogs, enhance liquidity and raise operational efficiency. Brokers contend that the five-day settlement would be to the advantage of bank-owned firms which find it easier to offer integrated banking and broking services; but private-client brokers would either have to hold a client's money on account or have access to swift money transmission services, both of which will raise their costs.

Competing continental stock exchanges will be pleased at the problems accompanying the launch of TAURUS—indeed, with any difficulties that might curtail the advance of the ISE in trading international equities. A major success story for the London market has been SEAQ International (SEAQI), the market information service launched in 1985 as temporary support for the growing telephone market in international stocks. By 1990 it had transacted £150 billion of foreign equities and 93 per cent of European cross-border activity. Essentially, SEAQI provides a collection point for quotations from competing international market-makers operating in London; but, by linking with commercial network operators such as Reuters and Pont Data, the ISE has provided a worldwide display of quotations.

Future SEAQI plans are extensive. Firstly, with the advent of sophisticated information systems the London market is more transparent than other bourses; on the UK domestic market small trades are published immediately and large, wholesale trades 90 minutes after they occur, yet on the international market publication is the following day. The intention is to create a single wholesale market for domestic and non-UK stocks with relatively low-key regulation as preferred by professional investors and participants. The retail domestic market would be subjected to closer scrutiny to satisfy investment regulators concerned about the adverse impact on investor protection caused by reporting delays. Secondly, whereas SEAQI currently provides an electronic information service, the intention is to develop reporting and confirmation arrangements with possible links to national settlement systems. However, the most significant and controversial planned change is to open SEAQI further to non-UK securities firms and possibly foreign stock exchanges, with the intention of establishing London as the world's foremost market for international equities and equity-based instruments. For it to succeed, more non-UK-based market-makers would need to participate, both in dealing and in the formulation of rules covering market operations. For foreign stock exchange involvement they are likely to require equal status in ownership and governance, as they resent losing business to London, yet recognize the risk of being left further behind without participation.

Undoubtedly, in the context of SEAQI London has benefited, among other things, firstly from deregulation in advance of its European competitors, secondly from the market-oriented nature of its financial system with the ability to assimilate risk and cater for large deals, thirdly from its location as one corner of the global time-zone triangle with New York and Tokyo, and fourthly from its reputation. In the latter context, the restructuring of the market and its supervision are significant features. The growth of international securities business in London and the widening of share ownership of member firms culminated in 1986 in the decision of the Stock Exchange and the International Securities Regulatory Organization (ISRO), representing bond and equity dealers, to coordinate activities. In order to comply with the 1986 Financial Services Act, two bodies were created: the Securities Association, a self-regulatory organization (SRO), to oversee the operations of Stock Exchange members and others in dealing with investors; and the International Stock Exchange of the United Kingdom and Republic of Ireland (ISE or Stock Exchange), a recognized investment exchange (RIE).

The merger and new name was seen as giving the Stock Exchange an opportunity to become the main focus for world trade in international equities. In February 1992 the ISE announced that thereafter members would be represented by their companies in so far as they are corporate members. Those members who are sole traders will have to join a new professional body, the Securities Institute, akin to the Law Society or Institute of Chartered Accountants, responsible for professional training and lobbying. Regulation of the market and members in their dealings will continue via the Securities and Futures Association (SFA), the SRO that evolved from the merger of the TSA (The Securities Association), and another SRO, the Association of Futures Dealers and Brokers (AFDB). The abolition of individual membership is seen as necessary to widen corporate membership so that those who use the Exchange have a role in running it, and to ensure that the market retains sufficient liquidity for international-scale operations.

In the initial aftermath of 'Big Bang' the performance of the ISE was impressive, with significant rises in the volume of business, numbers of large bargains, market visibility and capital raised. The average number of daily equity transactions virtually doubled to 58 000 in 1987 (Valentine 1988). Some 31 firms began trading as equity market-makers on 27 October 1986 and a year later there were 35, most of whom were quoting firm prices for large-size, major company security transactions on SEAQ. As expected, transaction costs fell sharply, with the average effective commission for domestic equities on institutional business halved from 0.4 to 0.2 per cent, and on very large deals above £2–£3 million rates of 0.125 per cent were obtainable (Ingram 1987). Thus, the market was able to absorb increasing volumes of activity, and, although customer business dominated, intra-market-maker activity became significant in value terms, accounting for half of total trade.

This situation changed with the crash of October 1987. Domestic trading dwindled, brokers' losses increased and capital raising activity slumped. Several firms, including the Virgin Group, withdrew from the market and the number of listed companies fell from 2961 in 1987 to 1781 in 1989. Between October

1987 and 1990 turnover halved to £196 billion and the numbers of market-makers fell to 24 as revenue and margins slumped (Euromoney 1992). Although average commission rates have continued to fall (to 0.19 per cent in 1990 on institutional deals), minimum commissions have risen to £20–£30 on small deals. In spite of a 'mini-boom' in early 1991 and a greater volume of trading, the underlying UK domestic market scenario has remained one of excess capacity to which market participants have been forced to adjust, trimming their labour forces accordingly. Those UK and foreign banks that scrambled to buy jobbers and brokers in the run-up to 'Big Bang' in 1986 saw brokerage as the key to profitability, paying vast sums in goodwill to buy into member firms. However, generous fixed commissions have been replaced by tough negotiated rates with market power in the hands of large investing institutions who trade sufficient volumes to generate a profit. Broking houses cut their spreads to attract business, but only at the cost of reducing market-makers' 'touch', the difference between buying and selling prices. Typical current strategies include specializing in the largest, most active 'Eurostocks', omitting many UK equities deemed unprofitable.

In the light of these trends, the ISE has recently reviewed its market-making operations. London has traditionally had systems that focus on marketability, i.e. a quote-driven system based on jobbers' and, after 'Big Bang', on market-makers' quotes on SEAQ. Many overseas, especially US, firms were accustomed to order-driven systems and the ISE has proposed concentrating market-making in the hands of 'matching principals'. These would match buy and sell orders as well as acting as market-makers. Investors would buy or sell immediately at the principal's quote or wait until a matching order appeared and deal without a spread. For those stocks considered too illiquid to be traded this way, a 'bulletin board' will exist on which traders can advertise orders. However, as Thomas (1989) suggests, a major reason for maintaining the quote-driven system is the success of SEAQI, which is potentially a prime mechanism for the integration of European markets. If further non-UK-based securities market-makers are persuaded to participate, it could lead to a federation of European markets with London supreme.

The 'Big Bang' may be seen as a success in terms of the ISE's international equity business. It trades almost as many overseas shares as it does domestic ones, its operating costs are lower than other centres, and its institutional investors, pension funds and insurance companies have been able to diversify their portfolios internationally and at lower costs. Notwithstanding the October 1987 'crash', the October 1989 'downturn' and occasional instances of insider dealing, the Exchange is generally considered as price-efficient and well-policed as any stock exchange. Nevertheless, the ISE faces potential long-term threats from various sources. For example, Scott-Quinn (1990) cites inter-market competition from overseas exchanges such as NASDAQ (National Association of Securities Dealers), the US over-the-counter market, or the Paris bourse with its computer aided trading system (CATS), not to mention disintermediated markets such as Reuters' Instinet offering investor–dealer direct access, and the growing futures and options markets in Europe. However, immediate problems lie closer to home, with the implementation of TAURUS and, arguably, the need for a more profitable and stronger domestic equity base on which to cement the ISE's aspirations as Europe's number one capital market.

8.2.2   UK derivative markets

Financial derivatives trading has become a major global growth industry as customers have become more confident and innovative in their use of futures and options products to take positions and hedge risks. Consequently competition among the exchanges that trade derivatives has grown fiercer. In financial futures, rivalry has been intense between the London International Financial Futures Exchange (LIFFE), the Marché à Terme International de France (MATIF) in Paris and the Deutsche Terminbörse (DTB) in Frankfurt, and is part of a wider battle for supremacy as Europe's premier financial centre. In equity options in 1991 the DTB overtook the London Traded Options Market (LTOM) and the European Options Exchange (EOE) in Amsterdam in volumes traded despite having been in existence for only two years. However, such competition has also spawned new cooperative alliances. In the USA, where financial futures began, the Chicago Board of Trade (CBOT) and Chicago Mercantile Exchange (CME) have cooperated on several joint ventures, notably Globex, a worldwide electronic futures trading system. In the UK the March 1992 merger of LTOM and LIFFE has produced the London International Futures and Options Exchanges (LIFFOE), now the third largest exchange after those in Chicago. The merger is seen as a means of rectifying London's perceived weakness in equity derivatives, a feature emphasized by the recent success of its main continental rivals.

Derivatives markets do not involve the buying and selling of claims themselves, but rather the purchase and sale of options and futures contracts in specific claims. The products traded have two fundamental characteristics: gearing and risk diffusion. The former implies that the capital invested in the derivative is less than the price of the underlying asset, yet changes in the price of the underlying asset are fully reflected in the price of the derivative. To illustrate, if in July an investor paid an 18p premium for an October *call* option to buy for 300p one Boots plc share currently trading at 293p, the hope would be that before the expiry of the option the share price would have risen above 318p. If the market price on expiry were 330p, the profit would be 12p or 4 per cent of the underlying share price, yet 67 per cent of the 18p outlay. Moreover, because the 18p option gives the right to claim a 12p profit, it will itself be valued at 30p on exercise. This leverage allows such speculative investments to be used to take advantage of specific profit opportunities or to insure a portfolio against risk. For example, the latter may occur if an investor wishes ideally to maintain shareholdings over the longer term but is concerned about short-term market trends. By the purchase of *put* options in the appropriate securities or index (e.g the Financial Times–Stock Exchange index, FTSE), the investor has the right to sell at a pre-determined price at some future date. If, as hoped, the share price continues to rise, the benefit of the appreciation will offset the option premium. If, however, prices fall, the adverse movement will be offset by the increase in value of the put options.

Futures and options both represent claims on assets to be effected at a future date. However, a *futures* contract is for the exchange of an asset or commodity on agreed terms at a specified future time: change in ownership will occur. An *option* gives the buyer the right, but not the obligation, to buy (or sell) an asset at a future date for a pre-determined price. The obligation is thereby restricted to the seller, or writer, of the option. If a buyer of an option chooses not to exercise it, the maximum loss is restricted to the purchase price of the option and the underlying asset will not change hands. In futures contracts neither party has a limit to its potential loss as they gain and lose symmetrically. Such leveraged instruments can exist technically in the form of private contracts between two parties. Indeed, Thomas (1989) cites conventional (or traditional) options as existing in London from as early as 1694. However, once purchased, there is no formal mechanism for their secondary trading during their life, hence the holder must either exercise the option or allow it to lapse. While traditional options still exist for some relatively illiquid stocks, they have been surpassed by the growth of formal exchanges, starting in the USA with the Chicago Board of Options Exchange (CBOE) in 1973, and followed five years later in Europe by the European Options Exchange (EOE) in Amsterdam and the London Traded Options Market (LTOM).

Both futures contracts and options are traded on organized markets in a wide range of commodities, including cattle, coffee, corn, pork bellies, rice, sugar and tin, but our concern is with financial derivatives. In London, before the opening of the new LIFFE/LTOM trading floor at Cannon Bridge in March 1992, all financial futures contracts had been dealt with at LIFFE since 1982. Financial options started on the ISE in 1978 and are essentially equity and FTSE index options, while the options traded on LIFFE since 1986 are mainly currency options, or options on interest rate/index futures. Although technically the options markets were collectively known as LTOM, this really refers to the ISE operation (Table 8.4). This distinction is retained in subsequent discussions, save for reference to the recent merger.

LTOM was London's first major experience of organized financial derivative trading, starting in 1978 with the trading of call options in 10 shares. During the peak year of equity option trading in 1987 some 53 companies had options on their equity traded, involving over 11 million contracts (Table 8.4). As their name suggests, the contracts traded on the market are options to buy ('calls') or sell ('puts') a certain quantity of securities (1 contract = 1000 shares) at a specified price ('exercise' or 'strike' price) at a future date. The equity options traded in London are 'American' options which can be exercised at any time

Table 8.4 Derivatives turnover on the major European exchanges, 1982–1990

Exchange	\multicolumn{9}{c}{Contracts traded ('000)}								
	1982	1983	1984	1985	1986	1987	1988	1989	1990
Traded options									
LTOM (UK)	455	606	1257	2171	5285	11 754	8 439	9 578	8 205
LIFFE (UK)				171	487	1 173	1 758	2 178	4 371
MATIF (France)							3 431	7 150	8 229
MONEP (France)						388	2 403	3 744	5 523
DTB (Germany)									6 688
EOE (Netherlands)	1354	3276	4927	6893	9540	10 525	8 279	13 153	10 230
SOFFEX (Switzerland)							1 528	6 140	9 074
Financial futures									
LIFFE (UK)	242	1365	2578	3372	6484	12 380	13 787	21 681	29 799
MATIF (France)					1714	12 018	12 890	18 581	20 016
DTB (Germany)									110
FTA (Netherlands)						67	127	376	553
MEFF (Spain)									189

before expiry. Their life is nine months with quarterly cycles of expiry dates, so that at any one time there will be contracts on the underlying share with three different expiry dates. For each class (call or put) and expiry date, an exercise price series is created at intervals that vary according to the underlying share price. Thus if, say, a share price is 212p, the exercise prices might be set at 200p, 220p and 240p (Table 8.5).

Options with exercise prices at any particular time below the current market price are 'in-the-money' options and 'out-of-the-money' if the market price exceeds the exercise price. The option premium is quoted in pence and is paid to the option 'writer' in return for supplying the underlying stock at the exercise price. Premia will vary mainly with the time to maturity, volatility of the share and current price.

In essence, the system of trading options is one of order-driven 'open out-cry' in a 'pit' formerly on the floor of the Stock Exchange or LIFFE (now at Cannon Bridge following merger of LTOM and LIFFE). The method involves a 'pitch' for each class of options around which a 'crowd', consisting of a pitch official, a board official, registered market-makers, broker-dealers and some sole traders, gathers. The pitch and board officials are to ensure an orderly market and execute public limit orders. Whereas the market-makers operate in the manner of old jobbers, quoting bid and offer prices, the broker-dealers come to the floor to execute client orders. Deals made are recorded on official dealing slips by both parties and are matched by the Exchange, which operates a clearing house to register and clear trades and to generate delivery of the underlying shares.

The purpose of the market is described by de Guingand (1987) as 'to enable

Table 8.5 Equity options quotations

		Market quotations as at 10 August 1992 (premia in pence)[a]					
		Calls			Puts		
		Aug.	Nov.	Feb.	Aug.	Nov.	Feb.
British	200	18	33	42	7	27	30
Aerospace	220	7	26	33	16	38	42
(212[b])	240	3	18	25	35	52	56
		Sep.	Dec.	Mar.	Sep.	Dec.	Mar.
Eurotunnel	300	37	56	80	9	20	27
(325[b])	330	20	38	67	23	35	42
		Oct.	Jan.	Apr.	Oct.	Jan.	Apr.
Fisons	160	25	32	38	12	20	23
(170[b])	180	16	22	27	23	31	35

	FTSE index (2325[c])							
	2150	2200	2250	2300	2350	2400	2450	2500
Calls								
Aug.	176	126	83	40	16	5	2	1
Sep.	195	149	110	77	49	27	16	7
Oct.	213	172	134	101	73	51	34	22
Nov.	—	193	156	123	95	71	53	37
Dec.	—	208	—	142	—	87	—	50
Puts								
Aug.	2.5	7	11	25	50	95	142	192
Sep.	12	21	31	48	72	106	146	193
Oct.	22	31	44	60	83	116	153	196
Nov.	—	40	53	70	94	123	157	199
Dec.	—	42	—	75	—	124	—	200

[a] Premiums are based on closing offer price.
[b] Underlying security price.
[c] Underlying index price.

ISE member firms and their clients to manage, cost- and capital-effectively, the price risks which arise from dealing in the various underlying securities which are traded on the Exchange, and also to provide them with diversified investment opportunities'. Options allow speculators to bet on their views that specific share prices are likely to move, but provide advantages of limited outlay, loss and the gearing effect outlined earlier. In contrast to such risk exposure, hedging investors use a wide range of option strategies to reduce risk. For example, if an institutional investor suspects a fall in the price of shares owned, it may write a call option to protect its position. Indeed, the majority of transactions involve institutional investors using the market for hedging purposes. Inevitably, investors offset their positions by making a reverse trade before expiry, thus reselling an option rather than exercising it.

As Table 8.4 illustrates, UK equity option trading grew steadily between 1978 and 1984 but then boomed in the mid-1980s, boosted by the advent of options on British Telecommunications shares and the 'bull' market of early 1987. Thereafter the October 1987 crash had such a dramatic adverse influence that by 1990 turnover was nearly half that of 1987. However, to a certain extent the downturn in UK equity options has been offset by the development of index options. The first stock index option based on the FTSE-100 was launched in 1984, virtually simultaneously with LIFFE's listing of FTSE futures contracts. The FTSE-100 index option provides a mechanism for speculation or hedging against general market movements over the short term and has grown in popularity accounting for one-third of 1990 LTOM turnover.

Contracts are traded in units of a 1000 at 1p per unit or £10 × FTSE-100 index value. As the index itself is not tradable, transactions are for cash, with the difference between the exercise price and the current value of the index taken and multiplied by £10. As an example, if in August the index stands at 2325, an investor who speculates on a market rise may buy a November 2350 call contract at a premium of 95p which gives him or her the right to buy the index at 2350 between then and the end of November. If on expiry the index rises to 2480, the exercise of the option would produce the difference between £24 800 and £23 500, i.e. £1300 less the option cost of £10/1p × 95p = £950, a profit before commission of £350. As a defensive, hedging measure against a market fall, an investor who holds shares with a market value of, say, £50 000 on which traded options are not listed may protect the investment by writing index call options. With the index at 2325 in August he or she may write, say, five October 2300 calls and receive a premium of 101p. If at expiry date the index stands at 2230, the options expire worthless and the writer retains the premium, i.e. 5 × £10/1 × 101p = £5050. If the value of the portfolio moves in line with the market, its value would be reduced to £50 000 × (2230/2325) = £47 957, a fall of £2043 but more than compensated for by the premium income.

The success of the FTSE-100 option prompted the introduction of the Euro-FTSE option with immediate success in 1990. This is a European-style option which can be exercised only on specific dates, unlike the American-style options of the FTSE-100 index, which can be exercised at any time during a specific period.

LTOM diversification into other option contracts has proved unsuccessful. Options on selected gilt-edged securities were introduced in 1985, and, significantly in an international context, currency and US equity options were launched in 1987 and French equity options in 1988. However, none proved successful and all were abandoned in 1989. The overall decline in LTOM activity and the growth of foreign competition, notably in Amsterdam, Paris and Frankfurt, prompted LTOM's eventual merger with LIFFE.

As Europe's longest-standing and most international financial futures exchange, LIFFE has had a crucial role in London's status as a major financial centre. The exchange has been in a continual state of evolution since its foundation in 1982 as innovative financial engineering has created new products and controversy. LIFFE has primarily traded financial futures, although options were added in 1985. Essentially, financial futures contracts are agreements to buy or sell fixed quantities of financial assets at pre-determined prices and dates, with the products normally currency, interest rates or stock index futures. The standardization of contracts enables participants to open and close positions by making offsetting contracts without the need to take delivery, and thus are used to hedge or take advantage of price movements. Trading on LIFFE traditionally operated by 'open outcry', with customer orders, once executed, being confirmed and recorded on clearing slips. The latter are collected by LIFFE officials and the details entered on to a computerized matching system. Matched deals are subsequently registered with LIFFE's clearing house, the ICCH (International Commodities Clearing House). Once trades are registered, the contractual obligations are with the ICCH, not the original counter-party.

The most actively traded futures contracts worldwide are interest rate futures, used by banks and treasury managers to hedge interest rate exposure, and by speculators who take views on interest rate movements. On LIFFE various short- and long-term contracts are traded, although as Table 8.4 shows the most numerous are short sterling, long gilt and *Bund* (German government bond), all of which also have option contracts. As examples, contracts on short-term instruments are quoted at 100 minus the interest rate on the underlying instrument. This preserves the inverse relationship between prices and interest rates: the lower the interest rate, the higher the futures price. For example, if a September three-month sterling interest rate future is priced at 91.50, this implies that an interest rate of 8.5 per cent can be secured for three months on a September time deposit. The minimum price movement (or tick size) is 0.01 per cent of the interest for three months, and if the unit of trade is £500 000, the implied tick value is £12.50. Thus, someone who buys five such contracts at 91.50 and closes the position with a reverse sale at 91.65 gains a profit of £12.50 × 5 × 15 ticks [(91.65–91.50)/0.01] = £937.50. With all LIFFE contracts margin payments are necessary; for example, on the above short-term sterling this is £750 and is maintained by variation margin payments as rates move.

Currency futures are in sterling, Deutschmarks, yen and Swiss francs, all of which are traded against the US dollar. Sterling contracts are for sums of £25 000, the buyer receiving this sterling sum and paying dollars depending upon the currency price. The tick size on the sterling contract is 0.01 cents per pound, i.e. $0.0001, which implies a tick value of $2.50 ($0.0001 × 25 000). Thus, the purchase of a sterling contract at 1.8215 and later closure at 1.8275 would create an exchange rate change of $0.0060 or 60 ticks, and a gain of 60 × $2.50 = $150 per contract. The advantage of currency futures is that the investor can transact small amounts at reasonable cost in a liquid market which allows for active currency risk management.

The third generic type of future traded is the stock index, which on LIFFE is the FTSE-100 index. Contract values are £25 per index point with the futures price quoted in index points; so with the index at 2200, the contract value is 2200 × £25 = £55 000. The tick size is 0.5 and the value is therefore £12.50. Thus, the purchase of 10 contracts at 2200 and their subsequent sale at 2215 would produce a gain of 10 × 30 (ticks) × £12.50 = £3750. Since the stock index does not exist physically, all settlement takes place for cash. The buyer of a stock index receives the difference between the value of the index and the previous futures price.

Stock indices have grown in popularity and controversy in recent years. Their popularity stems from the opportunity for investors to hedge shares or speculate on movements with a small cash outlay equal to the margin (£2500 on FTSE-100). Moreover, an investor can invest directly in the broad market without running the specific risk of individual securities. They are thus a highly liquid, relatively cheap method of obtaining a position similar to a diversified portfolio.

Some controversy has arisen, however, notably with reference to the role of stock indices in the 1987 crash, and the wider issue of whether the futures market is driving the equity market. Unlike equity markets, futures markets do not raise capital and hence do not have an allocative efficiency role in the conventional sense. However, they have a pricing function, and any inefficiency here affects their abilities to transfer risk. In the context of the 'crash', reference has already been made to the wide range of influential factors, specifically the adjustment of yields in the UK market (see Sec. 8.1.2). However, in seeking explanations for the marked downturn, considerable attention has also focused on the use of futures in the context of portfolio insurance and programme trading. The former involves using derivative contracts to lock in the value and/or return of a portfolio, often via creating a synthetic put option. Programme trading involves exploitation of discrepancies between futures and underlying assets.

Normally, if an investor anticipates a market rise he or she may buy index futures contracts to realize actual cash gains as well as normal gains on the share portfolio. If instead the market falls, as the buyer of futures contracts and the holder of a share portfolio, he or she will lose in both respects. Thus, in the event of a market fall, as in October 1987, not only did some speculators withdraw from the market, but portfolio insurers attempted to sell index futures contracts to safeguard their portfolios. Moreover, portfolio managers, who used computer programmes to monitor the markets and react accordingly, also began to sell shares. Tosini (1988) has described a 'cascade' process whereby heavy selling of such index futures contracts creates an undervaluation of the futures contract relative to the cash index. Stock index arbitrageurs buy the relatively underpriced futures and sell the overpriced shares, and so share prices fall further, inducing additional selling by portfolio insurers; and so it continues.

The events of October 1987 and thereafter have fuelled debate about market linkages. Griffiths (1991) cites the US Presidential Report into the crash as concluding that what had hitherto been regarded as separate markets—shares, share index futures and options—were really a Single Market. The linkages that had previously allowed arbitrage operations had lapsed and portfolio managers' capacity to insure their portfolios had vanished. In the UK, since 1988 the volume of FTSE-100 futures contracts has risen rapidly, and, as in July 1991, such futures have traded at a premium to the shares involved and have led the stock market higher by creating demand for the underlying shares. Thus, on the one hand futures markets may be seen to merely respond to what markets and traders want to do in the stock market, but to respond more quickly and more efficiently than the underlying market. Alternatively, perhaps derivatives should be considered primary instruments in their own right, especially given the price advantages to institutional investors of trading such markets, notwithstanding deregulation of the main exchange.

In trading various financial futures contracts, LIFFE has experienced rapid growth, especially since 1986 (Table 8.4). In terms of sterling products performance, the long gilt dominated until 1988, based on a notional 20-year maturity, a coupon of 9 per cent and a unit value of £50 000, and with delivery by any real gilt with 15–25 years to maturity in multiples of £50 000. Trading volumes have varied with UK economic performance and government funding policy to such an extent that the repayment of public indebtedness reduced trading volumes in 1988 and 1989. However, the onset of the recession and a return to Treasury borrowing from the gilt market should boost turnover in the early 1990s. As long gilt turnover fell, it was replaced by growth in the short sterling contract, a reflection of the surge in bank lending and greater interest rate volatility. This growth is likely to be maintained, notwithstanding ERM entry, while interest rates remain principal macroeconomic instruments. The FTSE-100 index future has grown steadily, especially since 1988, and, as institutional investors utilize more derivatives in portfolio management, its prospects for further development in the new LIFFOE appear bright. Indeed, various developments have spurred a shift to greater use of derivatives. For example, in the 1990 Budget, pension funds and authorized unit trusts were exempted from tax on trading income from futures and options. In July 1991 the SIB allowed authorized unit trusts to invest in two new categories of unit trust: FOFs (futures and options funds), able to invest up to 10 per cent of their assets in derivative products, and riskier GFOFs (geared futures and options funds), which can have up to 20 per cent of the fund's assets in futures and options, and which, unlike FOFs, do not have to cover expenses with the underlying securities.

Although sterling-denominated contracts have dominated, LIFFE has lived up to its name and operated a range of international products. The longest-established of these are US dollar products: the three-month Eurodollar interest rate based on a trading unit of US$1 million, and a Treasury Bond carrying an 8 per cent coupon and traded in US$100 000 units. Both have diminished in significance in the recent past largely through greater attention to European-oriented products, notably Deutschmark-related contracts, which were negligible in 1988 yet accounted for 40 per cent of LIFFE volume in 1990, with the *Bund* future (6 per cent notional German government bond) the most heavily traded LIFFE product. This trend is likely to increase, given the costs of German unification, although severe competition is likely from the DTB even though LIFFE had a two-year start in its Deutschmark trading. Thus, the Euro-Deutschmark and *Bund* contracts have been major contributors to LIFFE's growth and prestige.

Elsewhere international diversification has occurred with trading of the yen and Japanese government bond. The latter has never taken off and was seen partly as a mechanism for entry to the Tokyo Stock Exchange. The 1991 introduction of Euro-Swiss franc interest futures, lira bond and ECU bonds together with the Eurotrack 100 index reaffirms the significance of European products, and the position of LIFFE therein. Some of these aspects represent competitive reaction, notably in ECU and lira bonds, where MATIF had established such contracts earlier, and also with the proposed opening of the Italian derivatives exchange to trade lira bonds. Similarly, the Eurotrack 100 index has a European flavour based upon Europe's 100 largest companies and denominated in Deutschmarks. The introduction of the Eurotrack illustrates LIFFE's aim to provide greater equity derivative coverage, but again is evidence of exchange competition with MATIF and the EOE (Amsterdam) listing similar products in ECUs.

The vast majority of LIFFE's trades have been in futures contracts, but from 1985 the exchange began to offer options and by 1990 these accounted for 13 per cent of its turnover, most notably *Bund* and short sterling options. This growth, the aforementioned downturn in equity options on LTOM and the desire to operate as Europe's premier derivatives exchange encouraged the merger with LTOM in March 1992. Indeed, informal merger discussions had started as far back as September 1986, with both parties recognizing potential benefits from reduced costs, avoidance of duplication which confuses overseas investors, and the complimentary nature of the products traded. However, execution of the merger was problematic, in particular the establishment of a single clearing house to accommodate the different collateral, margin and default requirements of both exchanges, and overcoming the problem of transferring the complex LTOM market-making system, with its stock-borrowing privileges, to the new exchange.

Traditionally, options market-makers have borrowed stock from money-brokers. For example, if an option holder exercises an option to buy BP shares, the market-maker is then obliged to deliver these; but normally they will not be to hand: instead they will be borrowed from a money-broker. The shares will be delivered to the option holder, and other shares will be purchased at a later date for return to the money-broker who earns a fee on the business. LTOM market-makers were concerned that the same privileges would not be available under the merger, and that they would be disadvantaged *vis à vis* competitors who also make markets in the underlying equities. In addition, options traders formerly dealt with clients on the exchange floor, like the old stock exchange jobbers, but now they must conform to the futures markets' 'open-outcry' method with their prices visible to everybody in the 'pit', and they must take all orders. The merger has thus produced some uncertainties for the former LTOM members, who consider themselves the poor relations as the futures part of LIFFOE gathers momentum. Nevertheless, the growing institutional use of derivatives and the impetus from the new exchange gives further backing to London's position *vis à vis* its European rivals.

8.3 GERMANY

Germany is Europe's prime economic power, its currency is the anchor for the ERM, and, with a market capitalization of over DM600 billion, it has the world's fourth biggest equity market. Yet until recently Germany has lagged behind its major European competitors in terms of the development of both its financial markets and of Frankfurt as a major financial centre. Moreover, equity market capitalization represents just over one-quarter of GDP, which means that German industry is relatively poorly represented on its stock exchanges compared with companies in France, the UK or the Netherlands. Nevertheless, attempts to reform German financial markets are in progress, including heavy investment in technology and, significantly, the establishment of a major derivatives market.

8.3.1 The stock market

The strong sense of federalism in Germany has affected the development of a coherent financial market. Frankfurt is Germany's principal stock exchange, accounting for 70 per cent of all equity and bond trading, but the existence of seven other centres (Düsseldorf, Berlin, Munich, Hamburg, Stuttgart, Hanover, and Bremen) dilutes overall liquidity. Each of the regional exchanges is located in an autonomous *Land* and has reacted strongly against moves to centralize supervision and the creation of a holding company, *Deutsche Börse*, to oversee operations. Indeed, following unification, two of the new *Länder* in the East sought to open exchanges in Dresden and Leipzig. However, German companies have increasingly voiced discontent with such domestic market arrangements. Campbell (1991) quotes BASF, already listed on international exchanges, as questioning the need to pay fees to eight separate German exchanges, especially when the relevance of small exchanges such as Bremen is doubtful. Regionalism apart, German equity market growth has also been stunted in the past by company capital structure and investor attitudes. Only 2700 of Germany's two million businesses are public limited companies; moreover, only 650 are listed, of which just 38 are actively traded. Traditional close relations between German companies and their 'house banks' has meant that industry has been encouraged to use debt rather than equity finance, whereas many family-owned companies have tended to avoid listings through a desire to retain control. Investor preferences have favoured conservative investments with banks; therefore a mere 3.5 million Germans own shares. Moreover, the costly stock market structure and tax regime discriminated against equity investment and thus mitigated against the channelling of individual retail savings into equities.

Recently, attempts have been made to modify the traditional picture of an undercapitalized corporate sector and a bank-dominated financial system in which equities play a minor role. Legislation has been passed to encourage small and medium-sized enterprises easier market access, for example the Act concerning Risk Capital Investment Companies, and the Act on the Admission of Securities to the Official Stock Exchange, both introduced in 1987; and corporation tax has been reformed to avoid double taxation of dividends. More domestic support for equities has also come from 'special-purpose funds' set up by pension funds and insurance companies and managed by banks. These funds have grown in number, from 326 with funds of DM5 billion in 1978 to 1300 and funds of DM84 billion in 1988, and, significantly, they have shifted the focus of their investments from bonds to equities. In addition, foreign investment in German equities rose with the 'bull' markets of the mid-1980s; and, notwithstanding the 1987 crash, the fundamental attraction of the underlying German economy and the need for international diversification of share portfolios has given some impetus to equity market prospects.

The German equity market is organized into three parts. The Official Market (Amtlicher Handel) covers the larger, more liquid, shares and government bonds. The Second, or Regulated, Market (Geregelter Markt) deals in securities traded on the smaller regional exchanges outside of Frankfurt. The Free Market (Freiverkehr) trades unlisted securities. Prices of securities are traditionally determined on the Frankfurt Stock Exchange (FSE) by official brokers/jobbers (*Kursmaklers*) who have acted as intermediaries while being authorized to determine prices. Free brokers (*Freimaklers*), who also act as intermediaries but trade on their own account, risking their capital, are not authorized or obliged to determine and fix prices. *Kursmaklers* determine either standard or variable-price quotations. With the former they match buy and sell orders so as to execute the most deals, and each security has a standard price set each day. Variable-price quotes are used with high-turnover securities and are quoted continuously throughout trading sessions. Orders are traditionally transmitted by telex and telephone, then passed to the *makler* using order slips.

Various attempts have been made to update and improve the efficiency of the trading systems using available technology. However, coordination has often been lacking in the projects undertaken, cost-overruns have occurred, and attempts to move from floor to screen-based trading have been complicated by regional interests. An electric screen-based trading system IBIS (Interbank Information System) was launched by German banks in 1989 to provide a quick, reliable and cost-effective price quotation system for leading stocks. Fearful for their future existence under such a system, the *Kursmaklers* set up a rival price information system, MATIS (Makler-Tele-Information System), distributed via Reuters, and the *Freimaklers* established MIDAS (Market-Maker Information and Trading System), a quote-driven trading system as opposed to essentially a price-quotation one. MATIS and MIDAS were developed because the *maklers* were excluded from the original IBIS 'bank-only' scheme. However, IBIS proved very expensive and was sold to the FSE. A revised IBIS 2 (now Interborsen Handels and Information System) began operating in April 1991, and with the change of ownership the *Kursmaklers* have no need to operate a separate system. Meanwhile competition between MIDAS and IBIS has intensified, with MIDAS arguing that it is well-placed to recapture much of the overseas trading in German equities and able to list a wider range of securities, while IBIS, as part of the FSE, benefits from being recognized as an official German stock exchange. One area where the German equity market is relatively efficient is in the computerized settlement system introduced in 1970, which effects transactions within two days.

Thus, while the prospects for the German equities in the medium to long term are good, difficulties remain in developing the main market. Essentially, the market is thin, in spite of new equity capital amounting to DM98 billion raised between 1980 and 1989 (Deutsche Bundesbank 1991e), and is dominated by a handful of industrial companies, banks and insurers. Competition from overseas, notably SEAQI, has taken much business from Frankfurt, and internal competition also undermines its effectiveness. The regional market structure is costly, inefficient and unattractive for foreign firms which might otherwise seek listings. The banks, *Kursmaklers* and *Freimaklers* have seemingly varying objectives and disagree on the appropriate trading system. The banks play a powerful role in the market and maintain the high cost structure as they take 1 per cent out of the average commission of 1.33 per cent, a figure high by current European standards. This stems from the requirement that people wishing to trade on the market have to do so through a bank represented on the FSE, since the 'purchase and sale of securities for third parties is banking business' (Hamke 1990). In addition, unification is unlikely to boost the equity market given the poor state of East German industry. Indeed, the bulk of financing needed is being taken up by bond issues, for which the Germans appear to have an insatiable appetite.

8.3.2 The Deutsche Terminbörse (DTB)

A major success for Germany, and especially for Frankfurt, has been the Deutsche Terminbörse (DTB), the derivatives exchange which opened in January 1990. By the year-end it had traded over 6.6 million equity option contracts, and in the record month of June 1991 traded 1.1 million lots, a volume double that of LTOM. On this basis, the DTB is set to become Europe's foremost traded options market. Such success is remarkable considering the aforementioned problems of the German equity market, the conservative nature of domestic investors and the rapid growth of Deutschmark products on derivatives exchanges elsewhere. The last feature is significant in that, whereas most derivatives exchanges could exploit their domestic markets without competition, this situation was not available to the DTB because Deutschmark derivatives were already extensively and successfully operated 'offshore'. However, this in turn gave the DTB a rationale to repatriate such trade.

The DTB was established as an integrated options and futures exchange, although trading in the latter did not begin until November 1990 and has proved more difficult to establish. Two futures contracts were initially traded: a *Bund* future, similar to the 10-year one already traded on LIFFE, and the DAX stock index future. The latter is based on the DAX index of 30 leading German blue-chip stocks, and has gathered liquidity as it offers a market where other exchanges do not compete. Moreover, a DAX cash option was launched in August 1991 which should aid the growth of the DAX index future as well as promoting wider use of equity derivatives as a whole in Germany. The *Bund* future aimed to cut into LIFFE's trade in the same product; and although by June 1991 the DTB was taking only 16 per cent of total *Bund* futures trading, with the strong commitment of German banks to the DTB, there are hopes that its share of futures trading will rapidly increase. In December 1990 the DTB urged its member banks to support their home market in which they had invested heavily. However, the German banks had not been great users of derivatives until then, and, even if they were, there was no guarantee they would unwind favourable positions on LIFFE to transfer funds home. In August 1991 the DTB launched *Bund* options to enhance *Bund* trading, thus fuelling further competition between the exchanges.

The DTB *Bund* futures contract has a wider significance in that for the first time a derivative product is tradable simultaneously on a trading floor (LIFFOE) and via a computerized exchange (DTB). International rivals believe the DTB will eventually succeed because of the massive investment (DM110 million) in the exchange alone, and the greater transparency of computerized screen-based trading and integrated clearing that promotes efficient monitoring and market regulation. However, advocates of 'open-outcry' argue that it promotes greater liquidity and speed of execution, especially during busy periods. This is seen as particularly relevant for futures trades, whereas options, with their mathematical complexities, lend themselves more to computer trading. Computerization of the DTB may also be seen as a pointer to the domestic, regional, equity markets. Although administered from Frankfurt, members network into the system from locations throughout Germany; and, as Courtney (1992) observes, while outsiders consider the DTB to be a Frankfurt-based exchange, within the country the DTB is very much a national one.

The DTB's prospects appear mixed. The potential for its equity options on the major companies comprising the DAX-30 seems good. Here the computerized nature of the DTB and greater investor interest in equities may prove beneficial. However, in its fixed-income and interest rate futures the DTB will have a hard fight to repatriate trade lost to LIFFE and MATIF. Moreover, the DTB is far from truly internationalizing its portfolio to the extent needed to reinforce Frankfurt's claim to be the major European financial centre.

8.4 FRANCE

France's financial markets have undergone significant development in recent years with the overall reform of the Paris Bourse and the introduction of new derivative markets. These changes parallel deregulation in other spheres of the French economy, notably the 1986–87 privatization programme, a more market-based use of monetary policy and the recent easing of foreign exchange controls. However, the bank-dominated nature of the financial system remains, as evidenced in the context of French equity market reforms which have strengthened the services that banks offer.

8.4.1 Paris Bourse

The French stock market is the fifth largest in the world but is heavily concentrated on Paris, where 95 per cent of total turnover occurs. Although six regional exchanges are found in the major cities, these were merged into a single nationwide entity in 1991 as one stage in the reform process begun in the mid-1980s. For many years the Paris Bourse suffered from a Napoleonic legacy of a closed-shop mentality whereby member firms of *Sociétés de Bourse* were small, undercapitalized, private stockbroking firms concerned primarily with small-investor business. The brokers lacked resources to develop their trading operations, and hence the Bourse itself. Banks had the necessary distribution network and financial muscle but not the authority to trade.

Unlike 'Big Bang', the French reforms have involved a series of discrete changes over the past decade. A notable early step was the introduction of paperless trading in 1984, whereby computerized book units were created by authorized intermediaries, mainly banks. The most significant development, though, was the decision in 1987 to allow outsiders to buy progressively into member stockbroking firms. Subsequently most banks have acquired controlling interests, thus furthering their hold on the financial system. Indeed, all but 4 of the 58 member firms have linked with outside partners, and, with 13 foreign-controlled, non-French firms, control 30 per cent of French equity trading (Dawkins 1991).

In 1988 a market reorganization took place with the creation of two controlling bodies: the Société des Bourses Françaises (SBF) as the market operator, and Conseil des Bourses de Valeurs (CBV) as regulator. The latter works in conjunction with the Commission des Operations de Bourse (COB), effectively an overseer. In 1989 the latter was given additional powers to search and prosecute, for example where insider dealing occurs. The reorganization allowed bankers to become market-makers and trade on their own account, thus offering new profit opportunities to compensate for the loss of fixed commissions. In January 1992 a licence system was introduced whereby broker functions are segmented into, e.g., clearing and market trading. The purpose is to provide an outlet for small firms to offer a basic dealing capacity yet contract out the expensive settlement operations to an investment bank. The COB also sees segmentation as a way of preventing clients' accounts being used to cover losses elsewhere.

Market operations involve the categorization of stocks under a threefold system, essentially based on liquidity. The main listing, the Côte Officielle, involves spot (cash) and forward (end-of-month settlement) markets. The Second Marché launched in 1983, is similar to the UK's Unlisted Securities Market for smaller, growth firms, and there is a Marché Hors-Côte, an over-the-counter market in relatively illiquid stocks. In operational terms, the Paris Bourse is highly modernized with heavy emphasis on information technology. In particular, a computer-based order-driven system, Cotation Assisté et Continu (CAC), was introduced in 1986 with terminals on member firms' premises linked to the central Bourse computer. In 1990 a FF600 million fully electronic clearance and settlement system (RELIT) was unveiled which covers actively traded shares, with eventually a 5-day rolling settlement cycle compared with the previous average time of 13 days.

The considerable modernization and heavy investment in computer-based systems would suggest that Paris is well equipped to compete with other *bourses*. However, its performance so far has been variable. From a market capitalization of FF318.4 billion in 1983, turnover rose steadily to FF990.3 billion before the October 1987 crash. The latter brought disaster, and by the end of November turnover was down 36 per cent on its peak. More significantly, foreign investment fell drastically, thereby lowering the international status of the Bourse. The newly privatized companies and their army of small investors were particularly badly hit. Heavily oversubscribed on issue, these stocks did not generate the expected capital gains as many were issued in the months just before to the crash. Indeed, Cie Financière de Suez was listed in early November and opened 18 per cent below the issue price (Parrott 1988). However, in the context of raising funds and widening share ownership, the privatization programme has been successful, generating FF60 billion and increasing fourfold to 6 million the number of French shareholders in only six months. Moreover, the crash did not prevent links being established between banks and broking firms or discourage continued capital investment in the market.

Such linkages have furthered market concentration. Around 50 per cent of turnover now goes through the top five brokers, including Bacot-Allain-Farra, 90 per cent owned by J. P. Morgan. That such connections are necessary is evidenced by the failure of several broking firms in the late 1980s. Indeed, in

1988 one-third of Paris broking firms lost money and another one-third made profits of less than FF10 million, a poor return on their capital employed, especially with the need to set aside funds for the capital investment the market requires. The opportunities to link with brokers—and, indeed, from 1992 to apply for stock exchange seats—have given the banks a wider range of services. So far they have had some success in using their branch networks to sell securities and unit trusts.

However, problems remain. In the first place, securities trading remains relatively underdeveloped in France and there is a danger that it will remain essentially an interbank operation rather than an open market with active independent operators. Henrot and Levy-Lang (1990) suggest that it is in the banks' interest to develop an open market with both foreign and non-bank-dominated brokers, and cite the open ownership of the futures market, MATIF, in this context. In part, the problem arises from the structure of company finances. For a full listing, a company must in theory have 25 per cent of its capital in the hands of the public, yet few companies meet even the 10 per cent required for the Second Market. Most firms are tightly controlled through a series of holding structures so that ultimate power resides in the hands of individuals whose real equity stake is small. In an attempt to raise liquidity, the CBV proposed that companies should forgo their Paris Bourse listing if turnover in their shares fell below FF10 000 per day, although this was met with derision.

A second related issue is the lack of capacity for large institutional investors to trade substantive blocks of shares off the central market, a feature that is available to French investors via SEAQI in London. Paris operates a 'matching' price mechanism, whereby the arrival of a new order triggers transaction(s) if a matching order(s) exist on the centralized book. Such an order-driven system is less effective for trading large amounts than a quote-driven system such as operates in London, since the trade may not be fully satisfied. At present SEAQI handles 20 per cent of trades in France's top 50 listed companies, and has stimulated attempts to provide special facilities for block trades. Although new rules were introduced in 1991, these have been relatively unsuccessful as dealers still have to disclose the price at which they operate, whereas on SEAQI dealers may handle large quantities outside the official market, making disposal easier via private traders (Dickson 1991). The transfer of such business to London also emphasizes the high-cost nature of the Paris Bourse, a feature compounded by the need to recoup the outlays on the new operating technology. For example, a turnover tax is levied of between 0.15 and 0.3 per cent according to the size of the deal, whereas in London this tax is due for abolition when TAURUS takes effect, and in Frankfurt it does not exist at all.

Coexistent with deregulation of the equity market have been reforms to the issuance and management of primary government debt. These have involved widening the scope of the Treasury bill market, standardizing the issue procedure for government securities, and creating nominated primary dealers. Before 1986 Treasury bill issues were available only to the interbank market, but deregulation has opened these up to institutional and domestic investors. Significantly, in February 1991 a ministerial decree also allowed foreign companies, other than financial institutions, to issue their own *billets de Trésorie* in what represents the French equivalent of a commercial paper market. This furthers the popularity of this type of instrument in both its public and private forms. New issues of government securities have favoured the auction method and have involved a range of bonds of differing maturities and coupons, including indexed and zero coupon securities. The 13 new *spécialistes en valeurs du Trésor* (SVTs) or primary dealers are empowered to inform the Treasury of market developments, to sell Treasury securities and to ensure liquidity by acting as market-makers.

It is clear that the primary capital market has undergone significant deregulation by French standards in recent years. However, some legacies of the past remain in terms of its cost structure, and the hand of government is never far away. The equity market will continue to be a large market for domestic shares already traded, but in spite of the significant technological advances it seems likely to remain a somewhat small player in international securities.

8.4.2 French derivative markets

In recent years Paris has been the centre for two of the world's fastest growing derivatives markets: MONEP for traded options and MATIF for financial futures. MONEP (Marché des Operations Negociables de Paris) was founded in 1987 and trades a narrow range of domestic equity options and the CAC 40-stock index, a reflection of its status as a division of the Paris Bourse. Its high growth rate so far reflects the popularity of the CAC 40 as the world's fastest growing equity derivatives contract. Courtney (1992) suggests that expansion in equity options turnover *per se* will become more difficult, in that only 25 stock options are quoted on MONEP, of which 8 were added in 1990 including Cerns, EuroDisney, L'Oreal and CMB Packaging. Moreover, some of the quoted stocks are not very actively traded on the main market which affects the option business. In contrast, index options are relatively new and underdeveloped, as in the UK, and are expected to surpass equity options in the volume of business traded. In this respect MONEP shows parallels with LTOM which, although established longer, was eventually forced to reassess its future and merge with LIFFE.

The French financial futures exchanges MATIF (Marché à Terme International de France) was created in 1986 originally as the Marché à Term des Instruments Financiers and has retained its initials. It vies with LIFFE for the position of Europe's foremost financial futures exchange and, unlike MONEP, is currently developing internationally-oriented products. However, initially MATIF concentrated on the domestic market, trading the Notionnel bond and Treasury bill futures contracts. The former has so far been the most significant product traded on any European exchange and even in 1990 accounted for 56.6 per cent of MATIF activity. It is a fictitious security with the characteristics of a 10-year government bond with a 10 per cent coupon and contract value of FF500 000. At maturity the contract is closed by delivering bonds from the clearing house's list of eligible government bonds that are constantly quoted on the Bourse. Contracts mature at the end of the last month of each of the four quarters following the current month, i.e., for July 1992 contracts will be available end-December 1992, end-March 1993, end-June 1993 and end-December 1993. The success of the Notionnel reflects commitment to it from most French financial institutions, but more specifically from the Trading Hors Séance (THS) system introduced in 1988. This is effectively an over-the-counter market, allowing transactions to be cleared by the exchange's clearing house CCIFP (Chambre de Compensation des Instruments Financiers de Paris) before and after official dealing hours which ensures an active market. The medium-term prospects for the Notionnel contract depend upon the extent to which the Banque de France begins to issue a proportion of its funding in ECUs. Should this increase then a boost will be given to the MATIF's ECU bond contract at the expense of the Notionnel.

The other original domestic product, the 90-day Treasury bill, proved much less successful. It was available in nominal values of FF5 million, but lack of liquidity led to its withdrawal in 1988 and its replacement by the PIBOR (Paris Interbank Offered Rate) futures contract to provide for short-term interest rate exposures. Following a promising start trading fell away in 1990, partly because of competition from similar contracts such as short sterling Euro-Deutschmark and Eurodollars on LIFFE, and partly because the French were reluctant to use PIBOR as a reference rate for loans. Nevertheless, a PIBOR option was successfully launched in 1990 and has taken up some slack in PIBOR derivatives trading, and as a 'combined' derivative it may assume a more significant role. The entry into index futures occurred in 1988 with the launch of CAC 40 and its rise has been meteoric, mirroring the success of its option on MONEP. This rate of growth is likely to slow, but stock index derivatives appear popular and in the immediate future it may consolidate its position as Europe's foremost index derivative. In the longer term, however, competition from LIFFE and the DTB may prove significant.

The aforementioned domestic products limit the scope of MATIF's operations, and with the introduction of Euro-DM futures (1989) and options (1990) the exchange served notice of its international intentions. Initially trading was substantial, but it fell away under competitive pressure from LIFFE and the opening of the DTB in Frankfurt geared to attract Deutschmark-denominated derivatives trades. MATIF's international future now seems more promising in terms of ECU-derivatives trading. In 1990 the three-month ECU bond contract was launched, partly to reflect the Banque de France's commitment to raising a proportion of new funds in ECUs. As other public and corporate bodies raise more issues, the prospects for this hedging contract will increase and strengthen MATIF.

As with London, Paris has traditionally promoted separate futures and options exchanges in spite of similarities in some of the products traded and membership. However, the benefits of consolidation and merger have been decisive in London, and, as competition intensifies between European exchanges, the pressures to cooperate domestically may push MONEP and MATIF closer together.

8.5 SMALLER EUROPEAN FINANCIAL MARKETS

While London, Frankfurt and Paris vie to become the premier financial centre, other EC nations also are developing their financial markets. The following overview concentrates on selected centres, but readers are also referred to Chapter 10, notably the impending EC–EFTA linkage which brings important Scandinavian and other markets, such as Austria and Switzerland, within the wider EC sphere of influence.

8.5.1 Northern Europe: Benelux

In theory, the markets of Belgium, the Netherlands and Luxembourg should have a strong international focus, a reflection of the past trading significance of the first two and the 'offshore' status of the third. Of the three, the Netherlands has had the greatest aspirations to challenge the 'Big Three' European financial centres. However, while Amsterdam hosts the world's oldest stock exchange and Europe's oldest options exchange, its home market is small. Moreover, the famous Dutch multinationals, such as Philips and the oil majors, find it just as easy to trade in overseas financial markets. Competition from London is particularly noticeable; in 1989 more than 50 per cent of Dutch state bond trading took place there, and SEAQ conducted 25 per cent of share trading in the top 20 Dutch firms.

Such a loss of business prompted the Amsterdam financial community to produce a city blueprint including recommendations ranging from property development to tax changes. Key features have focused on Amsterdam's stock exchange with the abolition of stamp duty, new commission structures, fixed settlement dates, longer trading hours and an 'open order book' for large bond transactions. The latter combines a new screen-based quote system, designed to serve the professional wholesale market and the existing central floor order system for the retail market. Amsterdam has long maintained a unique equity and bond trading system whereby potential trading partners are bought together by a *hoekman*, a specialist intermediary. Under the new 'open order book' system, exchange members' bond orders (minimum Dfl2.5 million) and quotes (minimum Dfl5 million) are brought together by the *hoekman* to determine optimum prices, and thereby to transform the role of the *hoekman* into an interdealer broker. This creates a link between the old central, order-driven, floorbased market and the new quote-driven segment with market-makers. A series of mergers has reduced the individually relatively small and undercapitalized *hoekman* firms to more viable units in the new market, and a move towards a limited 'open order book' for shares is expected.

A major constraint on an active and liquid Dutch equity market remains the complex protection against corporate predators which stifles takeover activity. In spite of the Amsterdam Stock Exchange's attempts to lobby companies to dismantle their defences, artificial protection has remained, such as the ability to offer priority or preferred shares to friendly shareholders. However, full European integration and the rise of the corporate governance debate seem set to precipitate the dismantling of such protectionism.

One of Amsterdam's main claims as a major European financial centre lies in its options trading. The European Options Exchange (EOE) is still Europe's largest by contract volume, although each contract is 100 shares compared with 1000 on LIFE/LTOM. The EOE trades exclusively options with futures traded on the Financiale Termijnmarkt Amsterdam (FTA) owned by the same holding company but operationally distinct. EOE options trading is dominated by equity options (74 per cent of 1990 turnover) and stock index options (21 per cent); diversification into bond, bond index, and currency options has been attempted, although not altogether successfully. Indeed, much of the latter trading has been *ad hoc* over-the-counter and seems likely to continue with deals cleared via the EOE. The FTA was established in 1987 and has expanded rapidly via the growth of EOE stock index futures. However, both the EOE and FTA are dominated by domestic guilder products where there is limited scope for expansion. International product diversification has been very limited so far—merely the joint launch of the Eurotop 100 multinational equity index in 1991—but future strategy may focus on links with other exchanges, notably in Scandinavia, to provide a northern derivatives market to counter the power of London, Paris and Frankfurt.

Brussels' role as the administrative centre of the European Community and its favourable location juxtaposed between the major European powers might be expected to give it prominence as a financial centre. However, the Belgian financial system is relatively unsophisticated and is in the midst of a 'Big Bang' of market and institutional reforms. Blanden (1991) argues that the system has been dominated by banks making easy profits financing government borrowing and subsidizing the corporate sector via cheap loans. An open trading policy has encouraged a strong complement of foreign banks, but activity is characterized by large volumes and weak margins. Reforms began in 1989 with the abolition of the two-tier exchange rate system, a reduction in withholding tax and improvements to government bond issues. The most significant changes took effect in 1991 at the Brussels Stock Exchange and with the start of derivatives trading on BELFOX (Belgian Financial Futures and Options Exchange).

The Stock Exchange reforms have included the introduction of a computer-aided trading system (CATS) to replace the open-outcry procedure, lower commission scales, reducing fees by an average 30 per cent; and, the erosion of the stockbrokers' monopoly. Legislation has required the latter to incorporate themselves into limited-liability *sociétés de bourse*, which can be owned by banks or other financial institutions and thus provide the capital the market needs. Inevitably, the number of brokers has fallen by half through merger or exit from the business. The new *sociétés de bourse* were initially required to have a minimum capital of BFr25 million, a figure doubled by 1992. However, the initial response to the reforms has been disappointing, with a poor volume of trading and exchange revenue, and so further changes are planned, notably to increase the listing fees which are currently minimal. In part, the problems reflect the nature of trading, since the equity market is primarily a retail one with a high level of individual ownership of equities, unlike institutional dominance elsewhere. Consequently the market is thin and illiquid with often small trades heavily concentrated among a handful of firms such as Petrofina (energy) and Electrabel (utility). Indeed, overall market capitalization is only 2.6 per cent of the European equity market (Siaens and Goossens 1992).

In December 1991 BELFOX began trading financial futures on government bonds, with equity options on the leading six Belgian shares starting in 1992. In part this activity reflects the institutionalization of former OTC practices, although competition arose between Belgian banks and stockbrokers to first establish a derivatives exchange. Government intervention was needed to consolidate activity and establish BELFOX, an automated, integrated futures and options exchange. This may be seen as part of the government's ambition to liberalize the domestic financial market. However, market opportunities are limited: the Belgian bond market ranks sixth in Europe but is relatively small; there are only modest prospects for the BEL 20 index compared with, say, the CAC or FTSE; and there is limited scope for international growth unless via merger or joint venture with other similarly placed exchanges. Accordingly, in both its main equity and derivatives markets, Brussels plays a minor role by international standards.

Luxembourg has held a unique position as the European Community's main onshore 'offshore' financial centre. Tax and secrecy were undoubtedly important factors in its early growth, although local financiers argue that it is not a tax haven, notwithstanding the lack of withholding tax on dividends and interest payments. Nevertheless, many entities still register there and conduct their business in other international centres—including BCCI, which has tarnished the Duchy's image in recent times. Luxembourg has proved flexible, initially becoming the main European centre for quoting Eurobonds. Indeed, 70 per cent of the 10 000 securities listed on its stock exchange are corporate bonds and represent substantial business taken away, in particular, from its immediate neighbouring countries. The share market is minimal, listing only a few foreign companies.

In recent years the country has become a centre for the administration of UCITS (Undertakings for Collective Investment in Transferable Securities) and has almost a thousand investment funds registered in its domain. Future growth prospects are less certain since, although Luxembourg is an international banking centre with 190 banks registered there, including the European Investment Bank (EIB), it is essentially a niche centre, specializing in asset management and private banking. Moreover, it is vulnerable to tax changes and competition—notably from other 'offshore' centres, including Switzerland, the most prestigious such centre within the European time zone.

8.5.2   Southern Europe: Italy and Spain

Italian finance is in the throes of considerable change as it tries to move away from a purely bank-dominated model. Until the early 1980s the prime role of Italian banks was to supply funds to the public sector backed by a range of direct controls. This led to an inefficient, high-cost, yet protected banking environment unsuited to the European climate of deregulation and integration. Subsequently, attempts at a more open, market-oriented approach have been tried, accompanied by a reduction in controls and internationalization of the financial sector. However, in order to modernize their operations many Italian banks require additional capital; and, because of a stretched public sector and weak equity market, attention has focused on potential capital injections from foreign banks or domestic industry.

The weakness of the capital market stems from its inefficiency and lack of adequate regulation, which has given it a reputation for poor execution and insider dealing. The Milan Stock Exchange handles some 90 per cent of Italian equity trading, listing approximately 220 companies, although overall market capitalization is low considering the importance of Italian manufacturing industry, and compares unfavourably with other European markets. In part this reflects the fact that much of this business has found its way to SEAQI in London.

In an attempt to improve the market's image, new legislation was introduced in 1992 creating Societa di Intermediazone Mobiliare (SIM), a new form of securities firm involved in stockbroking and fund management, which will conduct stock trading, negotiation, placements and distribution, and will replace the former licensed brokers. All market transactions will be routed through SIMs and executed on the exchange floor. The SIMs must include authorized brokers but are set to be dominated by the banks in view of the higher capital requirements of the system. In addition, screen-based trading is being introduced and, perhaps the most contentious aspect of all, a new settlement system. The aim is to move away from the current fixed period to eventually a three-day rolling system. However, this will take time to deliver and is part of a move to eliminate all physical share transfers by using a computer-based share ownership system.

Although the changes are needed to bring the Milan Stock Exchange technologically into line with other financial centres, they may take time to alter attitudes at home and abroad. The Exchange's poor reputation has discouraged many smaller firms from seeking a quotation, added to which many companies and entrepreneurs are unwilling to cede partial control. Moreover, from an investor's perspective, the frequent public-sector deficits have tended to keep interest rates high and to offer tax incentives to attract private-sector savings away from equities, while more sophisticated investors have tended to invest internationally rather than rely on the narrow domestic equity base. Nevertheless, once the new systems show stability and enhanced returns, investor confidence may return and demonstrate the benefits of operative- and price-efficient markets.

In keeping with the rapid growth and democratization of the nation, the Spanish financial system developed radically in the 1980s. The banking sector was opened up and there are now around 50 foreign banks in Spain offering a variety of products from floating-rate notes to interest-bearing current accounts. In addition to those with large branch networks such as Barclays and Nat West, BNP and Credit Lyonnais, there has been a substantial expansion of investment banking operations. In a crowded market these may be classified as: overseas investment/merchant banks providing international equities and merger advice, such as Rothschilds and Goldman Sachs; the investment banking parts of foreign commercial banks such as Bankers Trust; and the merchant banking arms of Spanish banks such as Banco Santander de Negocios. Within the domestic banking sector, a process of rationalization and merger created five large, private-sector banks: Banco Santander, Banco Bilbao Vizcaya, Banco Central Hispano, Banco Popular and Banesto. The state-owned trade bank Banco Exterior has absorbed the state's industrial credit bank, BCI, and has itself been pooled with other public financial institutions within a new holding company, Banco Argentaria. Retail banking still dominates their operations despite attempts to boost fee income, although through their large industrial holdings they influence the banking and capital-raising activities of many firms. Thus, the Spanish banking sector has expanded considerably in recent years; yet equally the Spanish government has recognized the need to build up a sizeable, efficient capital market to supply the necessary development capital.

Spain has stock exchange trading floors in Barcelona, Bilbao and Valencia, although Madrid is by far the most significant market. During the early to mid-1980s the equity market boomed, and even in 1987, the year of the worldwide crash, it recorded a 9 per cent annual gain. To cater for this upsurge in activity, 1988 legislation created a securities commission, *Comision Nacional del Mercado de Valores (CNMV)* to oversee the market. A new trading structure was introduced such that existing brokers' licences were revoked and new specialist entities created. These were either *sociedades de valores*, brokers authorized to trade for themselves and clients, or *agencias de valores*, dealers who may act only for third parties.

The changes paved the way for banks and other institutions to take stakes in the new broking or dealing firms and bring needed liquidity. However, although most of the 51 broking firms formed powerful alliances with domestic partners, foreign entities were less forthcoming, fearing the market was saturated, especially with Spain's big banks running four of the five biggest brokers and those brokers doing the bulk of their business in the shares of the owning bank. At the start of 1992, fixed commissions which stood at 0.25 per cent of all transactions were abolished, and the intense competition saw these at least halve on major orders. Thus, the numbers of brokers are likely to be reduced drastically. The larger brokers can survive as the market widens but many independents may eventually disappear. Other structural changes included the formation of *sociedades rectoras* to administer the markets, charging members fees based partly on volume traded. These companies also took a 25 per cent stake in a company, Sociedad de Bolsa, created to run a new computer-aided trading system (CATS) to improve operational efficiency and the trading of active stocks. To enhance settlement, another company, Servicio de Compensacion y Liquidacion (SCL), was formed to run a new book entry registration, clearing and settlement system, aiming for a five-day settlement.

Derivatives trading began in Spain in 1989 with the creation of OM Iberia trading options in Madrid. However, shortly afterwards a futures exchange, Mercado de Futuros Financieros (MEFF) was established in Barcelona, fuelling further the rivalry between the two centres and raising questions about unnecessary duplication. In reality, the products traded were complementary, but, as elsewhere, the futures trading outperformed the options business with the most active contract on both exchanges the three-year government bond. After much debate, the two cities agreed in December 1991 to merge the exchanges and created a supervisory holding company, Mercado de Futuros Financieros SA (MEFFSA), based in Barcelona. Essentially, Madrid is now the centre for equity derivatives with Barcelona covering interest rate, currency and fixed-income trades. The Madrid operation began offering contracts on IBEX 35, the Spanish stock market index of the biggest 35 quoted companies, and had hoped to offer contracts on individual stocks. However, in reality the Spanish equities market is too narrow, with only 428 listed companies, many of whom are not actively traded. The Barcelona operation has gained from government support for derivatives development, and its prime product is a future on a notional 10-year government bond. However, less success has been gained with currency products, and both components of the joint exchanges remain domestically oriented with the limitations this implies in a European context.

Thus, the Spanish markets have developed in line with the expansion of the financial system in the 1980s. But, market capitalization remains low, at less than 30 per cent of GDP, and is heavily concentrated in a few major stocks, often banks, utilities or construction firms. Foreign involvement is limited although it provides the more active source of trading, possibly because the fiscal regime mitigates against equity investment given high capital gains tax rates. The fragility of developing financial markets such as Spain is seen with reference to the Danish 'no' vote in their 2 June 1992 referendum on the Maastricht Treaty. Arguably, the Treaty had been one spur for the Spanish 'bull' market in the late 1980s, with the anticipation that Spanish budget deficits would shrink and in turn reduce inflation and interest rates as a result of the EMU commitment and the Maastricht convergence criteria; a substantial stock market revaluation of up to 30 per cent was expected. However, with Maastricht thrown into doubt, the Madrid stock market fell by 5 per cent the week after the vote as Spain's commitment to convergence without a clear EMU framework thus came under scrutiny. Even more volatile were the Spanish derivatives markets. Until 3 June 1992 the largest number of daily contracts traded on notional 3-year and 10-year bonds was 17 000, but on that day 43 770 contracts were traded as investors became 'bearish'.

8.6 TOWARDS THE INTEGRATION OF EUROPEAN CAPITAL MARKETS?

The foregoing examination of European capital markets highlights their rapid growth, especially in derivatives products, yet also their progression along often similar lines, with the emphasis on liberalization and product innovation. However, the development of truly successful and continued markets and, indeed, financial centres stems largely from maintaining investor and participant confidence. This in turn derives from various factors, among which the following are noteworthy: the application of modern technology, appropriate legislation and supervision, and overall efficiency.

A key feature in the recent growth and integration of capital markets is the progress in communications and information technology which has cut transaction costs, quickened processing, improved surveillance and also enhanced global trading and competition. The gains of SEAQI at the expense of domestic exchanges in France, Germany and the Netherlands were noted in this respect. The move to screen-based trading, which is not of necessity location-specific, has brought fundamental changes to trading procedures; as Reed (1988) comments, 'a market-maker inputting prices of a security in Glasgow is just as much "the market" as a counterpart in London'. Moreover, clients as well as the industry's participants now have the opportunity to access large quantities of data but at very low cost. Since the systems suppliers are in active competition, the prospects are for even higher-specification products in the future. Exchanges and market operators are thus faced with difficult decisions as to the choice of trading, clearing and settlement system and the capital outlay required to maintain their competitive position.

Among the main integrating factors in capital markets is undoubtedly the liberalization of international capital operations, notably the reduction of exchange controls and the deregulation of financial markets. The latter particularly includes the dismantling of 'club' and cartel practices which have harboured fixed commission scales and restrictive practices. However, success depends upon appropriate regulation which takes time to implement. The 'Big Bang' in London loosened the ties that had confined practitioners to specific operations, but the new Banking and Financial Services Acts mean that large institutions involved in a range of financial services operations have had to report to a variety of statutory and self-regulatory bodies. This has proved costly and time-consuming, and inevitably has led to a reliance on observance of the spirit of the law rather than its detail in what is essentially a more relaxed and informal regulatory environment. In recent years, however, the major unifying force has undoubtedly come from EC legislative proposals to create an integrated Single Market for financial services where previously harmonization did not exist. Subsequent progress has involved the breaking down of national barriers, but with the imposition of new safeguards, and in the context of equity market integration, three sets of legislation are particularly noteworthy:

- The 'passport principle' of the right to set up/provide services anywhere in the EC under the *Investment Services Directive*
- Mutual recognition and minimum standards for company listings on stock exchanges under the *Admissions and Listings Directive*
- Minimum standards for company reports, prospectuses, information on share stakes and insider trading rules, covered in various *Reporting and Disclosure Directives*

In view of the foregoing moves towards integration, it is vital that acceptable levels of efficiency are achieved. European markets may be more informationally efficient in the EMH weak-, semi-strong- and strong-form senses, in that even European institutional investors are unable consistently to outperform the market and earn abnormal returns. However, while market efficiency in general has improved, instances of share price manipulation and insider dealing do still occur, and some markets remain 'thin' and illiquid, raising doubts about their allocative efficiency and pricing ability. Clearly, in an integrated market environment a poor reputation will lead to a loss of business to markets that are perceived to be more efficient, as the Italians have found to their cost.

The forces for financial market integration are thus gathering momentum, aided by economic convergence among member states and national equity market reforms. However, the latter have often been spurred not so much by Single Market opportunities as by competitive reaction to the dominance of the 'global triangle' based on New York, Tokyo and London, and notably by the loss of business to London. Indeed, integration should not be equated with cooperation since to date cooperative ventures between European markets have a poor record: rather, competition has driven market practices closer as successful operations are copied. Indeed, empirical evidence suggests that markets are so far relatively independent. For example, Solnik (1988) has shown that correlation coefficients between equity market returns are still relatively low, hence risk diversification is possible without sacrificing returns. However, it is noticeable that the Deutschmark bloc shows a strong regional interlinkage covering

Germany, Benelux and Switzerland, and, as European integration progresses, statistically significant increases in correlation coefficients between equity markets should develop. Any subsequent reduction in risk diversification opportunities would be offset by efficiency gains as market liquidity improves and choice widens among the European markets. Moreover, given that market covariance is unlikely to be unity, then scope for diversification will persist, especially when focused on specific industry sectors or market niches.

The *Euroquote* project is illustrative of the difficulties of formal cooperation. This Belgian company, owned by EC stock exchanges, was to provide a share price and information system networked to the 12 EC exchanges and, ultimately, was to serve as the vehicle for a competitive European trading system. While agreement was broadly reached on the system technology, fundamental differences occurred over its potential role. There was no justification for the infrastructure costs if it was to remain an information and price dissemination system, since existing systems already provide these or could be adapted accordingly. If it was to become a full trading system, then agreement would be needed on the appropriate market that investors require, while if it was to be linked to a European settlement system to simplify cross-border transactions, this would conflict with national developments, such as TAURUS in London. Fundamentally, there was the issue of whether formal links should be formed between national stock exchanges rather than building a new system. The London Stock Exchange was concerned that Euroquote as a trading system would compete with SEAQI, which currently accounts for 92 per cent of all EC cross-border trading. In the event, the project was postponed in 1991 because the major exchanges saw little commercial justification in it, some even arguing that it might enhance London's prominence if it operated in parallel to SEAQI yet carried the latter's prices.

The current dominant trend, therefore, is inter-country exchange competition as national stock markets fight to protect their share of equity trading in an international market environment. Moreover, resistance towards derivatives trading has been relaxed by governments who now recognize that an efficient derivatives exchange is essential to the functioning of the country's financial system in so far as it helps to disseminate risks and enhance the underlying cash market. Indeed, the establishment of the DTB supported by German financiers and government reflects the loss of Euro-DM futures business to LIFFE and a desire to repatriate such trade. Competition between derivatives exchanges is an outcome of internationalization and the success of financial futures, as illustrated by the September 1991 launch of MATIF's Italian bond futures contract within three weeks of an almost identical LIFFE one. With its concentration of exchanges, Europe exhibits the most competitive market worldwide, although to compete internationally requires national dominance, hence the tendency to consolidate domestically along the lines of the LIFFE–LTOM merger.

CONCLUSIONS

As the European Community has moved to unify its financial markets, so competition has strengthened among financial centres. Individual member states are liberalizing their financial systems and attempting to gain business by developing new exchanges, notably in derivatives. The logical extension of this trend may be seen as a wider distribution of activity, although, equally, the removal of restrictions might arguably encourage market forces to prevail and operations to polarize towards the larger, established markets, notably London. This raises problems for the appropriate location of institutions, i.e. whether relative to their customers, markets or competitors, and also for market behaviour, for example Amsterdam's ability to trade Dutch multinational companies' shares, or the range of MATIF's futures products in the light of competition from LIFFOE.

The foregoing examination of European financial centres suggests that London currently holds a dominant position. It was the pioneer in introducing the current spate of deregulation common throughout Europe, but has a long tradition of open markets and the provision of capital for industry via securities markets. It also has critical mass, with the world's largest foreign exchange market and dominant shares of international equities, Eurobonds, banking and fund management activities. Moreover, it is the main location for arranging note-issuance facilities, interest rate and currency swaps and forward-rate agreements. Further attractions include the use of English as the principal business language, and the high concentration of bankers, lawyers, accountants and other specialists who fuel its innovative and professional reputation. In general, in securities regulation and exchange operations the London markets are regarded as relatively efficient compared with those overseas. Indeed, the liquidity and size of its markets, and their ability to assume risk and provide immediacy in large trades, features that are so important to financial system operations, have made London a very attractive centre for European institutions.

On the other hand, London faces major challenges. In market technology some areas of dealing and settlement are vulnerable, notably the delayed launch of TAURUS. High property and wage costs in the past have caused problems, although the current commercial property glut is helping to alleviate the former; but a poor infrastructure remains. Recently the City's image has been tarnished by a string of scandals, notably the collapse of BCCI, Polly Peck, the Maxwell empire and the débâcle at Lloyds Insurance, all of which are regarded as symptomatic of how a loss of confidence in a market can drive business away. City practitioners might well argue that London's position could have been stronger with a more solid macroeconomic environment and greater political commitment to Europe. Late entry to the ERM and failure to sign for the third stage of monetary union might be cited as adverse influences on the campaign to gain the 'prize' of the location for the future EMI or ECB. However, sterling's September 1992 withdrawal from the ERM may well have dashed completely

London's hopes of hosting further European financial institutions—apart, that is, from the EBRD's having already been located there since April 1991.

With regard to other centres, Paris has invested more heavily in technology and infrastructure, and has introduced far-reaching reforms to its antiquated financial system, even though the spectre of state intervention hangs over the sector. The success of MATIF shows what can be done in a relatively short space of time, and Paris will continue to prove a competitive threat to London. Yet Frankfurt is now London's main European rival as it continues to develop its dominance over German financial markets, notably the fragmented regional stock exchanges. It has gained status from the strength of Germany's economic position and currency *vis à vis* Europe, and from unification and the current eastward concerns of the Community.

The location of the ECB is seen by some as particularly significant in that it would attract several hundred international banks, many of which have already located in London. The Bank of England fears an exodus if London loses out to one of its major rivals in this 'contest'. However, given the currency turmoil of September 1992, the concept and location of the ECB may be in jeopardy. Such a scenario could well benefit London in that monetary union might severely curtail its booming foreign exchange and derivatives business which gain from currency volatility. Indeed, a cynical perspective on the heightened market activity of 1992 might argue that it not only provided short-term windfall gains for the private-sector financial institutions involved, but also had a longer-term rationale in protecting future business for Europe's dealers. Certainly, any move to a single currency would severely dent foreign exchange profits for the major financial institutions. The currency upheavals illustrated the vast profits to be made when central banks are forced to defend a run on their currencies. If £1 billion was converted into Deutschmarks on Wednesday 16 September at the prevailing rate of DM2.7750 and reconverted back the next day at DM2.7075, it would have netted close to £25 million in profit.

Notwithstanding uncertainty over the future of the major European financial institutions such as the ECB, one might argue that competition among the leading European financial centres is in any event futile and harmful, and that instead they should seek ways to cooperate. The idea that 'prizes', such as the location of major EC institutions, will have significant implications for the financial services industry in a particular location is outdated. Indeed, an extreme perspective is our earlier observation that modern financial markets do not need to be location-specific at all, since fibre optics and telecommunications technology remove the need for a physical trading presence. Nevertheless, geographical concentration in financial services partly reflects the fact that financial markets and centres still rely heavily on people skills, and hence that confidence built up by tradition and personal contact is a vital ingredient for success. In this respect London still has a competitive edge.

FURTHER READING

The stock exchanges and derivative markets in the EC member countries are primary sources of material. Davis (1990) provides an industrial analysis of financial centres. Blake (1990) and Samuels *et al.* (1990) review the EMH and associated tests, while texts such as Gilbody (1988), Howells and Bain (1990) and Buckle and Thompson (1992) give a general insight into the nature of financial markets. Griffiths (1991) provides an examination of options and futures. See Courtney (1992) for European derivatives, and journals such as *Euromoney* and *The Banker* for regular guides to the European equity and derivatives markets.

NINE

FUNDING FOR INDUSTRY: AVAILABILITY, GOVERNANCE AND SHORT-TERMISM

The advent of the single financial market means that in theory all EC firms should have equal opportunities to raise funds. Together with moves towards UK-style securities markets charted in the previous two chapters, this brings into focus important and recurrent issues governing the relationships between companies and their suppliers of finance. For the past two decades, the UK financial system has been subjected to sustained criticism and investigation over its financial and ancillary support for industry, especially when compared with countries overseas, notably Germany. The Wilson Committee (1980) was established mainly in response to views in the 1970s that the inadequate performance of the British economy was a reflection of its financial system. More recently, the CBI City/Industry Task Force (CBI 1987) has examined relationships between the City and UK industry in the wake of a frenzied spate of takeover activity, and the Cadbury Committee (1992) has published a draft report on corporate governance, notably the control and information relationships between business, investors and advisers.

Much of the criticism has traditionally focused on bank–industry relations, particularly on the claim that UK banks are preoccupied with liquidity and are unwilling to provide long-term finance for industry. They are perceived as 'fair-weather' bankers, keen to make funds available when the economy and firms are progressing but reluctant to assist when times are hard and distress lending is required. As such, they are seen to take a short-term perspective in contrast to Germany and Japan, where relationships are nurtured over time. Additional criticisms are levied at the cost of loan interest and bank charges, and the quality of their services. A recent Institute of Economic Affairs (IEA) report (Capie and Collins 1992) entitled *Have the Banks Failed British Industry?* shows that the debate is still alive. However, in recent years the UK capital markets and major institutional investors too have come under attack. The markets are seen in some quarters as uncertain and volatile, prone to bouts of speculation. In spite of market efficiency tests, there is a belief that the stock market inaccurately prices securities, thus fuelling takeover activity which promotes short-term perspectives. Moreover, such activity also encourages professional, institutional investors to take a short-term outlook. The focus on portfolio return optimization encourages the acquisition and disposal of holdings to gain from price surges and mitigate losses. In turn, the argument is that this encourages company managers to focus on short-term profits at the expense of long-term growth and real investment in technology, so as to court favour with their institutional shareholders.

In this chapter we focus upon three issues central to this debate. Firstly, the availability of bank finance is considered in relation to the nature of funding, lending criteria and the specific needs of small business. Secondly, the issue is addressed of whether the provision of finance does or should confer control or influence over European industry. Comparisons are made between the UK, France and Germany in the context of company structure, and specific reference is made to the role of controlling boards, voting rights and agency relationships to consider issues of governance. Finally, the short-termism debate is examined in the context of technology, investor behaviour, capital markets and takeover activity.

9.1 AN OVERVIEW OF FUNDING FOR INDUSTRY

The financing strategy of a given firm will be influenced by a host of factors, some of which are indicated in Fig. 9.1. Not surprisingly, financing needs and packages will vary markedly between firms both within and across nations. Ultimately the chosen mix will reflect firm-specific characteristics such as the current financial situation and pending obligations, the dividend policy applied, the nature of the industry sector concerned, and the size and stage of development of the firm. Above all, the strategic orientation of the business may influence the requirement for new, mainly long-term, funds. The availability of finance will also reflect environmental forces; in particular, the relative influence of banks and markets in the system may condition the balance of debt to equity. Similarly, the prevailing economic climate may be conducive to rights issues if in the onset of a 'bull market'; or alternatively, it may favour low fixed-interest debt if higher or more volatile interest rates are expected.

The sources of industry finance may be classified in various ways, although three methods are commonly adopted: internal or external; short-, medium- or long-term; and bank or non-bank. *Internal funds* normally consist of undistributed profits, unremitted profits and accruals adjustments. Undistributed income

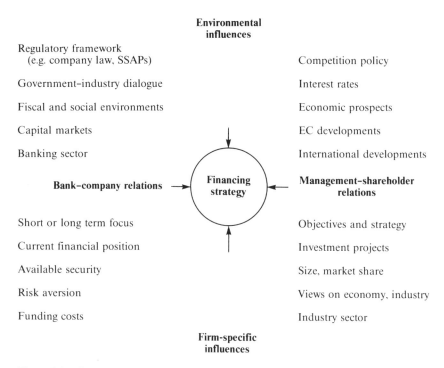

Figure 9.1 Influences on the demand for and supply of company finance

refers to the balance of the profit and loss account, before depreciation, stock revaluation and any additions to tax and dividend reserves. Such retained earnings are legally part of the shareholders' funds, but the decision to distribute or retain is effectively a managerial one, and unless shareholders have an active controlling interest and direct influence on management behaviour to encourage distribution, these funds are more akin to corporate savings. However, such 'savings' are often misguidedly regarded as cost-free since there is no transfer of money if the funds are retained, as there would be with interest or dividends. There is however an opportunity cost of consumption now (via full distribution to shareholders) or later (via investment now). Moreover, since shareholders require ample compensation for the risk capital they subscribe, such funds are not cheap. Clearly, managers need to establish an equitable balance between a company's retention and reinvestment policy and distributions to suit shareholder preferences.

The proportion of profit retained varies with overall profitability and is likely to show considerable cyclicality reflecting prevailing economic circumstances. In the UK in periods such as 1972–74, 1981–83 and 1989–91, when equity finance and profits have been under pressure, there has been heavy recourse to bank borrowing to top up the funding mix, in contrast to Germany, where conditions have been more stable from year to year.

The other sources of internal funds include net unremitted profits and accruals adjustments. The former represent domestic profits of overseas parent companies which have been retained, less profits due to domestic parent companies from overseas subsidiaries. Accruals adjustments represent tax collected but not yet paid and are a source of temporary funding. The prominence of internal funding reflects elements of prudence but also the need to provide for specific policies, notably depreciation, a particularly important item in a German context given the emphasis in that economy on replacing the capital stock with new technology.

External funds derive from various sources such as new equity issues or other corporate securities raised on capital markets, from domestic and overseas banks, insurance companies, trade financing organizations and government agencies. For convenience, these may be classified into short-, medium- and long-term finance, although opinions differ as to the appropriate divisions. The Bank of England (1985) considers borrowing under three years as short-term, three to ten years as medium and over ten years as long-term. In the context of trade finance, short-term is often less than six months, and many bank managers would review facilities annually. Similarly, medium-term in the context of, say, export finance schemes may be two to five years, but if particular countries or banks extend their cover, others may follow and terms can easily lengthen.

Short-term finance is essentially for the working capital needed in the daily operations of a business to cover the period between the payments to creditors and receipts from debtors. Clearly, any business must maintain adequate cash inflows to survive, since if it cannot pay its debts as they fall due it is at risk of liquidation by its creditors even if it is profitable. Ultimately, profit is an accounting concept whereas cash flow is a reality. Various sources of short-term funding exist including trade credit extended by suppliers and bill finance. *Factoring* companies offer financing as well as ancillary administrative, credit reference and insurance services. Normally bank subsidiaries will factor debts, that is purchase them as they arise, thus generating cash flow and reducing the customer's need to provide trade credit from its own resources. *Invoice discounting* involves sales of specific invoices to a factoring company or finance house. The customer receives an agreed proportion of the sum due, but is responsible for the collection of the debt and in this way maintains the normal business relationship with trade customers without the latter knowing about the factor's presence.

By far the most significant form of short-term funding is by way of *short-term loan or overdraft* facility. The latter has been traditionally the most widely used form of bank finance for British industry, accounting for over half of total lending in the mid-1970s by the London clearing banks (Freear 1989). Indeed, the Wilson Committee (1979) recognized the virtual absence of term lending to small businesses. The overdraft was originally conceived as a temporary working capital facility, particularly appropriate for seasonal fluctuations in cash

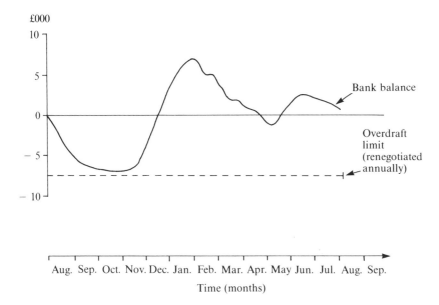

Figure 9.2 Operation of an overdraft

flow, or for bridging finance for the purchase of equipment or property pending the sale of an asset. A limit is agreed, with the customer able to draw cheques until it is reached. Under normal circumstances the account will swing between debit and credit, possibly with defined seasonal variations (Fig. 9.2). The system is simple—arrangements are negotiated very quickly without the need for a new account—and flexible, in that only the amounts needed are borrowed with interest charged solely on the daily debit balance.

A key feature of the overdraft facility is that it is intended to create mutual trust between banker and customer through its operation. Thus, it is the basis of the business customer–banker relationship in the UK. The major disadvantages are the need for renewal, the fact that it is technically repayable on demand, that security may be required, and that its cost can rise steeply with an upward movement in interest rates. Under normal circumstances facilities are renewed annually, and herein lies a change in focus from a temporary, self-liquidating advance purely for financing stocks or bridging needs. Indeed, the concept of a self-liquidating advance is illusory if the banking system is suffering a cash drain. Within the production chain, the ability of a manufacturer to repay an overdraft facility may depend on the sale of finished goods to a wholesaler, and, in turn, on the wholesaler's ability to raise bank credit. Therefore, the initial loan is self-liquidating only if credit is available for wholesalers—and, by extension, for retailers too. Hence, in the event of cash withdrawals, the failure of the wholesaler to gain credit might affect the manufacturer's ability to repay.

More significantly, the overdraft often gains a 'hard-core', semi-permanent element, especially when small firms use the facility to fund plant and equipment or other long-term assets. This is perceived as financially imprudent since there is always the possibility of loan recall, leaving a liquidity crisis or the forced sale of assets. Whether or not such an overdraft will be called depends on the bank's perception of the customer's situation. From the bank's perspective, the overdraft system as a whole creates uncertainty about the likely funds demanded, especially as only half the agreed limits are used at any one time. Banks must therefore retain low-yielding assets in sufficient quantities in case of a rise in overdraft usage (Morgan 1981).

Given these disadvantages, and in response to particular concerns of the Wilson Committee, the banks have introduced more fixed-term loans in keeping with the practice on the Continent, and involving formal repayment schemes with greater certainty of availability, term and cost. Short-term loan accounts, where the borrower takes on a fixed sum technically repayable on demand, but with repayment spread over a two- to three-year period, have tended to be superseded by the growth of contractual medium- and long-term lending for most businesses.

Medium-term loans are predominantly the province of the clearing banks and aim at fixed asset acquisition, to be secured either by fixed charges over those assets or by floating charges on the company's assets as a whole. Often the term loan formalizes the 'hard-core' component of the overdraft facility, thus forcing the customer to budget for the repayments but giving targets to reduce overall indebtedness. However, the advantage is that repayment can be tailored to meet expected cash flows via quarterly or semi-annual instalments, with or without a grace period, or may come from a single lump sum at maturity. Frequently such loans are negotiated at fixed rates of interest, thus providing greater certainty of cost. However, fixed rates are usually higher than variable ones often around 5 per cent over base, as against 2–5 per cent over base, and the borrower may lose out if the general level of interest rates falls. Fixed-interest-rate lending has tended to be less common in the UK than in Germany, where currency stability has traditionally reduced the volatility of interest rates. Also, the variable-rate base LIBOR became a standard in the 1970s for the rating of large-scale syndicated credits, and thus common in the London market as a whole.

The banking community is the major supplier of medium-term funding, whether by loans or through specialist trade, project or leasing finance. *Leasing* operations are conducted via bank subsidiaries and represent contractual obligations whereby the lessor retains ownership of the equipment, while the lessee has possession and use against the payment of lease rentals over a specified period. Medium-term leases are often 'operational' for equipment such as computers or cars, items subject to obsolescence and maintenance, and where the lease only partially covers the capital cost. Full-payout 'financial' leases involve amounts sufficient to cover the capital financing and profit element. Leasing can be used for long-term finance under 'sale and leaseback' arrangements where major assets, such as aircraft and ships, are sold by the manufacturer to a 'buyer', often a subsidiary company set up by a bank, and then leased back by the ultimate user over a long time period.

The major sources of *long-term funds*, leasing apart, involve a choice between forms of debt or equity, and provide the means whereby the major corporate assets can be acquired on which the development of the business depends; hence the availability of such finance is crucial. In the UK the main long-term debt derives from mortgage loans from institutional investors or corporate bonds and hybrid securities issued by the borrower in capital markets. Mortgage loans are normally for 20 years or more, and are specifically granted by insurance companies and pension funds for the purchase of land and buildings, normally for values in excess of £100 000.

The UK corporate bond market consists of debentures, unsecured loan stocks and 'hybrid' securities such as convertibles, debentures with warrants attached and preference shares. *Debentures* are secured, transferable loan stock which may be listed on the Stock Exchange and sold to investors. On issue, a trustee is appointed to look after the interests of the stockholders, so as to ensure the payment of interest. The security is either a fixed charge on specific assets (mortgage debenture) or a 'floating charge' on the business and those assets already pledged elsewhere. By offering well-secured debentures, the borrower can benefit by applying a lower rate of interest (Fig. 9.3a) than other funding methods of comparable maturity.

As the name implies, *unsecured loan stock* carries no security, and for the higher risk investors will require commensurate returns. As with secured loan stocks, a trust deed is drawn up, the terms of which may well incorporate covenants (negative pledges) restricting the company from issuing additional debt, or maintaining certain financial ratios in respect of liquidity, gearing, etc. Generally speaking, well established, sound enterprises will be able to raise funds successfully from institutional lenders, but each issue will be rated according to potential default risk which will affect its attractiveness. To enhance the take-up, such securities may be issued with a high coupon although this raises the cost of finance, or, conversely, sold at a deep discounted price to that at which it is redeemed.

In addition, the form of the loan stock might be made more attractive either by issue as a convertible or with warrants attached. Such hybrids have become popular often as 'middle-tier' or 'mezzanine finance' (Fig. 9.3b) for companies needing to raise significant sums but with only a relatively small capital base and with assets already pledged. *Convertibles* give the holders the right to convert stock into equities at specified rates and times, whereas *warrants* may be detached from the accompanying loan stock and used to subscribe for equity on favourable terms at some later date. For investors they represent an option to participate in the company at some future date if it progresses; but if they decline to do so, the interest received will be lower than could have been attained

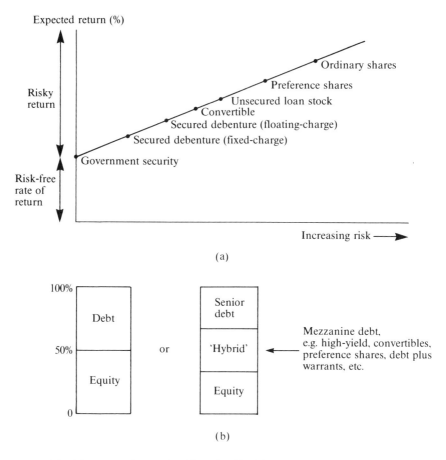

Figure 9.3 Risk, return and methods of financing (a) Risk and return (b) Nature of debt

under a comparable 'straight' loan stock. *Preference shares* are also hybrids, since their holders are part-owners of a company, rather than creditors, but receive a fixed dividend akin to fixed interest debt. They rank before ordinary shareholders in the event of liquidation but after all forms of debt, and cannot put the company into liquidation if their dividend is not forthcoming. Hence preference shares yield a higher return than debt. Their attraction is for corporate investors who can offset the advanced corporation tax (ACT) deducted from their preference dividend receipts against that payable on their own dividend payouts.

Irrespective of the amount of debt in a capital structure, there will be an element of *equity*. This represents the owners' interest and risk, since it acts as a cushion to meet creditors' needs if the firm fails. The generation of funds via the issue of share capital can provide a lesser obligation on the company than money borrowed by debt, but it implies ceding part ownership. For the share-holder, with restricted liability to the amount payable on the shares subscribed for, there exists a risk of loss to be offset by participation in the returns to the assets of the company for which he or she shares ownership. Most enterprises begin with an initial capital injection from the owner's resources aided by some borrowing. Where companies are established, share issues via an organized cap-ital market provide opportunities to raise large sums, both initially and later through rights issues, since the liquidity and marketability of listing generally make a company more attractive to prospective investors. In this way, the growth and development of the Stock Exchange in London, charted in Chapter 8 and Table 9.1, has given UK firms the chance to tap equity sources to a greater extent than many of their overseas counterparts.

The appropriate mix of debt and equity, or the capital structure decision, is a controversial issue, especially as differences between European nations are often linked to economic progress. In general, the prevailing view is that in France and Germany banks, often encouraged by governments, fostered close relationships and provided long-term, mainly fixed-rate, finance; thus capital markets remained relatively underdeveloped and narrow. In contrast, the UK banking sector has seen its primary role as the provision of short-term, mainly overdraft, finance. Until the emergence of the wholesale markets, the depend-ence upon retail deposits for funding meant that the sector was reluctant to lend long while obliged to meet depositor withdrawals on demand. Hence UK companies were encouraged to seek longer-term funding via the securities mar-kets. However, these distinctions have fuelled the criticisms of UK banks men-tioned at the start of this chapter and have led to the argument that low gearing in the UK is responsible for poor industrial performance. Samuels *et al.* (1975) suggested that higher debt—equity ratios would aid UK industry as they would reduce the cost of capital, debt being cheaper than equity (Fig. 9.3a).

In a historical context, UK gearing appears to have been much lower than that overseas. White (1984) reported capital gearing ratios for France, Germany and the UK of 65, 63 and 52 per cent respectively in 1970, and 72, 65 and 49 per cent in 1981. However, he acknowledged that German accounts add depreciation reserves to company liabilities rather than deducting them from assets, which understates the gearing ratio, and that there are differences in consolidation in France and Germany compared with the UK. Moreover, the above ratios dis-guise the fact that assets financed by leasing contracts were not capitalized in balance sheets. Since leasing was more popular in the UK at the time owing to favourable tax concessions, it may be seen as an alternative to borrowing. Sim-ilar findings relating to the UK and Germany were reported by the Deutsche Bundesbank (1984). It estimated that some 10 per cent of UK investment in plant and machinery was financed by leasing and pointed to a debt–equity capital (including reserves) mix of 51 to 49 per cent for the UK in 1981 and 81 to 19 per cent for Germany. Net capital gearing of German business (net financial debt as a proportion of total trading assets valued at historic cost) was over 60

Table 9.1 Value of securities quoted on the UK stock exchange and new capital issues, 1980–1991 (£billion)

	1980	1982	1984	1986	1987	1988	1989	1990	1991
Total of all securities quoted at market values	281	456	832	1248	1548	1427	1861	2106	2195
of which:									
Total company securities	211	350	671	1016	1285	1162	1570	1861	1923
of which:									
Loan capital	4	5	8	9	12	12	14	17	14
Preference and preferred capital	2	2	7	8	22	27	35	40	33
Ordinary deferred capital	205	343	656	999	1251	1123	1521	1804	1876
Total net new issues	0.8	1.6	2.3	9.0	15.4	7.1	7.9	2.8	*n.a.*
of which:									
Loan capital	-0.2	0.6	0.9	1.2	-0.2	0.9	3.3	-0.3	n.a.
Preference shares	–	–	–	–	0.7	1.0	0.9	0.4	n.a.
Ordinary shares	1.0	1.0	1.4	7.8	14.9	5.2	3.7	2.7	n.a.

Source: Annual Abstract of Statistics, 1992, T.17.11, 17.12.

per cent in 1982 compared with a low of 25 per cent in the UK, a reflection partly of the large proportion of SMEs in Germany.

Various obstacles to obtaining external equity finance have traditionally existed in Germany. In the first place, most businesses are sole proprietorships, partnerships or private limited companies since there exist stringent organizational requirements for public limited companies, the only ones able to raise equity in the capital markets. Secondly, returns on equities have discouraged investors via the double taxation of corporate equity capital and shareholders' wealth, the heavy transaction costs reducing profits, and, above all, the better return on fixed-interest investments in the low-inflation environment. Thirdly, and most pervasively, the influential banking community has not encouraged equity financing.

Among other sources of finance, a feature of the 1970s and early 1980s was the relatively small recourse to bond issues in both nations. In Germany most bond issues are by banks which on-lend the funds raised to their industrial customers; indeed, by 1982 corporate bonds outstanding were some DM3 billion compared with DM10 billion a decade earlier, with longer-term bank borrowing gaining in significance. In the UK the corporate bond market remained dormant for much of the 1970s and early 1980s, declining from a peak in 1965 when £415 million of debentures were issued to just £2 million in 1980 (Rutterford 1984). This shrinkage coincided with high and volatile levels of inflation and interest rates, creating uncertainty, and government gilt-edged stock issues which 'crowded-out' commercial borrowers.

Since the mid-1980s there has been some convergence in the methods of corporate finance provided in both nations. The 1984 Bundesbank report argued for a stronger equity base in both nations, especially to support emerging high-risk, technology-based, often capital-intensive firms. Table 9.2 illustrates the substantive 1980s growth in equity capital quoted on the UK market, including some £38.4 billion new ordinary shares raised over 1985–90. Much of this increase was associated with the takeover boom of the mid-1980s. For example, Saatchi and Saatchi raised some £574 million between 1984 and 1986 for acquisitions, and the subsequent financial collapse of the company meant that its shares, which had traded at 995p in April 1986, were quoted at only 16p in February 1991, thus reinforcing criticisms of 'short-termism' in the UK securities markets.

In Germany a similar equity growth has occurred, with some DM94.2 billion in new equity capital raised over 1985–90, of which 82 per cent was raised by commercial companies and 18 per cent by banks (Deutsche Bundesbank 1991e). This surge in equity financing represents a shift in corporate behaviour stimulated by improvement in company earnings and the boom affecting stock markets worldwide, and only temporarily interrupted by the 1987 crash. The emerging significance of shares as financing instruments is not immediately apparent from the composition of 'own funds' (Table 9.3), as in recent years substantial transfers to reserves have taken place reflecting high levels of

Table 9.2 Sources of enterprises' capital funds, UK, 1984–1991 (£millions)

	1984	1985	1986	1987	1988	1989	1990	1991
Internal sources								
Undistributed income	31 302	32 540	31 225	41 954	41 967	38 046	36 166	35 838
Net unremitted profits	-2 601	-1 141	-2 250	-3 777	-3 470	-5 505	-4 540	-3 349
Accruals adjustment	-71	-338	-225	-265	-585	1 298	2 006	5 489
Total internal funds (A)	28 630	31 061	28 450	37 912	37 912	33 839	33 632	37 978
External sources								
Ordinary shares	1 127	3 407	5 427	13 175	4 573	1 882	2 822	9 683
Bank borrowing	7 300	7 704	9 417	13 003	29 614	33 089	18 468	-3 389
Other loans/mortgages	576	876	1 453	2 760	3 783	9 212	8 393	3 764
Debenture/preference shares	248	816	490	534	1 207	5 648	3 403	5 051
Other capital issues	298	770	1 492	3 969	3 092	7 706	6 937	6 424
Other overseas investment	-3 124	-835	2 880	2 760	3 322	9 312	8 762	6 365
Total external funds (B)	6 425	12 738	21 159	36 201	45 591	66 849	48 785	27 898
% A/% B	82/18	71/29	57/43	51/49	45/55	34/66	41/59	58/42
Total funds	35 055	43 799	49 609	74 113	83 503	100 648	82 417	65 876

Source: CSO Financial Statistics T.8.2.

Table 9.3 Sources of enterprises' capital funds, FRG, 1988–1990 (DM millions)

	1988	1989	1990
Internal sources			
Capital increases of unincorporated			
enterprise and transfers to reserves	7 900	19 900	23 000
Depreciation	130 900	142 300	153 500
Transfers to provisions	16 100	39 700	33 000
Total internal funds (*A*)	154 900	201 900	209 500
External sources			
Capital of uncorporated enterprise	7 000	9 200	12 000
Debt: short-term	57 400	130 800	109 500
Debt: long-term	21 800	25 500	21 000
Total external funds (*B*)	86 200	165 500	142 500
% *A*/% *B*	64/36	55/45	60/40
Total funds	241 100	367 400	352 000

Source: Monthly Report of the Deutsche Bundesbank, November 1991, p. 17.

retained profits. Corporate profitability has stimulated the raising of equity capital by offering higher returns than on fixed-interest securities, a switch in the conventional pattern in Germany. Moreover, German universal banks facing enhanced competition have keenly sought new share underwriting business, thus assisting companies seeking listings. For established German companies equity financing has proved beneficial in recent years, but with only 500 listed companies and partnerships limited by shares, the benefits of a quotation remain concentrated.

Convergence is also occurring on the UK side, where more companies are varying their capital structures. For example, the dormant corporate bond market reawakened in the mid-1980s as rising company profitability encouraged firms to undertake long-term investment financed by borrowing. Moreover, the fall in inflation to low and sustainable levels allowed a return to fixed-interest funding as long-term interest rates fell and yields stabilized. Other contributory factors to the resurgence in debenture and preference share issues (Table 9.2) were the improvement in public-sector finances, which left more scope for other fixed interest borrowers; the abolition of exchange controls, which attracted foreign investors; and deregulation, which increased the number and size of market intermediaries, thus promoting liquidity in bond dealings. The stronger stock market *al.*so encouraged hybrids such as convertibles. However, as Table 9.3 shows, even these issues appear insignificant relative to the surge in short- and medium-term borrowing in the period 1987–90 which initially fuelled takeover activity (see Tables 9.2 and 9.4). As the economy turned down in 1990, companies adjusted their expenditure downwards and reduced their financial deficit, repaying loans in the face of high real interest rates.

Thus, the overall perception of UK companies as having low gearing and relying on their banks solely for working capital finance masks the greater recourse to long-term debt. Similarly, the traditional view of German companies operating in a bank-dominated environment with little use of equity funding appears to be less appropriate now. As the above tables indicate, the gearing levels of firms in both countries appear volatile and subject to the prevailing economic climate. However, while the aggregate data depicted here suggest that firms in both nations have had access to substantial and varied sources of funds, it belies the needs of varying kinds of firms, notably small and medium-sized ones.

9.2 FINANCE FOR SMALL AND MEDIUM-SIZED ENTERPRISES

Both the initial development of the European Community and the advent of the Single Market have been geared to large firms which can access the extended market and benefit from economies of scale. But concentration has not prevented the growth of small and medium-sized enterprises (SMEs), defined by the EC as those employing less than 500 people and accounting for over 90 per cent of European firms. There is however no universally agreed definition of a small firm, and in the UK the Committee of Inquiry on Small Firms (Bolton 1971) produced seven different definitions for the industries it covered. In manufacturing small firms were seen as those employing less than 200 people, although the Bolton Committee emphasized distinguishing features such as personalized management, independence and small market shares rather than statistical quantification in terms of turnover, assets or employment. The 1981 Companies Act did attempt a statistical definition: small firms were those with a turnover of under £1.4 million, assets not exceeding £0.7 million and less than 50 employees; medium-sized companies were those with a turnover of under £5.75 million, assets under £2.8 million and less than 250 employees.

Whatever the definition, small firms make major contributions to the domestic and hence European economy. Mayes (1989) cites the job creation effect, assistance to growth via increasing the pace of innovation and assimilating risk, and the direct growth impact of progression from small into medium and large firms. The Bolton Committee reported on the decline in the number of UK businesses, but since then there has been a dramatic turnaround, and between 1979 and 1988 the number of new VAT-registered businesses rose by 22 per cent or 285 000. Burns and Dewhurst (1986) suggest that UK enterprises of under 500 persons employed 37 per cent of the workforce (32 per cent in manufacturing and 50 per cent in services), although this is markedly less than in Italy (83 per cent), Germany (64 per cent) or France (60 per cent). They contend that the UK remains a land of big business in spite of the growth of small firms in recent years, especially in services and sub-contract work.

In Germany unincorporated businesses play a particularly important role in the economy, especially when craft trades and independent professionals are considered, and Bannock (1976) estimated there might be over 40 per cent more small businesses in Germany than in the UK even allowing for population differentials. Small and medium-sized businesses, referred to as the *Mittelstand*, are actively promoted by the federal government to compete with larger firms. Simon (1992) points to their success in export markets, especially for intermediate goods or niche products, and cites manufacturers of bookbinding textiles, offset printing machines, chain saws, and sunroofs as being world leaders in their fields. This greater importance of small businesses in Germany would be expected to be reflected in relatively greater reliance upon bank finance, in spite of the structural differences in the financial systems of the two nations.

Throughout Europe, one can envisage that the typical small business will be financed by the entrepreneur's personal equity stake, possibly with a relatively low level of retained profit. Heavy reliance will be placed upon trade and possibly instalment credit, factoring and leasing; but if these are in short supply then inevitably recourse is made to the bank overdraft or short-term loan. The characteristic shortage of long-term debt and general under-capitalization are often reflected in liquidity constraints. Early studies of small-firm financing pointed to a financing gap. In the UK the Bolton Committee (Bolton 1971) argued that small firms were disadvantaged in seeking external funds, in terms of both availability and cost, compared with their larger counterparts, yet it acknowledged also that many small firms failed fully to utilize the available funding. The Wilson Committee in 1979 reached similar conclusions, arguing that deficiencies in the availability of long-term finance hampered growth.

In Germany, Hunsdiek (1986) examined the financing problems of German high-technology firms in the early start-up and growth phases of their life-cycle and concluded similar results. The lack of a track record to obtain favourable credit terms, insufficient collateral to meet bank demands and a poor equity base creating high gearing were frequently cited, which, compounded with problems of cash generation after launch, led to liquidity difficulties. High gearing was seen as a constraint, not so much from the perspective of problems of acquiring debt or bank–industry relations as from the difficulties of raising the equity element. SMEs in Germany have traditionally had limited access to capital markets because of the high costs, aforementioned poor returns on equity investments for investors and, above all, restrictions placed on going public by the issuing banks. Thus, Hunsdiek argued that in Germany too an equity gap existed. Within their life-cycles small companies need long-term funding as soon as possible, since further investment needs will follow if they are successful at launching new products, and recourse to trade credit and other short-term funds will be insufficient.

Since the early 1980s, greater attention has been given in Europe to the long-term financing needs of SMEs; in the UK, for example, there has been the introduction of the Loan Guarantee Scheme, the development of the Unlisted Securities Market and the growth of venture capital. The Loan Guarantee Scheme (LGS) was a consequence of the Wilson Report recommendations and aimed to remove the constraints imposed by an inadequate track record, or lack of security, which would create too large a risk for the lending banks. Under the initial scheme introduced in 1981 for three years, the government provided £50 million per annum to guarantee 80 per cent of any medium-term loan (two to seven years) made by the clearing banks. The minimum and maximum limits on individual loans were £5000 and £75 000 and the borrower paid a 3 per cent government premium (later 5 per cent) above the commercial lending rate, ostensibly to cover the operation of the scheme and the inevitable claims arising from business failure. In 1984 the LGS was revised as failures rose; subsequently it has provided 70 per cent finance, later amended to 85 per cent cover for small companies in inner-city areas, and with the loan ceiling raised to £100 000 (Samuels *et al.* 1990).

The scheme works on the concept of 'additionality'; in other words, the presence of a bank guarantee allows the bank to provide incremental lending to potentially viable businesses which otherwise could not raise the money. The continuation of the scheme and the provision of £750 million in the 1980s to 23 000 firms suggests that it has filled a gap. In effect, such programmes provide 'quasi-equity' loans, additional to the owner's stake, but they are expensive and raise the company's gearing with attendant adverse effects on liquidity. They do not meet the need for straight equity funding for under-capitalized start-ups.

Another new source of funding to close the 'equity gap' was the introduction in November 1980 of the Unlisted Securities Market (USM), a second-tier market with less onerous listing requirements and smaller charges than the full stock market. Only a minimum of 10 per cent of a company's capital had to be made available (25 per cent for a full listing), and companies had to have traded for three years (five for full listing), although in exceptional circumstances firms without a trading record but with a commercially developed product could secure a quotation. The USM confers advantages in that the company's image and capital-raising capacity is enhanced; its shares become more marketable; its financing sources become more varied; the owners can cash in on their achievements to date by selling some of their equity; and employees can be rewarded by share option schemes. However, such firms are subject to greater public disclosure and financial performance requirements.

The USM was seen to meet the needs identified in the Wilson Report (1979) of those firms with growth potential, and where greater marketability of their shares would lower costs. The market essentially aimed at firms with a capitalization of less than £5 million and acted as a bridge to a full listing. In the first 10 years of its existence some 817 firms were admitted, of which 157 moved up to a full listing, 160 were acquired and 72 left. Deregulation has assisted market liquidity, and the USM has proved resilient to downturns, has maintained investor interest and has proved a cheaper method of raising funds than a full listing. Hutchinson *et al.* (1988) found USM quotations to be sought by firms wishing to overcome difficulties in accessing borrowing, with entrants displaying high gearing and low liquidity. However, Buckland and Davis (1990) contend that entrants show a range of financial structures, and argue that access to debt is a motive for entry since debt capacity is constrained by the lack of security attached to non-marketable equity. This reiterates a general issue found by the Wilson Report, that the UK clearing banks' security requirements were considered onerous by small firms, a point that is made manifest elsewhere in the introduction of the LGS.

In 1987 the Stock Exchange introduced a junior Third Market, designed to compete with the over-the-counter (OTC) markets in small unlisted companies. These were largely unregulated telephone markets which raised capital through sponsorship and traded shares on the basis of matched bargains. The Stock Exchange wished to bring as much share trading 'on-market' as possible and saw the Third Market as providing a regulated, prestigious and liquid market for smaller start-up companies, since the USM had proved a successful vehicle for established firms. The entry requirements were relatively attractive: no minimum equity percentage; no minimum size requirement; and a trading record of merely one year with unqualified audited accounts. However, in 1990 entry requirements to the USM were relaxed to two years and the Third Market was closed, most of its participants transferring to the USM.

The most significant efforts to close the 'equity gap' have undoubtedly come through the development of venture capital funds. By 1989 the UK venture capital industry was channelling £1684 million in equity-based funding to over 1300 companies, compared with just £66 million in 1981 (Murray 1991). Such growth has been spurred by the above USM developments, a generally 'bullish' economic climate, and the association with entrepreneurship and high-growth SMEs.

Venture capital covers a multitude of operations but is generally defined as 'a way in which investors support entrepreneurial talent and thus obtain long-term capital gain' (Shilson 1984). In terms of the finance element, a range of investment opportunities may be covered from general small business development to high-risk investment in new technology-based industry. The latter is the more common focus and its significance lies in opening up a source of external equity finance for small businesses formed to exploit new ideas or technology and offering rapid growth and high profit potential. A distinguishing feature from other equity investment is that of 'hands-on' involvement, in that the venture capital company provides basic business advice and contacts, especially in the early stages of the investment, and generally takes an active interest in the business.

The venture capitalist invests funds with a view to capital appreciation rather than income, through a financing package which may include ordinary or preference shares and hybrid debt. The return will come from the company concerned being listed on a stock market, being taken over or being sufficiently profitable for the venture capitalist's stake to be bought out. While these are potentially long-term sources of finance, the venture capitalist is looking for an exit route within a three- to six-year time span, and a return on the investment of at least 25 per cent per annum.

The industry encompasses over 120 venture capital organizations, of which 27 have over £50 million or more under their management. Many venture capital funds are 'captive' organizations forming part of larger financial organizations— clearing banks and institutional investors such as pension funds and insurance companies. However, since 1981 'independent' groups have tended to grow in number and significance as smaller, specialized firms focused on specific segments, such as Piper Trust (retailing), or on regions, such as Avon Enterprise and Yorkshire Enterprise. Groups that have access to in-house funds can use these to 'leverage' their fund-raising efforts, whereas the independent funds must seek a wider range of support. This was readily available in the mid-1980s, but since 1988 fund-raising has become more difficult in the changed economic climate and intense competition. There are also a number of state-owned agencies, such as English Estates and the Scottish and Welsh Development Agencies, which are funded by central government to serve specific regions.

In 1983 the government introduced a Business Expansion Scheme (BES) providing a tax incentive for personal equity investment in unquoted companies operating in selected fields. Individuals were able to obtain tax relief on investments of up to £40 000 per annum held for up to five years and could either invest directly or through approved BES funds which gave them benefits of portfolio diversification. The extension of BES tax relief allowed BES funds to quote competitive terms to companies requiring equity finance, but eventually the scheme ended when tax relief was phased out.

One specialized area of venture capital that developed in the 1980s was 'corporate venturing', whereby a large company with spare liquidity can purchase a minority stake in a small enterprise active in a technological area significant to the investing company. Sometimes the larger entity also provides management assistance, and the terms of the agreement may also include licensing or distribution arrangements, possibly with a sell-out to the larger company if the venture proves successful. Such corporate venturing—and, indeed, venture capital as a whole—is particularly suited to high-technology or science-based industries founded by technicians, engineers or scientists possessing a wealth of product and process knowledge but lacking company management skills. Arguably, a successful high-tech company needs at least two entrepreneurs: one a skilled engineer/technician and the other a skilled manager who can raise risk capital for the start-up and growth of the business.

Although the UK venture capital industry accounts for well over half the funding available in Europe, similar developments have also taken place on the Continent. In Germany, Hunsdiek (1986) noted that there were some 30 venture capital companies with a total investment of DM700 million, although few funds are geared to 'seed-bed' or 'start-up' finance, and the scale of the operation has yet to cope fully with the equity need identified earlier. For a long time the main focus of support has been via subsidized interest rates and state guarantees. An 'equity capital programme' was established in 1979 by the federal government whereby an equity investment of around 10 per cent by an entrepreneur setting up a firm could be trebled by public loans if the investment cost was up to DM120 000 (Kayser and Ibielski 1986). The mainstay of *Mittelstand* financing remains the banking community, especially at the regional and savings bank level.

Similar considerations apply elsewhere, although in France much more financing emphasis is placed upon short-term debt than in the UK or Germany. The main long-term support comes from government-subsidized loans for capital investment promoted through the Crédit National and regional development agencies, plus a wide range of 'aid' schemes with subsidies for marketing, training and technological development. Overall French industrial policy has focused on the larger companies. A policy of concentration in the 1970s led to the acquisition of many medium-sized firms by larger entities receiving state aid. In the early 1980s there was a spate of nationalizations based on the idea that the prosperity of firms was linked directly to state intervention (Szarka 1992). A liberalization phase has followed since 1986 with wholesale privatization, but again with little joy for small firms.

Specific EC assistance has burgeoned in recent years. The Commission set up a task force to coordinate the improvement of the environment for SMEs, including the provision of loans and grants. In 1986 an action plan was launched, and in June 1989 the Council adopted a programme covering 1990–93 with a budget of ECU110 million (Roney 1991). The enterprise policy includes the establishment of a new company, EUROCONFIN, to act as a clearing house for potential financial backers of SMEs. Cheap loans are also to be made available via the European Investment Bank. In addition there are innovation and new technology funds, such as BRITE, ESPRIT and SPRINT, and some 24 new funds are to be created to provide 'seed-bed' and venture capital funding. A European Venture Capital Association (EVCA) was founded in 1983 as a non-profit-making organization based in Brussels to manage and invest new venture capital in the EC, to finance innovation, and to coordinate existing provision (Budd and Jones 1991).

Throughout Europe, therefore, there appears to be a growing awareness of the financing needs of small SMEs, and the UK financial system should be as capable as most of meeting these. Certainly, with the resurgence of entrepreneurship in the 1980s and in the wake of the Wilson Report, more attention and resources have been devoted to the sector. Indeed, a whole industry—venture capital—has emerged to this end. Yet business surveys point to increasing concerns over the banking relationship, which go beyond the pure availability of funds. Indeed, given the wide range of bank-based sources, and the fact that over half the overdraft facilities are not fully utilized, there appears to be some reluctance to borrow, notwithstanding evidence that firms relying on bank credit have grown more rapidly. For example, Hankinson (1991), in a small-scale, localized survey of small engineering firms in Dorset and Hampshire, found that the 28 respondents in general rejected bank credit even though they felt it was potentially profitable. Many complained of the banks' 'unhelpful attitudes', and of failure to understand seasonal problems, of demanding excessive collateral, and of stressing track record rather than potential.

Doggett (1992), in a survey of SMEs in Hertfordshire and Essex, found that 80 per cent of the 189 respondents used overdraft facilities but hardly any made use of term loans, or indeed of any alternative sources of short-term funds such as factoring. He argues that this reflects a lack of understanding of financial structure by small companies plus a desire for banks to commit themselves only to a series of 'short-terms'. The study pointed to marked inertia on the part of customers, who expressed dissatisfaction with their banking relationship, yet had made little attempt to change or seek independent advice.

Where SMEs do borrow from their banks, the main problems often appear to centre upon the cost of funding and the security required. The Wilson Committee (1979) found no financial bias in respect of charging commensurate with the risks involved. However, they did find the banks excessively cautious, and this raised the cost for SME borrowers. During the 1980s there was such intense competition in lending to large companies that margins were minimal, often less than the 1 per cent over base deemed the very minimum to cover lending costs. As the recession developed, and with it bad debts and capital constraints, banks have been keen to boost their income.

One solution is to focus on those borrowers who are prepared to pay for the service at higher cost or who exhibit inertia. Since lending in most UK towns is concentrated among a small group of clearing banks with similar problems and outlooks, the market power available to the SME is often limited. Hutchinson and McKillop (1992) cite evidence which suggests that interest rate premia on SME lending have been disproportionately high and have cross-subsidized the large business sector. Added costs have come from bank charges, which were often negligible for businesses but have risen in cost and complexity in recent years. Banks contend that their loan margins must incorporate allowance for bad debts and that in times of recession this risk increases. The problem for the borrower is that involuntary demand for lending increases at a time when the costs of such loans are also rising.

The issue of security is often contentious. From the bank's perspective it is just one aspect of the lending decision, an insurance should the primary source of repayment fail. Banks argue that every loan should stand on its own and that lending solely against security would make them 'pawnbrokers'. Nevertheless, as Berry et al. (1987) found, the lending approach used by banks is heavily influenced by the size of company; in particular, bankers dealing with small companies appear more concerned with security and will go to considerable lengths to value and effect it. Attitudes vary according to whether the amount is within the discretion of the local branch manager and the particular bank's lending policy. Guarantees from directors of smaller companies are often sought since the provision of a guarantee evidences the directors' commitment to the proposal (Bloomfield 1991).

Although Hutchinson and McKillop (1992) consider that the collateral requested in the UK is too high, especially in comparison with the USA, where more attention is given to cash flow than assets, security requirements are no stricter than in Germany. Similar security is sought in both nations, such as mortgages over property or marketable financial assets, but for medium-term funding to small businesses greater emphasis is placed upon guarantees in Germany. The lending institutions themselves, notably the savings and cooperative banks, took the initiative in promoting the emergence of regional credit guarantee associations (CGAs) with the specific purpose of aiding small firms unable to obtain bank loans through lack of adequate collateral. The capital of such CGAs derives from banks, chambers of commerce, insurance companies and various private institutions, supplemented by loans from the *Länder* and central government. Significantly, requests for credit guarantees come from the bank evaluating the loan application, and arise where there is a possibility of rejection without collateral.

In terms of general lending procedures, similarities now exist between the UK and Germany. Traditionally in the UK, lending decisions followed a hierarchy, from branch to region to head office according to the amount and the bank managers' discretionary limits. More recently, bank reorganization has led to the creation of small business centres or advisers specializing in the sector. For example, Barclays has over 300 such centres in its 2700 outlets, and National Westminster has a small business adviser in each branch. Their role partly mirrors that of the German *Kundenberater* or customer adviser, who advises firms on the amount and conditions of a loan and assists in the application. Reference has been made to the emphasis on security in both nations but other factors are considered. In the UK the acronym CAMPARI (Character, Ability, Margin, Purpose, Amount, Insurance (security)) is widely applied as a screening frame, although emphasis is placed on the calibre of the applicant and viability of the proposal in a less rigid form than the German focus on financial criteria and the bank's lending portfolio.

With £30 billion in loans outstanding, and many overdraft facilities not fully utilized, it appears difficult to argue that there is a lack of available funding. This is even more the case, if, as Mayer suggests, most studies of the UK financial system conclude that banks would lend more if only prospective borrowers would come forth with suitable proposals. However, much lending is short-term, despite developments in the 1980s, and it is argued that longer-term relationships need to be formed between banks and customers for the good of the economy. This is also significant for larger entities, and in the following section we consider the role of financial institutions in relation to industrial management and control issues.

9.3 ISSUES OF GOVERNANCE

Differences in bank–industry relations between Germany, France and the UK reflect organizational structures as well as their respective financial systems. In Germany and France both single-and two-tier administrative boards of control may exist, depending upon the legal form and company size, whereas in the UK a single-tier board comprising executive and non-executive directors is the norm. In Germany the two-tier system occurs in the larger private and public companies (*Aktiengesellschaft* or AG) and consists of a management board (*Vorstand*), with similar functions to those of a UK board of directors, and a supervisory board (*Aufsichtrat*), made up of shareholders' and employees' representatives, bankers and industrialists representing its customers and suppliers. The supervisory board is legally empowered to appoint and control the management board, and to monitor company performance on behalf of the interests of employees and shareholders. Any major business changes or investment projects would normally be referred for supervisory board approval.

Dyson (1986) argues that the two-tier system was introduced in Germany in 1870 to underline the close relationships between industry and banking and to give the latter an element of control. However, the supervisory board's functions are now more often akin to advice and administration than control. Banks are widely represented on the supervisory boards; Cable (1985) cites them as holding 145 seats on the boards of the largest 100 companies. Of these seats, 94 belonged to the 'Big Three' universal banks. Bank representatives are valued for their advice and contacts as well as for their fund-raising capacities, and in return receive additional internal company information beyond that normally available to external financiers. Since supervisory board appointments are part-time and the boards meet quarterly, the commitment is not burdensome. Although full-time board members of industrial companies are occasionally appointed as part-time members of bank boards, the reverse is the norm.

Bank representation on supervisory boards is not necessarily associated with their shareholdings or proxy voting rights. Direct shareholdings derive from company rescues and capital reconstructions, such as those involving Krupp and AEG, and from arranging stock market quotations. The proportion of total quoted ordinary shares held by banks in their own right has averaged less than 10 per cent, although in individual companies the stakes may be quite large. Bannock (1981) suggests that at least 90 per cent of holdings are of over 25 per cent of the shares, which under German company law gives a power of veto. Moreover, greater voting power accrues to banks from the exercise of proxy rights where shareholders have deposited shares with them. Technically, written shareholder authorization is needed, but in practice, where no instructions are given to the contrary, the banks will use the voting rights as they see fit. As banks provide most of the stockbroking and safe custody services, a large proportion of shares are deposited with them, and thus also substantial proxy rights.

The various roles played by German banks as lenders, advisers, shareholders, holders of proxy votes and operators in the securities markets could confer both advantages and conflicts of interest. Cable (1985) tested the association between bank participation and profitability in a sample of the largest 100 German firms and concluded that a positive relationship existed, and went beyond the provision of credit alone; i.e., bank control as well as lending enhanced profitability. Nevertheless, conflicts can arise; notably, a bank lending to a profitable company may urge it to take on further borrowing rather than turn to the capital markets. On the other hand, bank support can prove useful as a defence against a hostile takeover bid, and long-term lending for capital investment, research and development are central to the perception that managers should take a long-term perspective in their business strategy. Thus German banks have considerable potential influence over companies, especially under the 'universal' banking system when as 'house banks' they can offer a full service range to customers. But this influence is often more apparent than real in so far as interference in the daily management of companies is concerned; instead, what they offer is support and advice.

In France most large limited companies, or *sociétés anonyme* (SA), have a single board akin to the German model. Private limited companies are usually owner-managed Société à Responsibilité Limitée (SARL) and rarely have a formal board, but may have managers with responsibilities similar to a supervisory board. The relatively infrequent meetings of single-tier boards gives considerably more power to the company managing director than in Germany or the UK (Lane 1989). This is in keeping with the autocratic nature of French management culture with the emphasis on the *patronat*, a term that has varied French connotations from 'boss' to 'paternalism' but reflects the predominant owner–manager basis of firms (see Szarka 1992). It is the state rather than financial institutions that has played a major role in industrial development; firstly by restructuring then by wholesale nationalization before recent liberalization. Thus, former civil servants or administrators play the role assigned to bankers on German boards, and banks are just one set of institutions, along with trade associations and chambers of commerce, that have an influence.

In the UK the single-tier board of directors is the formal strategic decision-making body, comprising internal executive directors and external non-executive ones. The former are representatives of top management, and delegation of responsibility to them may be highly specialized, although overall the chairman or managing director may wield considerable power, especially if the two roles are combined. Employee participation is rare although external non-executive directors may represent shareholders or business contacts. During the early 1980s more companies were encouraged to appoint non-executive directors, but research in 1987 (Bank of England 1988a) indicated that little progress had been made. The survey was based on *The Times'* 1000 firms, and of the 549 respondents, 68 per cent had boards of between six and eleven members, yet 44 per cent had less than three non-executive directors, and only 12 per cent more than six. Some 75 per cent of the non-executive directors covered by the survey had no professional relationship with the company and had not served it in a former executive position.

Bank representation on UK company boards has been traditionally minimal. Bannock (1981) estimated that there were 417 bank directors who held board positions in unquoted companies and 422 such directorships in quoted ones. However, the latter represents only 17 per cent of listed companies, less than half the proportion in Germany; moreover, it remains more common for banks to invite full-time directors of industrial and commercial companies to become part-time members of *their* boards than vice versa.

It would seem that many appointments have been for prestige and business contacts rather than for expertise and advice. The CBI City/Industry Task Force (CBI 1987), in trying to enhance understanding between the City and industry, recommended that greater care be given to the choice of non-executive directors, arguing that their independence could boost the board's overall credibility with shareholders. More recently, the Stock Exchange encouraged the formation of the Cadbury Committee (1992) on the financial aspects of corporate governance to introduce measures to improve the management of quoted companies. The Committee has produced a voluntary code of practice, the main requirements of which are:

- The appointment of non-executive directors of sufficient calibre to challenge decisions
- A clear division of duties at the head of a company to prevent an individual holding disproportionate powers
- Disclosure of the performance-related part of directors' pay
- An audit committee to review financial statements and the work of the auditors

The principal recommendation related to the role and significance of non-executive directors. For some years audit committees have been advocated, although only 38 per cent of the 549 respondents to the Bank of England survey had formed them. The Cadbury Committee suggested a company's audit and remuneration committee should comprise non-executive directors chosen for their independence. The CBI is concerned that the enhanced supervisory role given to non-executive directors will change the concept of a single-tier board, although it could be argued that, if the selection of audit committees is by the main board, where executive directors form a majority, true independence may not be attainable.

In general, the voluntary code provides the spirit of governance but lacks enforcement, although the Cadbury Committee argues that if it fails to gain adherence then regulation is likely to follow. The recommendation on a division of responsibility at the head of a company could be said to be ineffectual without restrictions preventing chief executives combining their role with that of the chairman. Similarly, the code fails to deal with the conflict in auditing a company's accounts, whereby an accountancy firm discounts the audit fee to provide other more lucrative services to the business (Piers and MacGillivray 1992). Nevertheless, the Cadbury Committee is essentially trying to incorporate into the board of directors' role the function of monitoring management on behalf of the shareholders, a task performed by supervisory boards abroad. As a prerequisite, this requires an understanding of what shareholders and managers require, which initially involves improved dialogue between the parties.

Finance theory may be used to consider the management–shareholder relationship in terms of wealth optimization and agency concepts. A traditional view of the firm is that it is a means to an end, a mechanism whereby the owners and providers of financial capital can be matched with real projects which utilize those funds and generate a profitable return. The classical view is that its corporate objective should be the maximization of shareholders' wealth; that is, managers should take decisions that add value to the firm, e.g. the purchase of assets that are worth more than they cost. Accordingly the *shareholder* approach advocates the maximization of the present value of the firm, a reflection of which is the share price. As shareholder returns also come from dividends, appropriate policies here are important, too.

There are however difficulties with this approach. In the first place, modern society places various demands upon business, and various groups have stakes in the firm: employees, managers, customers, suppliers, society in general and, of course, shareholders. All have differing perceptions of the appropriate objectives for the firm and hence may constrain achievement of the primary goal. Although collectively it is their interaction with the firm that produces its output, their relative bargaining strengths affect the allocation of returns. Therefore this *stakeholder* approach sees the shareholders as one of several, significant, competing groups, all of whose interests management must bear in mind. Secondly, in spite of the acceptance of the existence of various stakeholders in a business, shareholder wealth maximization underpins the theory of business finance. There are operational problems with this concept, since in reality objectives are rarely stated explicitly and various proxy targets may be involved, such as return on capital employed (ROCE), earnings per share (e.p.s.), etc. Yet value maximization is broader than such profit maximization, as it takes into account risk, the time value of money, and cash flow unaffected by profit accounting conventions. Accordingly, emphasis is placed on the value of the owners' ordinary shares in the firm, that is the share price, although maximizing this may produce costs, notably risks to the debt-holders and other creditors, and a short-term outlook.

A third area of difficulty is that as company size increases ownership becomes divorced from control, and shareholders abdicate decision-making in favour of 'professional' managers. However, managers' motives may diverge from shareholder wealth optimization and can encompass varied objectives such as size maximization, as measured in terms of sales, growth or market share and their own prestige and power; or security, as in minimal risk and return strategies; or satisficing, i.e. aiming for a satisfactory level of performance rather than an optimal one (see Cyert and March 1983). For their part, managers may argue that they are constrained by market forces; in particular, the trade-off between sales and value maximization depends upon their ability to influence prices and the availability of goods.

The relationship between management and shareholders may be viewed in terms of an agency contract. Managers are the agents of the owners as principals, even though the former effectively control the firm. A contractual arrangement exists, but agency problems arise because shareholder and management utility may diverge, since each stakeholder in a firm strives to maximize its own position. For example, managers may be interested in the growth or size of the firm because their salaries are linked accordingly, or promotion may depend upon project success which might in turn encourage a focus on short-term payback. Jensen and Meckling (1976) contend that the agency problem intensifies if managers do not own significant equity stakes in the business, and so, in order to ensure compliance with their objectives, shareholders must offer managers perks or incentives, such as bonuses, cars, luxury offices and, perhaps most pertinent of all, executive share options. Jensen and Meckling suggest that shareholders also incur additional agency costs in monitoring managerial behaviour, such as auditing procedures, control systems and budget constraints. However, management performance is also publicly checked, firstly by the capital market, which if efficient, monitors management operations actively and accurately via share price movements; secondly by the labour market, which ensures competition for management jobs; and thirdly by the threat of takeover activity, which hangs over poor performance.

The extent of agency problems will reflect shareholder as well as management capabilities and motives. In the UK the financial institutions have come to dominate share ownership, in spite of the spate of privatizations and tax incentives, such as employee share schemes to boost individual holdings. Whereas in 1979 only 7 per cent of the adult population held shares, this proportion had risen to almost 20 per cent by 1990; but few have large or diversified holdings, and often the motivation has been short-term gain from the rapid price rises of many new privatization issues. In terms of listed shares, some 70 per cent are held by institutions, and almost 60 per cent are in the hands of life assurance and pension funds. The trend towards institutional concentration of share ownership has financing implications in that institutional funds are concentrated into relatively few, large quoted companies. These firms enable risks to be spread and provide readily available information, but above all their shares are liquid and marketable, allowing large transactions to be put through at minimum unit cost and without necessarily disrupting the underlying share price.

For their part, the institutional investors as major shareholders are in theory able to influence company management; but for many years they have distanced themselves, preferring to trade equities *passively* in order to optimize their investment and portfolio. Recently, however, there has been pressure for *positive shareholding*, whereby shareholders use their influence to change management and undertake the corrective action necessary. The CBI City/Industry Task Force (CBI 1987) argued that there was a communications gap which could be improved by stronger links between the institutions and the City. Its recommendations included the establishment of investor relations programmes, the disclosure of more information in company reports and better channels for conveying disquiet over management performance. Such information flows are seen as vital to ensure that market information is sufficient to value securities effectively, and to ensure that management comprehends how its operations are rated. Positive shareholding is seen to bring tangible benefits apart from merely greater dialogue. For example, a company with poorly performing shares might gain from a new management. However, a poor performance is likely to be manifest in a lower share valuation and to attract a predator. Some share recovery might ensue, depending on the bid premium, and entice shareholders to sell. If the takeover succeeds and the company recovers, the benefit accrues to the new owners, whereas the old shareholders have forgone long-term profit rather than initiate a management change. Moreover, if a more active and concerted stance is taken, then arguably standards of corporate governance will improve, one manifestation of which might be better use of annual general and other meetings to air issues and encourage change.

9.4 SHORT-TERMISM

The major consequence of *negative or passive shareholding* is perceived to be 'short-termism'. Reference has already been made to this in the context of bank lending; but here the focus is firstly on the apparent unwillingness of financial institutional investors to encourage long-term investment, research and development, and secondly on their preoccupation with short-term profits, often fuelling takeover activity. The former concern stems from the apparent failure of British industry to fulfil its industrial potential, notably in technology-based manufacturing. Studies such as Eltis *et al.* (1992) have pointed to the superior economic performance of Germany and Japan *vis à vis* the UK in recent decades, whether measured in terms of unemployment, inflation, rates of return in manufacturing or, above all, productivity. Various contributory factors are frequently cited: a sounder macroeconomic policy base for industry; high domestic savings ratios; a competitive environment spurring innovation; superior use of labour and emphasis on workplace-related skills; a focus on total quality management; bank-dominated financial systems with close industry relationships; and continuous innovation. The latter factors are particularly important to our examination of 'short-termism'.

Innovation is seen in terms of intensive technical application in all sectors of the business, geared to constant incremental gains in productivity, quality and customer service. The Japanese are noted for actively seeking new technologies and being quick to market the resultant products, and whereas imitation was important in their early success, now 'in-house' research and development is significant. Eltis *et al.* (1992) cite Matsushita as employing 22 000 scientists and engineers in 51 laboratories, but also note the important networks of government laboratories in basic technologies. With regard to Germany, Patel and Pavitt (1989) refer to the technological sophistication of German exports and foreign direct investment, the higher efficiency of their production processes and the reliability and performance of their products. Among common features found by Simon (1992) in his analysis of highly successful *Mittelstand* companies were an emphasis on combining technology with proximity to customers, and a self-reliance upon technological development. He suggests that *Mittelstand* companies feel that undertaking their own research, even to the extent of creating their own materials or components, improves their manufacturing abilities.

The manifestation of technological differences between the UK and Germany can be seen in terms of research and development expenditure (R&D). Patel and Pavitt (1989) point to a volume of firm-funded R&D in Germany more than double that of the UK in the mid-1980s, and moreover a growth rate five times higher, implying a willingness to devote a higher proportion of profits to R&D, rather than a faster rate of growth of output or profit *per se*. Moreover, Dobie (1992) suggests that the recession has led to dramatic cutbacks in R&D expenditure and reveals that Britain's largest corporate R&D spender, ICI, ranked only thirty-fifth in the world. Traditionally British pharmaceutical companies, such as Glaxo, Smith Kline Beecham and Wellcome, have a good reputation for the successful exploitation of research; however, even these spent far less in 1991 than their overseas rivals, implying that R&D budgets are susceptible to short-term profit pressures.

One explanation for the lower R&D expenditure in the UK is the higher cost of capital relative to Japan, Germany and the USA. Clearly, an industrialist must be confident and able to convince his or her (long-term) investors that returns will cover the cost of capital, and thus yield a return above that obtainable from a series of (short-term) investments. Given the normal higher cost of equity than debt which follows from the risk–return trade-off in Fig. 9.3, then, *ceteris paribus*, higher gearing is associated with a lower cost of capital. As indicated earlier, gearing levels have been traditionally higher in other countries, notably Germany, than in the UK. Moreover, the real cost of equity will be higher if there is a risk attached to earnings from the cyclical state of the economy, as has been the case with the UK. Similarly, the cost of debt will rise if lenders perceive that inflation will erode their returns, yet borrowers demand more debt, expecting the real value of their repayments to fall over time. In this way, high inflation in the UK relative to that elsewhere is also reflected in the higher cost of debt here.

Additional factors may account for the lower R&D cost of capital elsewhere, such as favourable tax allowances against R&D expenditure, and perhaps closer bank–industry relationships. Lower margins and transaction costs may follow from an understanding of the importance of long-term investment to the firm and the economy's growth, and from a presence as a 'house bank'. The implication of a higher cost of capital for R&D is that a shorter time-scale operates. Projects become marginalized as they have to meet higher rates of return over shorter periods than companies operating at lower cost, especially given the popularity of payback as a method of investment appraisal (see Pike 1988). Economic uncertainty will tend to have a dampening effect on investment, so a combination of high capital costs, a lack of tax concessions and a volatile economy mitigate against R&D expenditure.

If a major effect of a high cost of capital and a short-term perspective is a lack of long-term investment, a major cause of 'short-termism' is seen to be the requirements of institutional investors. Their perceived concern for enhanced profits and current dividends encourages company managers to maximize short-term returns to maintain share values and issue the signals of good current performance that they feel the market desires. Consequently, managers devote insufficient attention to the creation of long-term shareholder wealth. Peter Williams, chairman of Oxford Instruments Group plc, in describing the institutional pressures on his highly successful company, contrasted the differing time horizons of the parties. (Williams 1991). Since 1984 the company has been developing a high-technology device for the mass production of semi-conductor memory chips, a risky, costly and long-term project. During that period Williams cites short-term pressures from bankers, analysts and investment bankers trading the company's stock who react adversely to write-offs of R&D costs against profits. Arguably, it is the responsibility of corporate managers to generate investor confidence, to build a reputation for long-term growth and, above all, to keep their shareholders informed, thus overcoming short-term pressures. Indeed, one significance of proper governance is that enhanced communication flows will enable a company to plan long-term and make R&D announcements without the need for interim share price support.

Nevertheless, institutional performance pressures do encourage negative shareholding and short-term perspectives. Most shares are held by institutions and managed by professional fund managers with the aid of analysts, who are monitored on the performance of their investments and recommendations. In a highly competitive environment, fund performance measurement is on a quarterly and annual basis, which is more conducive to holding shares as short-term trading assets than as long-term investment assets. By implication, underperforming shares, in the context of the fund's portfolio, are likely to be sold, or possibly to be held only in the expectation of a takeover bid premium. Thus the methods of performance evaluation seem at odds with the nature of shares as an investment, and this situation represents a failure of governance in so far as it feeds through to affect management decisions adversely.

A related area of concern is dividend policy. Dividends provide important signals on company performance but are also an important source of income for institutional investors, who need to meet current liabilities such as pension payments and insurance claims. The dividend payout ratio (dividends relative to cash flow) was high in the 1960s, low in the 1970s and very high from 1986, since when payments have risen at a rate five times faster than the increase in R&D expenditure. J. W. Lomax (1990) suggests that distributions tend to rise strongly in periods of hostile takeover activity and he postulates two explanations. Firstly, takeovers resolve the conflict between the preferences of managers favouring reinvestment for growth maximization and the high payouts required by shareholders to force managers to succumb to the discipline of the market in their project proposals. Firms that deviate from shareholder expectations become marked down and vulnerable. Whether correct or not, it may be argued that institutional investors should identify only those companies that can sustain or enhance payouts and should not pressurize corporate management to maintain high payout ratios in the face of deteriorating profits. A second explanation is that distribution increases represent false signals about future prospects made to appease shareholders so as to enable management to retain their positions, but again at the expense of long-term growth.

Fundamental problems have arisen with high UK dividend growth, some 6 per cent faster than inflation, and investor expectations of continued increases. Nowadays payouts are rarely based on management perceptions of future viable investment opportunities but rather on past payouts. While creditors and bankers might argue that falls in profits should stimulate greater falls in dividends, and while such views would probably be supported by management since retained earnings give them more internal control over funds, shareholders may well disagree. Mowby (1991) cites M&G, the investment fund management group, which wrote to several hundred companies in which it invests, urging them not to curtail dividends because of cyclical trading problems. It argued that dividend cuts are a sign of failure and that they jeopardize a company's long-term relationship with its shareholders. Indeed, an extreme view might be to suggest that poor performance is no excuse to forgo a dividend, on the grounds that money returned to shareholders could be better invested by them!

The most important measure of shareholder power, and a major focus for accusations of short-termism during much of the 1980s, is in the context of takeover activity. Before the 1960s the divorce of ownership from control had reached its extreme, as most companies were still owned directly by private shareholders without collective influence, and there was a general lack of competition to challenge management. Since then, however, successive bouts of merger and acquisition activity have occurred, notably in 1967–69, 1972 and 1986–89, fuelled increasingly by the growth in power of institutional shareholders, a climate of deregulation and the promotion of stock market activity.

Table 9.4 illustrates the growth of UK takeover activity in the 1980s, both in numbers and in the amount spent. A noticeable feature has been the small number of very large acquisitions, such as the 1986 takeover of Imperial Group by Hanson Trust for £2.56 billion and of Distillers by Guinness for £2.53 billion,

Table 9.4 UK merger and acquisition activity in the 1980s

	1983	1984	1985	1986	1987	1988	1989	1990	1991
Numbers of companies acquired	447	568	474	842	1 528	1 499	1 337	776	512
Expenditure (£ millions)	2343	5474	7090	15 362	16 486	22 741	27 005	7910	10 300

Source: CSO Annual Abstract of Statistics, 1992, T.17.25.

and the 1988 acquisitions of Rowntree by Nestlé for £2.67 billion and of Britoil by BP for £2.3 billion. Benzie (1989) suggests that takeovers involving expenditure of over £25 million accounted for 81 per cent of total expenditure in the period 1984–89. The figures in Table 9.4 do not relate to all acquisitions and mergers, since large numbers involve ownership changes in small and private companies. However, they illustrate the trend and involve quoted companies of public interest. Although the vast majority of takeovers were agreed and imply restructuring changes, often horizontal mergers for market development purposes, a small but significant proportion were the result of hostile approaches. These involved substantial premia over the pre-bid share price and relate most directly to accusations of short-termism.

Compared with the UK, the level of acquisition activity in France and Germany is much lower and hostile takeovers are virtually non-existent. Most German transactions involve purchases of majority stakes associated with developing economies of scale, and in France buy-outs, divestments and minority stake acquisitions are popular. However, in both nations the changes relate to industry restructuring rather than to corporate control as such. Indeed, mutual cross-shareholdings between companies are common with the understanding that hostile takeovers are not contemplated. In essence, there exist several impediments to management and ownership changes. Reference has been made to the dominance of small, often family-owned, businesses in both countries and to the dominance of the banking sectors relative to the securities markets. In Germany supervisory boards monitor management performance, but mainly in a positive, supportive way, thus giving an element of protection. The *Vorstand* normally has a five-year term with only exceptional grounds for dismissal, and the replacement of the supervisory board by the shareholders requires a 75 per cent majority vote. In France management rights are limited but severe restrictions can be placed upon share transfer and voting rights through changes to the company articles. Moreover, the state still retains an interest in many larger companies, thus complicating any potential takeover bid.

In a broader European context, the merger and acquisition boom of the late 1980s was initially not seen as a reaction to the advent of the Single Market. Nevertheless, cross-border activity has been sustained in contrast to the domestic downturn in most nations after 1989. This would appear to have resulted from moves towards strengthening market positions among leading companies, often through defensive mergers. The removal of barriers will undoubtedly generate greater competition in most markets. Thus, although many continental firms do not have a history of hostile takeovers, British management may still be under threat from short-term pressures as competition intensifies. For this reason, it is even more imperative that mutual dialogue and communication flows are reinforced between managers and shareholders, and between the City and industry.

CONCLUSIONS

During the past two decades the UK financial system has sustained criticism in its relationships with industry, so much so that various major committees have investigated the complaints. Three common themes appear: the lack of available funding, especially for small businesses; an arm's-length approach, which distances shareholders and financiers from industry management; and 'short-termism', seen as the cause of many of the UK's economic ills.

The clearing banks have borne the brunt of the criticisms, having been variously accused of not being supportive in times of crises, of failing to provide long-term developmental funding to small firms, and providing high-cost, low-quality services with an emphasis on onerous security requirements. Much of this seemingly harsh criticism stems from small companies constrained in their funding sources. However, the funding case against the banks seems dubious, given that supply exceeds demand, and considering the specific measures taken by banks to develop their small business centres and loans, together with other assistance including loan guarantees, the development of the USM and venture capital sources. Indeed, in a competitive banking environment the UK clearers are keen to lend; moreover, the increased provisions for bad debts imply that security requirements are not always that onerous! Certainly the impression is that sufficient funds are available, although not always as cheaply as the borrower would like given the UK's high interest rate tradition. In this context UK firms seem no more disadvantaged than their counterparts on the Continent.

With regard to governance issues, marked differences exist between the UK, France and Germany. The benefits of a two-tier board to oversee and support management appear pervasive. However, there is still a danger that the two parts could become distanced and that ineffective supervision could occur. Independent non-executive directors appointed to a single-tier board of directors would appear to offer a better method of monitoring management although supportive legislation seems necessary. Stronger corporate governance is seen as part of positive shareholding and might reduce the frequency of takeovers that have fuelled the short-termism debate in the UK. Macroeconomic features have also played their part, notably the volatility of the economy and the high cost of UK capital. Institutional investors must take much of the blame, with their susceptibility to short-term profit-taking, but ultimately management practices are responsible. Much of the 'short-term' attitudes would seem to stem from poor communications between industry, finance and shareholders, whether it be the small businessman dealing with the bank or the company chief executive talking with City institutions. To this end, communications changes in the board-room would be more beneficial than the management changes characteristic of recent takeover booms.

FURTHER READING

The Wilson Committee reports (1979, 1980) provide a background to the funding debate, although Capie and Collins (1992) examine bank–industry rela-tions in a historical context. On different types of finance, see standard financial management texts such as Brealey and Myers (1991), Samuels *et al.* (1990) or Rutterford and Carter (1988). Burns and Dewshurst (1986) provide an examina-tion of SMEs throughout Europe. For governance see Charkham (1989) and for European industry–stakeholder relations see Lane (1989). Szarka (1992) gives an insight into business culture in a French context. On the short-termism debate see Ball (1991) and Williams (1991), while a standard text on mergers remains Fairburn and Kay (1989).

PART
FOUR

FINANCE AND THE OVERSEAS SECTOR

THE WIDER COMMUNITY: RESOURCE GROWTH OR DILUTION?

If we look forward to the next decade and the fiftieth anniversary of the Treaty of Rome in the year 2007, a remarkably wider European Community than originally conceived seems likely. Already the original EEC of Six has doubled in size, and, is quite likely to do so again. From the geographical core bordering the Rhine, the Community will possibly spread outwards in all directions. So far the existing extensions have been essentially west and south, to encompass the UK and Ireland, Portugal, Spain and Greece, the geographical exceptions being Denmark and the assimilation of former East Germany following German unification. Additional applications for membership have come from Turkey (1987), Austria (1989), Cyprus and Malta (1990), and Sweden (1991). In October 1991 the seven EFTA nations, mainly Scandinavian nations to the north, signed a pact with the EC Twelve to create a *European Economic Area* (EEA), the world's largest free trade zone, possibly as a prelude to full EC membership. Furthermore, the unification of Germany and the breakup of the Soviet Union and its COMECON satellites have focused attention to the east.

Thus the European Community might appear to be on the verge of a significant expansion, eventually a Community of Twenty, all undoubtedly attracted by the prospect of a Single Market. According to the Treaty of Rome (Art. 237), 'any European state may apply to become a member of the Community', although the following principles apply: firstly, the applicant nation must be European; secondly, it must be democratic; thirdly, it must accept the political and economic objectives of the EC; and, fourthly, under the Single European Act, new members admitted after 1992 must be approved by the European Parliament. The geographical constraint so far has been at issue only in the case of Turkey; but more significant is the question of democracy, which delayed the second enlargement involving the Mediterranean members, and is likely to figure more prominently in any eastward developments. Many of the former European COMECON states are struggling to establish their new political identities, and while some success has been achieved in Hungary and Poland, the emergence of national and ethnic tensions in areas such as the Baltic states, and most tragically of all in former Yugoslavia, indicate the long road ahead.

Those who favour a wider Community advocate extension of full and associate membership to the geographic groupings mentioned above, possibly with looser economic and political ties. However, this may lead to a 'two-speed', Europe as some of the more advanced nations converge more rapidly. Delors envisages a series of 'concentric circles', with the EC Twelve at the core, the existing EFTA nations as an inner ring and Eastern Europe as an outer ring (Owen and Dynes 1992). An alternative approach is to focus on a deeper integration among existing EC members, moving them closer to the stated goals of economic and political union. As we saw in Chapter 1, this involves a struggle between federalist ideals and the desire of nations to retain their sovereignty as long as possible.

In this chapter we address the economic, notably financial, issues involved in any widening of the Community, in particular how the Community has coped with the enlargements to date, and whether it has the resources to sustain future expansion. Broadly three main groups of countries are considered in this context: the integration of the newer members of the EC; the Eastern European nations; and the EFTA group.

10.1 FROM SIX TO NINE

The first widening of the European Community occurred on 1 January 1973 when Britain, the Republic of Ireland and Denmark joined some 15 years after the Treaty of Rome. Norway had also submitted an application and participated in the negotiations, but, whereas the other three subsequently ratified the decision with a referendum of their populations, the Norwegian people voted narrowly against and their country remained outside.

The lengthy delay before the first enlargement stemmed partly from British attitudes at the time of the Treaty of Rome. Britain wanted a looser arrangement than a customs union, one that would provide EEC market access yet not endanger its preferential trading links with the Commonwealth. Politically, it wanted to maintain its sovereignty, an issue that has become more prevalent over time. However, as indicated in Chapter 1, economic reality led to a change of heart. Continental Europe made impressive progress in the early years of EEC existence; Britain did not. Moreover, many newly independent Commonwealth nations were seeking wider relationships in the interest of development, while their far-flung markets were becoming less significant for British produce. Ultimately, Community membership was seen as a reluctant necessity, an attitude that did not endear Britain to existing members, notably France. Although de Gaulle used his veto twice in the 1960s, ostensibly over severe British balance of payments weaknesses, the major motive was undoubtedly political. Fear that Britain might take a leading role at France's expense—and, more significantly, might weaken the Franco-German alliance—was also influential.

When Britain, Ireland and Denmark applied for membership in 1973 they hoped to compound their growing trade with the Six. Both Denmark and Ireland saw a potential diversification of their trade, much of which was with the UK. Indeed, Nevin (1990) implies that, with 40 per cent of Danish and 80 per cent of Irish exports destined for the enlarged EEC, these countries could have little doubt about the benefits of membership, especially with agricultural production likely to benefit from the CAP. However, Britain, with a population seven times greater than the other two combined, was the most influential new member.

British entry became possible once de Gaulle resigned in 1969, and negotiations began over the detail, rather than the principle, of membership, notably the impact on Britain's traditional Commonwealth and EFTA suppliers, and her expected contribution to the budget. In the event, a transitional seven-year period was agreed (1971–78), during which the full incidence of the budget would be deferred, rising from 8.6 per cent in 1973 to 18.9 per cent in 1987, and other policies were introduced to offset the cost to Britain of the CAP. French objections to British membership were placated by *quid pro quo* arrangements with existing members supporting British membership. This involved the agreement to use the 'own-resource' tax base for financing the CAP, and, together with renewed interest in monetary integration led by Germany, represented attempts to deepen the Community while allowing for its widening.

In the decade following enlargement, the Community's development faltered, a feature blamed often unfairly on the new members. Certainly, British economic performance was initially uninspiring. The steady decline in competitiveness, consistent balance of payments crises and relatively slow growth from the 1950s encouraged the application for membership but were not alleviated by it. Indeed, the downward trend continued, fuelled by world recession following the 1970s oil crises. Between 1973 and 1984 the UK's growth averaged only 1.5 per cent p.a., compared with 2.7 per cent p.a. in the period 1962–73; whereas EC growth fell on average from 4.5 per cent to 2 per cent for the corresponding period (Barnes and Preston 1988). Moreover, the UK trade balance with the EC worsened in spite of the oil exports, Goodman (1990) arguing that British industry and commerce was too complacent, too sheltered and too much dominated by slack management and overpowerful unions.

However, as we noted in Chapter 4, the main issue for the UK during the 1970s was the cost of the CAP and the resultant budgetary contributions. The incoming Labour government in 1974 promised in their manifesto to hold a referendum on continued membership and renegotiate the entry terms. While the referendum outcome endorsed popular support for membership, many politicians remained adamantly opposed and this helped to sour already strained relations. By 1979 the UK net contributions had risen dramatically, and, despite the new Conservative government's pledges to a more positive attitude, Mrs Thatcher's immediate reaction was to demand 'our money back' at the Dublin summit. There then began a difficult period of Community negotiations from 1980–1984, during which Britain received annual rebates before agreement was reached on a permanent settlement of the British problem. During the intervening period the intransigence of the UK government irritated other members, raising more questions over Britain's commitment to Europe. There was further acrimonious debate prior to the 'fourth resource' compromise at Brussels in 1988. While Britain did gain concessions, with expenditure more closely tied to income, the 1988 agreement made it clear that the country was isolated in its requests for strict expenditure curbs, since most members were not willing to hold back funds and block further integration.

This is not to suggest that the British government was against unity, but the approach was geared more to directing the integration process towards specific, narrow, market-based trade liberalization. In September 1988 in Bruges Mrs Thatcher set out a vision of Europe in which European integration was advocated so long as the principle of sovereignty was maintained, in which open markets and enterprise activity were favoured, and in which pragmatic resolution of policy should outweigh grand political design. In essence, she castigated the centralization of power in Brussels, and was reciting the by then dated strategy used to revive Britain in the early 1980s. By 1989 Europe was a major political issue in the UK, especially after the Delors Report was published. A series of Cabinet changes followed, including Nigel Lawson's departure as chancellor following Mrs Thatcher's refusal to allow sterling to join the ERM. She saw an eventual single currency as the ultimate surrender of financial control to Brussels. In 1990 concern was expressed among senior Conservatives that Britain's position in Europe was being eroded by such attitudes, and eventually the Prime Minister's position became untenable, leading to her eventual replacement by John Major.

A more pragmatic British approach has subsequently ensued with government support for the '1992' programme. However, the preference has remained for a broadening of the Community rather than speedier integration. The vital Maastricht summit in December 1991 further highlighted divisions between Britain and the other members, specifically in the context of British 'opt-out' clauses relating to the single currency in 1989 and the social charter. The impression of Britain alone being pre-occupied with issues of national sovereignty is misleading. Germany, with its unification and monetary policy concerns, has often expressed reservations about the pace of integration, and about the linkages between EMU and political union. More spectacularly, Denmark failed to ratify the Maastricht Treaty in a national referendum in June 1992.

From a European perspective, British accession to the Community was seen as a logical step; bringing in an island nation with a long international trading tradition, acting as a catalyst for Ireland and Denmark to join, and as a counterbalance to the dominance of France and Germany. In the UK, views differed at the time of entry between those who foresaw the wider market as providing a boost to the sickly UK economy, and those who feared that further import penetration and the loss of traditional markets would exacerbate the economic problems. The latter view has tended to prevail, fuelled by the perceived inequity of the CAP and budget. Grahl and Teague (1990) argue that British relations with the EC are symptomatic of the malaise. In essence, there has been no long-term perspective, with the Community judged in terms of short-term costs and benefits, although arguably the same is true on the other side, in that temporary solutions to the UK's own budget difficulties have existed for too long.

10.2   FROM NINE TO TWELVE: THE 'SOUTHERN ENLARGEMENT'

The presence of a growing and relatively successful customs union was bound to attract the developed, democratic nations nearby, hence the inevitable accession of Britain and Denmark. However, membership was arguably even more attractive for the Community's weaker, largely agrarian, neighbours, especially those in the south bordering the Mediterranean. They depended on the EC for their limited trade, but were equally looking to its members for political guidance as they struggled to establish some semblance of democracy.

Most of the initial EEC members were former colonial powers whose colonies and dependencies received special trading concessions under the Treaty of Rome. Indeed, until 1962 Algeria was still part of France, whose influence extended all along the North African coast. In the 1960s and 1970s a series of bilateral trading ties were formalized in the form of separate association or cooperation agreements between the EC and individual nations comprising virtually all the Mediterranean basin except for Libya and Albania. These agreements are known collectively as the *Global Mediterranean Policy* (GMP) and have certain common elements: unlimited duty-free access for industrial products originating from the countries concerned; concessions for their major agricultural exports; and financial aid via grants and loans from the European Investment Bank. The association agreements with Turkey, Malta and Cyprus were designed progressively to establish customs unions with the Community, although all three have since applied for full membership. The cooperation agreements with the Maghreb nations (Algeria, Morocco, Tunisia), Mashreq (Egypt, Jordan, Syria and Lebanon) and Israel cover customs-free trade but also industrial, technical and financial assistance.

The most significant Mediterranean developments have been the accessions of Greece (1981), Spain and Portugal (1986) to full membership, collectively the 'southern enlargement'. This represents a considerable challenge to the Community to prevent economic divergence between its wealthier industrial members and the newer, less developed trio. All three had shaken off the constraints of military dictatorship in the period 1974–77 and had embarked upon a process of modernization and democratization. However, they all faced considerable adjustment problems; for example, incomes were much lower than existing EC members, their industrial bases were limited and often technologically backward, and they feared they would be unable to compete with the northern members. For existing Community states the main economic threats posed by this enlargement were envisaged in the agricultural sector, with competition for the Mediterranean produce of France and Italy. A more general concern was that, as these nations were relatively poor, they were likely to contribute proportionately less to the Community budget yet require more by way of handouts. On the political side, there was concern about integrating 12 nations, the latest three of which had little experience of democracy.

10.2.1 Greece

The accession of Greece stemmed from the signature of an association agreement with the EEC 20 years earlier. In essence this was a pre-accession arrangement, which allowed for the partial harmonization of tariffs with a customs union to be established in stages, culminating in the removal of tariffs and quotas by 1974. The main exceptions were imports of EC industrial goods, which were to be adjusted to the common tariff over a period to 1984. Provision was made for equality of treatment between member states' agricultural products and those of Greece. However, relations were frozen when a military coup occurred in 1967, although tariff reductions continued as planned. Indeed, Greek manufactures experienced duty-free access to the UK six years ahead of schedule. During this period the Greek economy grew rapidly, boosted by US foreign investment, although Featherstone (1989) suggests that the demise of the military regime in 1974 was followed by widespread anti-US feelings which helped push Greece closer to the EC. In 1975 a full application for membership was lodged, partly because domestic industry was already suffering from enhanced EC exports and co-operation agreements signed by the EC with Greece's Mediterranean neighbours.

As with the 1973 enlargement, the EC granted Greece on entry in January 1981 a five-year transition to full membership (seven years for the free movement of tomatoes, peaches and labour), and agreed that it should not be a net contributor to the EC budget during that time. However, Greece was neither politically nor economically prepared for membership. The conservative government which had negotiated entry was replaced in October 1981 by the socialist opposition Panhellenic Socialist Movement (PASOK) which initially did not favour membership, arguing that it hindered Greek attempts at independence, and sought 'special concessions' for agriculture and industry protection. The EC conceded these, and, significantly, came to realize the need for an EC Mediterranean policy.

Prior to entry, the economic benefits of full membership were expected to be found mainly in large budgetary transfers to agriculture under the CAP, offset by a deterioration in the terms of trade from liberalization, exposing manufacturing weaknesses. Indeed, these benefits were greater than expected and helped to boost incomes dramatically. The gains came from higher product prices and subsidies, notwithstanding increases in inputs (fertilizers, feedstuffs) following inflationary pressures. The structural impact of accession was to favour citrus fruit, salad vegetables and olive oil production at the expense of livestock, notably beef and pork, where high animal feed costs reduced their attraction.

In manufacturing, Georgakopoulos (1986) estimated that production fell by 6 per cent and real investment by 20 per cent in the first three years after entry. In part, this was due to the unfavourable international economic climate brought about by the onset of the 1979 oil crisis. However, the domestic environment was equally unhelpful, with PASOK's anti-EC stance and its tolerance of high inflation. EC membership had led to the removal of domestic protection, yet in reality it offered no new market opportunities given the earlier tariff-free concessions to Greek exports from 1968 onwards. Moreover, Greece now had to adopt EC foreign aid policy whereby developing nations could sell on advantageous terms throughout the EC. Since some of these developing countries were located in the Mediterranean, they offered similar products at lower costs to Greek firms. Barnes and Preston (1988) estimate that by 1985 40 per cent of Greek manufacturing was loss-making, and industrial production was lower than in 1982. In more recent years the government has committed itself to privatizing at least 20 nationalized, debt-ridden companies administered by the state Industrial Reconstruction Organization, and, moreover, to allowing the state banks to dispose of holdings in many ailing companies.

Deregulation of financial services has been a priority since 1985 in order to raise efficiency and bring variety and innovation to the sector. As late as 1990, 21 state banks still existed, although the major corporate business was controlled by the 17 foreign banks. Recently four new private banks have been created, supported mainly by the ship-owning and insurance fraternity, and modelled on the successful Credit Bank (specializing in mortgage finance and investment banking) and Ergobank (leasing, computer services). For the state banks, foreign equity stakes are seen to bring both capital and new ideas. The Hellenic Industrial Development Bank has sold a 30 per cent holding to France's Crédit Agricôle which will also widen its scope for treasury management and training activities (Hope 1990).

The overall macroeconomic effects of entry appeared on balance to be negative for Greece in the early post-accession years. The balance of payments effect was confined mainly to the current account, since capital movements were not liberated, but showed a deterioration in the trade position *vis à vis* the EC. The CAP raised the cost of food imports as well as feedstocks, and trade liberalization reduced the protection afforded to domestic manufacturing. The growth in imports reduced demand for domestic output and ultimately income so that, inevitably, public debt rose and the currency depreciated. Indeed, whereas the average annual rate of depreciation before accession was 5.5 per cent (1972–80), Georgakopoulus (1986) estimates that it was 12.1 per cent thereafter.

Although consumers and taxpayers faced higher burdens, the agricultural sector benefited from EAGGF payments and farm incomes rose by 13 per cent in the first five years of membership. Moreover, Greece was able to solicit EC assistance for financial support, including ECU1.75 billion in the mid-1980s, in return for economic measures geared to reducing the remaining protectionist measures and the introduction of VAT from 1987. In addition, in 1984 another ECU2 billion was agreed under Integrated Mediterranean Programme (IMP) funding, thus illustrating the scale of adjustment needed to incorporate the weaker members into the Community.

10.2.2 Spain and Portugal

The physical proximity of Spain and Portugal may have influenced their route to full EC membership. Both nations first applied in the early 1960s; established preferential trading agreements with the EC 10 years later; shed their military dictatorships in the mid-1970s; reapplied for entry in 1977 under socialist governments; and had difficult and protracted negotiations before entry on 1 January 1986. It is perhaps fortunate that their eventual membership coincided with resolution of the UK budget contribution problem and the White Paper on the Single Market promoting a new forward-looking growth phase. This detracted from the reality that both prospective members were poor, with large inefficient agrarian and fishery sectors and a joint population of almost 50 million people.

Portugal's small size meant that its accession was easier than that of Spain despite the fact that it would be the EC's poorest partner and a potential net drain on common resources. The per capita income is even now barely half that of the UK and reflects a lack of past industrialization and foreign investment, the expensive legacy of colonialism which the country was slow to discard, and traditional concentration of power in the hands of a few major private companies. With the advent of a socialist government, large sectors of the economy were nationalized, and thousands of people returned from the former colonies and unemployment rose. Before accession an austerity stabilization programme was launched to rectify a severe balance of payments crisis accompanied by high inflation. This proved relatively successful in containing the economic problem and, moreover, encouraged the EC to provide financial support.

In 1980 provision had been made within the EC budget for EC96 million in pre-accession aid including grants for Portuguese agriculture and fisheries, plus additional EIB loans (Featherstone 1989). Following accession, a regional aid programme, Programa Especifico de Desenvolvimento da Industria Portuguesa (PEDIP), was invoked, geared to the modernization of the industrial base and involving ECU1 billion between 1988 and 1992 as part of the enlarged structural funds. Portugal was given a seven-year transition period for industrial goods and ten years for agriculture. The skeletal industrial sector, although in need of restructuring, should prove reasonably competitive, especially in low-cost labour-intensive sectors such as textiles. Agriculture, however, is very weak, with a myriad of smallholdings and generally poor physical environment. The resultant paradox is that the majority of the working population is employed in agriculture, yet nearly two-thirds of food requirements are imported, an expensive situation within the EC context.

The Portuguese financial system is undergoing transition which will enhance competition but also lead to rationalization. As elsewhere in the economy, profitability and competitiveness have been curbed by government intervention geared to financing budget deficits, operating monetary policy as its prime macroeconomic stabilizer, and maintaining nationalized banks. The banking sector has been penalized for large government borrowing requirements, by implicit taxation in the form of large idle balances required to be held as excess reserves with the central bank. These balances are then used to finance government debt, but bank customers ultimately suffer through lower deposit interest and a higher cost of credit. The profitability and efficiency of Portuguese banks has also been compromised by tight credit restrictions and high interest rates, reflected in the severe 'stabilization programme' in 1983–85. Whereas a policy shift followed aimed at boosting investment and growth via government expenditure, tight control over credit was maintained.

Since 1986 the Portuguese banking sector has developed along lines similar to that in Greece: greater private involvement, the creation of new banks, and the entry of foreign operators. Borges (1990) suggests that Portugal appears to be indicative of the irrelevance of scale economies in banking since the newer, smaller banks have outperformed the larger ones. He argues that this reflects the costly legacy of intervention policies and directives to state banks to fund nationalized industry, often without hope of repayment, and poor management. In contrast, the newer, smaller banks are seen to be better managed and more innovative; yet arguably they have focused on profitable niches in corporate and wholesale banking and do not carry the overheads of extensive branch networks. The advent of the Single Market will force further liberalization, including the ultimate dismantling of credit ceilings and a shift away from bank support for state-controlled 'lame ducks', but it will also bring in more foreign competition.

Such credit restrictions and high interest rates have constrained the development of financial markets. The Portuguese stock market has not recovered from the 1987 crash, since with high interest rates investors have favoured government bonds and eschewed equities. The exceptions are state entities that have been privatized where social fiscal benefits have existed. Market reforms have occurred, including in January 1992 a threefold split: an 'official market' or first tier, including a small group of 11 major companies (market capitalization over Esc500 million) listed on a new national computer-based pricing system, and 50 firms quoted under the old system in Lisbon and Oporto; a 'second market' or second tier for small and medium-sized companies (market capitalization of

Esc125–500 million); and a 'market without quotations' or third tier for those firms not meeting the Stock Exchange's criteria on liquidity. Other reforms have included a new independent securities exchange commission and an increase in the numbers of brokers. However, these moves appear futile so long as the bulk of the market is geared to servicing government funding needs.

Spain, on the other hand, is experiencing a radical transformation of its economy spurred by the move to democratic rule and, undoubtedly, EC membership. The seeds for economic growth were sown in the 1960s when industrialization was fostered by a combination of state-run heavy industry and foreign multinationals, the latter notably in chemicals, electronics and vehicle manufacture. Together with emergent service activities, notably tourism, this encouraged a migration from agriculture. However, during the 1970s oil-import-dependent Spain was seriously affected by the two oil crises with the result that growth slumped. The worsening economic situation was exacerbated by the decline in tourism which afflicted other related services and construction. Moreover, under the new socialist regime the lid was lifted on wage restraint so that, together with rising input costs, a pattern of cost–push inflation and rising unemployment ensued.

From 1982 industrial policy was geared to restructuring traditional sectors such as steel, shipbuilding, fertilizers, vehicle components and shoes, all of which were characterized by relatively unsophisticated technology, labour intensity and excess capacity. The objective was to improve efficiency and profitability, and to rationalize output in an effort to meet the future needs of a wider EC market. The measures adopted included redundancy and early retirement programmes, grants, loans and equity participation, regional incentives via the creation of 'urgent re-industrialization areas', technology support and general incentives for small and medium-sized businesses. By 1988 almost £4 billion had been spent and 84 000 jobs cut, but recovery was in progress.

From a traditionally conservative, regulated and protected system controlled by a handful of financial institutions which also owned large parts of industry, the Spanish financial sector has changed considerably in recent years. In Chapter 8 passing reference was made to the banking structure, with more specific attention paid to the evolving financial markets. In essence, the relative influence of the banking sector is still high, with developed money and government debt markets but underdeveloped capital markets. Between 1978 and 1983 the banking system suffered a severe crisis affecting 51 banks, of which 38 failed, many associated with the troubled Rumasa group. The second oil crisis precipitated the collapse, which was exacerbated by close bank–industry relations, a lack of lending diversification, bad management, fraud and inadequate central bank policing. The crisis slowed down the pace of deregulation and led to a period of concentration in the industry, including mergers such as that between Banco de Bilbao and Banco de Vizcaya.

The current system is now overbanked, with 16 000 branches serving 2000 customers each and effectively six types of bank, including the 'Big Six', i.e.

foreign and savings banks. Concentration has not led to greater market share; indeed, the large banks have suffered from competing across the whole range of banking services, and have lost ground to the growing savings banks as the latter have extended the scope of their activities. The Single Market is expected to produce significant price reductions as competition intensifies, especially for corporate business between the large domestic banks with their established client base and the foreign entrants with their international contacts and technological advantages. In the retail market Caminal *et al.* (1990) see greater competition at the higher net worth end between savings and commercial banks.

By the end of the 1980s, Spain appeared to be coping with integration into the Community, although it was still within the seven-year transition period for the removal of tariffs. Improved economic performance allowed the easing of credit restrictions although interest rates remained high. Membership of the ERM is a major step forward in Spain's development but imposes constraints on the maximum (and minimum) rates applicable in stabilizing the peseta. The rapid growth of the economy added to liberalization is of concern to the authorities lest credit expansion fuels imports and inflation with downward pressure on the currency. In spite of rapid industrialization, 15 per cent of the population work in agriculture; and this encouraged the creation of IMPs to help existing EC members' regions, i.e. Greece, southern Italy, and southern France, cope with Spanish accession. Spain enjoys a comparative advantage in many Mediterranean products and is a significant table wine producer; yet with almost 40 million inhabitants it is also a major food importer, especially of dairy produce and grain.

10.2.3 Trade and aid

For Greece, Portugal and Spain, accession has had significant initial ramifications. In general, membership was welcomed as an act of reconciliation after years in a political vacuum. All three countries received net inflows of funds from the Community, not only through the CAP but also in the form of structural support. As expected, their trade patterns altered towards the EC, although liberalization has encouraged import growth and a competitiveness which their industries and financial sectors are finding it hard to cope with. For the EC the 'southern enlargement' has provided an additional challenge to 'cohesion', i.e. to reduce regional disparities by promoting development of the weaker areas. Accordingly, this principle was incorporated into the 1986 Single European Act. Moreover, it produced new policy initiatives to enhance integration. These involved payments to members threatened by enlargement as realized by the IMPs.

The most ambitious project to support the weaker EC regions is the 'Cohesion Fund'. This is the first time aid has applied to entire countries and will be provided for Greece, Spain, Portugal and Ireland. For 1993 a budget of ECU1.5 billion was approved with an estimated ECU10 billion to be set aside for the period to 1997. The money is destined for environmental and infrastructure projects, including roads, bridges, telephone systems and railways, designed to bring these poorer nations into line with the EC average. To qualify, the four nations must reduce their budget deficits and reduce inflation to conform with agreed EMU convergence criteria. Nevertheless, some member states argue that vast sums could be frittered away on grandiose schemes before assessments can be made as to whether the amounts are well spent. In any case, the scale of this aid underlines the Community's concern to deepen integration among the Twelve, notwithstanding any wider linkages.

The 'southern enlargement' and completion of the Single Market programme have had implications for EC relationships with non-member Mediterranean countries, and, indeed with developing countries further afield. The regional significance of the southern members means that the EC is the major power bloc and has greater regional responsibility for political stability and economic development in the Mediterranean. This is manifest in calls for more Community humanitarian involvement in the Yugoslavian states, and for enhanced market access for non-member Mediterranean producers under association agreements, in spite of the demands of Greece, Spain and Portugal. These Global Mediterranean Policy (GMP) agreements form part of a wider EC trade policy towards the Third World or, more precisely, to former colonies or dependencies of the major EC members. Other components include agreements with some South American and Asian nations, principally via the Generalized System of Preferences (GSP) covering preferential treatment for their exports, and, above all, via the Lomé Convention's trade and aid programme.

Some 69 African, Caribbean and Pacific (ACP) nations are allowed free access for their exports to the Community under a series of successive five-year agreements begun in 1964. The current convention Lomé IV, is the first to run for ten years (1990–2000) and aims at giving greater stability to EC–ACP relations. Under the trade provisions of these conventions, the Community grants non-reciprocal, preferential access for ACP exports to EC markets, whereby 99 per cent of products enter without tariffs or quotas. While this appears generous, most ACP nations are not able to benefit from the concessions as they are unable to manufacture industrial goods to compete with the EC. Moreover, if a competitive threat does arise, the Community has the right to impose 'voluntary' export restraints to limit inflows. Strict rules of origin also apply which ACP nations argue make it difficult to export processed goods with higher added value. Currently, many ACP nations are particularly concerned about the impact of the Single Market programme which will harmonize EC policy and endanger established bilateral arrangements between members and specific countries, for example the export of Jamaican bananas to the UK. This may focus trade more between EC members.

The aid provisions of Lomé IV include ECU12 billion in the form of grants, soft loans and interest rate subsidies for the first five-year period, an increase of ECU3.5 billion on Lomé III. Some 90 per cent of the total aid will be disbursed through the European Development Fund (EDF) as non-repayable grants, thus providing significantly less conditionality than aid packages from many developed nations. Lomé IV also provides for extensions to the STABEX and SYSMIN schemes, which provide compensation payments when nations become export-dependent on specific products and when export earnings fall by prescribed amounts. An increased range of products was included, for example gold and uranium under SYSMIN, and Lomé IV raised the STABEX budget by ECU575 million to ECU1500 million, and SYSMIN from ECU415 million to ECU480 million.

The aid programme has often been criticized for its slow disbursement and lack of effectiveness rather than volume, since more has been spent on aid via the EDF than on the Community's own regional and social policy (Lintner and Mazey 1991). The ACP nations have traditionally had close ties with the EC, yet the economic disparities between the two groups have widened, bringing into question the effectiveness of the trade concessions and the aid provided. It might be argued that the relationship has been one of post-colonial dependency, although in reality there are now relatively few political conditions attached. In spite of increased amounts under Lomé IV, the long-standing ACP–EC relations are likely to suffer as the ACP nations' share of trade with the EC falls through integration of the latter, and as demands on EC resources increase nearer to home, notably from Eastern Europe.

10.3   THE 'EASTERN FOCUS'

With remarkable speed, Eastern Europe has discarded communism and 45 years of centrally planned economic systems, and turned westwards in an attempt to embrace the principles of the free market and open societies. If democracy is to be fostered, then the Community faces a major challenge to ensure that appropriate support is given for the massive reforms needed in these nations. In particular, the EC is under pressure to provide significant financial transfers and trade concessions, and even to allow for eventual membership. Indicative in this context is Hungary's Democratic Forum, which when elected in April 1990 immediately announced that membership of the EC was its foreign policy priority, a stance subsequently echoed by other Eastern European nations.

Before its demise in 1991, the Council for Mutual Economic Assistance (CMEA), known as COMECON, was the Eastern equivalent of the European Community in so far as it was a customs union. However, it was a union bound by ideology and dominated by the USSR as the major trading partner and source of political influence. Three of the ten members were non-European (Mongolia, Cuba and Vietnam), and those that were European varied considerably, as evidenced since COMECON's collapse. To generalize, the 'southern group' (Bulgaria, Romania and most of the central and southern states of the former Soviet Union) have remained relatively backward and have sought assistance from enhanced COMECON integration, whereas the 'northern group' (Poland, Hungary, Czechoslovakia, the Baltic states and the former East Germany) were more developed and favoured flexibility with trading links to the West. Indeed, many of this latter group had long-established cultural and commercial ties with the West which they saw communism as rudely interrupting. Thus, not surprisingly, they have shown the greatest desire to transform their societies rapidly and incorporate free-market ideals.

An important turning point in East–West relations came at the December 1989 summit conference when Presidents Bush and Gorbachev discussed German unification, although the defeat of Poland's Communist Party in the first semi-free elections six months earlier and Hungary's opening of its border with Austria in September 1989 were also significant events. East Germans began to flee west, and ultimately the demand for change in the German Democratic Republic (GDR) led to the opening of the Berlin Wall on 9 November 1989. The GDR differed from the other members of COMECON in that its population had a guaranteed right of access to the West, but as long as this was denied it was a viable Eastern Bloc economy. Between October 1989 and January 1990, 300 000 people emigrated to the Federal Republic of Germany (FRG), a situation that was untenable for both nations for any sustained period. Accordingly, in February 1990 Chancellor Kohl proposed that a 'monetary union and economic community' be established (Deutsche Bundesbank 1990b). This was agreed and was formalized into a treaty providing for German economic, monetary and social union (GEMSU), which became effective on 1 July 1990.

10.3.1 German Economic, Monetary and Social Union (GEMSU)

The advent of GEMSU hastened the desire for political unity, and, following ratification of a Unity Treaty by both Parliaments, on 3 October 1990 the GDR became part of the FRG, and thus part of the EC. In the subsequent period the enormity of the reform task and of unifying two disparate nations became apparent. The FRG had a relatively solid foundation for unification with a growth rate of over 4 per cent, good levels of company profits, strong demand, low inflation and a substantial balance of trade surplus (Table 10.1).

Until 1989 official GDR statistics gave a false impression that the economy was performing well, with real growth, stable prices, no budget or external deficit and full employment. However, many of the figures proved unreliable since they reflected a price structure determined by the government rather than the market. Indeed, Mayer and Thumann (1990) argue that the GDR's situation was significantly poorer, since the inflexibility of the economy meant it was unable to adjust properly to consumer demands, technological innovation and the external shocks of the 1970s and 1980s. The absence of market competition fuelled inefficiency and created welfare losses, while capital investment was often concentrated upon specific, politically justified industries rather than consumer goods or infrastructure needs. Moreover, wage rigidity and the lack of

Table 10.1 GEMSU and the German economies

	FRG	GDR[a]
Area (sq km)	250 000	108 000
Average population ('000)	61 450	16 666
Average employment, 1988 ('000)	27 354	8 980
Average employment, 1991 ('000)	29 173	4 190
Average unemployment, 1988 (%)	7.7%	[b]
Average unemployment, 1991 (%)	5.7%	10.4%
Average monthly wages, 1988	DM3876	M1290
Average monthly wages, 1990	DM3962	M1436
% consumer price change p.a., 1980–88	3	[b]
Cost of living index change, 1990–91	+3.5%	+8.4%
GNP growth rate, 1980–88	1.7%	4.2%
GNP, July 1990–Jan. 1991 (DM bn)	1 270	105
Manufacturing output: % annual change from 2nd half 1990 to 2nd half 1991	+5.4%	−12.8%
Foreign trade balance, 1988 (DM bn)	+40	+2
% of exports (imports) to/from CMEA nations, 1988	4 (5)	70 (69)
% of exports (imports) to/from CMEA nations, 1991	4 (5)	68 (60)

[a] From Oct. 1990 the GDR became the Eastern *Länder* of Germany.
[b] Concept not recognized in GDR.
Source: Statistical Yearbooks of Deutsche Bundesbank and DDR.

wage differentiation created poor morale, especially when living standards in the FRG were known to be far higher. Lipschitz and McDonald (1990) reiterate such conclusions and point to a clear setback in the GDR economy in the year prior to unification. Indeed, they suggest that the East German GNP was only 10 per cent of that in the FRG, that labour productivity was at almost 35 per cent of the FRG average, net pay was 50 per cent lower, and foreign debt was over US$16 billion or 10 per cent of GDP.

Against this background, the State Treaty on GEMSU was designed on three main principles. Firstly, the GDR would be wholly assimilated into, rather than merged with, the FRG. Thus, five new *Länder* were created and existing GDR institutional structures are to be discarded. Secondly, the objective would be to establish a 'social market economy' based around sound monetary and fiscal policies and private enterprise, yet with a social security system to meet basic needs. Thirdly, German unification would be consistent with the aims of European integration. The main features of the Treaty were the introduction of a common currency and unified monetary policy; integration of the real economies, including industrial restructuring; and institutional reform, including the establishment of new banking, tax and social security systems.

Monetary union had the most immediate effect when on 1 July 1990 the GDR mark was replaced by the Deutschmark. In theory, an alternative approach would have been to allow both currencies to coexist for a transitional period so as to soften the blow for German industry; however, the existence of two currencies would have not stopped emigration and GDR marks would have quickly become unacceptable. In any event, there was little time before political unity was to be secured. The appropriate conversion rate between the currencies presented a problem in view of the paucity of reliable information on the GDR's economic status. A balance was required between minimizing inflation risks, safeguarding the competitiveness of firms and yet containing budgetary pressures, while making budgetary union socially acceptable to all Germans. In essence, conversion rates had to be set so that the increased money supply in the enlarged nation would match the rise in productive capacity while distinguishing between financial stocks (e.g. savings) and flows (e.g. wages).

In the event, financial assets and liabilities were converted in principle at a rate of GDRM2:DM1. However, with savings deposits GDR residents could convert at 1:1 in amounts of M2000 for those under 14 years of age, M4000 (14–58 years) and M6000 (over 59). Conversion of all assets and liabilities would have implied large purchasing power gains for GDR savers, possibly generating an inflationary buying spree. Conversely, the large debts of enterprises needed to be reduced drastically to avoid further weakening their competitiveness by heavy debt service burdens. In the consolidated balance sheet of the banking system, the average conversion rate was 1.8:1; but as the assets of the banking system were converted at less than the liabilities, the gap was closed by an equalization fund established by the government.

The conversion of flows, notably wages and salaries, was stipulated in the Treaty as 1:1. This was because, firstly, there had been too little time to effect any sort of comprehensive price reform prior to currency conversion, and, secondly, available economic data indicated that the GDR labour productivity was on average about 40 per cent that of the FRG, yet so were GDR industry wages. However, the data were suspect; moreover, given labour mobility and competition in the new enlarged Germany, the conversion rate would not be a permanent influence on the price of labour. At an average conversion rate of 1.8:1 the extension of the currency area caused the Deutschmark money supply (M3) to rise by DM180 billion, a 15 per cent increase, higher than the 10 per cent considered appropriate. However, the new residents had previously been able to hold financial assets only in liquid, low-return form and so invested in interest-bearing assets thus reducing the impact.

With the advent of monetary union, the Bundesbank assumed sole responsibility for monetary policy and for introducing an independent commercial banking system based on free-market principles. Until April 1990, the banking system of the former GDR consisted of primarily the State Bank of the GDR and its branches plus a few centrally controlled specialist institutions (the German Foreign Trade Bank, German Trade Bank, Bank for Agriculture and the Food Industry), and various savings and cooperative ventures together with the Post Office. All these institutions were integrated into a centralized allocation, ceiling control and clearing system to serve centralized economic planning.

Since July 1990 the major West German banks have played a major role in the restructuring of the banking system, through establishing joint ventures and their own branches. At the time monetary union came into force, some 571 banks with 4552 branches existed in the new *Länder*. By 1991 only 493 of these banks existed, yet there were already 1259 branches of West German banks, and representative offices of foreign banks were also being established (Deutsche Bundesbank 1991d). The State Bank of the GDR lost its central bank function, and its temporary successor institutions (State Bank Berlin and German Credit Bank), as well as the German Foreign Trade Bank, have been wound up. The one-tier banking system has thus been transformed into a two-tier system subject to German banking law and hence also EC directives. The German government has indicated that its involvement will be limited to easing transitional problems. For example, the Treuhandanstalt (Trust Fund) privatization agency has guaranteed short-term liquidity loans by former GDR banks and has taken over the debt clearance of loans granted to former state-owned enterprises.

In terms of *economic union*, the Treaty set out the goals of private ownership, competition, factor mobility, market-pricing and trading principles in line with the EC. These objectives represented a severe challenge given the obsolete capital stock, inefficient trading, transport and communications systems, and large parts of industry producing uncompetitive goods. However, Tietmeyer (1990) argues that the most difficult burden remains a population indoctrinated by an education system that discouraged them from decision-making and initiative.

The heart of the adjustment process was seen to be the restructuring of industry. In 1990 the Treuhandanstalt (THA) was nominated as owner of all the former state-owned enterprises, with a mandate to restructure and privatize the viable ones and liquidate the rest. As the largest privatization programme ever, this vast task covered initially 8000 industrial companies (raised to 11 000 with the breakup of the larger entities), with 4 million employees, debt and liquidity problems. By April 1992, 6300 industrial firms had been sold, in part or whole, with 1200 closed or being prepared for liquidation. In spite of privatization proceeds totalling DM22 billion by April 1992, the cost of the programme is enormous, with some DM28 billion spent in 1991 alone and estimated costs of DM50 billion in 1992, and annual deficits of DM30 billion expected over 1992–94 (Buhl 1992). Clearly, future obligations will add significantly to German public-sector debt, and, not surprisingly, the THA has been criticized, with calls for stronger, direct government influence. Some fear that the combination of privatization and company rescue activities can lead to resource misallocation through cross-subsidization. However, given the large number of irrevocable commitments agreed, the THA policy will continue, besides which any significant semblance of nationalization will be soundly resisted as it would defeat the objective of the THA's work.

The third strand of GEMSU involved *social union*, the transformation of the GDR's social security system. Essentially, this involved the adoption by the eastern *Länder* of the FRG system. However, since pensions and unemployment benefits are linked to past wages in the former GDR, it was necessary to have a transitional phase with assistance for the new pension, insurance and unemployment schemes. Previously the state budget had been at the core of central planning, and thus significant alterations were necessary to adapt it to a market economy. Subsidies were phased out for energy, transport and housing; major state enterprises (railways, post) were taken out of the budget; and personnel expenditure reduced. At the same time, the new tax laws of the FRG were adopted.

The sheer scale of GEMSU has meant that substantial fiscal transfers have been made from west to east in addition to private investment. To finance the GDR's budget deficit, contribute to the social security system and fund industry restructuring and the GDR's foreign debt, transfers of some DM40 billion in 1990 and DM60 billion in 1991 were expected; this would increase the overall German budget deficit to DM100 billion by 1991 compared with DM21.5 billion in 1989 (Tietmeyer 1990). However, as a result of the worse-than-expected state of the new *Länder*, the actual budget deficit was DM90 billion in 1990 and DM120 billion in 1991, with West–East transfers estimated at DM140 billion in 1991 (Deutsche Bundesbank 1992a). It could be argued that such costs are short-term investment for the longer-term national benefit following economic revival in the eastern *Länder*. And, to the extent that the transfers raise productive potential, they will be acceptable, although if significant amounts are geared to consumption sizeable deficits will persist. The counterpart to the large deficit is the strong impetus to East German demand which has shifted FRG resources from the export sector to the eastern *Länder*. This helped to reduce the current account from a surplus of DM776 billion in 1990 to a deficit of DM33 billion in 1991, although the major factor was a surge in imports, mainly to the benefit of the other EC members.

GEMSU represented a huge and unique undertaking. The currency conversion proceeded relatively smoothly but the exposure to competition adversely affected eastern manufacturing whose sales fell while costs rose as employees pushed for wage increases. Unemployment rose steeply, and, with widespread liquidity crises for most companies, the costs of unification grew abruptly. Indeed, the worse-than-expected overall economic situation brought forward political unification by some months. Many problems remain, notably the continued restructuring of state-owned enterprises and the creation of a private-sector business culture. At the macroeconomic level government budget deficits will need containment, since otherwise these may lead to tighter monetary policy, higher interest rates and lower growth. The Bundesbank does not want recourse to the capital markets on the same scale as in 1991 (DM102 billion), and to avoid tax increases this implies potential expenditure cutbacks.

Although we speak of GEMSU as German integration, in reality the GDR was integrated into the European Community. So what are the implications for the integration process within the Community, and specifically for the EMS and EMU? The suddenness of unity, the 15 per cent expansion of the German money supply, the massive fiscal transfers to the eastern *Länder* and the potential release of purchasing power have disrupted the ERM, as discussed in Chapter 2. However, given the speed and magnitude of the operation, the impact on the Community might have been much more disruptive. Certainly German macroeconomic variables have worsened: the country now has a large fiscal deficit, a deterioration in the balance of trade surplus, an increase in inflation and higher than desirable interest rates. However, to the extent that the fiscal deficit has arisen partly from a substantial increase in German imports from other EC countries, this aspect of unification may be viewed favourably.

Unification may have implications for the Bundesbank's role and perceived independence. Its anti-inflationary credibility has been partly compromised by the large money supply increase arising from introduction of the Deutschmark in the GDR on the government's terms. Moreover, in the short-term rising unemployment in the new *Länder* may fuel pressure for the Bundesbank to ease interest rates in circumstances in which it feels the monetary situation would normally not prescribe. In the longer term, however, the relative power of the Bundesbank may be restored—indeed, increased—within a larger trading area, as many of the neighbouring countries, such as Hungary and Czechoslovakia, increase their Deutschmark trade.

Gros and Thygesen (1992) suggest that the lessons for EMU are limited. For example, GEMSU created a market economy and, more importantly, a capital market, allowing Deutschmark finance for investment. These features already figure in the EC, so implying that a common currency was more significant for the GDR than in the context of EMU. GEMSU also had an important trade liberalization effect which EMU will not, since the Single Market programme will have already preformed this function. The timing of the two operations is not comparable, since GEMSU occurred virtually overnight whereas EMS convergence, the Single Market programme and the phasing of EMU will have taken many years. The massive fiscal transfers were required because of the poor state of the GDR and were possible because they amounted to 'internal' German transfers. However, whereas such transfers to the GDR were not possible before GEMSU, that is not the case with EMU; indeed, large transfers are being made under the 'cohesion fund' to the poorer members of the EC Twelve.

10.3.2   EC support for Eastern Europe: trade and aid

German unification must be considered alongside attempts to generate reforms throughout Eastern Europe. The triggers are moves towards political liberalization in the USSR, which began in 1985 with Gorbachev's advocacy of *glasnost* (openness) and *perestroika* (transformation), strengthened by the aforementioned events in Poland and Hungary in 1989, and the abolition of the power monopoly of the Soviet Communist Party in early 1990. Pressures for political change have gathered momentum since German unification, notably during 1991, a difficult year with the disintegration of Yugoslavia, violent clashes in the newly independent Baltic states and the abortive coup against Gorbachev.

However, political change was sealed by the dissolution of the Soviet Union and the creation of the Commonwealth of Independent States (CIS) in December. The populations involved now appear no longer prepared to tolerate rigid communist doctrines and infrastructures which restrict personal freedoms and condone poor living standards. While political change has come swiftly, however, the transfer to a market economy is fraught with difficulty, particularly concerning what measures to undertake first and at what speed.

Five broad areas of reform are commonly required:

1. *Privatization and ownership transformation* involving, stimulating private-sector development, breaking up monopolies, liquidating non-viable businesses, changing the financial system, and introducing accounting systems and management expertise.
2. *Economic systems* to provide the macroeconomic foundations for reform through currency, trade and monetary and fiscal regimes. These developments also include the establishment of appropriate banking and finance systems, whereby the central bank functions distinctively from the commercial banks; an efficient tax system; and a legal framework to protect property rights and the new social contracts required.
3. The *physical infrastructure*, notably in the areas of transport and communications. Much of this requires substantial refurbishment, being old and inefficient.
4. *Environmental concern*, which needs fostering via legal controls. The legacy of inefficient, heavy industry operating regardless of resource misuse, health and safety concerns is a common feature of Eastern Europe.
5. *Appropriate social developments*, to provide support and protect vulnerable groups, while discouraging dependence. Existing consumer subsidy systems must be replaced by adequate health, education and housing.

Many of these structural and technological gaps are common to those faced by the GDR, but a solution such as GEMSU is not. Considering the scale of such needs, an issue is whether the 'short, sharp shock' of swift but disruptive change is better than a more gradual, phased transformation. Poland has opted for the former in view of its macroeconomic legacy of hyperinflation, budget deficits and shortages. A four part austerity programme was launched in January 1990: prices were liberalized to find their own market-clearing level; a massive privatization programme was launched; hyperinflation was to be controlled via credit restrictions and balanced prices; and the exchange rate was to be made convertible. While this has created high costs in terms of lower output, higher unemployment and high inflation (79 per cent in January 1990), there are signs of improvement: inflation has fallen, and the rudiments of a market economy and entrepreneurship are in place, overseen by a democratically elected government (Åslund 1990).

Czechoslovakia originally adopted a more cautious and slower approach to change, incorporating French-style indicative planning, developing privatization and arguing for a centre path between the command and full market economy. However, it then followed Poland's lead in adopting IMF guidelines for stiff economic policies geared to accelerate change. The argument for a rapid transition is that at a micro level, unless private ownership and appropriate company laws exist, once the breakdown of the command economy occurs, resources are appropriated by managers for personal gain. Employees seize their chance to press for wage rises unrelated to productivity, and soon the country declines into a situation of shortages and civil strife. The risks of delaying reform were seen in the former USSR, where Gorbachev's inability to press reforms left the military–industrial complex largely intact. Crises ensued because the major economic and financial objectives could not be met and so public support waned, leading to the prospect of the government not implementing the reforms, and in turn to greater economic and political instability.

In spite of the risks in the short term, there appears little alternative to radical change; but this is impossible without Western, especially EC, assistance on a massive scale in a range of forms including trade agreements, financial transfers, assistance with privatization, joint ventures, technology transfer and management expertise, accounting, and financial and legal advice.

In June 1988 a joint declaration of mutual recognition was signed establishing official relations between the EC and COMECON, thereby paving the way for new trade and cooperation agreements signed with East European nations over the next two years (see Appendix C). As bilateral trade agreements *within* the COMECON began to break down in 1990, intra-East European trade faltered, notably oil imports from the USSR. The unification of East and West Germany meant that Hungary and Czechoslovakia lost significant trade in the short term. Overtures were then made to the EC, which began to develop 'second-generation' association or European agreements. These provide for free trade but also include economic, technical and scientific cooperation, financial support and mechanisms for political negotiation. The aims are to assist with the introduction of currency convertibility, real pricing and privatization, yet avoid a spate of premature EC membership applications. The agreements stipulate free access to EC goods according to a flexible timetable to reflect the specific situation of individual countries, the establishment of multi-party political systems with free elections, and the introduction of market economies. The first 'European' agreements were negotiated with Hungary, Poland, and Czechoslovakia, reflecting their status as the 'front-runners' in Eastern reforms. Poland, for example, in 1990 eliminated all quantitative restrictions and suspended most of its duties at the 0 or 5 per cent level in an effort to boost trade.

Various sources of financial aid to Eastern Europe involve the EC. For example, at the global level EC nations are individually members of the International Monetary Fund (IMF) and the World Bank (IBRD), but in addition they provide assistance via the Poland and Hungary: Assistance for the Restructuring of their Economies (PHARE) programme, the European

Bank for Reconstruction and Development (EBRD) and the European Investment Bank (EIB). In providing any help, a conflict arises between the desire to further the reform process and integrate the Eastern nations into the world economy, and the need to avoid overt subsidy of ailing regimes as occurred in the 1970s. Hence much of the aid is project-related or subject to conditions.

A major breakthrough in East–West relations occurred in early 1992 when the IMF admitted to membership seven nations in the CIS, including Russia. Poland, Hungary and Czechoslovakia had joined in September 1990. Membership requires the provision of detailed economic information, and acceptance of IMF and advice and conditions imposed on loans. In return, the member country can open the door to larger resources from the commercial banking fraternity, as seen with Hungary and Poland's austerity programmes. In July 1992 Russia was allocated a US$1 billion loan as part of a US$24 billion facility, including US$4.5 billion from the IMF and IBRD, a US$6 billion Rouble Stabilization Fund available in 1993, and US$11 billion in food aid and export credits. The agreement required Russia to reduce its budget deficit from 17 to 5 per cent of GDP by the end of 1992 and to reduce inflation to single figures (then above 15 per cent). In general, the approach adopted seems to be that the more complete the reform programme, the more the IMF will lend, although there is a large element of good faith in this particular package, or perhaps it is fear of the consequences of failure. Russia has freed most prices and border controls on trade, but it is still far from a significant privatization, and without a viable banking or legal framework. One way forward may be for part of Russia's US$74 billion foreign debt to be swapped for equity rights in its vast mineral, industry and land resources, thus saving valuable hard currency and encouraging Western investors.

The EC coordinates the assistance offered by the G-24 OECD nations (EC, EFTA, New Zealand, Australia, Canada, USA, Japan and Turkey) under the PHARE programme, which has been extended to Bulgaria, Czechoslovakia and Romania. The EC's own contribution to PHARE is considerable, with ECU1 billion set aside in 1992 out of the Community budget. The fundamental objective is to support East European transformation through four priority areas— agriculture, industry and investment, environment, and training—in order to aid the reform process. Among the diverse schemes funded are the TEMPUS programme for trans-European mobility in higher education, ECU20 million for Polish imports of feedstuffs to relaunch a livestock farming programme, and ECU10 million for Bulgaria for basic medicines.

Prior to the IMF decision to widen its Eastern European membership, and in the wake of the dramatic events of 1989, the European Community was concerned as to how it could provide substantial funding support for short-term consumption as well as long-term investment. However, there was reluctance to fund large-scale macroeconomic programmes on the grounds that to be effective they would need to be coordinated by the IMF and the World Bank. The World Bank, or International Bank for Reconstruction and Development

(IBRD), as the name implies would appear a suitable vehicle for European redevelopment. However, its membership is determined by that of the IMF and its focus has tended to be more towards public-sector projects, although it has provided funding, for example, to Hungary and Poland in the form of loans for environmental development, energy, telecommunications and housing schemes.

In the event, the European Community decided to launch a new bank, the European Bank for Reconstruction and Development (EBRD), located in London, which came into existence in April 1991 with a capital base of ECU10 billion. Of this, 52 per cent is subscribed by the EC and EIB, approximately 11 per cent by other West European nations, 24 per cent from non-European members and 12 per cent by the recipient East European countries. As with most development banks, only a percentage (30 per cent) of the subscribed capital is paid up, the remainder acting as guarantees. The main purpose of this is to back loans raised on the capital markets, and to this effect it may raise 250 per cent of its subscribed capital.

The bank's primary purpose is to foster the transition towards open-market economies and promote private and entrepreneurial initiative in those Central and Eastern European nations committed to applying the principles of multiparty democracy, pluralism and market economics. Its role in part is that of a regional development bank, and during its first five years 40 per cent of its financing will be available for lending to the state sector to support infrastructure projects. In this capacity it will assume the mantle of the IBRD for Eastern Europe.

Some 60 per cent of the EBRD's loan and equity investments will be geared to the private sector, and in this respect it operates as a merchant bank. Direct equity stakes are allowed to foster the development of private-sector firms and up to 30 per cent of its total investments can be in equities. In addition, loans are available at commercial rates, the aim being to support projects that are not sufficiently attractive to obtain all the private capital they require, but which nevertheless show potential. Apart from funding, the bank offers guarantees and underwriting, and technical support for the preparation of loan proposals and advice on aspects of accounting, management and privatization. Many of the initial funding operations are likely to be co-financed with the other international agencies such as the IMF and IBRD or affiliates. As an example, its first project in June 1991 was an ECU35 million loan as part of a co-financing with the World Bank to the Bank of Poznan, Poland, for on-lending to heating-sector enterprises. This was to support a restructuring programme to improve the technological base, encourage energy conservation and reduce pollution. Although this particular project carried a sovereign guarantee from the Republic of Poland, the EBRD may finance without guarantees.

The need for the EBRD is disputable, inasmuch as various development banks and agencies already exist with a track record, and presumably could have had their funds augmented. Moreover, in this context the cost of establishing and staffing the EBRD, and of research efforts and visits, would seem unnecessary.

Nevertheless, the EBRD is seen to fulfil a funding gap. While the World Bank, EIB and the PHARE programme provide loans to enhance infrastructures and bridge the technological gap, and the IMF gives stabilization funding at the macroeconomic level, there is a specific need for finance and coordination of the privatization programme.

The EBRD is distinctive in that it incorporates investment in both the public and private sectors, although the emphasis is on the latter via the promotion of privatization and entrepreneurship. Indeed, direct loans for public-sector infrastructure projects are not emphasized in its operations, but where such projects are funded, an 'economic return' is required. The EBRD articles of association state that such projects should raise GNP by more than the cost, and the foreign exchange earnings of the country must rise by more than the increase in the annual cost of servicing the foreign debt. The EBRD is also the first multinational development bank to have been created expressly to support political goals, namely human rights and the drive for democracy, and to involve East and West on an equal footing. Thus, lending policy is influenced by political as well as economic progress, and recipients have to demonstrate a commitment to multi-party democracy and pluralism.

The European Investment Bank was established in 1958, via the Treaty of Rome, as the Community's long-term development bank but with lending responsibilities for the Mediterranean and ACP nations under association programmes. Given its lengthy existence, the EIB has regularly expanded its capital base which in January 1991 was ECU57.6 billion of which 7.5 per cent had been called. The bulk of its funding comes from borrowing on the capital markets; indeed, its borrowing policies have actively stimulated domestic markets. For example, it has accounted for 35 and 62 per cent respectively of the new 'matador' and 'navegador' (non-resident peseta and escudo) markets in Spain and Portugal. It has also promoted the use of the ECU through its use of 'jumbo' borrowing; in 1990 some seven issues totalling ECU2.4 billion were made.

The EIB is a non-profit-making bank with the interest rates levied on loans reflecting the bank's borrowing cost plus a 0.15 per cent margin for administrative expenses. Maturities are generally 4–12 years for industry and up to 20 years or more for infrastructure and energy projects. The EIB's main priority is to support projects promoting regional development, and since its establishment about two-thirds of its lending has gone to the Community's less developed regions, amounting to ECU27 billion in the past five years alone. Other objectives cover energy and environmental protection, transport and telecommunications infrastructure, support for projects that support industrial competitiveness and promote industrial integration, and the promotion of small and medium-sized enterprises. Lending to the last-named category is normally via global loans to commercial banks for on-lending in smaller amounts.

The domain of the EIB's activity was widened by German unification and the events in Eastern Europe. In 1990 some ECU215 million was lent to Poland and Hungary for a series of infrastructure modernization projects covering the gas, electricity, telecommunications and railway industries. This was part of an ECU1 billion facility authorized for these countries, and in April 1991 ECU700 million was made available for investment in Bulgaria, Czechoslovakia and Romania, the operations coordinated via the PHARE programme. Substantially more of such funding will probably be required in future, although much of it will emanate from the EBRD.

The economic rehabilitation of Eastern Europe will be a complex and lengthy challenge to the European Community. GEMSU was unique and was effected swiftly, but even so it highlighted the immense structural changes required. Many Eastern countries are keen to forge links with the Community, and to this end the more forward-looking ones such as Hungary, Poland and Czechoslovakia are knocking on the door for entry having signed association agreements with the EC. Substantial trade and aid developments are underway, with agencies such as the IMF, IBRD and EIB channelling large amounts of finance eastward. The aims must be to foster private initiative, and to this end the EBRD is an important development, acting as a catalyst for privatization and joint venture operations with Western investors, in such a way that the private sector in the Community promotes development. However, the sheer scale of the problems suggests that any further eastward extension of the Community in the short term will require such massive financial transfers that it would seriously impinge upon the Community resource base and hamper integration.

10.4   THE EC AND EFTA: THE 'NORTHERN EXTENSION'

The Single Market programme and the events in Eastern Europe have added a new dimension to the long-standing, yet often changeable, relationships between the EC and EFTA nations. The European Free Trade Area was formed in 1960 as a reaction to the creation of the EEC, its members fearing that the disappearance of tariffs within the Community would damage their exports. They all hoped that the development of a free trade area would stimulate trade between them, while some saw EFTA as a means to press for a wider European free trade area at later date without compromising on sovereignty or existing commitments. Three of the original members—Denmark, the UK and Portugal—subsequently left, while Finland and Iceland joined, thus cementing the Nordic and neutral emphasis. In keeping with the concept of a free trade area discussed in Chapter 1, the organization has been a loose arrangement, with members retaining their own bilateral trading relationships, and is run by a series of regular meetings without devolution of power to a central, supranational body.

10.4.1   Towards a European Economic Area (EEA)

During the 1960s EFTA promoted the concept of a single European-wide market. Its own internal market was strengthened by the formal completion of the free trade area in 1966 and this became very important for the smaller nations, inasmuch as for them it effectively resembled a trade-creating customs union. However, Britain remained attracted to the EEC and applied for membership along with Denmark and Ireland, followed later by Norway. Sweden, Austria and Switzerland sought associate EEC status conditional upon retention of neutrality. Such moves encouraged attempts to bring the two organizations closer together, an approach adopted in the 1965 Vienna Declaration, in which EFTA ministers advocated reducing trade barriers, harmonizing standards and co-operating in research and development.

The catalyst for still closer relations was the defection of Denmark and the UK in 1973, since together they accounted for over half of EFTA trade. As members of the EEC, their trade with the remaining EFTA bloc would now be subject to the common external tariff unless acceptable agreements could be reached. The EFTA nations, Denmark and the UK were clearly concerned at the prospect, but equally, the EEC Six saw the benefit of eliminating trade barriers, given that the small EFTA nations' exports would not seriously threaten EEC industry, yet tariff reductions would boost the already extensive EEC exports to EFTA. During the early 1970s, therefore, bilateral free trade agreements (FTAs) were adopted by the EEC with each of the EFTA nations. Collectively these created the largest free trade area in the world, a market of 375 million people, and by 1977 it covered virtually all trade in industrial products, the exceptions being sensitive items such as fish (Iceland, Norway), timber (Finland) and steel (Sweden), which were given special concessions. The agreements abolished customs duties and quantitative restrictions on trade in industrial goods manufactured or substantially processed in the Community or EFTA, gave guidelines on state aid and industrial competition, and were to be administered by bilateral joint committees. Rules of origin had to be introduced to avoid a situation whereby imports from non-members entered the free trade area via a low-tariff member only to be re-exported duty-free to members with higher external tariffs.

The introduction of the FTAs helped boost EC–EFTA trade and by 1986 some 25 per cent of EC exports were going to EFTA nations and some 60 per cent to the EC from EFTA (de Lange 1988). Although bilateralism was the major feature of the relationship, at the start of the 1980s EFTA members gradually began to speak with a common voice and the association gained an identity of its own. Thus, a multilateral dimension was added at the first joint ministerial meeting in April 1984 in Luxembourg, which called for the intensification of cooperation and the creation of a European Economic Space (EES) going beyond the FTAs. The concept smacked of rhetoric, but EFTA drew strength from the EC's role as its most important trading partner (Table 10.2) to press for the reduction in non-tariff barriers. Its priorities were seen in the areas of border formalities, technical trade barriers, rules of origin and trade documentation. Subsequently various agreements were reached notably to include EFTA in the Community's Single Administrative Document (SAD) geared to reducing the

Table 10.2 EFTA trade with the EC (% shares[a])

Trading partner	EFTA		Aus.		Swz.		Fin.		Nor.		Swe.		Ice.	
	M	E	M	E	M	E	M	E	M	E	M	E	M	E
EC	61	58	69	65	72	58	43	46	47	65	55	54	50	68
USA	7	7	4	3	6	8	6	6	8	7	9	9	14	10
Japan	5	3	5	2	4	5	2	1	4	2	5	2	6	6
Other	14	19	15	20	11	22	29	27	19	10	13	16	14	7
Intra-EFTA	13	13	7	10	7	7	20	20	22	16	18	19	16	9
Total	100	100	100	100	100	100	100	100	100	100	100	100	100	100

[a] M = imports, E = exports.

321

paperwork in cross-border trade, to simplify the rules on origin, and to agree on a mutual recognition of tests, inspections and certificates.

This multilateral framework of EC-EFTA relations gained importance when the EC published its 1985 White Paper on the Single Market. The EFTA nations were particularly concerned that they might lose their privileged access and face discrimination (Pedersen 1991). Indeed, it was feared that the Community's desire for deeper integration might mean the end for EFTA unless it accepted the Community's control of decisions at the supranational level. This, of course, assumed that the EC wanted EFTA to participate in the internal market, but in 1988 the EC made it clear the internal market was for member states only. Moreover, some of the poorer EC members such as Spain and Portugal were unhappy that relatively rich Scandinavian EFTA nations were obtaining preferential access to the Community without carrying any of its financial burdens. EFTA was also under internal pressure following Portugal's defection in 1986 and Austria's application for EC membership.

Efforts to improve relations were made in 1989, prompted by Jacques Delors, who sought a compromise between the existing free trade cooperation framework and full EC membership. He aimed to develop the European Economic Space (EES) concept, now renamed European Economic Area (EEA) because the word 'space' had connotations of emptiness! Delors referred to a structured partnership with common decision-making and administrative institutions (Wijkman 1991). The EEA accord would extend the principles of the Single Market to cover EFTA nations. Thus there would be free movement of goods, services, capital and labour by the end of 1992 based on EC legislation, together with cooperation measures to reduce social and regional inequalities, and common rules for surveillance, enforcement and the settlement of disputes. However, both parties would retain sovereignty over decision-making within their own organizations.

For EFTA, the EEA would promote further economic integration without constraining its members' freedom to conduct foreign business. However, it would also mean adopting EC regulations without having a vote in EC decisions, although procedures were to be created whereby EFTA could be 'consulted' with regard to legislation affecting its members. For the EC, the EEA talks were seen as a means to prevent a fresh round of new membership applications at a time when deeper integration via the Single Market programme was a priority. Progress was slow in 1990 and 1991, largely because of the fluid situation in Eastern Europe and EFTA's reluctance to forgo decision-making involvement. However, with the end of the 'Cold War' making the neutrality issue less significant, EFTA members began individually to consider full membership, with Sweden filing an application in 1991. Swedish preoccupation with neutrality may have protected its public from the harsher social and economic realities of EC membership, namely higher food prices and tax harmonization which might reduce social transfers.

Eventually, in October 1991 in Luxembourg, the EEA Treaty was signed after protracted negotiations over four areas of dispute. Firstly, the southern EC members had insisted upon financial support from the EFTA group, which was conceded. Secondly, Austria and Switzerland agreed to allow more EC heavy goods vehicles to cross their frontiers. Thirdly, the EC wanted more fishing rights in Norwegian and Icelandic waters. But Norway was willing to cede only 50 per cent of the increase the EC wanted. For the Norwegians the issue was a deeper one of the viability of fishing communities in the middle and northern parts of the country (Hailer 1991). Iceland is virtually completely dependent upon fishing and fish processing. Ultimately special concessions were made to these nations. Finally, the difficult issue of EFTA's involvement in decision-making without undermining EC control was circumvented by the creation of a new EFTA panel, comprising five EC and two EFTA judges responsible for evaluating breaches of EEA rules.

The EEA Treaty was due to come into effect with the internal market in January 1993 (see summary below). In return for access to the Single Market, the EFTA nations accept EC legislation and will be able to participate fully in decision-making only in so far as its members accede to EC membership. However, the EC indicated that negotiations with potential members would not start until after January 1993 and then, once approved by the EC, would need ratification by all parties. So a referendum would be required, which in Sweden's case is unlikely before the 1994 elections. Hopes of joining by 1995, therefore, appear optimistic.

The EEA challenges basic EFTA philosophy in that most members originally joined to avoid supranational control implied in the EEC. Yet for the EEA to function the EFTA nations have to enhance internal integration and take on additional commitments. In EFTA collective action has no real track record, whereas, following majority rule, it is the norm in the EC. If the EEA works then pressures will diminish for full EC membership, but if not the demise of EFTA seems assured.

The EC–EFTA Treaty   The treaty can be summarized as follows:

- From 1993, free movement of goods and services in the EEA
- From 1993, free movement of labour and capital in the EEA. Mutual recognition of qualifications. Capital movements in respect of *some* EFTA property and direct investment to face restrictions
- EC and EFTA to agree a system for classifying which goods are regarded as originating from within the EEA
- Special arrangements for trade in fish, energy, coal and steel. EFTA to maintain its own farm policies without joining the CAP
- EFTA to assume EC rules on company law, social policy, the environment, education, consumer protection, research and development, competition policy, procurement, mergers and state subsidy
- EFTA countries not able to vote on EC legislation

- An independent joint court to deal with EEA-related disputes and appeals on competition policy
- The EEA Council of Ministers to decide whether to extend new EC legislation to EFTA
- The treaty to be approved by the European Parliament and notified by the parliaments of all states involved. Treaty reviews every two years starting at the end of 1993

10.4.2   Financial services in EFTA

The EEA is expected to boost trade between the two organizations, not least of all in financial services. Here the potential attractions to the EC would appear to come from access to the 'onshore offshore centres' of Switzerland and Liechtenstein, and opportunities in the relatively rich Nordic nations. Switzerland is a major financial centre in its own right, focused on Geneva, Basle, Lugano as well as the main location in Zurich. The country's long history of banking, the diversity of its languages, its political neutrality and economic stability creating a strong currency—all have traditionally attracted foreign investors and capital. The country is essentially a financial entrepôt where foreign corporate borrowers have raised funds largely via bond and note transactions. Fiduciary transactions have been common whereby investments are made by a bank in its own name but for and at the risk of the customer. As foreign investments are exempt from the punitive Swiss withholding tax, most of the incoming fiduciary capital is invested abroad. Moreover, the financial centre has also been associated with private banking and portfolio management services built upon secrecy provisions and the nation's stability.

However, many of these operations face an uncertain future with changes in investment practices and growing competition. Schuster (1990) points to a growth in 'social' as opposed to 'personal' savings, that is savings by institutional investors such as pension funds and insurance companies, which invest in liquid capital markets with more regard for return than secrecy. Moreover, within the EEA both Switzerland and Liechtenstein, the tiny principality lodged between Austria and Switzerland, may eventually have to adapt to EC directives and greater transparency. Liechtenstein still allows for virtually total secrecy, although recent investigations, notably in the Robert Maxwell case, show that concern for its reputation allows for some discretional disclosure. Since 1991 Swiss bankers have been required to know the beneficial owners of accounts and to cooperate with authorities at home and abroad in criminal inquiries (Rodger 1992). Given EC directives on money laundering and sharing information on tax matters, the isolation of these centres is thus liable to change. Moreover, the Swiss franc is no longer as pre-eminent in terms of stability, nor is tax avoidance and evasion so dependent upon locations such as Switzerland.

Liechtenstein and Switzerland also face increased competition from 'offshore' centres in Europe (Fig. 10.1). Luxembourg is perhaps the most significant

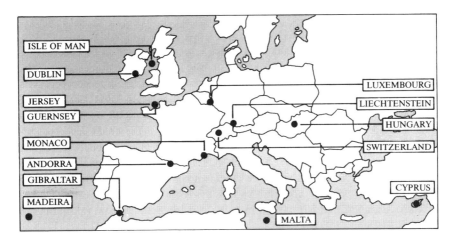

Figure 10.1 European offshore centres

such centre within the EC but it has experienced a decline in its Eurocurrency business following greater concentration in London and securitization. Instead, it is seeking more portfolio management activity, especially in UCITS and ECU-based operations, thus directly challenging Switzerland. Newer non-EC European contenders are also appearing, such as Malta, Cyprus and even Hungary. For these reasons, Switzerland has sought concessions to avoid becoming too constrained by EEA regulations, and may opt out of the treaty.

The Nordic region is suffering from the aftermath of liberalization of its banking sector in the mid-1980s, which led to a credit expansion with little regard for solvency. Added to this, the globalization of financial markets, the free movement of capital within the EEA and the EC's Second Banking Directive all fuel competitive pressures for domestic banks. In 1991 the top three Norwegian banks—Christiana Bank, Den Norske Bank and Fokus Bank—shared combined losses of NKr16 billion, four times greater than in 1990. Norway was forced to virtually nationalize the banking system, effectively taking over the top three. Although the aim is to 'denationalize' as soon as possible, this is unlikely until adequate capital resources can be raised privately. A state-backed bank insurance fund was established in 1991 with NKr11 billion to help prop up the banks, but the fund had fallen to NKr0.5 billion in March 1992 by calls made on it (Fossli 1992). Part of the problem stems from the semi-isolationist nature of the banking industry in the past, which has been based on maintaining the 'Big Three' without raising efficiency or modernizing operations. In addition, the recession has badly affected Norway's industry which has suffered record unemployment and commercial bankruptcies.

The Swedish and Finnish banking scenarios are equally grim. Nordbanken, the 70 per cent state-controlled Swedish bank, has registered record losses in the past two years, prompting management changes, cost-savings and job losses through restructuring. The bank was formed in June 1990 as a merger between state-controlled PKBanken and its provincial competitor Nordbanken. PKBanken had previously embarked on an aggressive expansion of business to widen its customer base away from the public sector but it grew too quickly, and moreover it paid too much for Nordbanken. In an attempt to compete with the largest Swedish commercial banks—Skandinavia Enskilda Banken (S-E Banken) and Svenska Handelsbanken—it expanded its credit excessively at a time when the economy was slipping into recession. S-E Banken has also suffered as it paid SKr4.7 billion for an option on 28.2 per cent of the shares of Skandia, the insurance company, with a view to creating an integrated financial services group, but was snubbed by Skandia and had to resell at a loss of SKr415 million. With excessive property exposure, S-E Banken also had to make bad debt provisions of SKr4.76 billion in 1991, causing a 30 per cent fall in operating profit (Webb 1992).

In Finland, Skopbank, the clearing bank for the savings banks, failed through exposure to Tampella, a loss-making forestry group, and losses on its share portfolio. A subsequent capital injection of FM1.8 billion by the savings banks was insufficient to cover losses, and further liquidity needs meant that the Bank of Finland was forced to take control in September 1991. Subsequently, it has sought to sell the 53 per cent holding acquired. Skopbank's problems coincided with the recession and low interest margins and have prompted the sort of changes needed throughout the Nordic region: a state deposit guarantee fund and tighter reporting procedures.

It is evident that deregulation of the Nordic financial markets in the 1980s was not accompanied by a corresponding strengthening of the regulatory framework and banking supervision. To this end, adoption of EC banking directives would be beneficial. It is clear that Nordic banking is in the midst of a crisis, but liberalization and restructuring may provide opportunities for EC banks, especially those offering equity participation.

CONCLUSIONS

Europe is undergoing rapid economic and political change with the EC at the core and pressures and opportunities on all sides. Successive enlargements have widened the scope but at the same time, through their specific concerns, have helped to deepen the integration of the Community. The British have been accused of being 'anti-European', displaying intransigence and hindering the integration process, but they have voiced concerns over the CAP and budget contributions which led to reforms and a needed strengthening of the structural funds. Considerable efforts have been made to accommodate the 'southern' nations, Portugal, Spain and Greece, with their previously undemocratic regimes. All three have benefited in their development, most notably Spain, but at a cost in terms of resource transfer, the latest manifestation of which is the

'Cohesion Fund'. However, the 'southern enlargement' has also brought demands from the other Mediterranean countries and the ACP states, who feel that their aid from the EC may be under threat, especially with competing requirements from the East.

Whereas the initial enlargements were phased over several years from initial application to accession, the developments in Eastern Europe have occurred with such rapidity and on such a scale that they threaten the EC's resources. GEMSU has given an insight into the problems faced in converting the legacy of centrally planned, ideology-fed systems into social market economies, yet it is just the tip of an iceberg, especially relative to the needs of the former Soviet Union. The Community has responded with significant technical, financial and managerial support, but the financial requirements are so vast that the new funds and institutions, such as the EBRD, are likely to be severely stretched.

The ending of the 'Cold War' has had an impact on the EFTA nations, given their strategic locations. The 'federalist' versus 'national sovereignty' debate has been a recurrent theme throughout the EC—and, indeed, in this text—but nowhere is it more apparent than in the context of EFTA, whose members have been determined to maintain their neutrality and not to devolve power to central, supranational bodies. However, the economics of the market-place are proving more pervasive than politics, and EC-EFTA relations have been strengthened by the EEA Treaty. This creates a major free trade zone to rival that in North America and has potential for resource growth via trade creation. While the EC remains concerned to deepen integration, this widening of Single Market access is subject to caveats on EFTA involvement. Indeed, as the geographical scope of the Community's influence continues to widen, the key decision-making will remain within the core EC members, especially where financial resources are involved.

FURTHER READING

The initial enlargements are covered in Pinder (1991), Goodman (1990) and Lodge (1992). On GEMSU the economic aspects are covered by Lipschitz and McDonald (1990), the EMU aspects in Gros and Thygesen (1992) and banking and finance in Steinherr (1992). For EC-EFTA relations see Wallace (1991).

DECISION-MAKING IN THE EUROPEAN COMMUNITY

The decision-making process depicted in Fig. A1 depends upon the nature of the proposed legislation. The general 'consultation' procedure for directives, regulations and Council decisions begins with the *Commission* initiating and drafting legislation in discussion with various advisory bodies and officials of member states. The Commission consists of 17 members appointed by the member states but pledged to independence of national concerns. Opinions are then sought from *ECOSOC (Economic and Social Committee)*, a consultative body comprising employers, workers and other interests, and from the *European Parliament*, made up of 518 MEPs elected from the member states. The amended proposal, if appropriate, will then be sent to the *COREPER (Committee of Permanent Representatives)*, which consist of national civil servants who will discuss the proposals and prepare them for the *Council of Ministers* where, according to the subject under discussion, the relevant ministers will decide whether to adopt or reject it. If adopted, the decision and legislation are published in the *Official Journal (OJ)*. Rejected proposals will need to be resubmitted via the above process for approval.

This procedure has been extended under the 1986 Single European Act, which provides for a 'cooperation' phase involving a second reading by Parliament within a strict timetable for matters essentially relating to the Single Market. This marks a significant increase in Parliament's powers and aids the processing of legislation, since, although extra stages are involved, proposals may now be adopted by qualified majority voting by Council. Following the first reading, the Council determines a 'common position' which it must justify to Parliament, which in turn then has three months to decide whether to confirm,

First reading: Consultation

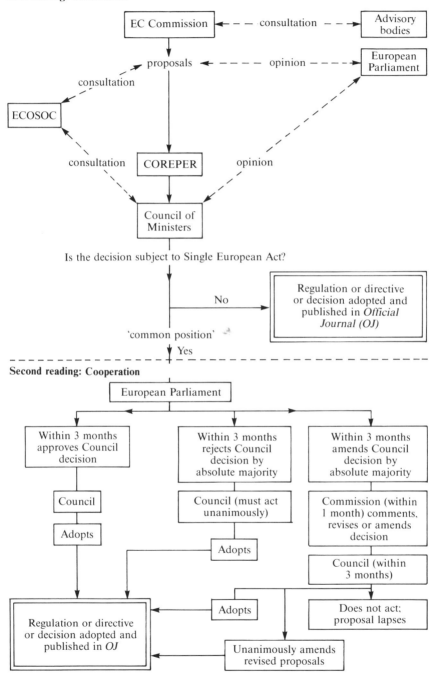

Figure A.1 Summary of the EC decision-making process

reject or amend under this 'second reading'. Parliamentary approval leads to referral back to the Council, which can adopt the legislation only by a unanimous decision. If Parliament proposes amendments by an absolute majority of its members, the Commission has one month to re-examine the 'common position' with regard to these amendments and modify the proposal. This is then submitted to Council for adoption, which can be by qualified only majority. Should the Commission reject Parliament's amendments, they can be revived by the Council via a unanimous decision.

THE RISE AND FALL OF BCCI

1972

BCCI Holdings is set up by Pakistani financier Agha Hasan Abedi with US$2.5 million capital, based in Luxembourg. Initial investors include Bank of America (25 per cent) and Middle East interests, including the ruling family in Abu Dhabi.

1972–1977

BCCI experiences rapid growth in the Middle East and the UK, aided by 1973 oil price rise and power of OPEC. Total assets rise from US$200 million in 1973 to US$2.2 billion in 1977. Aim is to create the world's largest bank by the year 2000. Operations are extended to Africa, Caribbean and Asian sub-continent, although the heart of the operation remains the London HQ.

1978

US Securities and Exchange Commission blocks takeover attempt of Financial General Bankshares (FGB) and accuses Abedi of failure to disclose details about BCCI. However, with the help of President Carter's friend Bert Lance, BCCI acquires 18 per cent of FGB via individual investor purchases. The Netherlands Antilles-based Credit and Commerce American Holdings (CCAH) and its Amsterdam-based subsidiary Credit and Commerce American Investment (CCAI) are established as vehicles to acquire FGB shares. BCCI denies any connection. Bank of England refuses BCCI a full banking licence and limits its UK branches to 45. Concern is expressed at its rapid growth.

1980

Bank of America sells its stake. Bank of England rejects BCCI's latest request for a full UK banking licence.

1982

FGB becomes First American Bankshares (FAB) on acquisition by CCAH and CCAI. Purchase is said to have been conducted by Clark Clifford, former US defence secretary and partner in lawyers Clifford and Warnke. Clifford becomes chairman of FAB.

1983

BCCI buys a Colombian bank with branches in Medellin and Cali, known centres for drugs and money laundering.

1985

Price Waterhouse (PW) audit of International Credit and Investment Company (overseas), a substantial shareholder in BCCI Holdings, reveals 'loan irregularities'. Significant Treasury losses are also shown. Bank of England approves BCCI decision to transfer its Treasury operation from London to Abu Dhabi.

1986

Saudi Arabia's Bin-Mahfouz family takes 10 per cent stake in BCCI, which is later raised to 20 per cent via investment companies. Ernst and Young, auditors of BCCI's holding company, complain of excessive management power and systems weaknesses.

1987

Basle supervisors from eight countries form a 'college' of regulators to oversee BCCI. PW are appointed sole auditors to BCCI. Findings suggest that US$32 million of drugs money was laundered between 1985 and 1987, a time when General Noriega of Panama was a customer.

1988

The Bin-Mahfouz family sell their stake in BCCI for US$528 million to representatives of the Abu Dhabi government. US customs operations lead to the eventual jailing of bank staff in Florida and London, and BCCI is subsequently fined a record US$15.3 million. Charges include conspiracy to defraud and money laundering.

1989

PW qualifies BCCI's 1988 accounts following Florida indictments. Abu Dhabi government subscribes to a US$180 million capital raising exercise by BCCI.

1990

May   PW discovers holes in BCCI's bank accounts with some US$2 billion under suspicion. The Abu Dhabi government subscribes US$400 million of new capital and acquires other holdings to take its stake to 77 per cent. Losses of almost US$500 million are announced, mainly through provisions against Third World debt. Following the results, the bank proposes a major restructuring and moves its HQ from London to Abu Dhabi. Some 4000 jobs are shed and the restructuring aims to slim BCCI down to three branches: London, Hong Kong and Abu Dhabi.

October   PW is led to further investigations which suggest widespread fraud. Abedi and his senior officer Swaleh Naqvi resign, although the latter remains to assist PW uncover some 6000 secret documents, the 'Naqvi files', in Abu Dhabi which are effectively a double set of books of who received loans and made deposits, i.e. 'the bank within a bank'.

1991

January   As the Gulf War develops, unrecorded deposits are revealed to the Bank of England amounting to US$600 million. The US Federal Reserve Board begins its formal investigation into BCCI's US activities but complains that the operation is hampered by the Bank of England's lack of cooperation.

4 March   The Bank of England appoints PW under Sec. 41(1) of the 1987 Banking Act to prepare a special report on potential false accounting at BCCI, separate from the annual audit.

June   The PW report reveals evidence of large-scale fraud over several years. Simultaneously, the Federal Reserve Board orders BCCI to divest itself of holdings in CCAH, the holding company of FAB, and to cease all US operations.

2 July   The Bank of England, in consort with other overseas authorities, notably in the Cayman Islands, France, Spain and Switzerland, seizes control of BCCI assets, thus effectively closing the bank. Subsequently in Luxembourg it is announced that BCCI staff were aware two months earlier that the authorities there were intending to close them down, given local losses of US$526 million compared with reserves of US$368 million. The potential losses faced by UK local authorities are expected to exceed £100 million, including £23 million by the Western Isles council. By mid-July questions are raised about the Bank of England's supervisory role and its seizure of BCCI's assets. Depositor action groups are formed, while in Abu Dhabi the government criticizes PW for failing to uncover the irregularities earlier, and the Bank of England for failing to allow a restructuring and not consulting Abu Dhabi before the closure. The Sheikh of Abu Dhabi claims that a revised plan was given to the Bank of England two days before the closure of BCCI. This envisaged BCCI being broken down into separate banks in London, Abu Dhabi and Hong Kong which then would have been sold as going concerns and the other businesses run down.

22 July The Bank of England petitions the High Court for the winding-up of BCCI under Sec. 92 of the 1987 Banking Act on the grounds that liquidation would be in the public interest as the bank is insolvent. Petition is adjourned for a week to allow Abu Dhabi officials to explore alternatives to winding-up provided consideration is given to depositor compensation. A political row ensues with the contention that the Prime Minister failed to act on information gleaned about BCCI's covert operations. In response, a Treasury inquiry is set up under Lord Justice Bingham. The High Court gives a four-month adjournment following a last-minute US$50 million compensation pending an Abu Dhabi rescue package. In the USA BCCI is fined US$200 million and criminal charges are issued against Abedi, Naqvi and BCCI itself.

August Luxembourg authorities threaten to liquidate BCCI unless the US$50 million package is extended to deposits outside of the UK. Clark Clifford, chairman of FAB, resigns.

September Thirty-five executives of BCCI are arrested in Abu Dhabi, including Naqvi, while in the USA a new indictment cites Naqvi and five other officials on US$14 million drug money laundering offences. Information reveals a worldwide network of BCCI-nurtured links at the highest political levels.

October In the face of deteriorating relations with the Bank of England, the Abu Dhabi authorities hint at not honouring a pledge of US$2.2 billion to BCCI creditors unless indemnities are forthcoming. This implies that creditors might receive virtually nothing when the bank is finally liquidated on 2 December, the rescue package having been abandoned.

November The Treasury and Civil Service Coordinating Committee hearings suggest it is untenable that regulation and supervision of a bank by the Bank of England do not constitute indicators of security.

December   There is a further adjournment of the hearing to the Bank of England's petition for the liquidation of BCCI SA to allow more time for a negotiated settlement for creditors.

1992

14 January   UK High Court issues compulsory winding-up order and follows similar action taken in Luxembourg and the Cayman Islands courts on 3 January. Possible payout could be 30–40 per cent of deposits following Abu Dhabi authorities' US$2.2 billion compensation plan and deposit protection schemes. Touche Ross announce that liquidation fees amount to US$50 million. In the USA, BCCI agree to a 'plea bargain' whereby they plead guilty to fraud, racketeering and drug money laundering, pay a US$10 million fine and hand over US$550 million of assets to the government in exchange for which the government will drop the US$200 million fine levied earlier and all existing/pending civil actions will be settled in US courts.

February   Abu Dhabi officials state that if the compensation package is rejected it will be withdrawn and not negotiated, thus leading to lengthy delays and litigation. Moreover, Abu Dhabi threatens massive actions against the Bank of England and PW. Report by the Bank of England on BCCI closure reveals that US$200 million was transferred by BCCI to futures company Capcom Financial Services Ltd, controlled by BCCI's former head of Treasury. Also, the National Commercial Bank of Saudi Arabia (NCB), owned by the Bin-Mahfouz family, is accused of hiding huge frauds at BCCI.

March   UK Securities and Investments Board (SIB) reports that it knew in March 1989 that Capcom was involved in money laundering, corruption and false accounting but did not link it to BCCI. It lists at least 18 accounts connected with artificial profits/losses. House of Commons Select Committee report severely criticizes Bank of England's regulation and supervision of BCCI. The central bank is accused of favouring reconstruction and reform, not restriction and closure. The report suggests that the Bank was well aware of the problems of BCCI in the 1970s and that PW had clear evidence of poor banking and deceitful transactions by 1990. A minority amendment to the report by Brian Sedgemore MP confirms views that the Bank of England should not have allowed BCCI to operate after March 1990 given (a) weaknesses in BCCI's accounting controls, (b) poor management, (c) the fact that auditors Ernst and Young had resigned, (d) drug money laundering and (e) the existence of terrorist finance accounts. Touche Ross, as liquidators, issue a writ against PW and Ernst and Young for negligence and breach of contract and duties over BCCI's 1985 and 1986 accounts.

May   A revised code of conduct for the London money markets is issued.

The Bank of England tells local authorities that they alone must assess the creditworthiness of banks with whom they deposit funds, whatever their money brokers advise.

June   Sheik Khalid Bin-Mahfouz, chief operating officer at NCB, is charged in New York of defrauding depositors in BCCI of US$300 million by helping to create a false picture of BCCI's health via purchases of US$900 million of shares in 1986 only to secretly repurchase them in 1988 at a profit of US$140 million. Some US$300 million of the sale proceeds came from depositors' accounts, recorded as a loan on BCCI's books, not a payment. NCB's New York operation is closed. Revised Basle Concordat is issued, including agreements by central banks to refuse access to branches of banks from countries where supervision is deemed inadequate. In the USA Clark Clifford is charged with misleading American bank regulators and accepting US$35 million in bribes. BCCI executives are also charged, including Robert Altman, chairman and president of BCCI's main US subsidiary in the 1980s, Abedi and Naqvi.

August   Bingham report is delayed but 'leaks' of the draft focus the blame on the Bank of England and the Abu Dhabi shareholders. The crucial delay in 1990 is highlighted. Evidence had emerged in April 1990 of holes in the balance sheet but it was not until October 1990 that Abu Dhabi began a formal examination. The Bank of England is criticized for not insisting on earlier, intensive investigations, and for delays between March and July 1991 over closure.

October   Bingham Report published and details a long series of mistakes or omissions by the Bank of England. The report argues that there has been too much concentration on what the Bank cannot do under the Banking Acts, that it was not diligent and vigorous enough in its pursuit of the truth, and relied too heavily on others. Recommendations include more effective internal communications, the creation of a Special Investigations Unit, greater on-site examination of banks, and better supervisory training. Some of these aspects are implemented immediately. Luxembourg Court approves $1.7 billion compensation plan formulated by BCCI's liquidators and its Abu Dhabi shareholders. On the assumption that creditors will not appeal against the decision, compensation payments may begin in 1993. Courts in the UK and Cayman Islands had already sanctioned the deal.

SOME RECENT DEVELOPMENTS IN EC–EAST EUROPEAN RELATIONS

March 1985 Mikhail Gorbachev is elected general secretary of the Communist Party of the USSR and introduces far-reaching reform ideas—*glasnost* and *perestroika*.

June 1986 Poland becomes a member of IMF.

June 1988 COMECON delegation signs a joint declaration with the EC agreeing on mutual recognition and allowing for agreements with each of the East European nations.

September 1988 Trade and cooperation agreement is drawn up between EC and Hungary with effect from December.

December 1988 Trade and cooperation agreement is drawn up between EC and Czechoslovakia.

January 1989 In Hungary, liberalization of company law allows possibilities for private enterprise. Foundation of political parties is allowed.

April 1989 Poland, ban is lifted on 'Solidarity' party, which wins all 161 seats open to independent groups in subsequent election.

July 1989 EC is given the task of coordinating Western aid to Poland and Hungary by G7. The Group of 24 is formed.

August 1989 Polish food prices are freed.

September 1989 Frontier between Austria and Hungary is opened to GDR citizens. Trade and cooperation agreement signed by Poland with EC.

November 1989 Act is passed declaring economic independence of the three Baltic states from the USSR. EC heads of government hold a special summit to discuss aid to Eastern Europe. The borders with FRG are opened to all GDR citizens. Demonstrations in Prague lead to demise of Communist party. Hungary declares a democratic constitution and applies for membership of the Council of Europe. Berlin Wall is breached.

December 1989 Trade and cooperation agreement is drawn up between EC and USSR. In Czechoslovakia, Vaclav Havel is elected first non-communist head of state for 40 years. In Bulgaria, the government promises free elections. In a revolution in Romania, the Ceausescus are toppled and executed. EC agrees to establish EBRD.

January 1990 Polish radical reform programme starts.

February 1990 Chancellor Kohl, FRG, proposes GEMSU. In USSR the Communist Party resolves to abolish its power monopoly. Poland applies for membership of the Council of Europe.

April 1990 EC Summit agrees arrangements to bring the GDR into the Community. New association agreements are to be offered to individual East European nations.

May 1990 Group of 24 agree to extend the PHARE programme to other Central and East European nations. GDR and Bulgaria sign trade agreements with the EC.

July 1990 GEMSU comes into effect.

October 1990 Germany is politically united.

November 1990 'European agreements' are established with Poland, Hungary and Czechoslovakia.

January–June 1991 Market-oriented programmes are implemented in Czechoslovakia, Romania, and Bulgaria.

April 1991 Foundations of EBRD are laid.

September 1991   EC allows reduction on import levies on produce from Hungary, Poland and Czechoslovakia.

December 1991   Dissolution of the Soviet Union is sealed by establishment of Commonwealth of Independent States (CIS).

REFERENCES

ABI (1991), *Insurance Statistics 1986–1990*, Association of British Insurers, London, September.

Abraham, J. P. and Lierman, F. (1991), 'European Banking Strategies in the Nineties: A Supply Side Approach', *Research Paper 91/8*, Institute of European Finance, University College of North Wales, Bangor, Gwynedd.

Anglo-German Foundation (1988), *New Technology-Based Firms in Britain and Germany*, Anglo-German Foundation for the Study of Industrial Society, London.

Ansoff, I. (1967), *Corporate Strategy*, Penguin, London.

Ardagh, J. (1990), *France Today*, Penguin, London.

Ardy, B. (1988), 'The National Incidence of the European Community Budget', *Journal of Common Market Studies*, 26: pp. 401–30.

Artis, M. J. and Taylor, M. P. (1988), 'Exchange Rates, Interest Rates, Capital Controls and the EMS', in F. Giavazzi *et al.* (eds), *The European Monetary System*, Cambridge University Press.

Åslund, A. (1990), *Systemic Change in Eastern Europe and East West Trade*, EFTA Economic Affairs Department Occasional Paper no. 31, EFTA, Geneva, June.

Bacon, R. and Eltis, W. (1978), *Britain's Economic Problem: Too Few Producers*, Macmillan, London.

Baldwin, R. (1989), 'Completing the European Single Market in 1992: How Cecchini Underestimates the Benefits', *Economic Policy*, 6(1): pp. 52–66.

Ball, J. (1991), 'Short-Termism: Myth or Reality?' *National Westminster Quarterly Review*, August: pp. 20–30.

Baltensperger, E. and Dermine, J. (1987), 'Banking Deregulation in Europe', *Economic Policy*, 4: 64–109.

―――― and ―――― (1990), 'European Banking, Prudential and Regulatory Issues', in J. Dermine (ed.), *European Banking in the 1990s*, Basil Blackwell, Oxford.

Bank of England (1985), *Money for Business*, 5th edn, Bank of England and City Communications Centre, London.

―――― (1988a), 'Composition of Company Boards', *Bank of England Quarterly Bulletin*, 28(2): pp. 242–5.

―――― (1988b), Banking Act 1987 Sec. 16: Statement of Principles, May.

—— (1990), 'Monetary Aggregates in a Changing Environment: A Statistical Discussion Paper', Discussion Paper no. 47, Bank of England, March.

—— (1991a), 'The Exchange Rate Mechanism of the EMS: A Review of the Literature', *Bank of England Quarterly Bulletin*, 31(1): pp. 73–82.

—— (1991b), *Report and Accounts*, Bank of England.

—— (1992a), 'The Maastricht Agreement on Eonomic and Monetary Union', *Bank of England Quarterly Bulletin*, 32(1): pp. 64–8.

—— (1992b), 'Institutions Included within United Kingdom Banks (at 31 December 1991)', Annex to *Bank of England Quarterly Bulletin,* 32(1).

—— (1992c), 'The Gilt-Edged Market: Developments in 1991', *Bank of England Quarterly Bulletin*, 32 (1): February, 56–59.

—— (1992d), 'The Net Debt of the Public Sector: end March 1992', *Bank of England Quarterly Bulletin*, 32(4): pp. 432–40.

Bannock, G. (1976), *The Smaller Business in Britain and Germany*, Anglo-German Foundation, London.

—— (1981), 'Banks and Industrial Management', Chapter 5 in *The British and German Banking System: A Comparative Study*, Anglo-German Foundation for the Study of Industrial Society, London.

Barnes, I. and Preston, J. (1988), *The European Community,* Longman, London.

Barr, D. G. and Cuthbertson, K. (1989), 'Modelling the Flow of Funds', Bank of England Discussion Paper, Technical Series, no: 21, February.

Barrell, R. (ed.), (1992), *Economic Convergence and Monetary Union in Europe*, Sage Publications, London.

Begg, D., Fischer, S. and Dornbusch, R. (1991), *Economics*, 3rd edn, McGraw-Hill, London.

Benzie, R. S. (1989), 'Takeover activity in the 1980s', *Bank of England Quarterly Bulletin,* 29(1): pp. 78–85.

Berry, A. J., Citron, D. B. and Jarvis, R. (1987), *The Information Needs of Bankers Dealing with Large and Small Companies: With Particular Reference to Proposed Changes in Legislation*, Research Report no. 7, Chartered Association of Certified Accountants, London.

Bingham Report (1992), *Inquiry into the Supervision of the Bank of Credit and Commerce Interantional* (Chairman Lord Justice Bingham), HMSO, London.

Blackburn, M. (1989), 'Euro-panic!', *Banking World*, June: pp. 30–1.

Blake, D. (1990), *Financial Market Analysis,* McGraw-Hill, London.

Blanden, M. (1990), 'Finding Common Cause', *The Banker*, October: pp. 45–6.

—— (1991), 'Small Bang in Belgium', *The Banker*, March: pp. 35–6.

Bloomfield, C. A. (1991), *Presenting Financial Proposals to Banks*, 2nd edn, Butterworths, London.

Boleat, M. (1986), *The Building Society Industry*, Allen & Unwin, London.

Boltho, A. (1990), 'Why Has Europe Not Co-ordinated its Fiscal Policies?' *International Review of Applied Economics*, 4(2): pp. 166–80.

Bolton, J. (1971), *Report of the Committee of Inquiry on Small Firms*, Cmnd. 4811, HMSO, London.

Borges, A. M. (1990), 'Portuguese Banking in the Single European Market', Chapter 9 in J. Dermine (ed.), *European Banking in the 1990s*, Basil Blackwell, Oxford.

Bourke, P. (1988), 'International Bank Regulation and the Small Country Problem: A Theoretical Perspective', Research Paper 88/12, Institute of European Finance, University College of North Wales, Bangor, Gwynedd.

Brealey, R. A. and Myers, S. C. (1991), *Principles of Corporate Finance*, 4th edn, McGraw-Hill, London.

Breckling, J. *et al.* (1987), 'Effects of EC Agricultural Policies: A General Equilibrium Approach: Initial Results', Australian Bureau of Agricultural Economics, Canberra. Upublished report.

Brown, C. V. and Jackson, P. M. (1990), *Public Sector Economics*, 4th edn., Martin Robertson, Oxford.

Bruce, P. (1984), 'Bonn Takes a Step Towards Privatisation', *Financial Times*, 15 November.

Buckland, R. and Davis, E. (1990), 'Bank Borrowing, Small Firms and the USM', Chapter 8 in E. P. M. Gardener (ed.), *The Future of Financial Systems and Services*, Macmillan, London.

Buckle, M. and Thompson, J. L. (1992), *The United Kingdom Financial System in Transition: Theory and Practice*, Manchester University Press, Manchester.

Buckwell, A. *et al.* (1982), *The Costs of the Common Agricultural Policy*, Croom-Helm, London.

Budd, S. A. and Jones, A. (1991), *The European Community: A Guide to the Maze*, 4th edn, Kogan Page, London.

Buhl, I. (1989), 'West German Privatisation Policy under Test', *Deutsche Bank Bulletin*, June: pp. 15–20.

——— (1992), 'Treuhandanstalt: Privatisation Still the Best Form of Reorganization', *Deutsche Bank Research Bulletin*, April: pp. 12–16.

Burniaux, J. M. and Waelbroeck, J. (1985), 'The Impact of the CAP on Developing Countries: A General Equilibrium Analysis', in C. Stevens and J. Verloren van Themaat (eds), *Pressure Groups, Policies and Development*, Hodder & Stoughton, London.

Burns, P. and Dewhurst, J. (eds) (1986), *Small Business in Europe*, Macmillan, London.

Burton, J. (1991), *Going the Whole Hog: VAT Finance of Local Government Services*, Centre for Business Economics Briefings, no. 1, European Business School, London, April.

Cable, J. (1985), 'Capital Market Information and Industrial Performance: The Role of West German Banks', *Economic Journal*, 95: pp. 118–32.

Cadbury Committee (1992), 'The Committee on the Financial Aspects of Corporate Governance' (Chairman Sir Adrian Cadbury), Draft Report, London, May.

Caminal, R. *et al.* (1990), 'Competition in Spanish Banking', in J. Dermine (ed.), *European Banking in the 1990s*, Basil Blackwell, Oxford.

Campbell, K. (1991), 'Plans to Centralise Provoke Old Squabbles', *Financial Times*, 11 October.

Capie, F. and Collins, M. (1992), *Have the Banks Failed British Industry?* Institute of Economic Affairs (IEA), Hobart Paper 119, London.

Castello-Branco, M. and Swinburne, M. (1992), 'Central Bank Independence', *Finance and Development*, 29(1): pp. 19–21.

CBI (1987), 'Investing in Britain's Future', *Report of the CBI/Industry Task Force*, CBI, London.

Cecchini, P. (1988), *The European Challenge: 1992: The Benefits of a Single Market*, Wildwood House, Aldershot.

Chant, J. (1992), 'The New Theory of Financial Intermediation', in K. Dowd and M. Lewis (eds), *Current Issues in Financial and Monetary Economics*, Macmillan, London.

Charkham, J. (1989), 'Corporate Governance and the Market for Companies: Aspects of the Shareholders' Role', Bank of England Discussion Paper, no. 44, Bank of England, November.

Cnossen, S. (ed.) (1987), *Tax Coordination in the European Community*, Kluwer, Deventer, (Netherlands).

Colwell, R. (1991), 'The Performance of Major British Banks, 1970–1990', *Bank of England Quarterly Bulletin*, 31(4): pp. 508–15.

Cooke, P. (1990), 'International Convergence of Capital Adequacy Measurement and Standards', Chapter 18 in E. P. M. Gardener (ed.), *The Future of Financial Systems and Services*, Macmillan, London.

Corbet, H. (1991), 'Agricultural Issue at the Heart of Uruguay Round', *National Westminster Bank Quarterly Review*, August: 2–18.

Courtney, D. (1992), *Derivatives Trading in Europe*, Butterworths, London.

Crystal, K. A. (1992), 'The Operation of Financial Markets', Chapter 4 in K. Dowd and M. Lewis (eds), *Current Issues in Financial and Monetary Economics*, Macmillan, London.

Cyert, R. M. and March, J. G. (1983), *A Behavioural Theory of the Firm*, Prentice-Hall, Hemel Hempstead, Herts.

Dale, R. (1984), *The Regulation of International Banking*, Woodhead-Faulkner, Cambridge.

Davis, E. P. (1990), 'International Financial Centres: An Industrial Analysis', Bank of England Discussion Paper no. 51, September.

——— (1991), 'The Development of Pension Funds: An International Comparison', *Bank of England Quarterly Bulletin*, (31)3: pp. 380–90.

Dawkins, W. (1991), 'Small Bang Fall-Out', *Financial Times*, 12 December.

de Boisseau, C. (ed.) (1990), *Banking in France*, Routledge, London.

de Guingand, A. (1987), 'The London Traded Options Market', *Interchange*, Autumn: pp. 17–24.

de Lange, H. (1988), 'Taking Stock of the EC/EFTA Dialogue', in J. James and H. Wallace (eds), *EC–EFTA: More than Just Good Friends?* De Tempel, Bruges.

Demekas, D. *et al.* (1988), 'The Effects of the CAP: A Survey of the Literature', *Journal of Common Market Studies*, 27(2): pp. 113–45.

Dermine, J. (1990), 'The Specialisation of Financial Institutions: The EC Model', *Journal of Common Market Studies*, 28(3): pp. 219–33.

Deutsche Bundesbank (1984), 'Business Finance in the United Kingdom and Germany', *Monthly Report of the Deutsche Bundesbank*, 36(11): pp. 33–42.

―――― (1990a), 'The Finances of the Länder Governments since the Start of the Tax Cuts in 1986', *Monthly Report of the Deutsche Bundesbank*, 42(4): pp. 20–8.

―――― (1990b), 'The Monetary Union with the German Democratic Republic', *Monthly Report of the Deutsche Bundesbank*, 42(7): pp. 13–28.

―――― (1990c), 'The Expenditure of the Central, Regional and Local Authorities since 1982', *Monthly Report of the Deutsche Bundesbank*, 42(7): pp. 38–46.

―――― (1990d), 'The New Principles I and Ia Concerning the Capital of Banks', *Monthly Report of the Deutsche Bundesbank*, 42(8): pp. 36–43.

―――― (1991a), 'One Year of German Monetary, Economic and Social Union', *Monthly Report of the Deutsche Bundesbank*, 43(7): pp. 18–30.

―――― (1991b), 'The Profitability of German Banks in 1990', *Monthly Report of the Deutsche Bundesbank*, 43(8): 14–31.

―――― (1991c), 'Trends in Public Sector Debt since the mid-1980s', *Monthly Report of the Deutsche Bundesbank*, 43(8): pp. 32–41.

―――― (1991d), 'The West German Economy under the Impact of the Economic Unification of Germany', *Monthly Report of the Deutsche Bundesbank*, 43(10): pp. 14–20.

―――― (1991e), 'The Significance of Shares as Financing Instruments', *Monthly Report of the Deutsche Bundesbank*, 43(10): pp. 21–8.

―――― (1991f), 'West German Enterprises' Profitability and Financing in 1990', *Monthly Report of the Deutsche Bundesbank*, 43(11): pp. 14–29.

―――― (1991g), *Annual Report for the Year 1990*, Frankfurt, April.

―――― (1992a), 'The Maastricht Decisions on the European Economic and Monetary Union', *Monthly Report of the Deutsche Bundesbank*, 44(2): pp. 43–52.

―――― (1992b), 'Deposit Protection Schemes in the Federal Republic of Germany', *Monthly Report of the Deutsche Bundesbank*, 44(7): pp. 28–36.

Diamond, D. and Dybvig, P. (1983), 'Bank Runs, Deposit Insurance and Liquidity', *Journal of Political Economy*, 91: pp. 401–19.

Dickson, T. (1991), 'Exposed by the Market's Transparency', *Financial Times*, 12 December.

Dixon, R. (1991), *Banking in Europe*, Routledge, London.

Dobie, C. (1992), 'British Firms Lag Behind Overseas Rivals', *The Independent* (Survey on Research and Development), 9 June, p. 18.

Dodds, J. C. (1987), *The Investment Behaviour of British Life Insurance Companies*, Croom Helm, London.

Doggett, P. (1992), 'Business Banking in 1992', *Management Accounting*, 70(4): pp. 48–50.

DTI (Department of Trade and Industry) (1992), *The Single Market: The Facts*, COI, London.

Dupont-Fauville, A. (1983), 'Nationalisation of the Banks in France: A Preliminary Evaluation', *Three Banks Review*, 139: pp. 32–41.

Durman, P. (1991), 'Royal in £110m Provision for Mortgage Loss', *The Independent*, 15 November.

Dyson, K. (1986), 'The State, Banks and Industry: The West German Case', in A. Cox (ed.), *The State, Finance and Industry*, Wheatsheaf, Brighton.

EC (European Community) (1986), *The Single European Act*, EC, Luxembourg.

―――― (1989), *A Common Agricultural Policy for the 1990s*, 5th edn, EC, Luxembourg.

—— (1989), *Europe without Frontiers: Completing the Internal Market*, European Documentation, Luxembourg.

—— (1990), *The Community Budget: The Facts in Figures*, 3rd edn, EC, Luxembourg.

—— (1992a), 'From the Single Market to Maastricht and Beyond: The Means to Match our Ambitions', Commission communication to the Council, COM (92) 2000, and Supplement 1/92 to *Bulletin of the EC*.

—— (1992b), 'Development and Future of the CAP', *Bulletin of the EC*, 5: pp. 53–9.

EC Commission (1977), *Report of the Study Group on the Role of Public Finance in European Integration* (MacDougall Report), EC, Luxembourg.

—— (1985), *Completing the Internal Market*, White Paper from the Commission to the European Council, Luxembourg.

—— (1987), *Recommendation concerning the Introdcution of Deposit-Guarantee Schemes in the Community*, 87/63. Luxembourg, 22 December 1986.

—— (1988), 'The Economics of 1992', *European Economy*, no. 35: pp. 103–168.

—— (1989), *Report on Economic and Monetary Union in the European Community* (Delors Report), Committee for the Study of Economic and Monetary Union, Luxembourg.

—— (1992a), *Proposed Council Directive on Deposit-Guarantee Schemes*, COM (92) 188, Luxembourg, 6 May.

—— (1992b), *Treaty on European Union (Maastricht Treaty)*. CONF-UP-UEM 2002/92, EC, Brussels.

EIS (European Information Service) (1992), 'Agriculture', press release no. 130, European Information Service, June, p. 13.

Eltis, W., Fraser, D. and Ricketts, M. (1992), 'The Lessons for Britain from the Superior Economic Performance of Germany and Japan', *National Westminster Quarterly Review*, February: pp. 2–22.

Emerson, M., Aujean, M., Catinat, M., Goybet, P., and Jacquemin, A. (1988), *The Economics of 1992*, Oxford University Press.

Euromoney (1992), *The 1992 Guide to the European Equity Markets*, Euromoney Publications, London.

Fairburn, J. A. and Kay, J. A. (1989), *Mergers and Merger Policy*, Oxford University Press.

Fama, E. (1980), 'Banking in the Theory of France', *Journal of Monetary Economics*, 6: pp. 29–39.

Featherstone, K. (1989), 'The Mediterranean Challenge: Cohesion and External Preferences', Chapter 10 in J. Lodge (ed.), *The European Community and the Challenge of the Future*, Pinter, London.

Financial Times (1991), 'Behind Closed Doors: BCCI: The Biggest Bank Fraud in History', reprint of feature articles, 9–16 November, Financial Times Business Information Ltd.

Fossli, K. (1992), 'Beleaguered and Disfigured', *Financial Times* Survey on Nordic Countries, 23 March, p. v.

Freear, J. (1989), *The Management of Business Finance*, 2nd edn, Pitman, London.

Garcia Crespo, M. (1991), 'Spain', Chapter 3 in F. J. L. Somers (ed.), *European Economies: A Comparative Study*, Pitman, London.

Gardener, E. P. M. (1990), 'Financial Conglomeration: A New Challenge for Banking', in E. P. M. Gardener (ed.), *The Future of Financial Systems and Services*, Macmillan, London.

—— and Molyneux, P. (1990), *Changes in Western Europe Banking*, Unwin Hyman, London.

Georgakopoulos, T. A. (1986), 'Greece in the European Communities: A View of the Economic Impact of Accession', *Royal Bank of Scotland Review*, no. 150: pp. 29–40.

Gessler Commission (1979), *Bericht der Studienkommission: Grundsatzfragen der Kreditwirtschaft*, Stollfuss Verlag, Bonn.

Gilbody, J. (1988), *The UK Monetary and Financial System*, Routledge, London.

Goodhart, C. (1987), 'Structural Changes in the British Capital Markets,' in C. Goodhart, D. Currie and D. Llewellyn (eds), *The Operation and Regulation of Financial Markets*, Macmillan, London.

—————— (1991), 'An Assessment of EMU', *Royal Bank of Scotland Review*, no. 170: pp. 3–24.

Goodman, S. E. (1990), *The European Community*, Macmillan, London.

Grahl, J. and Teague, P. (1990), *'1992': The Big Market*, Lawrence & Wishart, London.

Greenaway, D. and Shaw, G. K. (1983), *Macroeconomics: Theory and Policy in the UK*, Martin Roberson, Oxford.

Griffiths, H. (1991), *Financial Investments*, McGraw-Hill, London.

Grilli, V. *et al.* (1991), 'Political and Monetary Institutions and Public Financial Policies in the Industrial Countries', *Economic Policy*, 6(2): pp. 342–92.

Gros, D. and Thygesen, N. (1992), *European Monetary Integration*, Longman, London.

Guien, P. and Bonnet, C. (1987), 'Completion of the Internal Market and Indirect Taxation', *Journal of Common Market Studies*, 255(3).

Gupta, S. *et al.* (1989), 'The Common Agricultural Policy of the EC', *Finance and Development*, 26(2): pp. 37–9.

Haas, E. B. (1958), *The Uniting of Europe: Political, Social and Economical Forces 1950–1957*, Stanford University Press.

Hadjimatheou, G. (1987), 'Is Public Expenditure Growth a Problem?' *Royal Bank of Scotland Review*, no. 153: pp. 17–24.

Hailer, H. J. (1991), 'Scandinavia: Forging New Ties to Europe', *Deutsche Bank Bulletin*, October: pp. 6–11.

Hall, M. J. B. (1987), 'The Deposit Protection Scheme: The Case for Reform', *National Westminster Bank Quarterly Review*, August: pp. 45–54.

—————— (1989), *Handbook of Banking Regulation and Supervision*, Woodhead–Faulkner, Cambridge.

—————— (1991a), 'The BCCI Affair', *Banking World*, September: pp. 8–11.

—————— (1991b), 'The BCCI Affair', *Banking World*, October: pp. 11–14.

—————— (1991c), 'The BCCI Affair', *Banking World*, November: pp. 10–11.

—————— (1992a), 'The BCCI Affair', *Banking World*, February: pp. 10–11.

—————— (1992b), 'Spotlight on the Regulators', *Banking World*, July: pp. 15–21.

Hamke, M. (1990), 'Frankfurter Wertpapierbörse: History–Organization–Operation', Frankfurt Stock Exchange, September.

Hankinson, A. (1991), 'Them and Us', *Certified Accountant*, October: pp. 28–29.

Harden, I. (1990), 'Eurofed or "Monster Bank"?', *National Westminster Quarterly Review*, August: pp. 2–13.

Harrington, R. (1990), 'The Growth of Asset and Liability Management', in E. P. M. Gardener (ed.), *The Future of Financial Systems and Services*, Macmillan, London.

Harvey, D. R. and Thompson, K. J. (1985), 'Costs, Benefits and the Future of the Common Agricultural Policy', *Journal of Common Market Studies*, 24(1): pp. 1–20.

Hawkins, R. A. (1991), 'Privatisation in Western Germany, 1957 to 1990', *National Westminster Bank Quarterly Review*, November: pp. 14–22.

Heald, D. (1987), *Public Expenditure: Its Defence and Reform*, Basil Blackwell, Oxford.

Healey, N. M. and Levine, P. (1992), 'Unpleasant Monetarist Arithmetic Revisited: Central Bank Independence, Fiscal Policy and European Monetary Union', *National Westminster Quarterly Review*, August: pp. 23–37.

Henderson, R. (1989), 'The Deregulation of the Financial System: For Better or Worse?' Chapter 11 in M. Campbell *et al.* (eds), *Controversy in Applied Economics*, Harvester Wheatsheaf, Brighton.

Henrot, F. and Levy-Lang, A. (1990), 'Markets and Products in the Banking Sector', Chapter 4 in C. de Boisseau (ed.), *Banking in France*, Routledge, London.

Hewitt, G. (1988), 'Barclays de Zoete Wedd Takes the High Ground', *Banking World*, July: pp. 25–30.

Hitiris, T. (1991), *European Community Economics*, 2nd edn, Harvester Wheatsheaf, Brighton.

HM Treasury (1980), 'The Medium Term Financial Strategy', *Economic Progress Report*, April: pp. 1–6.

—————— (1986) 'Nationalised Industries', *Economic Progress Report*, July–August: pp. 5–7.

————- (1989), *An Evolutionary Approach to Economic and Monetary Union*, HMSO, London, pp. 1–6.

———— (1990), 'Privatisation', *Economic Briefing*, no. 1: pp. 4–6.

———— (1991), 'The European Community Budget', *Economic Briefing*, no. 2: pp. 12–14.

HM Treasury and Civil Service Select Committee (1992). See Bingham Report.

Hope, K. (1990), 'Windfall in Athens', *The Banker*, August: pp. 56–7.

Howcroft, J. B. and Lavis, J. (1986), *Retail Banking: The New Revolution in Structure and Strategy*, Basil Blackwell, Oxford.

Howells, P. G. A. and Bain, K. (1990), *Financial Markets and Institutions*, Longman, London.

Hulme, G. (1990), 'Contract Funding and Management in the National Health Service', *Public Money and Management*, 10(3): pp. 17–23.

Hunsdiek, D. (1986), 'Financing of Start-up and Growth of New Technology-based Firms in West Germany', *International Small Business Journal*, 4(2): pp. 10–24.

Hutchinson, P. *et al.* (1988), 'The Financial Characteristics of Small Firms which Achieve Quotation on the UK USM', *Journal of Business Finance and Accounting*, 15(1): pp. 9–20.

Hutchinson, R.W. and McKillop, D.G. (1992), 'Banks and Small to Medium-Sized Business Financing in the United Kingdom: Some General Issues', *National Westminster Quarterly Review*, February: pp. 84–95.

Ingram, D. H. A. (1987), 'Change in the Stock Exchange and Regulation in the City', *Bank of England Quarterly Bulletin*, 27(1): pp. 54–65.

Jensen, M. C. and Meckling, W. H. (1976), 'Theory of the Firm: Managerial Behaviour, Agency Costs and Ownership Structure', *Journal of Financial Economics*, 3: pp. 350–60.

Johnson, C. (1988), 'The Revolution in UK Banking', *Lloyds Bank Economic Bulletin*, 119: pp. 1–30.

Jones, C. (1988), 'Facing Up to the Challenge', *The Banker*, May: pp. 23–7.

———— (1989), 'Europe's Savings Banks: Think Vertical', *The Banker*, October: pp. 68–70.

Junz, H. B. and Boonekamp, C. (1991), 'What Is at Stake in the Uruguay Round?' *Finance and Development*, June: pp. 11–15.

Kay, J. A. and Silberston, Z. A. (1984), 'The New Industrial Policy Privatisation and Competition', *Midland Bank Review*, Spring: pp. 8–16.

———— and Thompson, D. J. (1986), 'Privatisation: A Policy in search of a Rationale', *Economic Journal*, 96(1): pp. 18–32.

Kayser, G. and Ibielski, D. (1986), 'The Federal Republic of Germany', Chapter 7 in P. Burns and J. Dewhurst (eds), *Small Business in Europe*, Macmillan, London.

Kennedy, E. (1991), *The Bundesbank*, RIIA, Pinter, London.

King, P. (1991), 'The Netherlands', *Euromoney*, October: pp. 78–84.

Lamb, A. (1986), 'International Banking in London, 1975–85', *Bank of England Quarterly Bulletin*, 26(3): pp. 367–78.

Lane, C. (1989), *Management and Labour in Europe*, Edward Elgar, Aldershot.

Lapper, R. (1991), 'Barriers Fall Across Europe', *Financial Times*, 26 February.

Laurie, S. (1989), 'Slicing it Right', *The Banker*, November: pp. 94–5.

Lewis, M. K. and Davis, K. T. (1987), *Domestic and International Banking*, Phillip Allan, Oxford.

Lindberg, L. (1963), *The Political Dynamics of European Economic Integration*, Stanford University Press.

Lintner, V. and Mazey, S. (1991), *The European Community: Economic and Political Aspects*, McGraw-Hill, London.

Lipschitz, L. and McDonald, D. (eds) (1990), *German Unification: Economic Issues,* IMF Occasional Paper, no. 75, IMF, Washington, December.

Llewellyn, D. (1988) 'Monetary Union in Europe: The Problems', *Banking World* 6(12): pp. 42–45.

———— (1992), 'Bank Capital: The Strategic Issue of the 1990s,' *Banking World*, January: pp. 20–25.

Lodge, J. (ed.) (1992), *The EC and the Challenge of the Future*, Pinter, London.

Lomax, D. F. (1991), 'A European Central Bank and Economic and Monetary Union', *National Westminster Quarterly Review,* May: 55–72.

Lomax, J. W. (1990), 'A Model of ICCs Dividend Payments', Discussion Paper no. 52, Bank of England, December.

Mair, D. (1991), 'Regional Policy Initiatives from Brussels', *Royal Bank of Scotland Review,* no. 169: pp. 33–43.

Marsh, P. (1990), *Short-Termism on Trial,* Institutional Fund Managers Association, London.

Mayer, C. (1987), 'Financial Systems and Corporate Investment', *Oxford Review of Economic Policy,* (3)4.

Mayer, T. and Thumann, G. (1990), 'Paving the Way for German Unification', *Finance and Development,* 27(4): pp. 9–11.

Mayes, D. G. (1989), 'Small Firms in the UK Economy', *Royal Bank of Scotland Review,* no. 164: pp. 15–34.

Metais, J. (1990), 'Towards a Restructuring of the International Financial Services Industry: Some Preliminary Empirical and Theoretical Insights', in E. P. M. Gardener, (ed.), *The Future of Financial Systems and Services,* Macmillan, London.

Morgan, E. V. (1981), 'The Supply of Funds for Industry and Commerce', Chapter 4 in *The British and German Banking System: A Comparative Study,* EAG, Anglo-German Foundation, London.

Mowby, S. (1991), 'Killing the Goose that Laid the Golden Egg?' *Financial Director,* 3: pp. 41–44.

Moyer, H. W. and Josling, T. E. (1990), *Agricultural Policy Reform: Politics and Process in the EC and USA,* Harvester Wheatsheaf, Brighton.

Mullineux, A. W. (1985), 'Do We Need the Bank of England?' *Lloyds Bank Review,* no. 157: 13–24.

—— (1987), *International Banking and Financial Systems: A Comparison,* Graham & Trotmann, London.

Murray, G. C. (1991), 'The Changing Nature of Competition in the UK Venture Capital Industry', *National Westminster Quarterly Review,* November: pp. 65–80.

Musgrave, R. A. (1969), 'Theories of Fiscal Federalism', *Public Finance,* 4: pp. 24, 521–32.

Neven, D. J. (1990), 'Structural Adjustment in European Retail Banking: Some Views from Industrial Organizations', in J. Dermine (ed.), *European Banking in the 1990s,* Basil Blackwell, Oxford.

Nevin, E. (1988), 'VAT and the European Budget', *Royal Bank of Scotland Review,* no. 157: pp. 37–45.

—— (1990), *The Economics of Europe,* Macmillan, London.

Oates, W. (1972), *Fiscal Federalism,* Harcourt, Bruce, Jovanovitch, New York.

—— (1977), 'Fiscal Federalism in Theory and Practice: Applications to the EC,' in EC Commission (1977).

Owen, R. and Dynes, M. (1992), *The Times Guide to the Single European Market,* Times Books, London.

Padua-Schioppa, T. *et al.* (1987), *Efficiency, Stability and Equity,* Oxford University Press.

Parker, D. (1991), 'Privatisation Ten Years On: A Critical Analysis of its Rationale and Results', *Economics,* 27, 4(16): pp. 154–162.

—— and Hartley, K. (1990), 'Competitive Tendering: Issues and Evidence', *Public Money and Management,* 10(3): pp. 9–15.

Parrott, M. (1988), 'France: A Bad Hangover', *The Banker,* January: p. 25.

Partington, I. (1989), *Applied Economics in Banking and Finance,* 4th edn, Oxford University Press.

Patel, P. and Pavitt, K. (1989), 'A Comparison of Technological Activities in West Germany and the United Kingdom', *National Westminster Quarterly Review,* May: pp. 27–42.

Pawley, M. *et al.* (1991), *UK Financial Institutions and Markets,* Macmillan, London.

Pedersen, T. (1991), 'EC–EFTA Relations: An Historical Outline', in H. Wallace (ed.), *The Wider Western Europe,* RIIA, Pinter, London.

Peston, R. and Holberton, S. (1992), 'Lloyds Encourages Review of Midland Bid', *Financial Times,* 29 April.

Piers, M. and MacGillivray, M. (1992), 'Cadbury Committee Offers Mixed News for Shareholders', *Financial Times*, 2 June.

Pike, R. (1988), 'The Capital Budgeting Decision', *Management Accounting*, October: pp. 28–30.

Pinder, J. (1991), *European Community,* Oxford University Press.

Pohl, K. O. (1988), 'Eine Konsequente Stabilitätspolitik hat uns das Vertraum des Auslands erhalten', *Deutsche Bundesbank: Auszuge aus Presseartiskeln*, 45.

Puxty, A. G. and Dodds, J. C. (1991), *Financial Management: Method and Meaning*, 2nd edn, Chapman & Hall, London.

Raymond, R. (1990), 'Money Market and Monetary Policy', Chapter 2 in C. de Boisseau (ed.), *Banking in France*, Routledge, London.

Reed, B. (1988), 'Future Systems Requirements in European Investment Markets', *Interchange*, Winter, pp. 32–44.

Richardson, H. W. (1978), *Urban and Regional Economics,* Penguin, London.

Rodger, I. (1992), 'Adapting to Modern Demands', *Financial Times*, Survey on Offshore Centres, 28 February: 9–10.

Roney, A. (1991), *The European Community Factbook*, Kogan Page, London.

Rudolph, B. (1990), 'Capital Requirements of German Banks and the European Community Proposals on Banking Supervision', in J. Dermine (ed.), *European Banking in the 1990s*, Basil Blackwell, Oxford.

Rutterford, J. (1984), 'The UK Corporate Bond Market: Prospects for Revival', *National Westminster Quarterly Review*, May: pp. 17–32.

────── and Carter, D. (eds) (1988), *Handbook of UK Corporate Finance*, Butterworths, London.

Rybcynski, T. M. (1984), 'The UK Financial System in Transition', *National Westminster Quarterly Review*, November: pp. 26–42.

────── (1985), 'Financial Systems: Risk and Public Policy', *Royal Bank of Scotland Review*, no. 148: pp. 35–45.

Samuels, J. M., Groves, R. E. V. and Goddard, C. S. (1975), *Company Finance in Europe*, Wilton Publications, London.

────── Wilkes, F. M. and Brayshaw, R. E. (1990), *Management of Company Finance*, 5th edn, Chapman & Hall, London.

Sayers, R. S. (1967), *Modern Banking,* 7th edn, Clarendon Press, Oxford.

Schuster, L. (1990), 'The Role of Swiss Banks in International Finance', in E. P. M. Gardener (ed.), *The Future of Financial Systems and Services*, Macmillan, London.

Scott-Quinn, B. (1990), 'A Strategy for the International Stock Exchange', *National Westminster Quarterly Review*, May: pp. 43–58.

Seiffert, E. (1991), 'The US Banking System in Transition', *Deutsche Bank Bulletin*, January: pp. 14–20.

Shackleton, J. R. (1984), 'Privatisation: The Case Examined', *National Westminster Quarterly Review*, May: pp. 59–73.

Shackleton, M. (1990), *Financing the European Community*, Chatham House Papers, RIIA, Pinter, London.

Shaw, E. R. (1990), The London Money Market, Heinemann, London.

Shilson, D. (1984), 'Venture Capital in the UK', *Bank of England Quarterly Bulletin*, June: pp. 207–11.

Shreeve, G. and Alexander, J. (1991), 'My Heart Belongs to Daddy', *The Banker*, February: pp. 8–12.

Siaens, A. and Goossens, J. (1992), 'Belgium', in *Guide to European Equity Markets 1992*, Euromoney Publications, London.

Simon, H. (1992), 'Lessons from Germany's Midsize Giants', *Harvard Business Review*, 70(2): pp. 115–23.

Solnik, B. (1988), *International Investments*, 2nd edn, Addison-Wesley, Wokingham, Berks.

Smith, D. (1987), *The Rise and Fall of Monetarism: The Theory and Politics of an Economic Experiment*, Penguin, Harmondsworth.

Spencer, J. (1986), 'Trade Liberalization through Tariff Cuts and the EEC: A General Equilibrium Evaluation', in T. N. Srinivason and J. Whalley (eds.), *General Equilibrium Trade Policy Modelling*, MIT Press, Cambridge, Mass.

Steinherr, A. (ed.) (1992), *The New European Financial Marketplace*, Longman, London.

Stigler, G. (1986), 'The Regularities of Regulation', in R. Dale (ed.), *Financial Regulation*, Woodhead-Faulkner, Cambridge.

Stone, I. (1991), 'The United Kingdom', Chapter 6 in F. J. L. Somers (ed.), *European Economies: A Comparative Study*, Pitman, London.

Szarka, J. (1992), *Business in France*, Pitman, London.

Terry, N. G. (1988), 'The Changing UK Pension System', *National Westminster Quarterly Review*, May: pp. 2–13.

Thomas, W. A. (1989), *The Securities Market*, Philip Allan, Oxford.

Thomson, K. (1991), 'France', Chapter 4 in F. J. L. Somers (ed.), *European Economies: A Comparative Study*, Pitman, London.

Thornhill, S. (1989), 'Small Business is Big Business', *Banking World*, June: pp. 17–21.

Tietmeyer, H. (1990), 'The Economic Integration of Germany: Problems and Prospects', Statement at the International Banking Seminar, Group of Thirty, Washington, DC, 24 September.

Timewell, S. (1990), 'Changing the Old Guard', *The Banker*, December: pp. 22–5.

—— (1991), 'BCCI: Unanswered Questions', *The Banker*, September: pp. 12–20.

Tobin, J. (1984), 'On the Efficiency of the Financial System', *Lloyds Bank Review*, no. 153: pp. 1–15.

Tosini, P. (1988), 'Stock Index Futures and Stock Market Activity in October 1987', *Financial Analyst's Journal*, 44: p. 31.

Tyers, R. (1985), 'International Impacts of Protection: Model Structure and Results for EC Agricultural Policy', *Journal of Policy Modelling*, 7(2): pp. 219–52.

—— and Anderson, K. (1986), 'Distortions in World Food Markets: A Quantitative Assessment', Background Paper for World Bank World Development Report, World Bank, Washington, DC.

Ugeux, G. (1989), 'Europe *sans Frontierès*': The Integration of Financial Markets', *Royal Bank of Scotland Review*, no. 162: pp. 9–25.

Valentine, S. (1988), 'The Stock Exchange after the Big Bang', *Long Range Planning*, 21(2): pp. 35–40.

Van den Bempt, P. (1991), 'National Fiscal Policies in an Economic and Monetary Union', *European Business Journal*, 3(1): pp. 10–18.

Wallace, H. (ed.) (1991), *The Wider Western Europe*, RIIA, Pinter, London.

Walters, A. (1990), *Sterling in Danger*, Fontana-Collins/IEA, London.

Webb, S. (1992), 'Trying Times', *Financial Times Survey on Nordic Countries*, 23 March, p. ii.

Welford, R. and Prescott, K. (1992), *European Business*, Pitman, London.

White, R. (1984), 'International Differences in Gearing: How Important Are They?', *National Westminster Quarterly Review*, November: pp. 14–25.

Wijkman, P. M. (1991), 'Economic Interdependence', in H. Wallace (ed.), *The Wider Western Europe*, RIIA, Pinter, London.

Williams, P. (1991), 'Time and the City: Short-Termism in the UK, Myth or Reality', *National Westminster Quarterly Review*, August: pp. 31–8.

Wilsadin, D. E. (1990), 'Budgetary Pressure in the EC: A Fiscal Federalism Perspective', *American Economics Association Papers and Proceedings*, May: pp. 69–74.

Wilson Committee (1979), *The Financing of Small Firms*, Interim Report of the Committee to Review the Functioning of Financial Institutions (Chairman Sir Harold Wilson), Cmnd. 7503, HMSO, London.

—— (1980), *Report* of the Committee to Review the Functioning of Financial Institutions (Chairman Sir Harold Wilson), Cmnd. 7837, HMSO, London.

Wolf, M. (1988), 'Painful Challenge, Important Gains', *Financial Times*, 17 November.

Wood, G. E. and Coleman, D. B. (1992), 'The EMU Treaty: Some Economic Reflections', in *The State of the Economy*, IEA Readings no. 37: pp. 117–135.

INDEX